Lecture Notes in Computer Science 16624

Founding Editors

Gerhard Goos
Juris Hartmanis

Editorial Board Members

The series Lecture Notes in Computer Science (LNCS), including its subseries Lecture Notes in Artificial Intelligence (LNAI) and Lecture Notes in Bioinformatics (LNBI), has established itself as a medium for the publication of new developments in computer science and information technology research, teaching, and education.

LNCS enjoys close cooperation with the computer science R & D community, the series counts many renowned academics among its volume editors and paper authors, and collaborates with prestigious societies. Its mission is to serve this international community by providing an invaluable service, mainly focused on the publication of conference and workshop proceedings and postproceedings. LNCS commenced publication in 1973.

Blair Archibald · Oszkár Semeráth

Editors

Graph Transformation

19th International Conference, ICGT 2026
Held as Part of STAF 2026
Rennes, France, July 1–2, 2026, Proceedings

 Springer

Editors
Blair Archibald
University of Glasgow
Glasgow, UK

Oszkár Semeráth
Budapest University of Technology
and Economics
Budapest, Hungary

ISSN 0302-9743　　　　　ISSN 1611-3349　(electronic)
Lecture Notes in Computer Science
ISBN 978-3-032-29729-7　　　ISBN 978-3-032-29730-3　(eBook)
https://doi.org/10.1007/978-3-032-29730-3

This Springer imprint is published by the registered company Springer Nature Switzerland AG
The registered company address is: Gewerbestrasse 11, 6330 Cham, Switzerland

If disposing of this product, please recycle the paper.

Preface

This volume contains the proceedings of ICGT 2026, the 19th International Conference on Graph Transformation, held on July 1 – July 2, 2026 at the University of Rennes in France. ICGT 2026 was affiliated with STAF (Software Technologies: Applications and Foundations), a federation of leading conferences on software technologies.

The use of graphs and graph-like structures as a formalism for specification and modelling is widespread in computer science and many fields of computational research and engineering. Examples include: software architectures, pointer structures, state space and control/data flow graphs, UML and other domain-specific models, computer network layouts or architectural models, topologies of cyber-physical environments, quantum computing and molecular structures, and graph databases. Often these graphs undergo dynamic change, reconfiguration, and evolution, which may be captured by different kinds of graph manipulation.

ICGT fosters research and collaboration between people working with graphs, graph transformation, and applications of graphs. We accept research not just in theoretical foundations, but also in the application of established graph formalisms and tools including in other novel areas. The conference serves as a well-established scientific publication outlet, a platform to boost inter- and intra-disciplinary research, and a pathway for new ideas.

ICGT 2026 continued the series of conferences previously held in Barcelona (Spain) in 2002, Rome (Italy) in 2004, Natal (Brazil) in 2006, Leicester (UK) in 2008, Enschede (The Netherlands) in 2010, Bremen (Germany) in 2012, York (UK) in 2014, L'Aquila (Italy) in 2015, Vienna (Austria) in 2016, Marburg (Germany) in 2017, Toulouse (France) in 2018, Eindhoven (The Netherlands) in 2019, online in 2020 and 2021, Nantes (France) in 2022, Leicester (UK) in 2023, Twente (The Netherlands) in 2024, and Koblenz (Germany) in 2025, following a series of six International Workshops on Graph Grammars and Their Application to Computer Science from 1978 to 1998 in Europe and in the USA.

This year, the conference requested papers in the following categories: research papers, describing new and unpublished contributions to the theory and applications of graph transformation, and short tool and vision papers, demonstrating the main features and functionalities of graph-based tools and reporting on new research directions or ideas that are in an early or emerging stage. Additionally we had a journal-first track accepting proposals for related articles from the last 4 years.

ICGT 2026 received 19 submissions, each reviewed by three Program Committee members and/or additional reviewers. The review process followed a single-blind protocol. This year, we had an additional revision phase to allow authors to respond to feedback and improve papers to an acceptable level to allow publication. Following extensive discussions, the Program Committee selected 13 research papers (9 technical track and 4 tool/vision track) for publication in these proceedings.

The topics of the accepted papers cover a wide spectrum including new approaches to hypergraphs, improvements to the understanding of conflict analysis and parallel transformations, verification of graph transformation and of programs using graphs, and advancements in graphs for neural applications and stochastic rewriting.

During the conference, we were delighted to host an invited talk by James Clarkson from Neo4j.

We would like to thank everyone who contributed to the success of ICGT 2026, including the members of our Program Committee, our additional reviewers, and our invited speakers. We are grateful to Reiko Heckel, the Chair of the ICGT Steering Committee, for his valuable suggestions; the organising committee of STAF 2026 for hosting and supporting ICGT 2026; conf.researchr.org, for hosting our website; and EasyChair, for supporting the review process and the preparation of the proceedings.

May 2026   Blair Archibald
                                                         Oszkár Semeráth

Organization

Program Committee Chairs

Blair Archibald	University of Glasgow, UK
Oszkár Semeráth	Budapest University of Technology and Economics, Hungary

Program Committee

Paolo Bottoni	Sapienza University of Rome, Italy
Andrea Corradini	Università di Pisa, Italy
Stefania Dumbrava	ENSIIE Paris-Évry, France
Maryam Ghaffari Saadat	Freelance Software Developer, UK
Holger Giese	Hasso Plattner Institute at the University of Potsdam, Germany
Raffaela Groner	Chalmers — University of Gothenburg, Sweden
Reiko Heckel	University of Leicester, UK
Barbara König	University of Duisburg-Essen, Germany
Leen Lambers	Brandenburgische Technische Universität Cottbus-Senftenberg, Germany
Detlef Plump	University of York, UK
Arend Rensink	University of Twente, The Netherlands
Daniel Strüber	Chalmers — University of Gothenburg, Sweden, Radboud University Nijmegen, The Netherlands
Gabriele Taentzer	Philipps-Universität Marburg, Germany
Steffen Zschaler	King's College London, UK

Additional Reviewers

Jens Kosiol	Philipps-Universität Marburg, Germany
Federico Vastarini	Independent Researcher
András Vörös	Budapest University of Technology and Economics, Hungary

Contents

Tool and Vision Papers

Technical Papers

LR-Based Parsing of Hypergraph Languages: A Positional Grammar Approach

Gennaro Costagliola[✉] [iD], Mattia De Rosa [iD], and Salvatore La Torre [iD]

University of Salerno, Fisciano, (SA), Italy
{gencos,matderosa,slatorre}@unisa.it

Abstract. We further investigate the use of LR-based parsing for languages generated by hyperedge replacement grammars (HRGs). Previous work successfully used predictive shift-reduce (PSR) parsing. Here, we turn our attention to positional LR (pLR) parsing. This approach has been devised to parse many kinds of non-string languages mainly in the domain of visual languages, such as iconic, box, box-and-arrows, and statechart-like languages, among others. Moreover, several tools based on positional parsers have been implemented so far.

In this paper, we give formal rules to translate HRGs into positional grammars: we first provide a simple translation to generic positional grammars and then define an algorithm to transform these grammars into well-formed positional grammars, i.e., grammars that are guaranteed to be parsable according to the positional parsing methodology. We show how the pLR parsing methodology applies to hypergraph languages, demonstrate that the well-forming transformation always guarantees parser construction, and analyze its time and space complexity. As a further contribution we implement our approach in a prototype tool, demonstrate it on the running example, and report on its application to a set of HRGs and sentences.

1 Introduction

Graph grammars extend the theory of formal languages from strings to graph-structured objects, providing powerful formalisms for specifying and recognizing classes of graphs. *Hyperedge replacement grammars* (HRGs) [21,27] occupy a prominent position among the various graph-grammar frameworks that have been proposed over the decades: they generalize context-free string grammars to hypergraphs by recursively replacing labelled hyperedges with right-hand-side hypergraphs, retaining many of the attractive closure and decidability properties of their string-based counterparts [18,21].

A central computational challenge in working with HRGs is the *parsing problem*: given a grammar and an input hypergraph, determine whether the hypergraph belongs to the language generated by the grammar and, if so, recover a derivation.

B. Archibald and O. Semeráth (Eds.): ICGT 2026, LNCS 16624, pp. 3–24, 2026.
https://doi.org/10.1007/978-3-032-29730-3_1

Several parsing strategies for HRGs have been studied in the literature, from general chart-based membership procedures to predictive methods for restricted grammar classes. In particular, Lautemann [31] established the general complexity barrier, Chiang et al. [2] refined dynamic-programming HRG parsing, and PTD/PSR parsing [22–24] (implemented in Grappa [28]) transfers LL/SLR-style ideas to hypergraphs, with GPSR [29] providing a generalized alternative when determinism is not available.

Independently, positional grammars and positional LR (pLR) parsing provide an LR-based framework for non-string and visual languages [6,8,10]. This line of work has developed explicit pLR-parsability criteria, conflict management techniques, and mature tool support for visual-language parsing [11–14].

Despite the shared LR-parsing heritage, the two strands of research, PSR/PTD parsing for HRGs on the one hand, and positional parsing for visual languages on the other, have so far evolved largely in parallel.

In this paper, we bridge this gap by providing a formal translation of HRGs into positional grammars, together with a well-forming algorithm that makes the *pLR* parsing methodology applicable to hyperedge replacement languages. The underlying intuition for this connection appeared in a work-in-progress report [17] that relied on a preliminary work reported in two Master Thesis [33,34]. There, the reduction from hyperedge replacement grammars to positional grammars and the role of hyperedge orderings in enabling deterministic parsing were first outlined but only at an informal level. We investigate further this intuition and develop a full methodology, with formal machinery and algorithmic treatment.

Our contributions are as follows:

1. we give a detailed translation from an arbitrary HRG into an *equivalent* positional grammar;
2. we introduce an algorithm to transform any positional grammar into a *well-formed* one, i.e., one that is guaranteed to be parsable by the positional parsing methodology, and discuss its time and space complexity of the transformation;
3. we implement our approach in a prototype tool and demonstrate it on the running example, reporting on its application to a set of HRGs and sentences.

The remainder of the paper is organized as follows. In Sect. 2, we discuss related work. In Sect. 3, we recall the necessary background on HRGs. Section 4 is devoted to give an overview of the approach we propose. In Sect. 5, we first recall the notion of positional grammars and then give our translation from HRGs to positional grammars. In Sect. 6, we propose an algorithm to automatically translate an arbitrary positional grammar into a well-formed one, thus allowing us to reuse off-the-shelf tools for parsing positional grammars. In Sect. 7, we report on the implementation and the experimental evaluation of the resulting prototype tool. Section 8 concludes the paper.

2   Related Work

Hyperedge Replacement Grammars and Parsing. For the foundations of HRGs we refer to the work by Habel [27] and the following book chapter by Habel et al. [21]. Lautemann [31] showed that the membership problem for general HRGs is NP-complete. This motivated later work on more specialized algorithms. Chiang et al. [2] refined chart-based HRG parsing and analyzed its complexity in detail, also providing the Bolinas toolkit. Earlier recognition results for more restricted settings were obtained by Vogler [37] and Drewes [19].

More relevant for our work is the predictive parsing line by Drewes, Hoffmann, and Minas: [22] predictive top-down (PTD) and predictive shift-reduce (PSR) [23,24] parsing. This work transfers classical compiler-construction techniques to hypergraphs, yielding efficient deterministic parsers when specific grammar-side conditions are satisfied. The corresponding parser generator is Grappa [28]. Hoffmann et al. [29] give a general PSR (GPSR) which although may incur in exponential worst-case behaviors.

Positional Grammars and pLR Parsing. Independently of the HRG literature, positional grammars were introduced to extend LR-style parsing to non-linear and visual languages [5,6]. A general LR-like methodology was developped by Costagliola et al. [7,8,10] who provide a developed parsing framework rather than only a representational formalism. Conditions for pLR parsability were studied in [12], and later work addressed run-time conflict detection [13], extensions of the formalism [4], and tool support for visual-language editors and compiler generation [11,14,15].

Comparing with Existing Approaches. Several recent works obtain efficient graph parsing by restricting the grammar formalism or the generated class of graphs. Examples include tree-verifiable graph grammars [3], graph-language models with controlled non-structural reentrancies [20], local graph expansion grammars under additional restrictions [25], and regular graph grammars [26]. There are also HRG-related approaches such as string generating hypergraph grammars [36] and their extensions with word-order restrictions [35] that impose order constraints to improve parsing properties.

Our contribution is orthogonal to both lines of work. We do not define a new parsable subclass of HRGs nor modify the generative semantics of hyperedge replacement. Instead, we provide a semantics-preserving translation from arbitrary HRGs to positional grammars, followed by a transformation to well-formed positional grammars so that the existing pLR methodology can be reused. Here, well-formedness is a property required of the target positional grammar for pLR parsing, not an additional restriction on the source HRG language class. The linear order introduced in our construction is therefore purely operational: it supports positional scanning without turning HRGs into an ordered graph-grammar formalism.

3   Hypergraphs and Hyperedge Replacement Grammars

Hypergraphs extend the notion of graphs by allowing single edges (called *hyperedges*) to connect an arbitrary number of vertices. A *hypergraph* is essentially a set of hyperedges, where each hyperedge is an ordered sequence of vertices along with a label. In this work, we adopt a definition of a labelled hypergraph that is common in the field of graph rewriting systems [21], where a standard operation is the replacement of a hyperedge with an entire hypergraph. For this, we also require that each hypergraph has a set of distinguished vertices called *external vertices* that act as stitching points in edge replacements.

Formally, fix a finite alphabet Σ. A Σ-labelled *hypergraph* H is (V, X, E) where V is a set of nodes, $X \subseteq V$ is a set of *external vertices* and E is a set of *hyperedges* of the form $a(v_1, \ldots, v_n)$ with $a \in \Sigma$, $n \in \mathbb{N}$ and $v_1, \ldots, v_n \in V$. For a hyperedge $e = a(v_1, \ldots, v_n)$, the *label* of e is $\lambda(e) = a$ and the *type* of e is $\tau(e) = n$. A *graph* is a hypergraph containing only hyperedges of type 2 (called *edges*).

Note that we deviate from the standard definition of hyperedges using tuples instead of multisets. However, this difference is immaterial since we interpret such tuples as an encoding of a multiset: the vertex ordering in the tuple is only used in the translation to positional forms and is ignored when comparing hyperedges.

A graphical representation of a labelled hyperedge $a(v_1, \ldots, v_n)$ is a diagram containing a box labelled with a connected to round nodes corresponding to the vertices $v_1, \ldots, v_n$ such that the link to vertex v_i is labelled with i for $i \in [1, n]$ (see Fig. 1a). Such links are called *tentacles* and the labels associated with them denote the position of the corresponding vertex in the tuple. A graphical representation of a hypergraph is obtained accordingly, denoting the external vertices with filled round nodes.

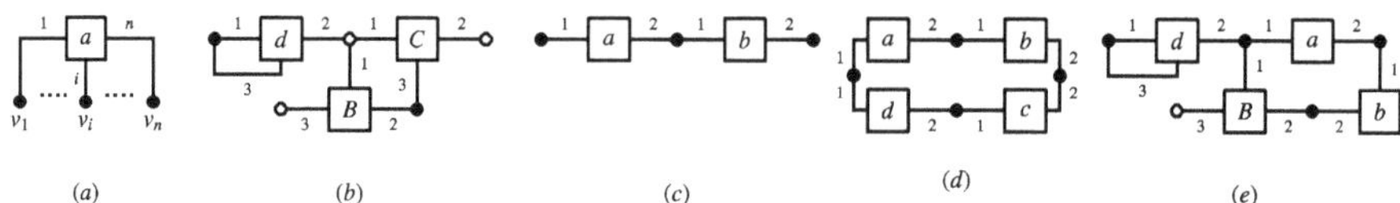

Fig. 1. Graphical representations of: (a) hyperedge $a(v_1, \ldots, v_n)$; (b) hypergraph H' [17], (c-e) hypergraphs H'', H''' and $H'[C \to_\mu H'']$.

Figures 1b-d give the graphical representation of three hypergraphs. As a simplification, we omit the names of the vertices. Hypergraph H' in Fig. 1b has five vertices, two of which are external, and three hyperedges of type 3 labelled respectively with d, C and B. Hypergraph H'' in Fig. 1c is a standard chain graph with three vertices linked through two edges. Hypergraph H''' in Fig. 1d is also a graph and has four vertices and edges that form a simple cycle. All vertices in H'' and H''' are external.

A hyperedge replacement grammar has the form of a context-free grammar where each production defines the replacement of a hyperedge e with a hypergraph H_e. When a production is applied in a hypergraph H containing e, the resulting hypergraph is obtained by removing e from H and then attaching the two graphs by forcing the external vertices of H_e and the vertices of e to coincide according to a given mapping μ. Given two Σ-labeled hypergraphs $H_i = (V_i, X_i, E_i)$ with $i \in [1,2]$, a hyperedge $e = a(u_1, \ldots, u_n) \in E_1$, and a map $\mu : [1,n] \to X_2$, we denote with $H_1[e \to_\mu H_2]$ the graph obtained from H_1 by the *hyperedge replacement* of e with H_2 via the map μ. Figure 1e gives the graphical representation of the hypergraph resulting from the replacement of the hyperedge $C(v_1, v_2, v_3)$ with the hypergraph H'' by the mapping μ defined as $\mu(1) = v_1$, $\mu(2) = v_2$ and $\mu(3) = v_3$ where v_1, v_2, v_3 are resp. the three vertices of H'' shown from left to right in Fig. 1c.

We fix an alphabet $\Sigma = \mathcal{N} \cup \mathcal{T}$ where $\mathcal{N}$ and $\mathcal{T}$ are disjoint sets and respectively denote the *non terminal* and *terminal* symbols.

A *production* over Σ is $A \to_\mu H$ where $A \in \mathcal{N}$, $H = (V, X, E)$ is a Σ-labeled hypergraph and $\mu : [1,n] \to X$ for some integer $n > 0$.

For two Σ-labeled hypergraphs $H_i = (V_i, X_i, E_i)$ with $i \in [1,2]$, and a production $p = A \to_\mu H$, we say that H_2 is *derived* from H_1 by $A \to_\mu H$, denoted $H_1 \Rightarrow_p H_2$, if a hyperedge $e = A(u_1, \ldots, u_n) \in E_1$ exists such that $H_2 = H_1[e \to_\mu H]$. We also write $H_1 \Rightarrow H_2$ denoting that a production p exists such that $H_1 \Rightarrow_p H_2$.

As usual we denote with $\Rightarrow^+$ and the transitive closure of the derivation relation $\Rightarrow$ and with $\Rightarrow^*$ its transitive and reflexive closure.

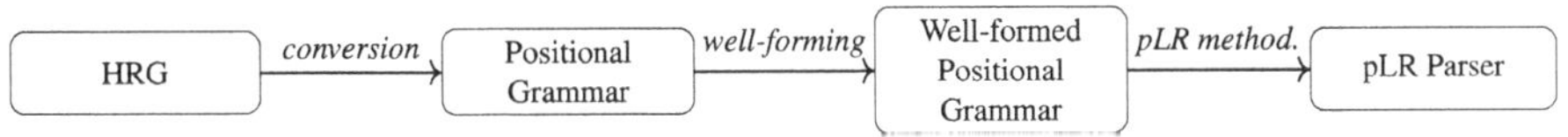

Fig. 2. Pipeline from HRG to pLR parser.

A *hyperedge replacement grammar* (HRG) G over $\mathcal{N} \cup \mathcal{T}$ is $(\mathcal{N}, \mathcal{T}, \mathcal{P}, \mathcal{A})$ where $\mathcal{P}$ is a finite set of productions and $\mathcal{A} \in \mathcal{N}$ is the *axiom*. A hypergraph generated by G is H such that $\mathcal{A} \Rightarrow^* H$. The language of G, denoted $L(G)$, is the set of all the $\mathcal{T}$-labeled hypergraphs generated by G, i.e., all the generated hypergraphs that are labeled with terminal symbols.

4   Our Approach

We address the computational problem of parsing HRGs by reducing it to parsing well-formed positional grammars. We achieve this by following the approach outlined in Fig. 2. We start by introducing positional forms to encode graph structures and then positional grammars to generate them. We then give a procedure to convert any HRG into a semantically equivalent positional grammar, that is, such that the generated positional forms are the encodings of all and only the hypergraphs generated by the given HRG. Next, we identify a class of well-formed positional grammars that are guaranteed to be suitable for pLR parsing, and design an algorithm to transform any positional grammar into an equivalent well-formed one. Finally, an off-the-shelf pLR parser for positional grammars is used as backend engine to parse the encodings of the hypergraphs: if the input hypergraph is an instance of the input HRG, the resulting parse tree can be translated back to a parse tree of the HRG.

We observe that in the translation from HRGs to positional grammars, we need to linearize symbols on the right-hand side of the productions and in general not all the linearizations lead to parsable positional grammars. We will take care of this in our translations.

In the rest of the paper, for simplifying the presentation, we assume that hypergraphs are connected. Note that this is without loss of generality: the different components can be linked by adding dummy edges. Further, we will use the following running example.

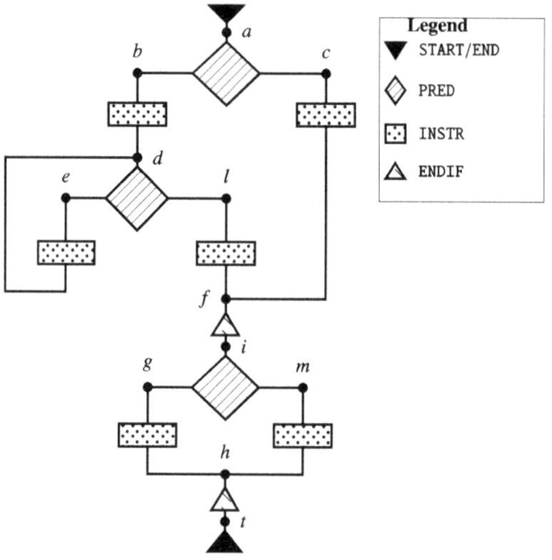

Fig. 3. A hypergraph generated by the HRG of Example 1.

Example 1 (ASIMPLEHRG). Consider the following HRG for a simple flowchart language, adapted from [24] with an additional ENDIF token. We use words with upper case letters for terminals and capitalized letters for non terminals, vertices are denoted with lower case letters, the external vertices are those listed for the hyperedge in the left-hand part of a production, and the mapping is implicitly given by using the same vertex name on both sides of a production:

(1) $\text{PROGRAM}() \rightarrow \texttt{START}(x)\ \text{STATS}(x,y)\ \texttt{END}(y)$
(2) $\text{STATS}(x,y) \rightarrow \text{STATEM}(x,y)$
(3) $\text{STATS}(x,v) \rightarrow \text{STATEM}(x,y)\ \text{STATS}(y,v)$
(4) $\text{STATEM}(x,y) \rightarrow \texttt{INSTR}(x,y)$
(5) $\text{STATEM}(x,y) \rightarrow \texttt{PRED}(x,v,y)\ \text{STATS}(v,x)$
(6) $\text{STATEM}(x,z) \rightarrow \text{STATS}(y,w)\ \texttt{PRED}(x,y,v)\ \text{STATS}(v,w)\ \texttt{ENDIF}(w,z)$

It generates structured flowcharts for programs of a simple language containing sequences of instructions including *while cycle* and closed *if-then-else* constructs. Each generated hypergraph starts with hyperedge $\texttt{START}$ and ends with hyperedge $\texttt{END}$ (production (1)). The body of a flowchart is composed of a sequence of one or more hyperedges STATEM (productions 2–3), where each hyperedge STATEM takes the form of a single instruction (production 4), a while-loop construct (production 5), or an if-then-else construct closed by the terminal $\texttt{ENDIF}$ (production 6). Figure 3 shows a structured flowchart generated by the above grammar and containing one while-loop and two if-then-else constructs. $\qquad\square$

5   From Parsing Hypergraphs to Parsing Positional Forms

In this section, we start by introducing a simplified version of positional grammars, where attributes are all of the same type over a singleton domain and with the *identity* as the only allowed relation (that thus can stay implicit in our notation). We then introduce an encoding of the hypergraphs into positional forms and conclude the section with a translation of HRGs into equivalent positional grammars.

5.1   Positional Grammars

An *attributed symbol* s is a standard symbol augmented with a sequence of attributes, where each *attribute* is a container (such as a variable for a programming language). Further, we denote with n_{as} the number of attributes of s and with $s(\mathsf{i})$ its i-th attribute for $\mathsf{i} \in [1, n_{as}]$. In the following, we also refer to this interval as I_s. An *attributed alphabet* is an alphabet of symbols with attributes.

For a sequence $\sigma = s_1 \ldots s_n$ of attributed symbols over Σ, a *connector* at position i of σ is $\mathsf{k}^z\lrcorner$ that connects to attributes $s_j(\mathsf{k})$ and $s_i(\mathsf{l})$ such that $j = i + z - 1$ and $j \leq i$. The index j (resp., i) denotes the position of the *source* (resp. *target*) symbol of a connector.

The indices k and l refer, respectively, to the k-th attribute of the source and the l-th attribute of the target. The *offset* $z \leq 1$ is such that, except for $z = 1$, $|z|$ is exactly the number of attributed symbols between s_j and s_i, being $z = 1$ the case when the source and the target positions coincide. In the following, to simplify the notation we omit the offset 0, therefore we will use $\mathsf{k}\lrcorner$ as a connector between two symbols a and b to denote that attribute $a(\mathsf{k})$ is linked to attribute

$b(\mathsf{l})$. In order to define positional forms, we first introduce weak positional forms as a larger class.

For an attributed alphabet Σ, a *weak positional form* is $r_1 s_1 r_2 s_2 \ldots r_n s_n$ where:

- $\sigma = s_1 \ldots s_n$ is a sequence over Σ;
- for $i \in [1, n]$, $r_i = \rho_1 \wedge \ldots \wedge \rho_{n_i}$ is a conjunction of *connectors* at position i of σ such that r_1 contains at most connectors with offset 1.

A *positional form* is a weak positional form such that for $i > 1$, r_i has at least one connector with offset strictly less than 1.

A *positional grammar* is $G = (\mathcal{N}, \mathcal{T}, \mathcal{P}, \mathcal{A})$ where:

- $\mathcal{N}$ is a finite set of *non-terminal* attributed symbols,
- $\mathcal{T}$ is a finite set of *terminal* attributed symbols, with $N \cap T = \emptyset$,
- $\mathcal{A} \in \mathcal{N}$ is the axiom,
- $\mathcal{P}$ is set of production rules of the form $A \rightarrow_\delta \omega$, where $A \in \mathcal{N}$, $\omega = r_1 s_1 r_2 s_2 \ldots r_n s_n$ is a positional form over $\mathcal{N} \cup \mathcal{T}$ and δ maps attributes of A to attributes within ω, i.e., $\delta : I_A \rightarrow \{(i, \mathsf{h}) \mid i \in \{1, \ldots, n\}, \mathsf{h} \in I_{s_i}\}$.

To define the language generated by a positional grammar G, we define a derivation as a sequence of rewriting steps that constructs a weak positional sentential form.

A derivation step, denoted by $\Rightarrow_p$, transforms a positional form $\gamma = \alpha r A \beta$, into a new positional form $\gamma' = \alpha \omega' \beta'$ by applying a production rule $p : A \rightarrow_\delta \omega$ such that the following holds:

1. the sequence ω' conforms to ω in the sense that if ω is of the form $r_1 s_1 \ldots r_n s_n$ then ω' is of the form $r'_1 s_1 \ldots r'_n s_n$; similarly, β' conforms to β;
2. the connectors of r (i.e., those with target position coinciding with that of A) are relocated within ω according to the mapping δ thus yielding ω'; in particular, the target position is assigned by the δ mapping and this may possibly cause the update of the connector offset (the number of positions between the source and the target increases unless δ points to the first position of ω); in addition, for the self connectors of r (i.e. those with offset 1 which have both source and target positions coinciding with that of A) also the source position is reassigned according to δ and an inversion of the relation may be required;
3. the connectors within β that have their source positions in the prefix $\alpha r A$ are also updated thus producing β', namely:
   a. for the connectors with source position in α, we just update the offset to account for the possible increase of the distance due to the insertion of ω between source and target positions;
   b. for the connectors with source position coinciding with that of A, we update the source position and the offset according to the position within ω assigned by the δ mapping.

The formal definition of the above transformation does not give further insights and in contrast may result in a quite heavy notation. We thus omit it here.

We use $\Rightarrow$ when a reference to a particular production in the derivation step is not needed, and with $\Rightarrow^*$ we denote the reflexive and transitive closure of $\Rightarrow$. A sequence generated by a positional grammar $G = (\mathcal{N}, \mathcal{T}, \mathcal{P}, \mathcal{A})$ is ω such that $\mathcal{A} \Rightarrow^* \omega$. If a sequence contains only terminal symbols, i.e., from $\mathcal{T}$, it is called a *sentence*. The language of G, denoted $L(G)$, is the set of all the sentences generated by G.

Example 2 (A POSITIONAL GRAMMAR FOR STRUCTURED FLOWCHARTS). Consider the following positional grammar (terminals are upper case and non terminals are capitalized):

(1) PROGRAM$\to_{\delta_1}$ START 1_1 STATS 2_1 END
$$\delta_1 = \emptyset$$

(2) STATS$\to_{\delta_2}$ STATEM
$$\delta_2: \text{STATS}(1) \mapsto (1, \text{STATEM}(1)), \quad \text{STATS}(2) \mapsto (1, \text{STATEM}(2))$$

(3) STATS$\to_{\delta_3}$ STATEM 2_1 STATS
$$\delta_3: \text{STATS}(1) \mapsto (1, \text{STATEM}(1)), \quad \text{STATS}(2) \mapsto (2, \text{STATS}(2))$$

(4) STATEM$\to_{\delta_4}$ INSTR
$$\delta_4: \text{STATEM}(1) \mapsto (1, \text{INSTR}(1)), \quad \text{STATEM}(2) \mapsto (1, \text{INSTR}(2))$$

(5) STATEM$\to_{\delta_5}$ PRED 2_1 $\wedge$ 1_2 STATS
$$\delta_5: \text{STATEM}(1) \mapsto (1, \text{PRED}(1)), \quad \text{STATEM}(2) \mapsto (1, \text{PRED}(3))$$

(6) STATEM$\to_{\delta_6}$ STATS 1_2 PRED 3_1 $\wedge$ 2^{-1}_2 STATS 2_1 $\wedge$ 2^{-2}_1 ENDIF
$$\delta_6: \text{STATEM}(1) \mapsto (2, \text{PRED}(1)), \quad \text{STATEM}(2) \mapsto (4, \text{ENDIF}(2))$$

It generates the same structured flowcharts as the HRG of Example 1: production (1) frames the program between START and END; productions (2)–(3) sequence statements; production (4) handles atomic instructions; production (5) encodes a while-loop via the bidirectional connector 2_1 $\wedge$ 1_2, which simultaneously threads the loop body and closes the back-edge; production (6) encodes if-then-else branching, merging both branch exits into ENDIF via 2_1 $\wedge$ 2^{-2}_1.

The derivation obtained by applying productions (1), (2), (6), (2), (4), (2), (4) in this order yields the weak positional sentence

START INSTR 1_2 $\wedge$ 1^{-1}_1 PRED 3_1 $\wedge$ 2^{-1}_2 INSTR 2_1 $\wedge$ 2^{-2}_1 ENDIF 2_1 END

which is not a positional sentence since no connectors occur between START and INSTR. $\qquad\square$

5.2   Encoding Hypergraphs as Positional Forms

In this section, we discuss our encoding of hypergraphs by positional forms. We use attributed symbols to capture the hyperedges: each tentacle is captured by an attribute. Then connectors link attributes corresponding to tentacles attached on a same vertex: for a pair of hyperedges e and e' that are incident on a same vertex via the i-th and the j-th tentacles respectively, and that are listed in this order in the sequence, we use a connector i^z_j at the position of the attributed symbol encoding e' (thus relating the attributes i and j of the respective symbols) and provided that the attributed symbol encoding e precedes that of e' with offset z.

For example, for the hypergraphs H', H'' and H''' from Fig. 1b-d, we get:

- $\omega = 1^1\_3\ d\ 2\_1\ C\ 2^{-1}\_1 \wedge 3\_2 \wedge 1\_1\ B$ encodes H';
- $\omega' = a\ 2\_1\ b$ encodes H'';
- $\omega'' = a\ 2\_1\ b\ 2\_2\ c\ 1^{-2}\_1 \wedge 1\_2\ d$ encodes H'''.

In the rest of this section, we describe our method to systematically encode hypergraphs into positional forms. A key step in this method is the notion of *link-graph*.

A link-graph is a graph with no external nodes where each node correspond to a hyperedge and each edge captures the incidence of two hyperedges on a same vertex. Namely, for each pair of hyperedges e and e' that are labeled with l_e and $l_{e'}$ respectively and are incident on a same vertex via the i-th and the j-th tentacles respectively, there is an edge with label $\{l_e(i), l_{e'}(j)\}$ that connects the corresponding vertices.

Formally, let $H = (V, X, E)$ be a hypergraph. The *link-graph* of H is the graph $\mathcal{L}(H) = (V', X', E')$ where:

- $V' = \{v_e \mid e \in E\}$;
- $X' = \emptyset$, i.e., there are no external nodes;
- The set E' contains exactly an edge $e = \lambda(n_{e'}, n_{e''})$ for each possible choice of two (not necessarily distinct) hyperedges $e, e' \in E$ that are incident on a same vertex $v \in V$ such that, denoted $e' = a'(v'_1, \ldots, v'_{n'})$ and $e'' = a''(v''_1, \ldots, v''_{n''})$: $v = v'_i = v''_j$ for some $i \in [1, n']$ and $j \in [1, n'']$, and $\lambda = \{a'(i), b'(j)\}$.

Figure 4a shows an example of the *link-graph* for hypergraph H' from Fig. 1b. By associating the label of a hyperedge to the corresponding node in the link-graph, and then mapping the label of a type-n hyperedge to an attributed symbol with n attributes, we can naturally interpret the edges of a link-graph as connectors between attributes of attributed symbols and in turns a linearization of a link-graph (i.e., the ordered sequence of its vertices explored in a standard graph traversal) results in a positional form.

For example, the labels on the path $d\ \{d(2), C(1)\}\ C\ \{B(2), C(3)\}\ B\ \{B(1), C(1)\}\ C$ produce the positional form $d\ 2\_1\ C\ 3\_2 \wedge 1\_1\ B$ (for the ease of presentation, we denote the attributed symbol corresponding to a hyperedge label with the label itself).

We now turn the intuition given in the above example into a procedure to compute a positional form corresponding to a hypergraph.

Let $H = (V, X, E)$ be a hypergraph and $e = a(v_1, \ldots, v_n) \in E$, we compute an equivalent positional form ω_H starting from e as follows:

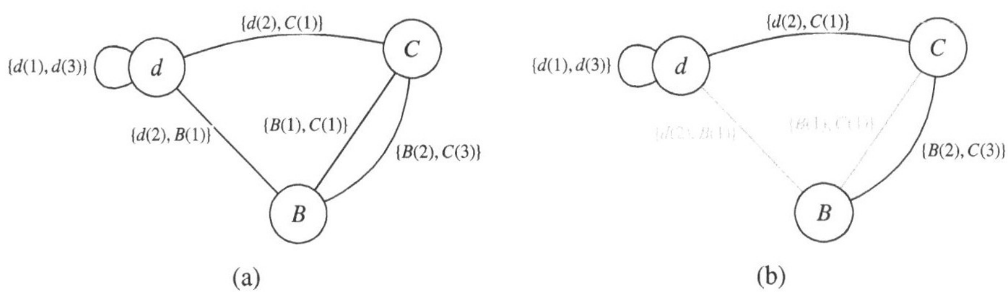

Fig. 4. (a) Example of the *link-graph* for hypergraph H' from Fig. 1b. For the ease of presentation we have explicitly labeled each vertex with the label of the corresponding hyperedge. (b) A possible spanning tree of the link-graph (green edges).

1. compute the link-graph $\mathcal{L}(\mathcal{H})$;
2. construct a positional form ω with only one connector for each attributed symbol; for this, we set an initial positional form $\omega = a$ (recall a is the label of the starting hyperedge) and then when computing a spanning tree starting from the node of $\mathcal{L}(\mathcal{H})$ corresponding to e iteratively update the positional form; namely, whenever a new vertex is explored, we update ω by appending $i^{-n}\_j\, b_2$ where $\{b_1(i), b_2(j)\}$ is the label of the edge used for discovering the vertex and $n \geq 0$ the number of attributed symbols following b_1 in ω;
3. complete the positional form ω by appending a connector as a conjunct at the position of a symbol for each remaining edge of the link-graph; namely, for each not visited edge of $\mathcal{L}(\mathcal{H})$, denoted with $\{b_1(i), b_2(j)\}$ its label, if the distance between b_1 and b_2 in ω is $n \geq 0$, then update ω by appending the connector i^{-n+1}_j as a further conjunct right before b_2.

In order to get a minimal positional sentence for a given hypergraph, the above procedure is completed by deleting connectors, inserted in step 3, that are derivable from other connectors (by transitivity).

As an example, we reconsider the hypergraph H' from Fig. 1b with the starting hyperedge d. Its link graph is given in Fig. 4a. Figure 4b shows (in green) a spanning tree rooted at d, which corresponds to the simple path $d\,\{d(2), B(1)\}\, B\,\{B(1), C(1)\}\, C\}$ that in turns give rise to the positional form $d\,2\_1\,B\,1\_1\,C$ at the end of step 2.

According to step 3, each remaining edge in Fig. 4b yields a potential new connector. However, the connection between $d(2)$ and $C(1)$ is discarded as it can be derived by transitivity from the other connectors (namely, by $\{d(2), B(1)\}$ and $\{B(1), C(1)\}$).

The resulting final and minimal positional form for the hypergraph H' from Fig. 1b, derived from the given spanning tree, is therefore: $1^1\_3\,d\,2\_1\,B\,1\_1 \wedge 2\_3\,C$.

5.3   From HRGs to Positional Grammars

To translate an HRG into an equivalent positional grammar, we essentially map each edge of type n to an attributed symbol with n attributes, and encode the right-end parts of the productions as shown in the previous section.

Formally, let $G = (\mathcal{N}, \mathcal{T}, \mathcal{P}, \mathcal{A})$ be an HRG and denote with $\mathcal{E}$ the set of hyperedges used in the productions in $\mathcal{P}$. Define Σ as the set of all and only the attributed symbols s_e such that $e \in \mathcal{E}$ and $n_{a\,s_e} = \tau(e)$, i.e., the number of attributes of s_e coincides with the number of tentacles of e. Let γ be the bijection that maps each edge in E to the corresponding symbol in Σ, i.e., $\gamma(e) = s_e$.

We define the positional grammar $G_\gamma = (\mathcal{N}_\gamma, \mathcal{T}_\gamma, \mathcal{P}_\gamma, \mathcal{A}_\gamma)$ as follows:

- $\mathcal{N}_\gamma = \{\gamma(e) \mid e = a(v_1, \ldots, v_n)$ and $a \in \mathcal{N}\}$;
- $\mathcal{T}_\gamma = \{\gamma(e) \mid e = a(v_1, \ldots, v_n)$ and $a \in \mathcal{T}\}$;
- $\mathcal{P}_\gamma$ is the set of all the productions of the form $A \rightarrow_\delta \omega$ such that there is a production $e \rightarrow_\mu H \in \mathcal{P}$ where $H = (V, X, E)$ and: (i) ω is the positional form computed from H according to the translation from the previous section (mapping hyperedges into attributed symbols by γ), and (ii) $\delta(i) = (j, \mathsf{k})$ where $\mu(i) = v \in V$, $e \in E$ is mapped to the j-th symbol in ω and e is incident on v by its k-th tentacle;
- $\mathcal{A}_\gamma = \gamma(\mathcal{A})$.

A hypergraph may have different encodings in terms of (weak) positional forms: attributed symbols may be listed in different orders and still we encode the same hypergraph as long as the connectors capture the incidence relation of the hyperedges (and thus the link-graph). Thus, in order to prove the equivalence of G_γ with the starting HRG G, we need to introduce the notion of permutation of a (weak) positional form.

For a bijection $\pi : [1, n] \rightarrow [1, n]$, a *permutation by π* of a sequence $s_1 \ldots s_n$ is a sequence $s'_1 \ldots s'_n$ obtained by rearranging its symbols according to π, i.e., such that $s'_1 \ldots s'_n = s_{\pi(1)} \ldots s_{\pi(n)}$.

Note that the bijection π maps the positions of the permuted sequence into those of the original sequence, and not the other way around. This will allow us to denote such bijections simply as tuples indicating the sequence of positions of the original sequence in the permuted one. For example, for a sequence $s_1\,s_2\,s_3\,s_4$ the bijection for the permutation $s_3\,s_1\,s_2\,s_4$ is denoted as $(3, 1, 2, 4)$.

We extend the notion of permutation to positional forms as follows. A *permutation by π* of a positional form $\omega = r_1\,s_1\,r_2\,s_2 \cdots r_n\,s_n$ is a sequence $\omega^\pi = r'_1\,s'_1\,r'_2\,s'_2 \cdots r'_n\,s'_n$ where:

- $s'_1 \ldots s'_n$ is a permutation by π of $s_1 \ldots s_n$ and
- the connectors within ω are rearranged according to this permutation, i.e., for $h \in [1, n]$ and each connector $\mathsf{k}^z\_\rfloor$ of r_h, denoting i and j the indices such that $h = \pi(i)$ and $h + z - 1 = \pi(j)$ (recall that $h + z - 1$ is the index of the source of the connector):
  1. if $j \leq i$ (i.e., the permutation keeps the same relative order between source and target of the connector), then r'_i contains the connector $\mathsf{k}^{z'}\_\rfloor$ where $z' = j - i + 1$;

2. otherwise (i.e., the permutation inverts the relative order between source and target of the connector), r'_j contains the connector $\mathsf{l}^{z'}\_\mathsf{k}$ where $z' = i - j + 1$;

no other connectors occur within ω^π.

By a simple proof by induction we can show the following theorem.

Theorem 1. *Let G be an HRG. If $H \in L(G)$ then $\omega \in L(G_\gamma)$ exists such that ω is a permutation of ω_H. Vice versa, if $\omega \in L(G_\gamma)$ then $H \in L(G)$ exists such that ω_H is a permutation of ω.*

It can be noted that the positional grammar in Example 2 can be constructed as an equivalent grammar from the HRG of Example 1 by using the procedure described in this section, with one exception: one of the two connectors of the conjunction $2\_1 \wedge 2^{-2}\_1$ in production (6) is omitted, since it can be derived from the other connectors in the same production.

6 Parsing Positional Forms with off-the-Shelf Parsers

Efficient parsing of positional grammars relies on the fact that only positional forms are handled: parsing is guided by connectors which ensures efficient deterministic rule exploration. However, as noted in Example 2, even starting from a positional form a derivation may yield a weak positional form that is not positional: by effect of a production the new form may have no connectors even at a position other than the first one.

In general, a well-formed positional grammar is not straightforward to construct and it may be significantly less succinct than an equivalent non-well-formed one. Therefore, we provide and implement a standard translation of a positional form into an equivalent well formed one.

In this section, we recall the notion of well-formed positional grammars, then give a key notion of our transformation (the permutation of positional forms) and conclude with our transformation algorithm.

6.1 Well-Formed Positional Grammars

From now on, without loss of generality, we will only consider positional grammars $G = (\mathcal{N}, \mathcal{T}, \mathcal{P}, \mathcal{A})$ without *useless* symbols and with axioms that may only start a derivation, i.e., such that:

1. non-terminals are all *accessible*: for every $A \in \mathcal{N}$, there exist $\alpha, \beta \in (\mathcal{N} \cup \mathcal{T})^*$ such that $\mathcal{A} \Rightarrow^* \alpha A \beta$;
2. non-terminals are all productive: for every $A \in \mathcal{N}$, there exists $w \in \mathcal{T}^*$ such that $A \Rightarrow^* w$;
3. the axiom $\mathcal{A}$ does not appear on the right-hand part of a production of G.

Well-formed grammars are defined as follows.

Definition 1 (Well-Formed Positional Grammar). *A positional grammar* $G = (\mathcal{N}, \mathcal{T}, \mathcal{P}, \mathcal{A})$ *is well-formed if:*

for every pair of productions in $\mathcal{P}$ of the form $A \to_\delta r_1 s_1 \omega_A$ and $B \to_{\delta'} \omega_1 r A \omega_2$,

where ω_A, ω_1 and ω_2 are positional forms and $\omega_1 \neq \varepsilon$,

there is a connector i^z_h in r with $z < 1$ such that $\delta(\mathsf{h}) = (1, \mathsf{k})$ for some $\mathsf{k} \in I_{s_1}$. $\qquad\qquad\square$

Well-formedness adds a crucial constraint on the attribute flow: if a production accesses a non-terminal A through one or more of its attributes (say $h_1, h_2, \ldots$) via non-loop connectors then it is sufficient that, in every production defining A, at least one of these attributes is mapped via δ to an attribute of the first symbol in the right-hand part of the production. This ensures preservation of positional forms in the derivations as stated by the following proposition.

Proposition 1. *Every sequence generated by a well-formed positional grammar is a positional form.*

A direct consequence of this proposition and the sentence derived at the end of Example 2 is that the grammar given in that example is not well-formed.

6.2 Making Positional Grammars Well-Formed: Prefix-Connected Permutations

We can use the notion of permutation introduced in Sect. 5.3 to transform a positional grammar into a well-formed one. We recall that a permutation of a (weak) positional form only alters the positions of the symbols while keeping the connectors. However, a permutation of a positional form may not be positional since some positions other than the first one may end up having no connectors. By requiring an additional property, it is possible to guarantee instead that a permutation of a positional form is still positional.

For a positional form $\omega = r_1\, s_1\, r_2\, s_2 \cdots r_n\, s_n$, a bijection $\pi : [1, n] \to [1, n]$ is *prefix-connected w.r.t.* ω if for every $i \in [2, n]$, the symbol $s_{\pi(i)}$ is *connected* (either as a source or as a target) to some symbol in the set $\{s_{\pi(1)}, \ldots, s_{\pi(i-1)}\}$ by at least one connector of ω. A *prefix-connected permutation of* ω is a permutation by π of ω for some prefix-connected bijection π. It is simple to verify that the following holds.

Proposition 2. *A prefix-connected permutation of a positional form is positional.*

To ensure well-formedness, In the next section, we will replace productions with others where the positional forms on the right-hand side of the starting production is permuted starting from a given position.

For a positional form $\omega = r_1\, s_1 \cdots r_n\, s_n$ and $h \in [1, n]$, a *h-rooted permutation of* ω is a permutation of ω of the form $r_1'\, s_1' \cdots r_n'\, s_n'$ such that $s_1' = s_h$.

Proposition 3. *Given a position h and a positional form ω, it is always possible to build at least a h-rooted prefix-connected permutation of ω.*

For a production $p = A \to_\delta \omega$, a j-*permutation of p* is $A \to_{\delta'} \omega'$ where: (1) for $\delta(\mathsf{j}) = (h, \mathsf{k}_h)$, ω' is a h-rooted permutation of ω and (2) δ' preserves the mapping δ after the permutation, i.e., denoted π the bijection mapping the positions of ω' to those of ω, we let $\delta'(\mathsf{i}) = (h', \mathsf{k}')$ whenever $\delta(\mathsf{i}) = (\pi(h'), \mathsf{k}')$ for $\mathsf{i} \in I_A$.

6.3   Translation Algorithm

We introduce the following terminology. A *driver set* is a minimal set of connectors that ensures connectivity within a positional form, that is, such that each symbol in the positional form is connected to one that strictly precedes it. Note that, any driver set for a positional form has exactly one connector for each attributed symbol except for the one in the first position that has no drivers (there is no previous symbol for it). Each connector in a driver set is called a *driver*, and the *driver attribute of a symbol* is the target attribute of the driver connector reaching that symbol. Each connector that is not a driver is called a *tester*. As an example, for $1^1\_3\ d\ 2\_1\ B\ 1\_1 \wedge 2\_3\ B$ the drivers are 2_1 and 1_1, while 1^1_3 and 2_3 are testers. Moreover, the driver attributes of B and C are both 1.

It is worth noting that in a link-graph the edges corresponding to a minimal choice of drivers form a spanning tree.

In the rest of the paper we will assume that in a positional form, the drivers are always listed as the first conjunct among the connectors preceding a symbol. For a positional form ω and a driver set $\mathcal{R}$, the *signature of ω w.r.t. $\mathcal{R}$* is the sequence obtained by ω by deleting all the testers.

Let $G = (\mathcal{N}, \mathcal{T}, \mathcal{P}, \mathcal{A})$ be a positional grammar, Algorithm 1 creates a new well-formed positional grammar $G' = (\mathcal{N}', \mathcal{T}, \mathcal{P}', \mathcal{A}1)$ such that $L(G) - L(G')$. In the following, we assume that the axiom has at least one attribute in position 1 to be considered as the starting attribute. Grammars that do not have such a property can be transformed by adding a new axiom $\mathcal{A}'$ and a production $\mathcal{A}' \to_\delta \#\,1\_1\mathcal{A}$ where $\#$ is a fresh symbol (we just discard the symbol $\#$ in the generated sentences to obtain the original language).

Algorithm 1 constructs a well-formed positional grammar G' equivalent to a given positional grammar G. The transformation ensures that the resulting grammar satisfies the well-formedness property while preserving the generated language.

The algorithm employs a worklist-based approach to systematically process non-terminals paired with their driver attributes defined in the grammar. Initially, the worklist is empty and the new set of non-terminals $\mathcal{N}'$ contains only $\mathcal{A}1$. The procedure GENERATE_PRODUCTIONS is first invoked on the pair $(\mathcal{A}, 1)$.

For each non-terminal A with driver attribute j, the procedure iterates over all productions of A in the original grammar G. For each production p, it computes the j-permuted production, which reorders the right-hand side according to j. Then, for each non-terminal B appearing in the permuted right-hand side, the

---

Algorithm 1: Construction of an equivalent well-formed positional grammar

---

Input: A positional grammar $G = (\mathcal{N}, \mathcal{T}, \mathcal{P}, \mathcal{A})$
Output: A well-formed positional grammar G' such that $L(G) = L(G')$.
let $\mathcal{N}' = \{\mathcal{A}1\}$, $\mathcal{P}' = \{\}$, worklist $= \{(\mathcal{A}, 1)\}$
while *worklist contains unvisited elements* **do**
    read a pair (A, j) from worklist and mark it as *visited*
    `generate_productions`(A, j)
return $G' = (\mathcal{N}', \mathcal{T}, \mathcal{P}', \mathcal{A}1)$

Procedure `generate_productions`(A, j)
    Input: a non terminal A and an integer $\mathsf{j} \in I_A$
    Output: updated sets $\mathcal{N}'$, $\mathcal{P}'$ and worklist
    foreach *production $p : A \rightarrow_\delta \omega$ in $\mathcal{P}$* **do**
        let $A \rightarrow_{\delta'} \omega'$ be a j-permuted production of p with $\omega' = r_1 s_1 \ldots r_n s_n$
        foreach *non terminal $s_i = B$ in ω'* **do**
            if *(i = 1)* **then**
                let k be such that $\delta'(\mathsf{j}) = (1, \mathsf{k})$
            else
                let k be the driver attribute of s_i
            rename s_i to $B\mathsf{k}$ in ω'
            add $B\mathsf{k}$ to $\mathcal{N}'$
            add pair (B, k) to worklist
        add $A\mathsf{j} \rightarrow_{\delta'} \omega'$ to $\mathcal{P}'$

---

algorithm determines its driver attribute k: if B is the first symbol, k is derived from the destination function δ'.

Each non-terminal B is then renamed concatenating B and k, i.e., $B\mathsf{k}$, the renamed non-terminal is added to $\mathcal{N}'$, and the pair (B, k) is added to the worklist for subsequent processing. The algorithm continues until all pairs in the worklist have been visited, ensuring that every reachable (non-terminal, driver attribute) combination is processed exactly once.

Example 3 (A WELL-FORMED POSITIONAL GRAMMAR). Applying Algorithm 1 to the non-well-formed positional grammar of Example 2, one possible well-formed grammar it may return—depending on the choice of j-permuted productions—has the same first five productions, with production (6) replaced by:

$$(6') \ \text{STATEM} \rightarrow_{\delta_6} \text{PRED } 2\_1 \ \text{STATS } 3^{-1}\_1 \ \wedge \ 2\_2 \ \text{STATS } 2\_1 \ \text{ENDIF}$$

$$\delta_6 \colon \text{STATEM}(1) \mapsto (1, \text{PRED}(1)), \ \text{STATEM}(2) \mapsto (4, \text{ENDIF}(2))$$

One can verify that the same derivation as in Example 2, with production (6) replaced by (6'), produces the following positional sentence:

$$\text{START } 1\_1 \ \text{PRED } 2\_1 \ \text{INSTR } 3^{-1}\_1 \ \wedge \ 2\_2 \ \text{INSTR } 2\_1 \ \text{ENDIF } 2\_1 \ \text{END}$$

6.4   Time and Space Complexity Analysis

Let $n_{\mathcal{N}}$ be the number of non terminals, $|\mathcal{P}|$ be the size of $\mathcal{P}$ and n_a be the maximum number of attributes associated with any non-terminal.

Each entry in the worklist is a pair (A, j) where $A \in \mathcal{N}$ and j is an attribute index of A. Since each non-terminal has at most n_a attributes and each of them can appear as a driver attribute, the worklist contains at most $n_{\mathcal{N}} \cdot n_a$ distinct pairs. The visited marking mechanism ensures each pair is processed exactly once.

For each pair (A, j) extracted from the worklist, the algorithm iterates over all productions from A. For each such production:

- computing a j-permuted production takes time linear in the size of the production;
- the inner loop iterates over all the symbols in the right-hand part, and for each non-terminal found, determining the driver attribute and updating the data structures takes $O(1)$ time (assuming constant-time set operations with hashing).

Overall, each production $p \in \mathcal{P}$ with left-hand side A may be processed once for each attribute of A, i.e., at most n_a times. Therefore, the total processing time is bounded by $n_a \cdot |\mathcal{P}|$. Assuming n_a constant (which is often the case in practice), the time complexity simplifies to $O(|\mathcal{P}|)$.

The algorithm requires $O(n_{\mathcal{N}} \cdot n_a)$ space for the worklist and the visited markers, plus $O(n_a \cdot |\mathcal{P}|)$ space for storing the new productions in $\mathcal{P}'$, as each original production may generate up to n_a new productions of the same size as the original ones.

It is worth noting that the algorithm considers one of the many possible feasible j-permuted productions (the first one respecting the required property), without attempting to identify the "best" j-permuted production with its "best" driver set. As a consequence, the resulting well-formed grammar may be very large. In order to minimize the number of productions, it would be desirable to construct j-permutations such that the number of pairs (A, j) to process is minimized, i.e., the number of pairs visited in the worklist to reach a solution is the smallest achievable by any sequence of choices. We leave this optimization problem for future work.

7   Implementation and Evaluation

Implementation. Our conversion algorithms from HRGs to well-formed positional grammars have been implemented as part of a language toolchain built on top of the XText framework [1]. The choice of XText was motivated by its native support for the Language Server Protocol (LSP) [1], which enables the distribution of a single language server compatible with all major code editors (e.g., VS Code, Rider) without requiring editor-specific adaptations. The toolchain exposes two distinct artifacts. The first is a *language server* that handles all editor-facing features through the LSP interface. The second is a standalone *transformation executable* that performs the actual conversion from the HRG down to the well-formed positional grammar and can be integrated into editor workflows by triggering an automatic transformation upon file save.

For the last step, i.e., the generation of an LR-based parser from a well-formed positional grammar, we developed a new tool comprising about 18k lines of C-sharp code. The tool extends the Elkhound [32] implementation of the GLR(1) parser to support positional parsing by applying the pLR methodology described in [9,16]. As a result, it is also capable of parsing visual languages described by ambiguous positional grammars and returning one or more parse trees for their sentences. In particular, the tool runs in the JetBrains Rider IDE, integrated with the LSP (Language Server Protocol) transformation program, and allows the user to edit a HRG, automatically convert it into an equivalent well-formed positional grammar, and build a pLR parser for it. Similarly to the traditional LR parsing methodology, this procedure always provides a parser, either deterministic or non deterministic, how it can be argued from [9,16].

As an example, our tool transforms the HRG of Example 1 into the well-formed positional grammar of Example 3. Even though the corresponding pLR parsing table presents conflicts, the tool builds a deterministic parser by resolving shift/reduce conflicts in favor of shifts following YACC policy [30]. Figures 5a and 5b show respectively, the input hypergraph of Fig. 3 and the parse tree returned by the tool.

Evaluation. We have executed experiments on two sets of benchmarks to evaluate the correctness of our translation. Grammars and hypergraphs from the two sets are of comparable sizes.

Base Benchmarks. A first set of benchmarks comprises 27 HRGs and 132 hypergraphs, taken either from the literature or explicitly designed to challenge the tool. We used this set as a first test bench for our prototype tool. All the HRGs were successfully translated. We then generated a pLR parser for each grammar and tested against the considered hypergraphs. All the experiments produced the expected results: each hypergraph was correctly accepted/rejected.

Grappa Benchmarks. A second set of benchmarks comprises 34 HRGs shipped with the Grappa workbench [28]. They account for roughly one third of the overall Grappa set of HRGs. We excluded grammars in a format that is not yet supported by our prototype or that are not context-free.

For each considered grammar, we extract from the Grappa workbench all the corresponding hypergraphs. This yields 184 instances (i.e., pairs of grammars and hypergraphs) of the HRG parsing problem that we use as a test suite. For each grammar, we also generate a suitable Grappa parser among the available ones, translate the grammar to the corresponding positional form, and generate the corresponding generalized pLR parser.

We run the test suite and compare the outcomes of our prototype and Grappa. The two tools agree on about **98 %** of the considered instances. In

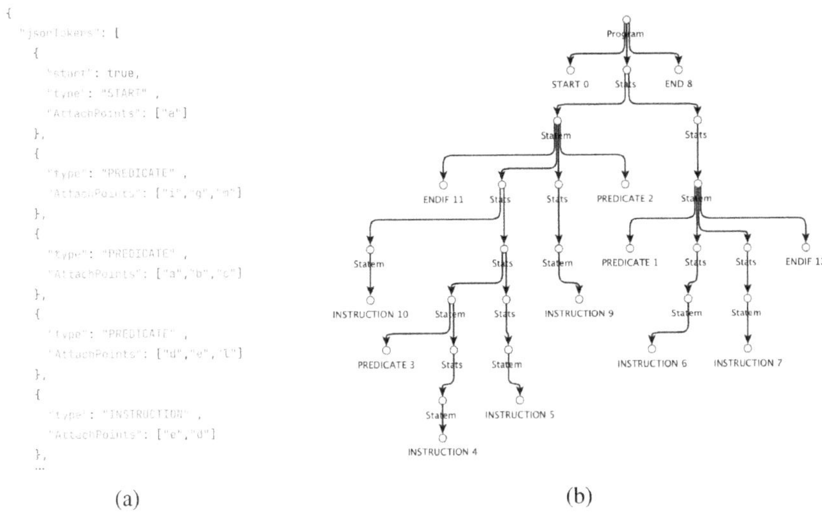

(a)   (b)

Fig. 5. (a) Portion of the encoding of the hypergraph from Fig. 3, and (b) corresponding parse tree (with terminals starting from 0).

particular, 128 pairs are accepted and 52 are rejected by both parsers. For the remaining 4 instances, our parser rejects the input hypergraphs while the Grappa parser accepts them. By a manual inspection on one of them, the answer of our tool looks correct. However, the manual inspection of the outputs is not a trivial task and is prone to error by itself. Therefore, we think that this requires further investigation.

8   Conclusions

In this paper, we have connected predictive shift-reduce parsing for hyperedge replacement grammars and positional LR parsing for visual languages, so far two independent lines of research on LR-based parsing of non-string languages.

Our main contributions are threefold. First, we have provided a systematic translation from arbitrary HRGs into equivalent positional grammars, showing how hypergraphs can be faithfully encoded as positional forms. Second, we have designed an algorithm that transforms any positional grammar into a well-formed one— guaranteed to be parsable by the pLR methodology—and we have shown that this transformation runs in linear time (assuming constant-arity hyperedges). Third, we have implemented the full pipeline and evaluated it on several input grammars and sentences.

Beyond the immediate technical results, bridging these two formalisms opens to a cross-fertilization that could be beneficial to both research fields. On one hand, results developed in the context of positional parsing, such as runtime conflict detection [13], become directly applicable to hypergraph languages. On the other hand, techniques from the HRG parsing literature, such as the free edge choice optimization [24], can inform new strategies for improving positional parsers.

We see a few future work directions. First, our well-forming algorithm just selects one feasible permuted production. Establishing whether minimizing the total number of generated productions leads to fewer parser conflicts, or whether carefully choosing the permutations yields a deterministic parser more readily, are both open questions. Second, extending the approach to generalized pLR parsing would allow handling ambiguous HRGs, where conflicts are managed rather than eliminated; in this setting, the size of the grammar is likely to be meaningful for the overall complexity.

Finally, the connection established in this paper now enables a direct empirical comparison between positional parsers and existing graph-parsing approaches such as the Grappa toolchain and PSR [28]; a comparison across a wider set of benchmarks would clarify the practical tradeoffs between the two families of techniques.

Acknowledgements. This work was supported by FARB 2023–25 grants of Università degli Studi di Salerno.

Disclosure of Interests. The authors have no competing interests to declare that are relevant to the content of this article.

References

1. Bettini, L.: Implementing Domain-Specific Languages with Xtext and Xtend, 2nd edn. Packt Publishing, Birmingham (2016)
2. Chiang, D., Andreas, J., Bauer, D., Hermann, K.M., Jones, B., Knight, K.: Parsing graphs with hyperedge replacement grammars. In: Proceedings of the 51st Annual Meeting of the ACL (Volume 1: Long Papers), pp. 924–932 (2013). https://aclanthology.org/P13-1091/
3. Chimes, M., Iosif, R., Zuleger, F.: Tree-verifiable graph grammars (2024). https://arxiv.org/abs/2402.17015
4. Costagliola, G.: Extended positional grammars: a formalism for describing and parsing visual languages. In: Ferri, F. (ed.) Visual Languages for Interactive Computing, pp. 102–116. IGI Global (2008). https://doi.org/10.4018/978-1-59904-534-4.ch005
5. Costagliola, G., Chang, S.K.: DR parsers: a generalization of LR parsers. In: Proceedings of the 1990 IEEE Workshop on Visual Languages (1990). https://doi.org/10.1109/WVL.1990.128401
6. Costagliola, G., Chang, S.K.: Parsing 2D languages with positional grammars. In: Proceedings of the 2nd Int. Workshop on Parsing Technologies, pp. 235–243 (1991)
7. Costagliola, G., Chang, S.K.: Using linear positional grammars for the LR parsing of 2-D symbolic languages. Grammars **2**, 1–34 (1999)
8. Costagliola, G., De Lucia, A., Orefice, S., Tortora, G.: A parsing methodology for the implementation of visual systems. IEEE Trans. Softw. Eng. **23**(12), 777–799 (1997). https://doi.org/10.1109/32.637392

9. Costagliola, G., De Lucia, A., Orefice, S., Tortora, G.: A parsing methodology for the implementation of visual systems. IEEE Trans. Softw. Eng. **23**(12), 777–799 (1997). https://doi.org/10.1109/32.637392
10. Costagliola, G., De Lucia, A., Orefice, S., Tortora, G.: Positional grammars: a formalism for LR-like parsing of visual languages. In: Marriott, K., Meyer, B. (eds.) Visual Language Theory, pp. 171–191. Springer (1998). https://doi.org/10. 1007/978-1-4612-1676-6_5
11. Costagliola, G., Deufemia, V.: Visual language editors based on LR parsing techniques. In: Proceedings of the 8th International Conference on Parsing Technologies, pp. 78–90 (2003)
12. Costagliola, G., Deufemia, V., Ferrucci, F., Gravino, C.: On the PLR parsability of visual languages. In: Proceedings IEEE Symposium on Human-Centric Computing Languages and Environments. pp. 48–51. IEEE (2001). https://doi.org/10.1109/ HCC.2001.995234
13. Costagliola, G., Deufemia, V., Ferrucci, F., Gravino, C.: Run-time conflict detection in visual language parsing. J. Comput. Lang. **57**, 100943 (2020). https://doi. org/10.1016/j.cola.2020.100943
14. Costagliola, G., Deufemia, V., Polese, G., Risi, M.: Building syntax-aware editors for visual languages. J. Visual Lang. Comput. **16**(6), 508–540 (2005). https://doi. org/10.1016/j.jvlc.2005.06.001
15. Costagliola, G., Tortora, G., Orefice, S., De Lucia, A.: Automatic generation of visual programming environments. IEEE Comput. **28**(3), 56–66 (1995). https:// doi.org/10.1109/2.366162
16. Costagliola, G., Deufemia, V., Polese, G.: A framework for modeling and implementing visual notations with applications to software engineering. ACM Trans. Softw. Eng. Methodol. **13**(4), 431–487 (2004). https://doi.org/10.1145/1040291. 1040293
17. Costagliola, G., Vastarini, F.: Parsing hypergraphs using context-free positional grammars. Electron. Proc. Theoretic. Comput. Sci. **440**, 1–5 (2026). https://doi. org/10.4204/eptcs.440.1
18. Courcelle, B., Engelfriet, J.: Graph Structure and Monadic Second-Order Logic – A Language-Theoretic Approach. Cambridge Univ, Press (2012)
19. Drewes, F.: Recognising k-connected hypergraphs in cubic time. Theoret. Comput. Sci. **109**, 83–122 (1993). https://doi.org/10.1016/0304-3975(93)90065-2
20. Drewes, F., Björklund, H., Ericson, J.: Generation and polynomial parsing of graph languages with non-structural reentrancies. Comput. Linguist. **49**(4), 841–880 (2023). https://doi.org/10.1162/coli_a_00488
21. Drewes, F., Habel, A., Kreowski, H.J.: Hyperedge replacement graph grammars. In: Rozenberg, G. (ed.) Handbook of Graph Grammars and Computing by Graph Transformation, vol. I, pp. 95–162. World Scientific (1997) . https://doi.org/10. 1142/9789812384720_0002
22. Drewes, F., Hoffmann, B., Minas, M.: Predictive top-down parsing for hyperedge replacement grammars. In: Parisi-Presicce, F., Westfechtel, B. (eds.) ICGT 2015. LNCS, vol. 9151, pp. 19–34. Springer, Cham (2015). https://doi.org/10.1007/978-3-319-21145-9_2
23. Drewes, F., Hoffmann, B., Minas, M.: Predictive shift-reduce parsing for hyperedge replacement grammars. In: de Lara, J., Plump, D. (eds.) ICGT 2017. LNCS, vol. 10373, pp. 106–122. Springer, Cham (2017). https://doi.org/10.1007/978-3-319-61470-0_7

24. Drewes, F., Hoffmann, B., Minas, M.: Formalization and correctness of predictive shift-reduce parsers for graph grammars based on hyperedge replacement. J. Logic. Algebraic Methods Program. **104**, 303–341 (2019). https://doi.org/10.1016/j.jlamp.2018.12.006
25. Drewes, F., Stade, Y.: On the power of local graph expansion grammars with and without additional restrictions. Theoret. Comput. Sci. **1015**, 114763 (2024). https://doi.org/10.1016/j.tcs.2024.114763
26. Gilroy, S., Lopez, A., Maneth, S.: Parsing graphs with regular graph grammars. In: Proceedings of the 6th Joint Conference on Lexical and Computational Semantics (*SEM 2017), pp. 199–208. Association for Computational Linguistics (2017). https://doi.org/10.18653/v1/S17-1024
27. Habel, A.: Hyperedge Replacement: Grammars and Languages, LNCS, vol. 643. Springer (1992)
28. Hoffmann, B., Minas, M.: Generating efficient predictive shift-reduce parsers for hyperedge replacement grammars. In: Seidl, M., Zschaler, S. (eds.) STAF 2017. LNCS, vol. 10748, pp. 76–91. Springer, Cham (2018). https://doi.org/10.1007/978-3-319-74730-9_7
29. Hoffmann, B., Minas, M.: Generalized predictive shift-reduce parsing for hyperedge replacement graph grammars. In: Martín-Vide, C., Okhotin, A., Shapira, D. (eds.) LATA 2019. LNCS, vol. 11417, pp. 233–245. Springer, Cham (2019). https://doi.org/10.1007/978-3-030-13435-8_17
30. Johnson, S.C.: YACC: yet another compiler-compiler. Tech. Rep. Computing Science Technical Report 32, Bell Laboratories, Murray Hill, NJ, USA (1975)
31. Lautemann, C.: The complexity of graph languages generated by hyperedge replacement. Acta Informatica **27**, 399–421 (1990). https://doi.org/10.1007/BF00289017
32. McPeak, S., Necula, G.C.: Elkhound: a fast, practical GLR parser generator. In: Duesterwald, E. (ed.) CC 2004. LNCS, vol. 2985, pp. 73–88. Springer, Heidelberg (2004). https://doi.org/10.1007/978-3-540-24723-4_6
33. Piscitelli, A.: Multidimensional languages, a grammar specification for the definition of multidimensional languages. Master's thesis, Università di Salerno, Fisciano (SA), Italia (2019). https://alfy91.github.io/files/master-thesis.pdf. Accessed 27 April 2026
34. Reccia, L.: A formal grammar definition to describe Multidimensional Languages. Master's thesis, Università di Salerno, Fisciano (SA), Italia (2020). https://cluelab.di.unisa.it/old/images/stories/papers/reccia_thesis.pdf. Accessed 27 April 2026
35. Riedl, M., Seifert, S., Fischer, I.: String generating hypergraph grammars with word order restrictions. In: Corradini, A., Ehrig, H., Montanari, U., Ribeiro, L., Rozenberg, G. (eds.) ICGT 2006. LNCS, vol. 4178, pp. 138–152. Springer, Heidelberg (2006). https://doi.org/10.1007/11841883_11
36. Seifert, S., Fischer, I.: Parsing string generating hypergraph grammars. In: Ehrig, H., Engels, G., Parisi-Presicce, F., Rozenberg, G. (eds.) ICGT 2004. LNCS, vol. 3256, pp. 352–367. Springer, Heidelberg (2004). https://doi.org/10.1007/978-3-540-30203-2_25
37. Vogler, W.: Recognizing edge replacement graph languages in cubic time. In: Ehrig, H., Kreowski, H.-J., Rozenberg, G. (eds.) Graph Grammars 1990. LNCS, vol. 532, pp. 676–687. Springer, Heidelberg (1991). https://doi.org/10.1007/BFb0017421

Conditional Borrowing Hyperedge Replacement

Frank Drewes[1] , Berthold Hoffmann[2] , and Mark Minas[3]([envelope])

[1] Umeå universitet, Umeå, Sweden
`drewes@cs.umu.se`
[2] Universität Bremen, Bremen, Germany
`hof@uni-bremen.de`
[3] Universität der Bundeswehr München, Neubiberg, Germany
`mark.minas@unibw.de`

Abstract. In graph grammars based on borrowing hyperedge replacement (BHR), a production replaces a hyperedge by a hypergraph that contains borrowed nodes, which are later contracted with other nodes of the graph being derived. In contrast to context-free hyperedge replacement, this allows graph languages of unbounded treewidth to be defined. Here we further equip the productions of BHR grammars with conditions, which are specified by graph formulas that may require (or forbid) the existence of paths of arbitrary length in the graphs of the language. This is defined in such a way that the top-down parsers for BHR grammars devised in earlier work can be extended to verify these conditions.

Keywords: Graph grammar · Hyperedge replacement · Graph condition · Graph parsing

1 Introduction

Hyperedge replacement (HR) grammars [13] are a well-established formalism for rule-based generation of graph languages. HR grammars have attractive properties, in particular the existence of efficient parsing algorithms for certain subclasses, e.g., predictive top-down parsing (PTD, [4]) and predictive shift-reduce parsing (PSR, [5]). To a large extent, this is due to the fact that, by context-freeness, the result of a derivation depends only on which productions are applied to which nonterminal hyperedges; it is independent of the order in which those productions are applied. Formally, this means that HR is *confluent* in the sense of Courcelle [1]. Context-freeness is a very nice property both for the theory of HR languages and for the development of efficient parsing algorithms, but it also limits the generative power of HR grammars, excluding many graph classes of practical and theoretical interest.

A weakness of pure hyperedge replacement is that it generates only graph languages of bounded treewidth. Contextual hyperedge replacement (CHR, [2])

B. Archibald and O. Semeráth (Eds.): ICGT 2026, LNCS 16624, pp. 25–45, 2026.
https://doi.org/10.1007/978-3-032-29730-3_2

was introduced to overcome this limitation by allowing right-hand sides of productions to contain *contextual nodes*. When a production is applied, contextual nodes in its right-hand side are *contracted*, i.e., fused with previously generated nodes elsewhere in the graph. While this adds expressive power, it has the disadvantage of breaking confluence. Since contextual nodes can only be contracted with previously generated nodes, the order in which productions are applied to the nonterminal hyperedges in a graph suddenly matters. In particular, this makes it difficult to find natural subclasses to which the mentioned PTD and PSR parsing techniques can be generalized. The only subclass of this kind known to us is the class of *acyclic* CHR grammars [7], which are difficult to work with both algorithmically and practically because acyclicity is a non-trivial semantic property of CHR grammars.

Borrowing hyperedge replacement (BHR, [3]) overcomes the bounded tree-width limitation in a related but different way. It allows right-hand sides of productions to contain so-called borrowed nodes. Only after the completed derivation, these nodes are contracted with non-borrowed nodes of the generated graph. This means that a similar effect is achieved, but now with a generation process that is simply hyperedge replacement with an added "post-processing" step, thus maintaining confluence. It can be shown that BHR grammars can simulate acyclic CHR grammars [7].

The flexibility of BHR comes at a price. Since the contraction of borrowed nodes is entirely uncontrolled, BHR grammars provide no means to guarantee desired structural properties of the generated graphs when it comes to substructures involving edges incident with borrowed nodes. In particular, this holds for properties that require or forbid the existence of path-like structures. This observation motivates the present work: we aim to strengthen the descriptive power of BHR grammars in a manner compatible with the "philosophy" of BHR grammars, which is to decouple the non-context-free aspects from the underlying context-free generation process.

To this end, we equip BHR productions with the ability to introduce so-called condition edges. These condition edges locate places where the generated graph must satisfy certain structural conditions, such as the existence or non-existence of paths between nodes. This follows the ideas outlined in [19], where the integration of logical constraints into CHR grammars was advocated as a means of increasing expressiveness without sacrificing conceptual clarity.

It is important not to confuse our type of conditions with traditional application conditions. Whereas application conditions restrict the applicability of a production when it is to be applied, conditional BHR grammars first generate a graph with borrowed nodes and condition edges in an entirely context-free and thus confluent manner, using ordinary hyperedge replacement. Afterwards, borrowed nodes are contracted with potential target nodes in a way satisfying the structural requirements on the resulting graph expressed by the condition edges. In this way, a clear separation is maintained between the confluent generation process of the underlying HR grammar and the enforcement of additional structural conditions.

The resulting formalism, conditional BHR, allows for the concise specification of graph languages beyond the scope of plain BHR grammars. The conditional BHR grammar for statecharts presented in Sect. 4 of this paper demonstrates that this approach is applicable in realistic modeling scenarios rather than being of mere theoretical interest.

In addition, conditional BHR grammars lend themselves to top-down parsing, of which PTD parsing is a deterministic and thus efficient variant. PTD parsing requires the grammar to satisfy certain conditions, worked out for HR grammars in [4] and for acyclic CHR grammars in [6]. Since BHR grammars are at least as powerful as acyclic CHR grammars, and conditional BHR grammars provide the former with significant additional control over the generated structures, it is our aim to extend PTD parsing to conditional BHR grammars. In addition to introducing conditional BHR grammars, the present paper takes the first step into this direction by sketching how a (nondeterministic) top-down parser for conditional BHR grammars can work. Due to space restrictions, the formal definition of such a parser and its further development into a PTD parser have to be left to future work.

The remainder of this paper is structured as follows. Next, we define BHR grammars that use graph expressions in their production rules (in Sect. 2). In Sect. 3, we recall how graph formulas specify properties of graphs, and equip BHR grammars with conditions specified by shallow graph formulas. The conditional BHR grammar for statecharts in Sect. 4 demonstrates that our concepts are useful in practice. Then we outline how conditions can be verified during the run of a top-down parser for BHR grammars (in Sect. 5). In Sect. 6, we discuss related work and indicate directions of future research.

2 Borrowing Hyperedge Replacement

We let $\mathbb{N}$ denote the set of non-negative integers and $[n]$ the set $\{1, \ldots, n\}$ for all $n \in \mathbb{N}$. A^* denotes the set of all finite sequences over a set A; the empty sequence is denoted by ε. For a sequence $s \in A^*$, $[s]$ denotes the set of all members of A occurring in s. If $f\colon A \to B$ is a function, $f^*\colon A^* \to B^*$ denotes the function defined by $f^*(a_1 \cdots a_n) = f(a_1) \cdots f(a_n)$. As usual, for a binary relation $\leadsto \subseteq A \times A$, we let $\leadsto^n$ $(n \in \mathbb{N})$, $\leadsto^+$, and $\leadsto^*$ denote the n-fold composition with itself, its transitive closure, and its reflexive-transitive closure, respectively.

2.1 Graphs and Graph Concatenation

We consider edge-labeled hypergraphs (which we simply call graphs), i.e., edges are attached to sequences of nodes. To be able to concatenate graphs in the way originally proposed by Engelfriet and Vereijken [10], we supply each graph with two sequences of distinguished nodes, its front and rear interfaces.[1]

---

[1] In contrast to [13], however, we do not also divide the attached nodes of edges into sources and targets.

A ranked set (Σ, rank) consists of a finite set Σ of elements and a function $\mathit{rank}\colon \Sigma \to \mathbb{N}$, which assigns a rank to each element $a \in \Sigma$. The pair (Σ, rank) is usually identified with Σ, keeping rank implicit.

Definition 1 (Graph). Let Σ be a ranked set of symbols. A *graph* over Σ is a tuple $G = (\dot{G}, \bar{G}, \mathit{att}_G, \mathit{lab}_G, \mathit{front}_G, \mathit{rear}_G)$, where $\dot{G}$ and $\bar{G}$ are disjoint finite sets of *nodes* and *edges*, respectively, $\mathit{att}_G\colon \bar{G} \to \dot{G}^*$ attaches sequences of nodes to edges, $\mathit{lab}_G\colon \bar{G} \to \Sigma$ labels edges with symbols so that $|\mathit{att}_G(e)| = \mathit{rank}(\mathit{lab}_G(e))$ for every edge $e \in \bar{G}$, and the node sequences $\mathit{front}_G, \mathit{rear}_G \in \dot{G}^*$ are the *front* and *rear* interface, respectively, of G.

An a-edge is an edge labeled by the symbol a. Given a graph G and an edge $e \in \bar{G}$, we denote by $G - e$ the graph obtained from G by deleting e. Given a subset Δ of Σ, we denote by $G|_\Delta$ the graph obtained from G by deleting all edges $e \in \bar{G}$ such that $\mathit{lab}_G(e) \notin \Delta$.

The *type* of a graph G is $(|\mathit{front}_G|, |\mathit{rear}_G|)$. The set of all graphs of type (m, n) is denoted by $\mathbb{G}_\Sigma^{(m,n)}$. Furthermore, $\mathbb{G}_\Sigma = \bigcup_{m,n \in \mathbb{N}} \mathbb{G}_\Sigma^{(m,n)}$. A subset of $\mathbb{G}_\Sigma$ is a *graph language*, and one of $\mathbb{G}_\Sigma^{(m,n)}$ is a graph language of type (m, n).

For graphs $G, H \in \mathbb{G}_\Sigma$, a *morphism* $m\colon G \to H$ is a pair $(\dot{m}, \bar{m})$ of functions $\dot{m}\colon \dot{G} \to \dot{H}$ and $\bar{m}\colon \bar{G} \to \bar{H}$ such that $\mathit{lab}_G = \mathit{lab}_H \circ \bar{m}$, $\mathit{att}_H \circ \bar{m} = \dot{m}^* \circ \mathit{att}_G$, $\mathit{front}_H = \dot{m}^*(\mathit{front}_G)$, and $\mathit{rear}_H = \dot{m}^*(\mathit{rear}_G)$; m is called *injective* or *surjective*, respectively, if both $\dot{m}$ and $\bar{m}$ are, and it is called an *isomorphism* if $\dot{m}$ and $\bar{m}$ are both bijective. Two graphs $G, H \in \mathbb{G}_\Sigma$ are called *isomorphic*, written $G \cong H$, if there is an isomorphism $m\colon G \to H$.

The graph Id_k with $\bar{\mathit{Id}}_k = \varnothing$, $\dot{\mathit{Id}}_k = [k]$, and $\mathit{front}_{\mathit{Id}_k} = 1 \cdots k = \mathit{rear}_{\mathit{Id}_k}$ is the *identity graph (on k nodes)*.

We follow Engelfriet and Vereijken [10] in defining a concatenation operation for graphs.

Definition 2 (Graph Concatenation). Let $G \in \mathbb{G}_\Sigma^{(i,k)}$ and $H \in \mathbb{G}_\Sigma^{(k,j)}$ be disjoint graphs, i.e., $\dot{G} \cap \dot{H} = \varnothing = \bar{G} \cap \bar{H}$ (otherwise appropriate isomorphic copies of G and H are used). Let C be the graph given by $\dot{C} = \dot{G} \cup \dot{H}$, $\bar{C} = \bar{G} \cup \bar{H}$, $\mathit{att}_C = \mathit{att}_G \cup \mathit{att}_H$, $\mathit{lab}_C = \mathit{lab}_G \cup \mathit{lab}_H$, $\mathit{front}_C = \mathit{front}_G$, and $\mathit{rear}_C = \mathit{rear}_H$. Then the *concatenation* $G \cdot H$ of G and H is the graph obtained from C by fusing each node in rear_G with the corresponding node in front_H. Thus $G \cdot H \in \mathbb{G}_\Sigma^{(i,j)}$.

We recall frontal subgraphs in [8].

Definition 3 (Frontal Subgraph). Let $H \in \mathbb{G}_\Sigma^{(i,j)}$. A graph $G \in \mathbb{G}_\Sigma^{(i,k)}$ with $\dot{G} \subseteq \dot{H}$ and $\bar{G} \subseteq \bar{H}$ is a *frontal subgraph*[2] of H if

- $\mathit{lab}_G(e) = \mathit{lab}_H(e)$ and $\mathit{att}_G(e) = \mathit{att}_H(e)$ for all $e \in \bar{G}$, and
- $\mathit{front}_G = \mathit{front}_H$.

---

[2] Note that some edges of H may be attached to nodes that do not occur in the rear of G; Thus, in general, H is not the concatenation $H = G \cdot H'$ with some graph H'.

2.2 Specifying Graph Languages by Graph Expressions

We now recall the definition of graph expressions in [8]. Similarly to regular expressions for string languages, graph expressions construct graph languages from singleton languages with the operations union, concatenation, and Kleene star on graphs. In graph expressions, we will use the notation known from regular expressions for these operations.

Definition 4 (Graph Expressions). Let $i, j, k \in \mathbb{N}$.

- The *(typed) concatenation* of graph languages $\mathcal{L} \subseteq \mathbb{G}_\Sigma^{(i,k)}$ and $\mathcal{M} \subseteq \mathbb{G}_\Sigma^{(k,j)}$ is $\mathcal{L} \cdot \mathcal{M} = \{G \cdot H \mid G \in \mathcal{L}, H \in \mathcal{M}\}$.
- The *(Kleene) star* $\mathcal{L}^*$ of a graph language $\mathcal{L} \subseteq \mathbb{G}_\Sigma^{(i,i)}$ is the smallest graph language containing Id_i and, for all graphs $G \in \mathcal{L}$ and $H \in \mathcal{L}^*$, the graph $G \cdot H \in \mathcal{L}^*$.

Note that graph concatenation is associative. For $\mathcal{L} \subseteq \mathbb{G}_\Sigma^{(i,i)}$, we may also abbreviate the n-fold iterated concatenation of $\mathcal{L}$ with itself by $\mathcal{L}^n$, i.e., $\mathcal{L}^0 = \{Id_i\}$ and $\mathcal{L}^{n+1} = \mathcal{L} \cdot \mathcal{L}^n$ for $n \in \mathbb{N}$.

The set $\mathbb{E}_\Sigma^{(i,j)}$ of *graph expressions ex* of type (i, j) over Σ and the languages $\mathcal{L}(ex)$ they denote are defined inductively, as follows:

1. $\varnothing \in \mathbb{E}_\Sigma^{(i,j)}$ with $\mathcal{L}(\varnothing) = \varnothing$.
2. If $G \in \mathbb{G}_\Sigma^{(i,j)}$, then $G \in \mathbb{E}_\Sigma^{(i,j)}$ with $\mathcal{L}(G) = \{G\}$.
3. If $ex_1, ex_2 \in \mathbb{E}_\Sigma^{(i,j)}$, then $ex_1|ex_2 \in \mathbb{E}_\Sigma^{(i,j)}$ with $\mathcal{L}(ex_1|ex_2) = \mathcal{L}(ex_1) \cup \mathcal{L}(ex_2)$.
4. If $ex_1 \in \mathbb{E}^{(i,j)}$ and $ex_2 \in \mathbb{E}_\Sigma^{(j,k)}$, then $ex_1 ex_2 \in \mathbb{E}_\Sigma^{(i,k)}$ with $\mathcal{L}(ex_1 ex_2) = \mathcal{L}(ex_1) \cdot \mathcal{L}(ex_2)$.
5. If $ex \in \mathbb{E}_\Sigma^{(i,i)}$, then $ex^* \in \mathbb{E}_\Sigma^{(i,i)}$ with $\mathcal{L}(ex^*) = \mathcal{L}(ex)^*$.

We let $\hat{\mathbb{E}}_\Sigma^{(i,j)}$ be the subset of $\mathbb{E}_\Sigma^{(i,j)}$ obtained by considering, in case 2 above, only graphs $G \in \mathbb{G}_\Sigma^{(i,j)}$ such that $front_G$ is free of repetitions. Hence, the graph languages $\mathcal{L}(ex)$ for $ex \in \hat{\mathbb{E}}_\Sigma^{(i,j)}$ contain only graphs whose front interfaces are repetition-free.

To save parentheses in expressions, we use the convention that the Kleene star binds stronger than concatenation, which binds stronger than union.

Example 1 (Cycles and Wheels). The following graph expressions in $\hat{\mathbb{E}}_\Sigma^{(0,0)}$ and $\hat{\mathbb{E}}_\Sigma^{(1,1)}$ (over a single binary edge label that is invisible) specify cycles of arbitrary length $\ell \geq 1$, of type $(0, 0)$, and *wheels* with an arbitrary number $n \geq 2$ of spokes (as in [13, page 92]), of type $(1, 1)$, respectively.

As usual, we draw nodes as circles and non-binary edges as boxes, the boxes containing the edge label and being connected to their attached nodes by lines; binary edges are drawn as arrows and have their label ascribed, or are distinguished by the way the arrow is drawn (e.g., thick or thin, as in the Wheel expression). The front and rear nodes of each graph are indicated by connecting them by double lines to the left and right edge, respectively, of the box underlying the graph, ordered from top to bottom.

2.3   Recalling Borrowing Hyperedge Replacement

To re-cast the definition of borrowing hyperedge replacement, and later to define conditional borrowing hyperedge replacement, we use annotated graphs, where edges are labelled not only with the terminal symbols Σ considered so far, but also with symbols from a ranked set $X = N \cup \{\Box\} \cup C$ such that Σ, N, $\{\Box\}$, and C are pairwise disjoint. The additional labels will be used for the following purposes:

- *nonterminal names* in N indicate places for hyperedge replacement;
- The *borrow symbol* $\Box$ (of rank 1) designates the attachment of a $\Box$-edge as a *borrowed node*, to be contracted with another node later on;
- *condition names* in C indicate places where conditions must be satisfied.

Edges labeled with these symbols are accordingly called nonterminal, borrow, and condition edges, respectively.

For $Y \subseteq X$, we will refer to the set of graphs over $\Sigma \cup Y$ by $\mathbb{G}_\Sigma(Y)$; its restriction to graphs of type (m, n) are denoted by $\mathbb{G}_\Sigma(Y)^{(m,n)}$. For graph expressions, the corresponding notations $\mathbb{E}_\Sigma(Y)$ and $\hat{\mathbb{E}}_\Sigma(Y)$ is defined in the obvious similar way.

For $A \in N$ of rank k, the *nonterminal atom of A*, denoted by $\langle A \rangle$, consists of k nodes and an A-edge e such that $att_{\langle A \rangle}(e) = front_{\langle A \rangle}$ and $rear_{\langle A \rangle} = \varepsilon$. Let G be a graph. For a node sequence $\alpha \in \dot{G}^*$, we let $\alpha : G = (\dot{G}, \bar{G}, att_G, lab_G, \alpha, rear_G)$ and $G : \alpha = (\dot{G}, \bar{G}, att_G, lab_G, front_G, \alpha)$ denote the graphs where $front_G$ and $rear_G$ is set to α, respectively. In particular, $G : \varepsilon$ is the graph G with an empty rear interface.

Definition 5 (Borrowing Hyperedge Replacement). A *borrowing hyperedge replacement graph grammar* (*BHR grammar* or just *grammar*, for short) is a tuple $\Gamma = (\Sigma, N \cup \{\Box\}, \pi, S)$, where Σ and N are as above,
1. π is a mapping $\pi \colon N \to \mathbb{E}_\Sigma(N \cup \{\Box\})$ defining *productions* such that, for every $A \in N$, $\pi(A)$ is of type $(rank(A), n)$ for some $n \in \mathbb{N}^3$, and its borrowed nodes do not appear in its front, and
2. $S \in N$ is the *start symbol*.

Consider a graph G with a nonterminal A-edge $e \in \bar{G}$. *Replacing e by $P \in \mathcal{L}(\pi(A))$* yields $H = ((G - e) \colon att_G(e)) \cdot (P \colon \varepsilon)$. We then write $G \Rightarrow_A H$. We write $G \Rightarrow_\pi H$ if $G \Rightarrow_A H$ for some A-edge in G.

---

[3] The rear of $\pi(a)$ is irrelevant; this liberty makes productions easier to write.

A *contraction* of a graph G is a surjective morphism $\xi\colon G' \to G''$, where G' is obtained from G by removing all borrow edges, $\dot{G}'' = \{v \in \dot{G} \mid v$ is not borrowed$\}$, $\bar{G}'' = \bar{G}'$, $\bar{\xi}$ is the identity, and $\dot{\xi}(v) = v$ for all $v \in \dot{G}''$. Consequently, a contraction fuses each borrowed node with any node that is not borrowed, and removes all borrow edges. Then we write $G \rightsquigarrow G''$.

The *language* of Γ is defined as

$$\mathcal{L}(\Gamma) = \{G' \in \mathbb{G}_\Sigma \mid \langle S \rangle \Rightarrow_\pi^* G \rightsquigarrow G'\}.$$

We observe that the application of a production yields a graph with an empty rear. In particular, $\mathcal{L}(\Gamma) \subseteq \mathbb{G}_\Sigma^{(m,0)}$ where m is the rank of S.

Borrowing hyperedge replacement corresponds to contextual hyperedge replacement *with* confluence [7]. Note that contractions in the BHR grammars of [6] are more restrictive in that borrowed nodes must not be contracted with nodes inserted in the same production. In the settings of this paper, this restriction can be enforced by conditions in *conditional* BHR grammars, as defined in the next section. Moreover, the productions in [6] have graphs as their right-hand sides only. In contrast, the productions defined above admit arbitrary expressions on the right-hand side, potentially involving alternatives and Kleene star operators, like in [10, Def. 10]. This enables a more syntactically convenient and compact specification.

3   Conditional Borrowing Hyperedge Replacement

The practical usefulness of borrowing hyperedge replacement grammars is severely limited by the fact that contractions allow borrowed nodes to be contracted with arbitrary non-borrowed nodes. These grammars provide no way to formulate structural conditions that the graph needs to obey once these contractions have taken place. Below, we introduce conditional borrowing hyperedge replacement as a remedy.

Conceptually, the way conditions are used in conditional borrowing hyperedge replacement is orthogonal to the generation process of Definition 5: any formalism specifying graph languages can be "plugged in". However, to be of practical use such a formalism should be expressive enough to specify non-trivial conditions, but not too powerful to allow for a reasonably efficient implementation. In this paper, we use a weaker version of the graph formulas of [8], disallowing nested quantifiers.[4]

Definition 6 (Shallow Graph Formulas). For $m \in \mathbb{N}$ and a ranked set Σ of edge labels, the set $\mathbb{SF}_\Sigma^m$ of *shallow graph formulas* of type m over Σ (simply called *formulas* in the following) is defined inductively as follows:

(1) *true*, *false* $\in \mathbb{SF}_\Sigma^m$;

---

[4] As shown in [8, Theorem 3] the uniform membership problem for unrestricted graph formulas is PSPACE complete because of the arbitrarily deep quantifier nesting.

(2) if $ex \in \mathbb{E}_\Sigma^{(m,i)}$ for any $i \in \mathbb{N}$, then $\exists ex \in \mathbb{SF}_\Sigma^m$;
(3) if $fo, fo' \in \mathbb{SF}_\Sigma^m$, then $\neg fo$, $fo \vee fo'$, and $fo \wedge fo'$ are in $\mathbb{SF}_\Sigma^m$.

We let $\mathbb{SF}_\Sigma = \bigcup_{m \in \mathbb{N}} \mathbb{SF}_\Sigma^m$ denote the set of all formulas over Σ.

A graph G of type (m,n) *satisfies* a graph formula fo of type m, written $G \vDash fo$ if one of the following holds:

- $fo = \exists ex$ such that some graph $H \in \mathcal{L}(ex)$ is a frontal subgraph of G,
- $fo = \neg fo'$ such that $G \vDash fo'$ does not hold,
- $fo = fo' \vee fo''$ such that $G \vDash fo'$ or $G \vDash fo''$ (or both), or
- $fo = fo' \wedge fo''$ such that $G \vDash fo'$ and $G \vDash fo''$.

The structure of shallow formulas corresponds to the nested conditions (over injective graph morphisms) of [14–16,22], but without nested quantifications of the form $\exists(P,C)$ and $\forall(P,C)$.

Nested conditions may require (or forbid) structures in a graph, but only of bounded size, which is equivalent to first-order logic on graphs. Shallow graph formulas allow to specify graph conditions that require or forbid the existence of subgraphs of arbitrary size, e.g., of paths of arbitrary length [12].

We now motivate the definition of *conditional borrowing hyperedge replacement grammars* (conditional BHR grammars).

For the discussion in this paragraph, let us temporarily consider condition names as additional terminal symbols. Now, let $\Gamma = (\Sigma \cup C, N \cup \{\Box\}, \pi, S)$ be a BHR grammar, let $\langle S \rangle \Rightarrow_\pi^* G$ be a derivation for some graph $G \in \mathbb{G}_\Sigma(C \cup \{\Box\})$, and let $H \in \mathbb{G}_\Sigma(C)$ be a contraction of G, i.e., $G \rightsquigarrow H$. We aim to turn Γ into a *conditional BHR grammar* by interpreting the condition edges of H as constraints that must be fulfilled for H (without the condition edges) to belong to the graph language generated by Γ.

Each condition is specified by a graph formula and referred to by a condition name. To explain the underlying idea, consider an arbitrary condition edge $e \in \bar{H}$ with label $c = lab_H(e) \in C$. Intuitively, the graph formula fo referred to by c is then checked against the graph H at the position indicated by the attachment of e. More precisely, we test whether

$$H' \vDash fo \quad \text{for} \quad H' = att_H(e) : H,$$

that is, whether fo is satisfied by H when evaluated starting at the sequence of nodes attached to e.

Definition 7 (Conditional Borrowing Hyperedge Replacement). A *conditional borrowing hyperedge replacement grammar* (*conditional BHR grammar*, or *cBHR grammar* for short) is a quintuple $\Gamma = (\Sigma, X, \pi, S, \phi)$,[5] where:

1. $\pi \colon N \to \hat{\mathbb{E}}_\Sigma(X)$ is a mapping defining *productions* such that, for every nonterminal $A \in N$, $\pi(A)$ is of type $(rank(A), n)$ for some $n \in \mathbb{N}$, and its borrowed nodes do not appear in its front;

---

[5] Recall that $X = N \cup \{\Box\} \cup C$ comprises the nonterminal symbols, the borrow symbol $\Box$, and the condition names.

2. $S \in N$ is the *start symbol*;
3. the *condition assignment* ϕ is a function $\phi\colon C \to \mathbb{SF}_\Sigma$ such that $\phi(c) \in \mathbb{SF}_\Sigma^k$ with $k = rank(c)$ for every condition name $c \in C$.

We say that a graph $H \in \mathbb{G}_\Sigma(C)$ *satisfies* ϕ, and write $H \vDash \phi$, if

$$att_H(e)\colon H \;\vDash\; \phi(lab_H(e)) \tag{1}$$

for every condition edge $e \in \bar{H}$. The reader should note that $\phi(lab_H(e))$ is a formula over Σ. Condition edges in H are thus invisible to it, i.e., whether or not (1) holds does not depend on the condition edges present in H.

The *language* generated by Γ is defined as

$$\mathcal{L}(\Gamma) = \big\{ G'|_\Sigma \mid G' \in \mathbb{G}_\Sigma(C) \text{ with } \langle S \rangle \Rightarrow_\pi^* G \rightsquigarrow G' \text{ and } G' \vDash \phi \big\}.$$

Example 2 (Snails). Figure 1 depicts graphs in which nodes are represented as small circles and (binary) undirected edges as lines between them. As usual, each undirected edge can be modeled by a pair of antiparallel directed edges. We distinguish two terminal edge types drawn as thin or thick lines (as in Fig. 1).

The graphs $S_0, S_1, S_2, \dots$ are called *snails*[6] in [13, p. 92], where it is shown that the language $\mathcal{S}$ of all snails cannot be generated by any hyperedge replacement (HR) grammar. We further argue:

Lemma 1. $\mathcal{S}$ *cannot be generated by any BHR grammar.*

Proof. Assume, for contradiction, that $\mathcal{S}$ is generated by some BHR grammar Γ. Since every HR grammar is a special case of a BHR grammar, the non-generability result for HR grammars implies that Γ must make use of borrowing and contraction. In particular, there must exist a snail, say S_k, that is obtained by a contraction fusing a borrowed, non-isolated node u with a non-borrowed node v. As S_k contains more than one node, we may instead contract u with a different non-borrowed node $v' \neq v$, yielding another graph with the same number of nodes generated by Γ. This graph cannot be a snail because it is obtained by picking any node and a non-empty subset of the edges incident with this node, redirecting them to another node. Clearly, this destroys the snail structure regardless of the choice of these edges. $\qquad\square$

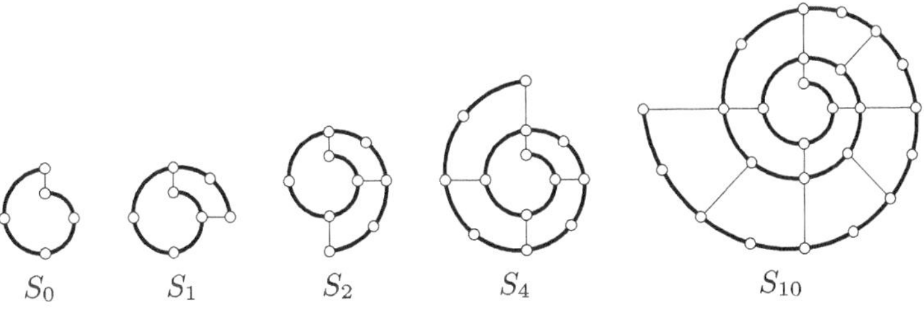

Fig. 1. Five snails.

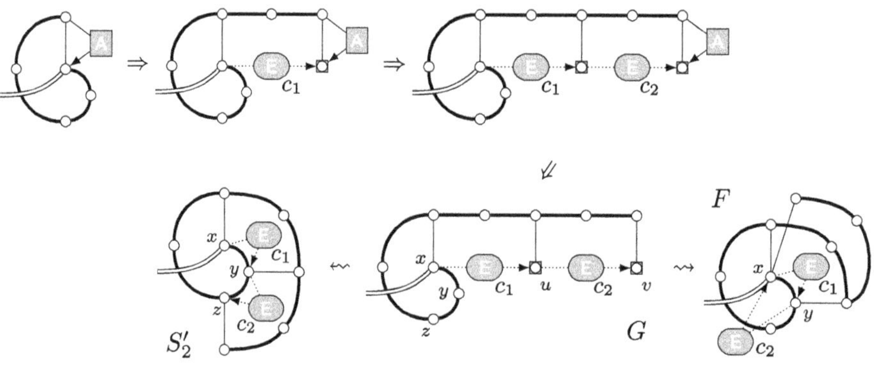

Fig. 2. The conditional BHR grammar $\Gamma_{\mathcal{S}}$ generating snails.

However, $\mathcal{S}$ can be generated by the cBHR grammar $\Gamma_{\mathcal{S}}$ in Fig. 2. Besides two kinds of binary terminal edges, the grammar uses two nonterminals (where S is unary, and A is binary), and a binary condition E. The only borrowed node is indicated by enclosing it in a square. Fig. 2 shows the two productions defined by mapping π, and one condition specified by ϕ. Nonterminal A-edges are drawn as rectangles and condition E-edges with rounded corners. Condition edges are connected to their attached nodes with dotted lines. The second attached node is indicated by the arrow.

Fig. 3. Three derivation steps and two contractions with the snail grammar $\Gamma_{\mathcal{S}}$.

Figure 3 shows three derivation steps with $\Gamma_{\mathcal{S}}$, yielding the terminal graph G. Each of the two borrowed nodes u and v in G can be merged with any of the nine non-borrowed nodes in G, so there are 81 possible contractions of G. Figure 3 shows just two of these, yielding graph S_2' by merging u with y and v with z, and graph F by merging u with y and v with x. Note that the constraints imposed by the condition edges c_1 and c_2 of S_2' are both satisfied:

$$xy\colon S_2' \vDash \phi(E) \quad \text{and} \quad yz\colon S_2' \vDash \phi(E).$$

This proves that $S_2 = S_2'|_\Sigma$ is a valid snail, i.e., $S_2 \in \mathcal{L}(\Gamma_{\mathcal{S}})$. In contrast, $F|_\Sigma$ is not a valid snail, and $F|_\Sigma \notin \mathcal{L}(\Gamma_{\mathcal{S}})$ because of the following:

$$xy\colon F \vDash \phi(E), \quad \text{but} \quad yx\colon F \vDash \phi(E) \text{ does } \mathbf{not} \text{ hold.}$$

---

[6] More precisely, they should be called *snail shells* or, even better, *ammonites*.

The latter follows from the fact that two edges drawn as thin lines are attached to node x, which is prohibited by $\phi(\mathsf{E})$. Note that omitting ϕ_2 from $\phi(\mathsf{E})$, i.e., using $\phi(\mathsf{E}) = \phi_1$ instead, would make $F|_\Sigma$ a valid graph, even though it is not a snail. $\qquad\Box$

4   A Conditional BHR Grammar for Statecharts

UML state machines [21] are used to specify system behavior in terms of state transitions that occur in response to events. They are derived from State-charts [18], which extend classical finite automata with hierarchical structuring mechanisms such as composite states. In the following, we do not elaborate on the precise semantic differences between UML state machines and Statecharts; instead, we just use the term *statechart*.

To show that conditional BHR grammars can generate graph languages of practical relevance, let us now discuss in some detail how to generate statecharts with meaningful structural properties (see (C1)–(C3) below).

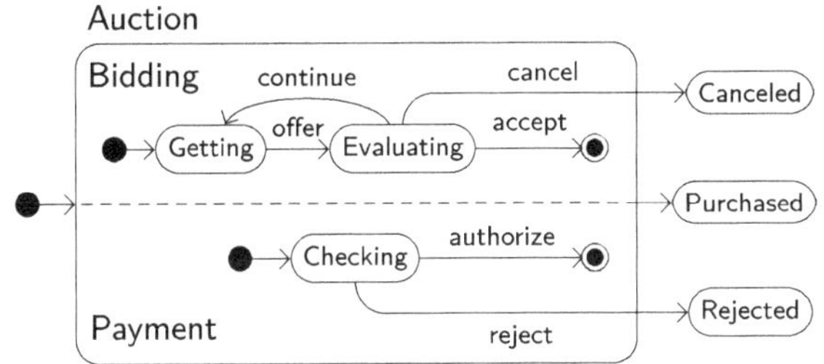

Fig. 4. A statechart modeling an auction.

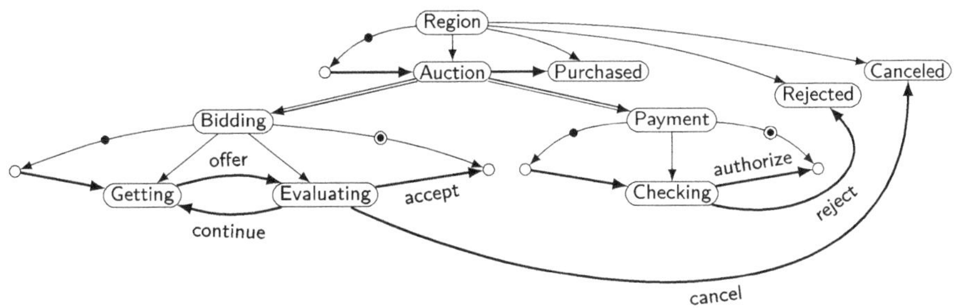

Fig. 5. The graph representing the auction statechart in Fig. 4.

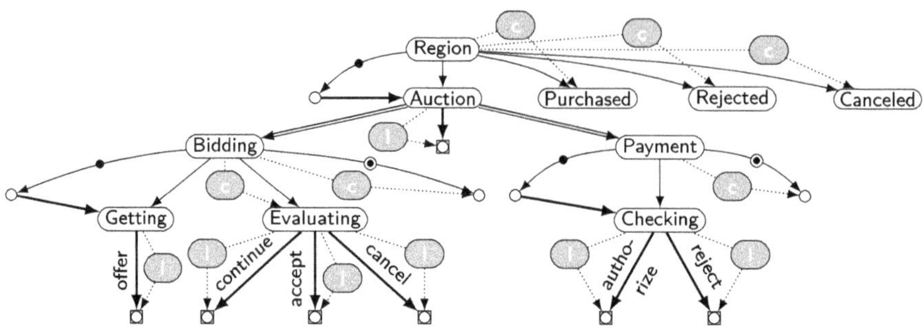

Fig. 6. The graph that can be derived by the productions in Fig. 7 and contracted to the auction graph shown in Fig. 5. The condition labels conn and legal have been abbreviated to c and l, respectively.

A statechart as in Fig. 4 consists of states and transitions between them. A filled black circle • denotes an *initial* state, whereas a state represented by ⊙ denotes a *final* state. Rectangles with rounded corners represent either *simple* or *composite* states. Composite states differ from simple states in that they contain one or more *regions*. Each region serves as a container for its own states and transitions. A composite state with exactly one region is called a *simple composite* state; a composite state with multiple regions is called an *orthogonal* state. In orthogonal states, regions are separated by dashed lines. When a composite state becomes active, all of its regions become active simultaneously, and they execute independently of one another.

The statechart in Fig. 4 models an auction process and comprises five top-level states: the initial state on the left, the orthogonal state Auction, and the three simple states Canceled, Finished, and Rejected. The state Auction contains two regions, Bidding and Payment, each with its own initial and final states. Its intended semantics is beyond this paper and not considered here.

We require transitions of a statechart to satisfy the following conditions:

(C1) A chart must be *connected*, meaning its inner states and optional final state must be reachable from the initial state via transitions. However, reachability can be complicated, as shown in Fig. 4. There is no sequence of transitions from the top-level initial state to the top-level Canceled state. Rather, the latter is reached from the contained state Evaluating, which is indirectly reachable through the initial state of region Bidding.

(C2) Transitions must not target initial states.

(C3) Transitions may cross the border of regions and states, but they are only *legal* if they do not go to initial states, and do not enter any of the regions of an orthogonal state "from outside".

These conditions yield well-structured statecharts with predictable control flow and unambiguous execution semantics. They are more restrictive than the requirements by the UML state machine specification. But at least (C1) and (C2) are consistent with, and in the case of (C2) directly reflect, the interpretation of Harel's statecharts as reactive models.

Figure 5 shows how we represent the auction statechart as a graph. It is essentially a tree with nodes representing states or regions and edges representing containment. However, it also has crosscutting edges representing transitions. The root node describes the region of the entire statechart, containment is indicated by thin arrows. Arrows pointing to initial and final states carry • and ⊙. Transitions are drawn as thick arrows. Double-lined arrows point from orthogonal states to their regions.

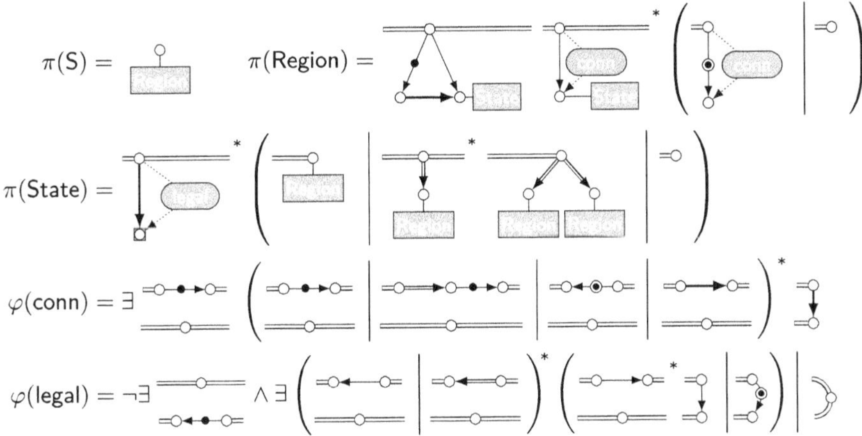

Fig. 7. A conditional BHR grammar for statecharts

As described below, the language of statechart graphs is defined by the productions and conditions in Fig. 7. These productions derive tree-like graphs where transition edges are attached to borrowed nodes instead of their intended target nodes. Then, a contraction turns these transition edges into crosscutting transitions. The condition edges conn and legal make sure that the resulting graph satisfies the conditions (C1), (C2), and (C3).

Figure 6 shows the tree-like graph that can be derived by the productions starting at the start symbol S. This graph can then be contracted to the auction graph in Fig. 5. The idea behind the productions is as follows: A nonterminal Region-edge is attached to a node if it represents a region. Each region contains a unique initial state and at least one additional state. The latter is represented by a node and an attached nonterminal State-edge. A region may also contain an arbitrary number of additional states and an optional final state. These states must be reachable from their initial state, as required by (C1); this condition is expressed by binary conn-edges. Finally, every state may have an arbitrary number of outgoing transitions to other states, represented by borrowed nodes. A legal-edge describes the condition that the borrowed node will eventually be contracted with a legal node that fulfills conditions (C2) and (C3). Each state node is either a region by itself (in which case it is a simple composite state) or it is an orthogonal state containing at least two regions, or it is just a simple state.

To see how connectedness is specified by conn-edges, consider such an edge with its attached nodes, say x and y. Its condition $\phi(\mathsf{conn})$ is satisfied if state y is reachable from the initial state of region x. In the simplest case, y is reachable from the initial state via a sequence of transitions, i.e., thick arrows. However, $\phi(\mathsf{conn})$ also covers the more complicated cases where y is reachable across region and state boundaries. Note in particular the final-state edge occurring in $\phi(\mathsf{conn})$ that allows to continue with the enclosing simple composite state as soon as its final state has been reached.

Finally, legal-edges prevent contractions that produce transitions between illegal states. Note that $\phi(\mathsf{legal})$ has the form $\neg\exists\rho \wedge \exists(\psi|\theta)$. The part containing ρ prevents transitions from entering initial states, as required by (C2), and ψ ensures condition (C3). The final part, θ, permits both nodes of a legal-edge to be identified by contractions, yielding looping transitions.

5   Checking Conditions During Parsing

We now indicate by means of an example how a parser for BHR grammars can be extended so that it verifies the annotations of a conditional BHR grammar. Our discussion is based on a top-down parser for the snail grammar in Example 2; for a general definition of these parsers (without conditions), the reader is referred to [6]. We note here that, despite the fact that the integration of condition checking is only explained by means of the snail example, no use is made of any peculiarities of this example. Hence, the technique generalizes to arbitrary cBHR grammars.

When a graph parser attempts to construct a derivation for a cBHR grammar that matches the input graph, it treats nonterminal and condition edges in particular ways. To facilitate this process, we assume that every production, $\pi(A)$, has the form $ex_1|\cdots|ex_n$, where $ex_1,\ldots,ex_n$ are its *alternatives*. Similarly to the transformation of context-free grammars in EBNF, it is straightforward to show that this assumption implies no loss of generality. Furthermore, each alternative is a sequential concatenation of graphs that all have a particular form: if such a graph contains a nonterminal or condition edge, then it contains only one edge. Figure 8 shows the productions π' for the snail language, rewritten from those in Fig. 2 to make them convenient for parsing. In the following, we silently assume that the given cBHR grammar is in such a "parser friendly" form.

A parser is defined as a pushdown automaton operating on an *input graph* $G \in \mathbb{G}_\Sigma$ and maintaining a stack that plays a similar role as the stack of a pushdown automaton recognizing a context-free string language. Each state reachable by the parser is formalized as a *configuration* described below. Each operation performed by the parser (called *move* in the following) changes its configuration, written $\kappa \vdash \kappa'$ where κ and κ' are the configurations immediately before and after the operation, respectively.

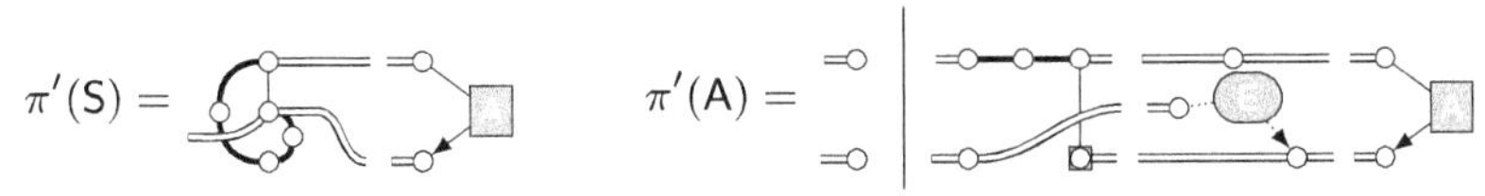

$$\pi'(\mathsf{S}) = \qquad\qquad \pi'(\mathsf{A}) = \qquad\qquad$$

Fig. 8. The production rules for snails used for parsing

A parse is a sequence $\kappa_0 \vdash \kappa_1 \vdash \cdots \vdash \kappa_n$ of moves starting at a *start configuration* κ_0. A parse *terminates* at κ_n if no more move is possible. Such a parse is *accepting* if κ_n is an *accepting configuration*. A terminated parse *fails* if it is not accepting. A parser accepts G if there is an accepting parse for G, otherwise the parser fails.

We now introduce configurations of our cBHR parser for the input graph G. A configuration is a four-tuple $(\nu, \bar{U}, \dot{U}, \sigma)$ where $\nu \in \dot{G}^*$ is the *focus* where the next move of the parser will take place. The subsets $\dot{U} \subseteq \dot{G}$ and $\bar{U} \subseteq \dot{G}$ designate those nodes and edges of G that are yet *unconsumed*. Finally, σ is the (contents of the) *stack*, containing a sequence of graphs; the first graph is the top of stack.

In the start configuration $\kappa_0 = (\nu_0, \bar{U}_0, \dot{U}_0, \sigma_0)$, no edges and nodes of the input graph have been consumed, and the stack contains the start graph $\langle S \rangle$ of the grammar, i.e., $\nu_0 = front_G$, $\bar{U}_0 = \bar{G}$, $\dot{U}_0 = \dot{G}$, and $\sigma_0 = \langle S \rangle$. A configuration $(\nu, \bar{U}, \dot{U}, \sigma)$ is accepting if the entire graph has been consumed, and the stack is empty, i.e., $\nu = \sigma = \varepsilon$ and $\bar{U} = \dot{U} = \varnothing$.

Figure 9 shows a terminating parse for the graph F of Fig. 3 with the productions π' in Fig. 8 and the condition $\phi(E)$ shown in Fig. 2. In Fig. 9, we draw the components $\nu_i, \bar{U}_i, \dot{U}_i$ of a configuration as the single graph $\nu_i : G$ wherein we designate the consumed edges $\bar{G} \setminus \bar{U}_i$ by drawing them as dashed arrows, and mark the consumed nodes $\dot{G} \setminus \dot{U}_i$ by crossing them out.

We note here that the snail grammar is a particularly simple case because it is *right-linear* in that the non-terminal right-hand sides have only one nonterminal edge, and that edge occurs in the last component of the concatenation. As a consequence, the stack is of bounded depth. However, for the present discussion this is sufficient because we merely intend to illustrate the integration of the verification of conditions into the parser.

Let us now discuss the moves shown in Fig. 9. As long as the stack is not empty, the parser tries to perform moves, by popping and examining the top of stack. In the following, we denote the topmost graph on the stack of the ith configuration by T_i (starting with $i = 0$), and the input graph by G.

Move 1 *expands* the topmost nonterminal graph $T_0 = \langle S \rangle$ by pushing the corresponding right-hand side $\pi'(S)$ onto the stack after popping T_0 from it.

Move 2 *matches* the terminal graph T_1 on the top of the stack to a corresponding subgraph of G by marking the matched edges and nodes as consumed. Note the role played by the focus: it restricts the matching since the front of T_1 must be mapped to the focus. Note also that the focus is moved to the image of $rear_{T_1}$ in the resulting configuration.

Move 3 chooses the second alternative of $\pi'(A)$ for expansion, and its sequentially concatenated graphs are pushed onto the stack.

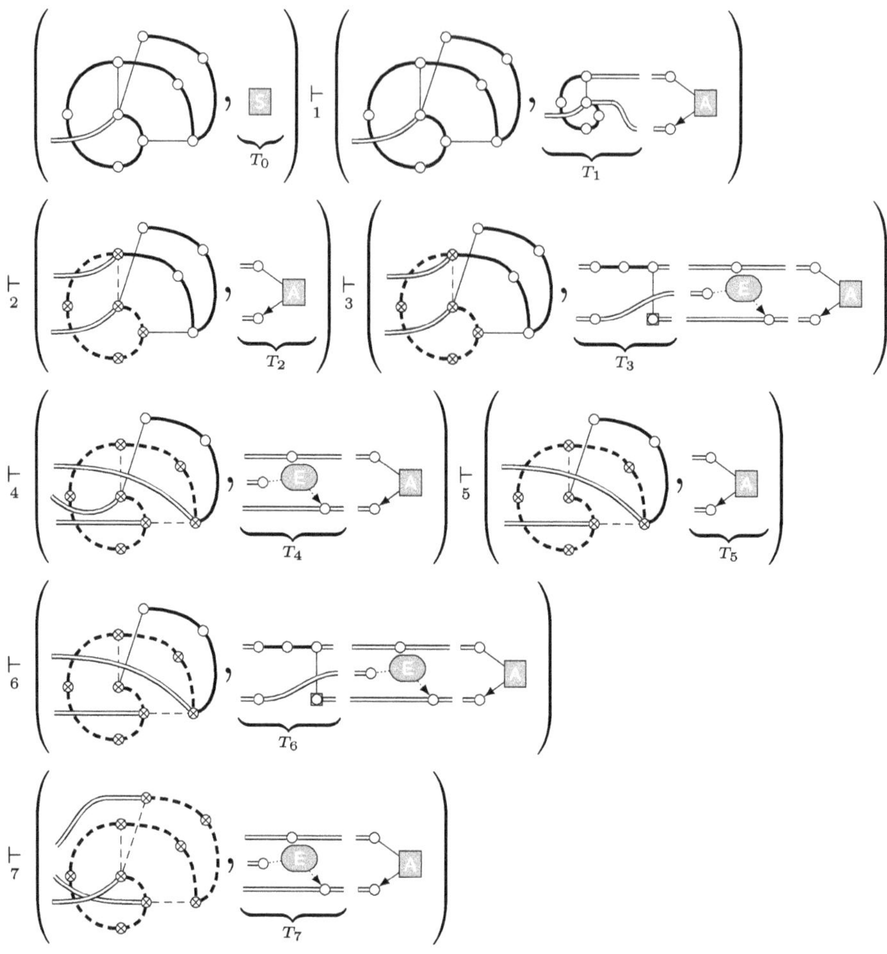

Fig. 9. A failing parse of the snail F of Fig. 3.

Move 4 matches T_3, which contains a borrowed node, at the current focus. Note
that the borrowed node is mapped to a node that has already been consumed by a previous match. In general (but not in successful parses of
the snail grammar), borrowed nodes may also be mapped to nodes which
have not yet been consumed. Such nodes would then remain unconsumed.

Move 5 *verifies* the condition $\phi(E)$ on the input graph at the current focus.[7]
The condition is satisfied, hence the parser proceeds.

Move 6 expands (again) the second alternative of $\pi'(A)$.

---

[7] Verification can be done by executing the alternating graph automaton $\mathfrak{A}(\phi(E))$ that
can be generated from the condition, see [8].

Move 7 matches once more a terminal graph with a borrowed node, where the borrowed nodes has already be consumed earlier.

At his point, G has been consumed completely. Thus, if the stack would be empty, the parser would accept G.

After reaching this configuration by Move 7, the next move would be to pop T_7 from the stack and verify the condition $\phi(E)$ on G at the current focus. In this case, the condition is not satisfied, so the move cannot be performed. The parse therefore terminates and fails, as it is not in an accepting configuration.

However, the failure of a parse does not in general imply that the input graph is invalid (although F is indeed not a valid snail). An input graph may admit multiple terminating parses; if one parse fails, another may still be accepting. Therefore, the parser is inherently nondeterministic. In particular, the parser moves are nondeterministic in the following ways:

(a) In an expand move, any of the alternatives of a production can be chosen. In moves 3 and 6, the terminating alternative of $\pi'(A)$ could have been chosen, but this would have led to failure, as the input graph has not been consumed completely.
(b) In a match move, a terminal graph may have several valid matches in the input graph; each of them can be chosen. (The snail grammar is special in that just one match is possible at each step, provided that the input graph belongs to the language.)

Furthermore, there is more than one way in which a parse may fail in a configuration:

(i) Its stack may be empty although the input has not entirely been consumed.
(ii) Its input may be consumed completely although its stack is not yet empty.
(iii) A terminal graph on top of the stack may not have a match in the input graph.
(iv) The verification of a condition during a verify move may fail.

In such a situation, the general top-down parser must backtrack, undoing moves and trying different ones. In the above example, all of the parses eventually fail, showing that G is not a valid snail.

Backtracking is inefficient. For the case of HR grammars, the authors have therefore introduced *predictive top-down (PTD) parsers* as a remedy [4]. PTD parsing requires the parser to be able to apply moves deterministically. More precisely, call a parser configuration *promising* if there is an accepting sequence of moves. Now, assume that the parser is in a promising configuration.

(1) If the next move is an expansion, looking ahead into the yet unconsumed part of the input graph must enable the selection of an alternative of the corresponding production such that the next configuration is also promising.
(2) If the next move is a match move, look ahead must enable the selection of a match yielding a promising successor configuration. (In [4] the stronger *free edge choice* property is used, ensuring that *every* match has this property.)

Then, backtracking is not needed: a parse only fails if the initial configuration was not promising, meaning that the input graph does not belong to the language.

PTD parsing requires a static grammar analysis that either rejects a grammar as non-PTD or results in efficient look-ahead procedures for (1) and (2).

Example 3 (Deterministic Parsing of Snails). The parsing of snails can be made deterministic as follows: (a) The PTD parser identifies the front node of the start symbol by locating S_0 (see Fig. 1) as a subgraph and selecting the node incident to exactly one thick and one thin edge. This criterion uniquely determines the node, except in the case of S_0 itself or when the input graph is invalid. The parser proceeds if exactly one such node is identified. Otherwise, it accepts the input graph if and only if it is S_0; in all other cases, it fails. (b) The choice between the productions for A can be guided as follows: if the first node of the focus is incident to an unconsumed thick edge, the recursive production has to be chosen for expansion. (c) The condition E in this production makes the match of the terminal graph deterministic.

In future work, we plan to (a) formalize the parser sketched above as a backbone for PTD parsing and prove its correctness, and (b) based on this, extend PTD parsing to cBHR grammars. To accomplish the latter, a suitable static grammar analysis must be devised which takes advantage of the conditions in a cBHR grammar. This is both an opportunity and a challenge. On the one hand, conditions may restrict expansion and match candidates sufficiently to make a cBHR grammar PTD parsable where the corresponding BHR grammar would not be PTD parsable. On the other hand, the grammar analysis is destined to be considerably more involved.

Eventually, the extension of the existing implementation of PTD parsing in Grappa[8] to cBHR grammars would make the ideas developed here available for practical applications and conclude this line of research.

6   Conclusions

We have extended the productions of borrowing hyperedge replacement grammars by conditions represented by condition edges. A condition edge indicates a place in the graph where an associated condition, in this paper expressed as a shallow graph formula, is required to hold. Such a condition is verified on the derived graph rather than when a production is applied. As a consequence, derivations remain confluent, and the conditions can be verified during parsing.

Since the verification of conditions is orthogonal to the derivation process, any decidable formalism for expressing properties of graphs with front interfaces could be used in place of shallow graph formulas. However, the conditions needed to define the statechart grammar (Fig. 7) indicate that such conditions should be able to require or forbid paths of arbitrary length.

So the well-known nested conditions of Habel, Pennemann, and Rensink [14–16,22] do not suffice. Several extensions of this formalism could be considered:

---

[8] https://www.unibw.de/inf2/grappa.

The nested HR-conditions of Habel and Radke [17,24], the monadic second-order (M-) conditions by Poskitt and Plump [23], the μ-recursive conditions of Flick [11], or the navigational logic of Orejas *et al.* [20]. However, the verification of these extensions is based on theorem proving, whereas shallow graph formulas can be checked by alternating graph automata [9]. (Even if shallow graph formulas would turn out to be not powerful enough, unrestricted (systems of) graph formulas defined in [9] can be checked in the same way.)

Acknowledgments. This work has been supported by the Swedish Research Council under grant no. 2024-05318 and by the Wallenberg AI, Autonomous Systems and Software Program WASP.

Disclosure of Interests. The authors have no competing interests to declare that are relevant to the content of this article.

References

1. Courcelle, B.: An axiomatic definition of context-free rewriting and its application to NLC graph grammars. Theoret. Comput. Sci. **55**, 141–181 (1987). https://doi.org/10.1016/0304-3975(87)90102-2
2. Drewes, F., Hoffmann, B.: Contextual hyperedge replacement. Acta Informatica **52**, 497–524 (2015). https://doi.org/10.1007/s00236-015-0223-4
3. Drewes, F., Hoffmann, B., Minas, M.: Contextual hyperedge replacement. In: Schürr, A., Varró, D., Varró, G. (eds.) AGTIVE 2011. LNCS, vol. 7233, pp. 182–197. Springer, Heidelberg (2012). https://doi.org/10.1007/978-3-642-34176-2_16
4. Drewes, F., Hoffmann, B., Minas, M.: Predictive top-down parsing for hyperedge replacement grammars. In: Parisi-Presicce, F., Westfechtel, B. (eds.) Graph Transformation - 8th International Conf., ICGT 2015. LNCS, vol. 9151, pp. 19–34. Springer (2015). https://doi.org/10.1007/978-3-319-21145-9_2
5. Drewes, F., Hoffmann, B., Minas, M.: Formalization and correctness of predictive shift-reduce parsers for graph grammars based on hyperedge replacement. J. Logical Algebraic Methods Programm. (JLAMP) **104**, 303–341 (2019). https://doi.org/10.1016/j.jlamp.2018.12.006
6. Drewes, F., Hoffmann, B., Minas, M.: Rule-based top-down parsing for acyclic contextual hyperedge replacement grammars. In: Gadducci, F., Kehrer, T. (eds.) Graph Transformation - 14th International Conference, ICGT 2021. LNCS, vol. 12741, pp. 164–184. Springer (2021). https://doi.org/10.1007/978-3-030-78946-6_9
7. Drewes, F., Hoffmann, B., Minas, M.: Acyclic contextual hyperedge replacement: decidability of acyclicity and generative power. In: Behr, N., Strüber, D. (eds.) ICGT 2022. LNCS, vol. 13349, pp. 3–19. Springer, Cham (2022). https://doi.org/10.1007/978-3-031-09843-7_1
8. Drewes, F., Hoffmann, B., Minas, M.: Graph formulas and their translation to alternating graph automata. In: Endrullis, J., Tichy, M. (eds.) Graph Transformation – 18th International Conference, ICGT 2025. LNCS, vol. 15720, pp. 112–132. Springer, Cham (2025). https://doi.org/10.1007/978-3-031-94706-3_6
9. Drewes, F., Hoffmann, B., Minas, M.: Systems of graph formulas and their equivalence to alternating graph automata. In: Lambers, L., Semeráth, O. (eds.) Proceedings of the Sixteenth International Workshop on Graph Computation Models

(GCM 2025). EPTCS, vol. 440, pp. 123–156, January 2026. https://doi.org/10.4204/EPTCS.440.4

10. Engelfriet, J., Vereijken, J.J.: Context-free graph grammars and concatenation of graphs. Acta Informatica **34**(10), 773–803 (1997). https://doi.org/10.1007/s002360050106

11. Flick, N.E.: Proving Correctness of Graph Programs Relative to Recursively Nested Conditions. Ph.D. thesis, University of Oldenburg, Germany (2016). https://nbn-resolving.org/urn:nbn:de:gbv:715-oops-29769

12. Gaifman, H.: On local and non-local properties. In: Stern, J. (ed.) Proc. of the Herbrand Symposium, Logic Colloquium. Studies in Logic and the Foundations of Mathematics, vol. 105, pp. 105–135. North-Holland (1982). https://doi.org/10.1016/S0049-237X(08)71879-2

13. Habel, A.: Hyperedge Replacement: Grammars and Languages, LNCS, vol. 643. Springer (1992). https://doi.org/10.1007/BFb0013875

14. Habel, A., Pennemann, K.-H.: Nested constraints and application conditions for high-level structures. In: Kreowski, H.-J., Montanari, U., Orejas, F., Rozenberg, G., Taentzer, G. (eds.) Formal Methods in Software and Systems Modeling. LNCS, vol. 3393, pp. 293–308. Springer, Heidelberg (2005). https://doi.org/10.1007/978-3-540-31847-7_17

15. Habel, A., Pennemann, K.H.: Correctness of high-level transformation systems relative to nested conditions. Math. Struct. Comput. Sci. **19**(2), 245–296 (2009). https://doi.org/10.1017/S0960129508007202

16. Habel, A., Pennemann, K., Rensink, A.: Weakest preconditions for high-level programs. In: Corradini, A., Ehrig, H., Montanari, U., Ribeiro, L., Rozenberg, G. (eds.) Graph Transformations, Third International Conference, ICGT 2006, Natal, Rio Grande do Norte, Brazil, September 17-23, 2006, Proceedings. LNCS, vol. 4178, pp. 445–460. Springer (2006). https://doi.org/10.1007/11841883_31

17. Habel, A., Radke, H.: Expressiveness of graph conditions with variables. Elect. Comm. of the EASST **30** (2010). https://doi.org/10.14279/tuj.eceasst.30.404, International Colloquium on Graph and Model Transformation (GraMoT'10)

18. Harel, D.: On visual formalisms. Comm. ACM **31**(5), 514–530 (1988)

19. Hoffmann, B., Minas, M.: Defining models – meta models versus graph grammars. Elect. Comm. of the EASST **29** (2010). https://doi.org/10.14279/tuj.eceasst.29.411, 6th Workshop on Graph Transformation and Visual Modeling Techniques (GT-VMT'10), Paphos, Cyprus

20. Navarro, M., Orejas, F., Pino, E., Lambers, L.: A navigational logic for reasoning about graph properties. J. Log. Algebraic Methods Program. **118**, 100616 (2021). https://doi.org/10.1016/j.jlamp.2020.100616

21. Object Management Group: OMG Unified Modeling Language (OMG UML), Version 2.5.1. https://www.omg.org/spec/UML/2.5.1 (2017), OMG File ID: Formal/2017-12-05

22. Pennemann, K.H.: Development of Correct Graph Transformation Systems. Dissertation, Carl-von-Ossietzky-Universität Oldenburg (2009). https://nbn-resolving.org/urn:nbn:de:gbv:715-oops-9483

23. Poskitt, C.M., Plump, D.: Verifying monadic second-order properties of graph programs. In: Giese, H., König, B. (eds.) Graph Transformation - 7th International Conference, ICGT 2014. LNCS, vol. 8571, pp. 33–48. Springer, Cham (2014). https://doi.org/10.1007/978-3-319-09108-2_3
24. Radke, H.: A Theory of HR* Graph Conditions and their Application to Meta-Modeling. Dissertation, Carl-von-Ossietzky-Universität Oldenburg, March 2016. https://nbn-resolving.org/urn:nbn:de:gbv:715-oops-28845

Higher-Order Graph Transformation Utilizing Diagram Categories

Lars Friederichs[(✉)] and Aaron Lye

German Aerospace Center DLR, Institute for the Protection of Maritime
Infrastructures, Bremerhaven, Germany
`{lars.friederichs,aaron.lye}@dlr.de`

Abstract. In this paper we propose a general approach for higher-order
graph transformation utilizing diagram categories. This approach encom-
passes earlier attempts while blurring the boundary between graphs
(data) and graph transformation rules (code), mimicking a similar phenomenon found with higher-order functions in (functional) programming
in order to increase expressiveness. We show that our formalism captures
some common constructions like rule parallelization and still fits into the
paradigm of adhesive categories, thus benefiting from existing theory.

Keywords: Graph Transformation · Higher-order rewriting · Diagram
Categories · Adhesive Categories · Parallelization · Amalgamation

1 Introduction

1.1 Motivation

Higher order functions are an essential tool in many programming language to
increase code readability and maintainability. We can observe that the usage
of higher order functions in any sufficiently expressive programming language
blurs the boundaries between code and data, in that functions that describe
behaviour on data can themselves be viewed as data to be used or returned by
other functions. This is especially visible in purely functional programming languages like *Lean* in which functions are given by formulas on their inputs which
can be examined for analysis in other functions or proofs. The most extreme
case can be found in the *LISP* family of languages in which code in the form of
abstract syntax trees and data are equally made up of nested lists the core primitive data type and namesake of these languages. As such they can be freely
picked apart and modified in macros. This phenomenon provides our key inspiration and guideline for what higher-order graph transformations should look
like: *Higher order graph transformations should provide a unified viewpoint on
graphs (data) and graph transformation rules in the form of spans (code).*

B. Archibald and O. Semeráth (Eds.): ICGT 2026, LNCS 16624, pp. 46–67, 2026.
https://doi.org/10.1007/978-3-032-29730-3_3

1.2 Related Work

The so-called double-pushout approach to graph transformation introduced in [1] has a vast theory (cf. e.g. [2,3]). Manipulation of graph transformation rules has been discussed since the early beginnings of graphs transformation (cf. [4, 5]). However, the theory lacks a proper notion of higher-order transformation, i.e., rule-based modification of graph transformation rules themselves. But there have been some attempts. Petri nets can be considered as monoids. Moreover, they can be combined with algebraic specifications leading to the concept of algebraic high-level nets. In [6] algebraic high-level net transformation systems have been discussed. This enables to build up algebraic high-level nets from basic components and to transform them using graph transformation rules.

In [7], Hoffmann has shown that variables can be used to define advanced ways of DPO graph transformation. Hoffman considers extensions of rules with attribute variables, clone variables, and graph variables, respectively. In each case, the variables in a rule are instantiated in order to obtain a set of rule instances which defines the transformation relation. As graph transformation has a well-developed theory, this approach promises to lift results of that theory from instances to rules with variables. The approach is also related to hierarchical graph transformation with variables (cf. [8]). In these graphs, distinguished hyperedges contain hypergraphs that can be hierarchical again. Rules are made more expressive by variables which allow to copy and remove hierarchical subgraphs in a single rule application. The framework extends the well-known double-pushout approach from flat to hierarchical graphs. Pushouts and pushout complements of hierarchical graphs and graph morphisms can be constructed recursively.

One of the approaches mentioning higher-order graph rules is presented in [9]. Göttler defines a model called two-level graph grammars, where there are meta-rules, which are the ones that modify parts of other rules, and hyporrules, representing the rules being modified. Göttler presents an algorithmic set-theoretic graph-rewriting approach, which corresponds neither to the DPO nor the SPO approach. The approach mixes characteristics of both DPO and SPO (such as deletion in unknown context and explicit notion of preservation). Göttler also presents a way of representing graph transformation rules by means of a single graph (divided into regions for the left-hand side, connection and right-hand side).

In [10] modifications of graph rules and in graph grammar specifications is discussed in the framework of high-level replacement systems. The proposed concepts of higher-order rewriting are the so-called local transformations. The approach is to use of graph transformations over parts of other rules to induce rule modifications.

In [11,12] rule-based transformation of graph transformation rules is discussed. The main contribution is a notion of double-pushout transformation for graph rewriting rules. The authors consider rule transformation as DPO diagrams in the category $T\text{-}Span$ of typed graph spans where span morphism are defined as in [13]. Spans in $T\text{-}Span$, i.e., spans of spans of typed graphs, were the primary objects investigated. The authors note that the existing theory on adhesive categories extends naturally to *T-Span* since it is well known that functor categories $[\cdot, \mathcal{C}]$ are adhesive if $\mathcal{C}$ is. The proposed concept is only able to transform a single rule and rule rewriting and regular rewriting happen in two distinct *phases*.

From the point of view of structure, the presented approach can be seen as a particular kind of triple graph rewriting [14] due to the fact that the notion of span rewriting and triple graph rewriting coincide.

1.3   Contribution

In this paper we propose an approach for higher-order graph transformation able to capture simultaneous rewriting of graphs and rules on graphs which is based on the concept of diagram categories. We show that a restriction of this construction fits into the paradigm of adhesive categories while encompassing and expanding upon previous work regarding higher-order rule rewriting of [11,12].

A rule r over some category $\mathcal{C}$ can be seen as a functor $r\colon (\bullet \leftarrow \bullet \rightarrow \bullet) \rightarrow \mathcal{C}$; similarly we can re-interpret a single object $G \in ob(\mathcal{C})$ to be given by a functor $\Delta_G\colon \bullet \mapsto G$. *Here and in the following when using* $\bullet$ *or* $\bullet \leftarrow \bullet \rightarrow \bullet$ *or any graph in place where a category is expected, we mean the free category generated by this graph.* The main idea is then to view a set of rules and possibly multiple graphs as a functor to $\mathcal{C}$ from an index category which can be written as a coproduct over these simple index categories

$$\mathcal{I}_{n_s, n_p} := \left(\coprod_{i=1}^{n_s} (\bullet \leftarrow \bullet \rightarrow \bullet) \right) \amalg \left(\coprod_{i=1}^{n_p} \bullet \right) \qquad \text{(for some } n_s, n_p \in \mathbb{N}_0)$$

and make this unified viewpoint into a category over which we can again consider replacement using spans as rules. Specifically we would need to be able to define morphisms between such objects.

The paper is organized as follows. Section 2 provides the definition needed to make sense of the main idea and provides details about the construction of pullbacks and pushouts as they are essential in DPO rewriting. In Sect. 3 we explore some properties of pushouts diagrams in extensive categories as preparation for the proof in the following section. Next in Sect. 4 we take a closer look at $Diag^{\mathcal{D}}(\mathcal{C})$ for a category $\mathcal{D}$ whose objects are exactly the $\mathcal{I}_{n_s, n_p}$ defined above and prove it to be adhesive if the base category $\mathcal{C}$ is. After some examples in Sect. 5, we explore how a less restricted version could be used to capture some structuring mechanism commonly seen in the literature in Sect. 6

2   Category of Diagrams

In this section we will first define the categorial construction used for our approach on higher order (graph) transformations namely the category of diagrams over some base category $\mathcal{C}$ (Definition 1). Afterwards we examine how pullbacks

(Theorem 1) and pushouts (Theorem 3) are formed in this category. We conclude with a proof that under relatively small additional assumptions the category of diagrams is extensive (Theorem 4).

2.1 Category of Diagrams $Diag(\cdot)$

Definition 1. *Let $\mathcal{C}$ be some base-category and $\mathcal{D} \subseteq \underline{Cat}$ a subcategory of the category of all small categories. We define the category of diagrams $Diag^{\mathcal{D}}(\mathcal{C})$ to be the category whose objects are given by pairs $(\mathcal{I}, F_{\mathcal{I}})$ of a small category $\mathcal{I} \in \mathcal{D}$ and a functor $F_1 \colon \mathcal{I} \to \mathcal{C}$. For two such objects $(\mathcal{I}_1, F_1)$ and $(\mathcal{I}_2, F_2)$ the morphisms between them are pairs (G, α) of a functor $G \colon \mathcal{I}_1 \to \mathcal{I}_2 \in \mathcal{D}(\mathcal{I}_1, \mathcal{I}_2)$ and a natural transformation $\alpha \colon F_1 \implies F_2 \circ G$, i.e. a set of morphisms $(\alpha_X \colon F_1(X) \to F_2 \circ G(X))_{X \in ob(\mathcal{I}_1)}$ such that the right diagram of (1) commutes for all morphism $f \colon X \to Y$ in $\mathcal{I}_1$.*

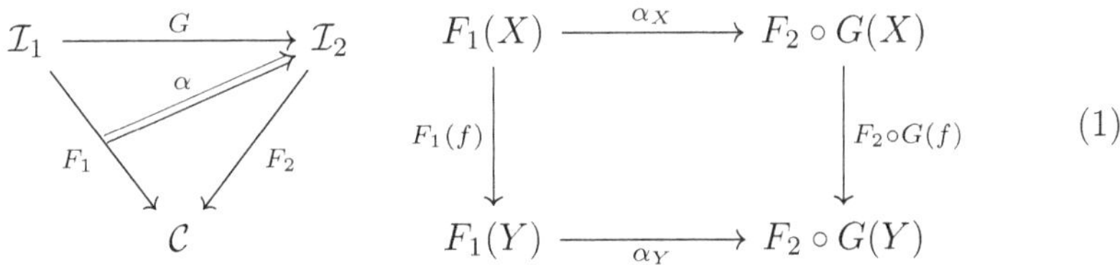

$$\tag{1}$$

A similar definition of a diagram category already appeared in the founding work of category theory by MacLane and Eilenberg [15] but there the focus was on using this diagram category as a domain to express taking limits as a functor. In [16] the authors already showed that category $Diag(\mathcal{C})$ (i.e. for $\mathcal{D} = \underline{Cat}$) has small limits of shape $\mathcal{I}$ if the base category $\mathcal{C}$ has small limits of shape $\mathcal{I}$ and if $\mathcal{C}$ is cocomplete so is $Diag(\mathcal{C})$.

Now we want to see how some common constructions in $Diag^{\mathcal{D}}(\mathcal{C})$ look like in detail, so that a user of higher order transformations in this context would know what properties to check. Furthermore, using the tools from this section and Sect. 3 we show that a restriction to certain shapes of index categories $\mathcal{I}$ more general than $\bullet \leftarrow \bullet \to \bullet$ is adhesive if the base category $\mathcal{C}$ is in Sect. 4.

2.2 Pullbacks in $Diag(\cdot)$

Theorem 1. *Let $\mathcal{C}$ and $\mathcal{D} \subset \underline{Cat}$ be categories with pullbacks then $Diag^{\mathcal{D}}(\mathcal{C})$ has pullbacks.*

While the construction of pullbacks as componentwise was already indicated in Remark 2.8 of [16] we aim to provide a more complete picture and intuition of how and why these work.

Proof. Let $(\mathcal{I}_1, F_1) \xrightarrow{(G_1, \alpha_1)} (\hat{\mathcal{I}}, \hat{F}) \xleftarrow{(G_2, \alpha_2)} (\mathcal{I}_2, F_2)$ be a cospan in $Diag^{\mathcal{D}}(\mathcal{C})$. Now take $\mathcal{I}_0$, H_1, H_2 such that the left diagram in (2) is a pullback in $\mathcal{D}$ and for every $X \in ob(\mathcal{I}_0)$ take $F(X)$, $(\beta_1)_X$ and $(\beta_2)_X$ such that the right diagram in (2) is a pullback in $\mathcal{C}$.

$$
\begin{array}{ccc}
\mathcal{I}_0 \xrightarrow{\;H_1\;} \mathcal{I}_1 & & F(X) \xrightarrow{\;(\beta_1)_X\;} F_1 \circ H_1(X) \\[2mm]
\Big\downarrow{\scriptstyle H_2} \quad \circlearrowleft \quad \Big\downarrow{\scriptstyle G_1} & & \Big\downarrow{\scriptstyle (\beta_2)_X} \quad \circlearrowleft \quad \Big\downarrow{\scriptstyle (\alpha_1)_{H_1(X)}} \\[2mm]
\mathcal{I}_2 \xrightarrow[\;G_2\;]{} \hat{\mathcal{I}} & & F_2 \circ H_2(X) \xrightarrow[\;(\alpha_2)_{H_2(X)}\;]{} \begin{array}{c}\hat{F}\circ G_1\circ H_1(X) \\ = \\ \hat{F}\circ G_2\circ H_2(X)\end{array}
\end{array}
\qquad (2)
$$

For a morphism $f\colon X \to Y$ in $\mathcal{I}_0$ consider the cube in (3). The front, back, right and bottom faces commute and the front and back faces are pullbacks in $\mathcal{C}$ by construction above. Then

$$
\begin{aligned}
(\alpha_1)_{H_1(Y)} \circ (F_1 \circ H_1(f)) \circ (\beta_1)_X &= (\hat{F} \circ G_1 \circ H_1(Y)) \circ (\alpha_1)_{H_1(X)} \circ (\beta_1)_X \\
&= (\hat{F} \circ G_2 \circ H_2(Y)) \circ (\alpha_1)_{H_2(X)} \circ (\beta_2)_X \\
&= (\alpha_2)_{H_2(Y)} \circ (F_2 \circ H_2(f)) \circ (\beta_2)_X
\end{aligned}
$$

and since the front face is a pullback there exists one and only one morphism $F_0(f)\colon F_0(X) \to F_0(Y)$ such that $(F_1 \circ H_1(f)) \circ (\beta_1)_X = (\beta_1)_Y \circ F_0(f)$ and $(F_2 \circ H_2(f)) \circ (\beta_2)_X = (\beta_2)_Y \circ F_0(f)$ making the whole cube commute.

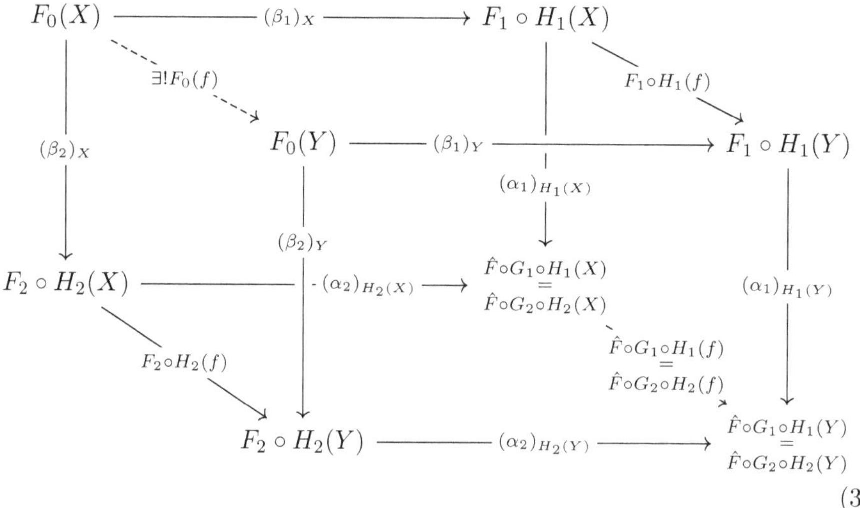

$$(3)$$

Because of the uniqueness of $F_0(f)$ we know that F_0 is compatible with composition of morphisms and thus a well-defined functor $\mathcal{I}_0 \xrightarrow{F_0} \mathcal{C}$. Note that the commutativity of the top and left faces are exactly the conditions needed to make the families of morphisms β_1 and β_2 into natural transformations $F_0 \overset{\beta_1}{\Longrightarrow} F_1 \circ H_1$ and $F_0 \overset{\beta_2}{\Longrightarrow} F_2 \circ H_2$ respectively. Therefore, the pairs (H_1, β_1) and (H_2, β_2) are morphisms in $Diag^{\mathcal{D}}(\mathcal{C})$. They make the left diagram in (4) commute since the front and back faces of the cube in (3) commute.

$$
\begin{array}{ccc}
(\mathcal{I}_0, F_0) \xrightarrow{(H_1,\beta_1)} (\mathcal{I}_1, F_1) & \qquad & (\mathcal{I}', F') \xrightarrow{(H_1',\beta_1')} (\mathcal{I}_1, F_1) \\
\downarrow{\scriptstyle (H_2,\beta_2)} \quad \circlearrowleft \quad \downarrow{\scriptstyle (G_1,\alpha_1)} & & \downarrow{\scriptstyle (H_2',\beta_2')} \quad \circlearrowleft \quad \downarrow{\scriptstyle (G_1,\alpha_1)} \\
(\mathcal{I}_2, F_2) \xrightarrow{(G_2,\alpha_2)} (\hat{\mathcal{I}}, \hat{F}) & & (\mathcal{I}_2, F_2) \xrightarrow{(G_2,\alpha_2)} (\hat{\mathcal{I}}, \hat{F})
\end{array}
\tag{4}
$$

Now let $(\mathcal{I}', F') \in ob(Diag^{\mathcal{D}}(\mathcal{C}))$ and morphisms $(H_1', \beta_1') \colon (\mathcal{I}', F') \to (\mathcal{I}_1, F_1)$ and $(H_2', \beta_2') \colon (\mathcal{I}', F') \to (\mathcal{I}_2, F_2)$ such that the right square in (4) commutes. Then since the left diagram in (2) is a pullback in $\mathcal{D}$ there exists one and only one functor $G \colon \mathcal{I}' \to \mathcal{I}_0$ such that $H_1' = H_1 \circ G$ and $H_2' = H_2 \circ G$. Finally, let $Z \in ob(\mathcal{I}')$

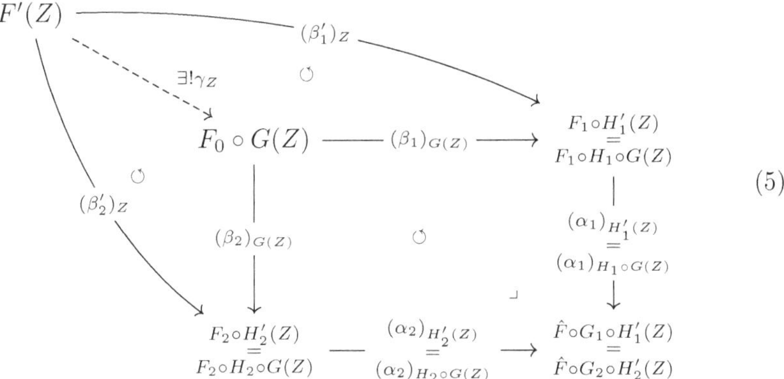

$$\tag{5}$$

then the outer square in (5) commutes by assumption on F', β_1' and β_2'. Furthermore, we get the inner square of (5) by construction of G which is also a pullback square in $\mathcal{C}$ by construction of F_0, so there exists a unique morphism $\gamma_Z \colon F'(Z) \to F_0 \circ G(Z)$. Since the γ_Z are unique they also fulfil the condition for the family of morphisms γ to be a natural transformation $F' \overset{\gamma}{\Rightarrow} F_0 \circ G$ and thus $(G, \gamma) \colon (\mathcal{I}', F') \to (\mathcal{I}_0, F_0)$ is a morphism in $Diag^{\mathcal{D}}(\mathcal{C})$ such that $(H_1, \beta_1) \circ (G, \gamma) = (H_1', \beta_1')$ and $(H_1, \beta_1) \circ (G, \gamma) = (H_1', \beta_1')$. It is unique since its components are unique. Therefore, we can conclude that the left diagram in (4) is in fact a pullback and since the choice of cospan $(\mathcal{I}_1, F_1) \xrightarrow{(G_1,\alpha_1)} (\hat{\mathcal{I}}, \hat{F}) \xleftarrow{(G_2,\alpha_2)} (\mathcal{I}_2, F_2)$ was arbitrary it means $Diag^{\mathcal{D}}(\mathcal{C})$ has all pullbacks. $\qquad\square$

2.3 Monomorphisms in $Diag(\cdot)$

Theorem 2. *Let $\mathcal{C}$ and $\mathcal{D} \subset \underline{Cat}$ be categories that admit pullbacks. A morphism $(G, \alpha) \colon (\mathcal{I}_1, F_1) \to (\mathcal{I}_2, F_2)$ in $Diag^{\mathcal{D}}(\mathcal{C})$ is a monomorphism if and only if G is a monomorphism in $\mathcal{D}$ and for every $X \in ob(\mathcal{I}_1)$ α_X is a monomorphism in $\mathcal{C}$.*

Remark 1. In particular if $\mathcal{D} = \underline{Cat}$, then the monomorphisms in $\mathcal{D}$ are the functors that are faithful and injective on objects.

Proof. We know that (G, α) is a monomorphism in $Diag^{\mathcal{D}}(\mathcal{C})$ iff the diagram

$$
\begin{array}{ccc}
(\mathcal{I}_1, F_1) & \overset{Id}{\longrightarrow} & (\mathcal{I}_1, F_1) \\
\downarrow{\scriptstyle Id} & \circlearrowleft \qquad \lrcorner & \downarrow{\scriptstyle (G,\alpha)} \\
(\mathcal{I}_1, F_1) & \underset{(G,\alpha)}{\longrightarrow} & (\mathcal{I}_2, F_2)
\end{array}
$$

is a pullback in $Diag^{\mathcal{D}}(\mathcal{C})$. From the proof of Theorem 1 we know that this is the case iff the diagram on the left of (6) is a pullback in $\mathcal{D}$ and for every $X \in ob(\mathcal{I}_1)$ the diagram on the left of (6) is a pullback in $\mathcal{C}$.

$$
\begin{array}{ccccccc}
\mathcal{I}_1 & \overset{Id}{\longrightarrow} & \mathcal{I}_1 & \qquad & F_1(X) & \overset{Id}{\longrightarrow} & F_1(X) \\
\downarrow{\scriptstyle Id} \; \circlearrowleft & \lrcorner & \downarrow{\scriptstyle G} & & \downarrow{\scriptstyle Id} \; \circlearrowleft & \lrcorner & \downarrow{\scriptstyle \alpha_X} \\
\mathcal{I}_1 & \underset{G}{\longrightarrow} & \mathcal{I}_2 & & F_1(X) & \underset{\alpha_X}{\longrightarrow} & F_2 \circ G(X)
\end{array}
\tag{6}
$$

This is the case iff G is a monomorphism in $\mathcal{D}$ and for every $X \in ob(\mathcal{I}_1)$ α_X is a monomorphism in $\mathcal{C}$. $\qquad\square$

Remark 2. Note that the existence of pullbacks in $\mathcal{C}$ and $\mathcal{D}$ in Theorem 2 is required to conclude that if the diagram is a pullback in $Diag^{\mathcal{D}}(\mathcal{C})$ then the diagrams in $\mathcal{C}$ and $\mathcal{D}$ are pullbacks. If these pullbacks exist in $\mathcal{C}$ and $\mathcal{D}$, then any pullback in $Diag^{\mathcal{D}}(\mathcal{C})$ must be of the form described in Theorem 1 by the universal property of the pullback. If pullbacks in $\mathcal{C}$ and $\mathcal{D}$ are not guaranteed to exist then a diagram in $Diag^{\mathcal{D}}(\mathcal{C})$ may still be a pullback without the individual parts being pullbacks so the conclusion in the proof of Theorem 2 would fail.

2.4   Pushouts in $Diag(\cdot)$

Theorem 3. *Let $\mathcal{C}$ be a cocomplete category, $\mathcal{D} \subset \underline{Cat}$ be a category with pushouts, then $Diag^{\mathcal{D}}(\mathcal{C})$ has pushouts.*

The construction in the following proof is adapted from Remark 2.8. in [16] where an overview about the construction of products, equalizers and their duals in $Diag(\cdot)$ are given. We have applied this directly to pushouts as coequalizers of two morphisms into a coproduct and provide a complete proof not reliant on high level facts about adjoint constructions.

Proof. Let $(\mathcal{I}_1, F_1) \xleftarrow{(G_1, \alpha_1)} (\mathcal{I}_0, F_0) \xrightarrow{(G_2, \alpha_2)} (\mathcal{I}_2, F_2)$ be a span in $Diag^{\mathcal{D}}(\mathcal{C})$. First take $\mathcal{I}_i \xrightarrow{H_i} \hat{\mathcal{I}}$ to be a pushout of G_1 and G_2 in Cat. We set $K_0 \colon \hat{\mathcal{I}} \to \mathcal{C}$ to be the left Kan extension of F_0 along $H_1 \circ G_1 = H_2 \circ G_2$ and $K_i \colon \hat{\mathcal{I}} \to \mathcal{C}$ to for $i \in \{1,2\}$ be the left Kan extension of F_i along H_i together with their universal natural transformation η_0, η_1 and η_2.

$$
\begin{array}{cc}
\mathcal{I}_0 \xrightarrow{\ F_0\ } \mathcal{C} & \mathcal{I}_i \xrightarrow{\ F_i\ } \mathcal{C} \\[2ex]
\begin{array}{c} H_1 \circ G_1 \\ = \\ H_2 \circ G_1 \end{array} \searrow\ \overset{\exists!\eta_0}{\Downarrow}\ \nearrow K_0 := Lan_{H_1 \circ G_1} F_0 & H \searrow\ \overset{\exists!\eta_i}{\Downarrow}\ \nearrow K_i := Lan_{H_i} F_i \\
\hat{\mathcal{I}} & \hat{\mathcal{I}}
\end{array}
\qquad (7)
$$

As $\mathcal{I}_i$ is small for $i \in \{0,1,2\}$ and $\mathcal{C}$ is small and cocomplete, the left Kan-extension $K_0(X)$ for $X \in ob(\hat{\mathcal{I}})$ can be calculated on objects as $colim((H_1 \circ G_1/\Delta_X) \xrightarrow{forget_X} \mathcal{I}_0 \xrightarrow{F_0} \mathcal{C})$. Where $(H_1 \circ G_1/\Delta_X)$ is the comma category over the cospan $\mathcal{I}_0 \xrightarrow{H_1 \circ G_1} \hat{\mathcal{I}} \xleftarrow{\delta_X} \bullet$ and $\Delta_X \colon \bullet \mapsto X$. For a morphism $f \colon X \to Y$ in $\hat{\mathcal{I}}$ note that f induces a functor $\theta_f \colon (H_1 \circ G_1/\Delta_X) \to (H_1 \circ G_1/\Delta_Y)$ with $forget_X = forget_Y \circ \theta_f$. Then the universal cocone $(K_0(Y),(\xi_Z \colon F_0 \circ forget_Y(Z) \to K_0(Y))_{Z \in ob((H_1 \circ G_1/\Delta_Y})$ over $F_0 \circ forget_Y$ given by the construction of K_0 on objects gives rise to a cocone $(C,(\xi_{\theta_f})_{Z \in ob((H_1 \circ G_1/\Delta_X}$ over $F_0 \circ forget_X$ and thus a unique morphism $\zeta_f \colon K_0(X) \to K_0(Y)$ due to the universality of the choice of $K_0(X)$. Similarly, $K_i := colim((H_i/\Delta_X) \xrightarrow{forget_X} \mathcal{I}_i \xrightarrow{F_i} \mathcal{C})$ for $X \in ob(\hat{\mathcal{I}})$.

For α_1 and α_2 we now get unique natural transformations $\gamma_1 \colon K_0 \Rightarrow K_1$ and $\gamma_2 \colon K_0 \Rightarrow K_2$ respectively by the universal property of the left Kan extension K_0 that make the left diagram in (8) commute for $i = 1$ and $i = 2$ respectively.

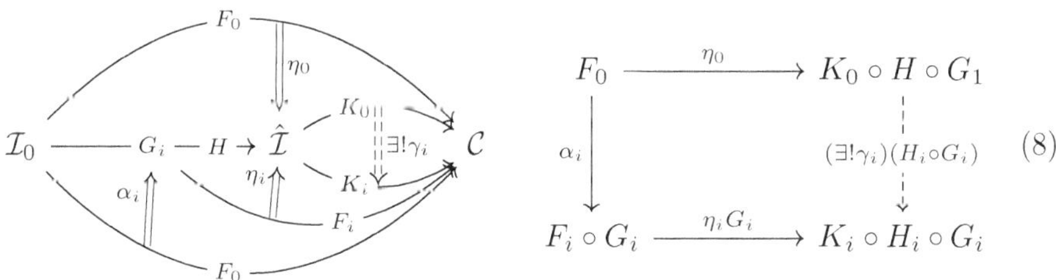

$$
\begin{array}{ccc}
F_0 & \xrightarrow{\ \eta_0\ } & K_0 \circ H \circ G_1 \\
\alpha_i \downarrow & & \downarrow (\exists!\gamma_i)(H_i \circ G_i) \\
F_i \circ G_i & \xrightarrow{\ \eta_i G_i\ } & K_i \circ H_i \circ G_i
\end{array}
\qquad (8)
$$

Finally we can take the pushout $\hat{F}$ of γ_1 and γ_2 in the functor category $[\hat{\mathcal{I}}, \mathcal{C}]$ as in the left diagram of (9) which is calculated componentwise. With that we get the square on the right of (9).

$$
\begin{array}{ccccc}
K_0 \xrightarrow{\ \gamma_1\ } K_1 & \qquad & (\mathcal{I}_0, F_0) \xrightarrow{\ (G_1,\alpha_1)\ } (\mathcal{I}_1, F_1) \\[1ex]
\gamma_2 \downarrow \quad \circ \quad \downarrow \beta_2 & (G_2,\alpha_2) \downarrow \quad \circ \quad \downarrow (H_1,(\beta_1 H_1)\circ\eta_1) & & & (9) \\[1ex]
K_2 \xrightarrow[\ \beta_2\ ]{} \hat{F} & & (\mathcal{I}_2, F_2) \xrightarrow[(H_2,(\beta_2 H_2)\circ\eta_2)]{} (\hat{\mathcal{I}}, \hat{F})
\end{array}
$$

The functors commute by construction of H_1, H_2 and $\hat{\mathcal{I}}$ and for the natural transformations we get

$$(\beta_1 H_1 \circ G_1) \circ (\eta_1 G_1) \circ \alpha_1 \overset{(i)}{=} (\beta_1 H_1 \circ G_1) \circ (\gamma_1 H_1 \circ G_1) \circ \eta_1$$
$$\overset{(ii)}{=} (\beta_2 G_2 \circ G_2) \circ (\gamma_2 H_2 \circ G_2) \circ \eta_2$$
$$\overset{(iii)}{=} (\beta_2 H_1 \circ G_1) \circ (\eta_2 G_2) \circ \alpha_2,$$

so the square actually commutes in $Diag^{\mathcal{D}}(\mathcal{C})$. Here equations (i) and (iii) are given by the construction of the γ_i and (ii) is given by the construction of the β_i as part of a pushout in $[\hat{\mathcal{I}}, \mathcal{C}]$. Now to check that this actually defines a pushout let $(\mathcal{I}_1, F_1) \xrightarrow{(H_1', \beta_1')} (\mathcal{I}', F') \xleftarrow{(H_2', \beta_2')} (\mathcal{F}_2, F_2)$ another diagram over $\mathcal{C}$ with morphisms such that $(H_1', \beta_1') \circ (G_1, \alpha_1) = (H_1', \beta_1') \circ (G_1, \alpha_1)$. Since the square in the following diagram on the left is a pushout by construction we get a unique functor H' so that everything commutes.

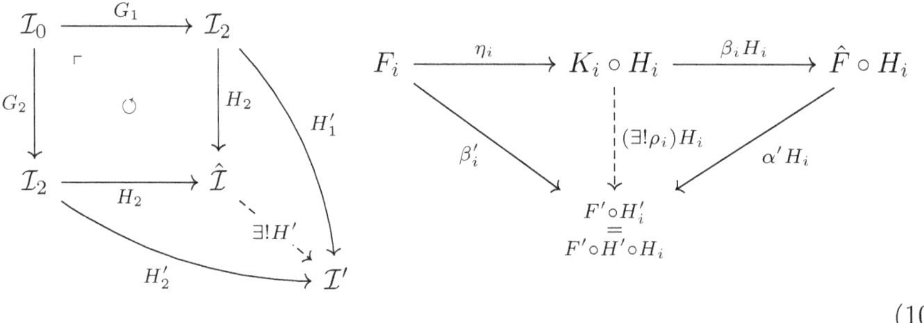

$$\tag{10}$$

Induced by the β_i' the universal property of the left Kan extensions K_i yield unique natural transformations $\rho_i \colon K_i \overset{\rho_i}{\Rightarrow} F' \circ G'$ making the left triangle of the right diagram in (10) commute. Then since $(\beta_1' G_1) \circ \alpha_1 = (\beta_2' G_2) \circ \alpha_2)$ by assumption on the β_i' the universal property of the left Kan extension K_0 gives us a unique natural transformation $\zeta \colon K_0 \Rightarrow F' \circ H'$ as in the left diagram of (11) with $(\rho_1 \circ \gamma_1)(H_1 \circ G_1) = \zeta(H_1 \circ H_1) = (\rho_2 \circ \gamma_2)(H_2 \circ G_2)$.

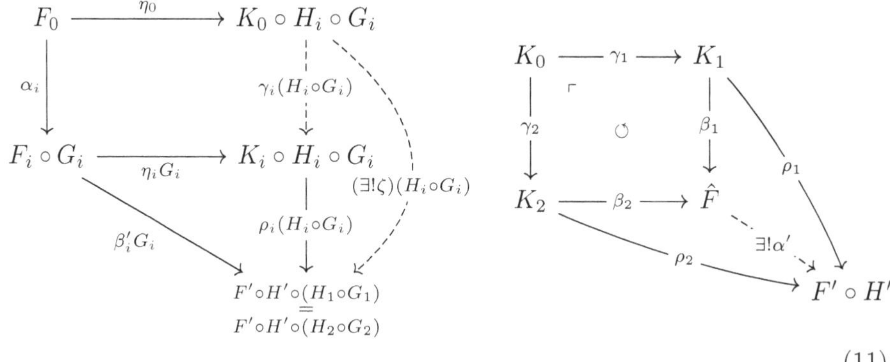

$$\tag{11}$$

Therefore we have $\rho_1 \circ \gamma_1 = \rho_2 \circ \gamma_2$ and since the square in the right diagram of (11) was constructed to be a pushout in $[\hat{I}, \mathcal{C}]$ of γ_1 and γ_2 we get a unique natural transformation $\alpha' \colon \hat{F} \Rightarrow F' \circ H'$ so that everything commutes. This then also means that the outer triangle in (10) commutes and thus $(H', \alpha') \colon (\hat{\mathcal{I}}, \hat{F}) \to (\mathcal{I}', F')$ is the unique morphism in $Diag^{\mathcal{D}}(\mathcal{C})$ such that $(H', \alpha') \circ (H_i, \beta_i) = (H'_i, \beta'_i)$ for $i \in \{1, 2\}$. In total this means that the constructed square is in fact a pushout, and consequently since the initial choice of span was arbitrary that $Diag^{\mathcal{D}}(\mathcal{C})$ has pushouts. $\qquad\square$

Remark 3. From the construction of pushouts via Kan-extension in the proof of Theorem 3 we can see that by limiting ourselves to *finite* categories as index categories (i.e. objects of $\mathcal{D}$) we can relax the requirement to the category $\mathcal{C}$ to *finite* cocompleteness.

Remark 4. The Kan-extensions used in the construction of pushouts can require construction of arbitrary colimits in $\mathcal{C}$. Because of this we believe that with $\mathcal{D} = \underline{Cat}$ relatively small (even *finite*) examples might exist where a pushout is not a pullback stable under pullbacks which would mean $Diag^{\underline{Cat}}(\mathcal{C})$ is not adhesive in general even if $\mathcal{C}$ is.

Remark 5. If the initial object in $\underline{Cat}$, namely the empty category $\emptyset$, is in $\mathcal{D}$ then regardless of the existence of an initial object in $\mathcal{C}$, $Diag^{\mathcal{D}}(\mathcal{C})$ has the initial object of $\mathcal{D}$ together with its unique functor to $\mathcal{C}$ as an initial object. In examples of classical DPO graph rewriting the empty graph often appears as a context graph K, similarly we likely always want $\emptyset$ to be in $ob(\mathcal{D})$ to have access to a similar mechanism in higher-order graph transformation.

Then and under the conditions for Theorem 3 $Diag^{\mathcal{D}}(\mathcal{C})$ is even finite cocomplete.

2.5 Extensiveness of $Diag(\cdot)$

Theorem 4. *Let $\mathcal{C}$ be a category and $\mathcal{D} \subseteq \underline{Cat}$ an extensive subcategory, then $Diag^{\mathcal{D}}(\mathcal{C})$ is extensive.*

Proof. First let $(\mathcal{I}_i, F_i) \xrightarrow{(\iota_1^{\mathcal{I}}, id)} (\mathcal{I}_1 \amalg \mathcal{I}_2, F_1 \amalg F_2)$ be a coprojection in $Diag^{\mathcal{D}}(\mathcal{C})$ and $(K, \gamma) \colon (\hat{\mathcal{I}}, \hat{F})$ some morphism.

$$
\begin{array}{ccc}
(\hat{\mathcal{I}}, \hat{F}) & \qquad \mathcal{I}'_i \xrightarrow{\ H_i\ } \hat{\mathcal{I}} \\
\big\downarrow{\scriptstyle (K,\gamma)} & \quad {\scriptstyle G_i}\big\downarrow \quad \circlearrowleft \quad \big\downarrow{\scriptstyle K} & \qquad (12)\\
(\mathcal{I}_i, F_i) \xrightarrow{\ (\iota_1^{\mathcal{I}}, id)\ } (\mathcal{I}_1 \amalg \mathcal{I}_2, F_1 \amalg F_2) & \quad \mathcal{I}_i \xrightarrow{\ \iota_i^{\mathcal{I}}\ } \mathcal{I}_1 \amalg \mathcal{I}_2
\end{array}
$$

Since $\mathcal{D}$ is extensive we know that pullback $\mathcal{I}_i \xleftarrow{G_i} \mathcal{I}'_i \xrightarrow{H_i} \hat{\mathcal{I}}$ exists in $\mathcal{D}$. To get a pullback in $Diag^{\mathcal{D}}(\mathcal{C})$ we would need to take a pullback at every $X \in ob(\mathcal{I}'_i)$ of

$$
F_1 \circ G_1(X) \xrightarrow{id} (F_1 \amalg F_2) \circ \iota_i^{\mathcal{C}} \circ G_1(X) \xleftarrow{\gamma_{H_1(X)}} \hat{F} \circ H_i(X),
$$

but this exists and is simply given by

$$F_i \circ G_i(X) \xleftarrow{\;\gamma_{H_i(X)}\;} (F_i'(X) := \hat{F} \circ H_i(X)) \xrightarrow{\;id\;} \hat{F} \circ H_i(X)$$

Therefore $Diag^{\mathcal{D}}(\mathcal{C})$ has pullbacks along coprojections. Now let there be a commutative diagram as (13) in $Diag^{\mathcal{D}}(\mathcal{C})$.

$$
\begin{array}{ccccc}
(\mathcal{I}_1', F_i') & \xrightarrow{\;(H_1,\beta_1)\;} & (\hat{\mathcal{I}}, \hat{F}) & \xleftarrow{\;(H_2,\beta_2)\;} & (\mathcal{I}_2', F_2') \\
\Big\downarrow & & \Big\downarrow & & \Big\downarrow \\
{\scriptstyle (G_1,\alpha_1)} & \circlearrowleft & {\scriptstyle (K,\gamma)} & \circlearrowleft & {\scriptstyle (G_2,\alpha_2)} \\
\Big\downarrow & & \Big\downarrow & & \Big\downarrow \\
(\mathcal{I}_1, F_1) & \xrightarrow{\;(\iota_1^{\mathcal{I}},id)\;} & (\mathcal{I}_1 \amalg \mathcal{I}_2, F_1 \amalg F_2) & \xleftarrow{\;(\iota_2^{\mathcal{I}},id)\;} & (\mathcal{I}_2, F_2)
\end{array}
\tag{13}
$$

Assume first that the left and right squares are pullbacks. Since $\mathcal{D}$ is extensive and the squares are also pullbacks in $\mathcal{D}$ we know that $\mathcal{I}_1' \xrightarrow{H_1} \hat{\mathcal{I}} \xleftarrow{H_2} \mathcal{I}_2'$ is a coproduct diagram. Furthermore, for $X \in ob(\mathcal{I}_i')$ the right diagram of (14)

$$
\begin{array}{ccc}
\mathcal{I}_i' & \xrightarrow{\;H_i\;} & \hat{\mathcal{I}} \\
\Big\downarrow{\scriptstyle G_i} \quad \circlearrowleft & & \Big\downarrow{\scriptstyle K} \\
\mathcal{I}_i & \xrightarrow{\;\iota_i^{\mathcal{I}}\;} & (\mathcal{I}_1 \amalg \mathcal{I}_2)
\end{array}
\qquad
\begin{array}{ccc}
F_i'(X) & \xrightarrow{\;(\beta_i)_X\;} & \hat{F} \circ H_i(X) \\
\Big\downarrow{\scriptstyle (\alpha_i)_X} \quad \circlearrowleft & & \Big\downarrow{\scriptstyle \gamma_{H_i(X)}} \\
F_i \circ G_i(X) & \xrightarrow{\;id_{G_i(X)}\;} & (F_1 \amalg F_2) \circ \iota_i^{\mathcal{I}} \circ G_i(X)
\end{array}
\tag{14}
$$

is a pullback in $\mathcal{C}$. Consequently, the $(\beta_i)_\bullet$ as pullbacks of id must be isomorphisms in $\mathcal{C}$ and therefore the $\beta_i \colon F_i' \Longrightarrow \hat{F} \circ H_i$ are natural isomorphisms.

$$
\begin{array}{ccc}
(\mathcal{I}_1', F_1') \xrightarrow{\;(\iota_1^{\mathcal{I}'},id)\;} (\mathcal{I}_1' \amalg \mathcal{I}_2', F_1' \amalg F_2') \xleftarrow{\;(\iota_2^{\mathcal{I}'},id)\;} (\mathcal{I}_2', F_2') \\
{\scriptstyle (H_1,\beta_1)} \searrow \qquad \Big\downarrow{\scriptstyle \exists!(M,\beta)} \qquad \swarrow {\scriptstyle (H_2,\beta_2)} \\
(\hat{\mathcal{I}}, \hat{F})
\end{array}
\tag{15}
$$

Now consider the coproduct diagram of the $(\mathcal{I}_i', F_i')$ in $Diag^{\mathcal{D}}(\mathcal{C})$ in the upper row of (15) and the induced morphism $(M,\beta) \colon (\mathcal{I}_1' \amalg \mathcal{I}_2', F_1' \amalg F_2') \to (\hat{\mathcal{I}}, \hat{F})$. Then

$$
\beta_X = \begin{cases} (\beta_1)_X & \text{if } X \in ob(\mathcal{I}_1') \\ (\beta_2)_X & \text{if } X \in ob(\mathcal{I}_2') \end{cases}
\qquad (\text{for } X \in ob(\mathcal{I}_1' \amalg \mathcal{I}_2'))
$$

so β is a natural isomorphism. $M \colon \mathcal{I}_1' \amalg \mathcal{I}_2' \to \hat{\mathcal{I}}$ is an isomorphism in $\mathcal{D}$ since both $\hat{\mathcal{I}}$ and $\mathcal{I}_1' \amalg \mathcal{I}_2'$ are coproducts of the $\mathcal{I}_i'$. Therefore, (M,β) is an isomorphism in $Diag^{\mathcal{D}}(\mathcal{C})$ and thus the upper row of (13) is a coproduct diagram.

Conversely, assume that the upper row of (13) is a coproduct diagram. Then $\mathcal{I}_1' \xrightarrow{H_1} \hat{\mathcal{I}} \xleftarrow{H_2} \mathcal{I}_2'$ is also a coproduct diagram and thus the squares on the left of (14) are pullbacks in $\mathcal{D}$. Additionally, the $(\beta_i)_X$ are isomorphisms. But any commutative square where two non-adjacent morphisms are isomorphisms is a pullback so the right diagram in (14) is also a pullback for all $i \in \{1,2\}$ and $X \in ob(\mathcal{I}_i)$. Therefore, both squares in (13) are pullbacks $\square$

Remark 6. Note that $\mathcal{D} = \underline{Cat}$ is extensive.

3   On Extensive Categories

We will now present some theorems about extensive categories that ultimately help to prove the adhesiveness of our construction. For this we will first introduce some notation:

Notation 1 Let $\mathcal{C}$ be any category.

- We denote coprojections (if the coproduct exists) as $\iota_i^X \colon X_i \to \coprod_{i \in I} X_i$.
- Let $f_i \colon A_i \to B_i$ be some morphisms we use $\coprod_\iota^{i \in I} f_i$ to mean the unique map induced by the maps $\iota_i^B \circ f_i \colon A_i \to \coprod^{i \in I} B_i$ by the universal property of the coproduct $\coprod^{i \in I} A_i$. (Also $f_1 \amalg_\iota f_2$ in the binary case.)

Theorem 5. *Let $\mathcal{C}$ be an extensive category and $f_i \colon X_i \to Y_i$ for $i \in \{1,2\}$ some morphisms. $f_1 \amalg_\iota f_2$ is a monomorphism if and only if f_1 and f_2 are monomorphisms.*

Some of the following theorems are relatively straightforward to prove, so the proofs are left to the Appendix (if one is included).

Theorem 6. *Let $\mathcal{C}$ be an extensive category. If the pullback diagrams on the right of (16) exist then the pullback of the diagram on the left of (16)*

$$
\begin{array}{ccccccc}
B_1 \amalg B_2 & & A_i & \xrightarrow{\ \ f_i\ \ } & B_i & & \\
\big\downarrow{\scriptstyle p_1 \amalg_\iota p_2} & & \big\downarrow{\scriptstyle g_i} & \circlearrowleft & \big\downarrow{\scriptstyle p_i} & & (16) \\
C_1 \amalg C_2 & \xrightarrow{\ q_1 \amalg_\iota q_2\ } D_1 \amalg D_2 & C_i & \xrightarrow{\ \ q_i\ \ } & D_i & &
\end{array}
$$

is exactly given by $B_1 \amalg B_2 \xleftarrow{\ f_1 \amalg_\iota f_2\ } A_1 \amalg A_2 \xrightarrow{\ g_1 \amalg_\iota g_2\ } C_1 \amalg C_2$.

Theorem 7. *Let $\mathcal{C}$ be any category. If the pushout diagrams on the right of (17) exist then the pushout of the diagram on the left of (17)*

$$
\begin{array}{ccccccc}
A_1 \amalg A_2 & \xrightarrow{\ f_1 \amalg_\iota f_2\ } B_1 \amalg B_2 & A_i & \xrightarrow{\ \ f_i\ \ } & B_i & & \\
\big\downarrow{\scriptstyle g_1 \amalg_\iota g_2} & & \big\downarrow{\scriptstyle g_i} & \circlearrowleft & \big\downarrow{\scriptstyle p_i} & & (17) \\
C_1 \amalg C_2 & & C_i & \xrightarrow{\ \ q_i\ \ } & D_i & &
\end{array}
$$

is exactly given by $B_1 \amalg B_2 \xrightarrow{\ p_1 \amalg p_2\ } D_1 \amalg D_2 \xleftarrow{\ q_1 \amalg q_2\ } C_1 \amalg C_2$.

Theorem 8. *Let $\mathcal{C}$ be an extensive category. And let for $i \in \{1,2\}$ the left diagram in (18) be a pushout that is stable under pullbacks*

$$
\begin{array}{ccc}
A_i \xrightarrow{\;f_i\;} B_i & \qquad & A_1 \amalg A_2 \xrightarrow{\;f_1 \amalg_\iota f_2\;} B_1 \amalg B_2 \\
\Big\downarrow{\scriptstyle g_i} \quad \circlearrowleft \quad \Big\downarrow{\scriptstyle p_i} & & {\scriptstyle g_1 \amalg_\iota g_2}\Big\downarrow \quad \circlearrowleft \quad \Big\downarrow{\scriptstyle p_1 \amalg_\iota p_2} \\
C_i \xrightarrow{\;q_i\;} D_i & & C_1 \amalg C_2 \xrightarrow{\;q_1 \amalg_\iota q_2\;} D_1 \amalg D_2
\end{array}
\tag{18}
$$

then the right diagram in (18) is also a pushout stable under pullback.

Proof. Applying Theorem 7 we know that the right diagram in (18) is a pushout. Now let $h^D \colon \hat{D} \to D$ some (base-change) morphism. Since $\mathcal{C}$ is extensive we know there exists $\hat{D}_1, \hat{D}_2 \in ob(\mathcal{C})$ and $h_i^D \colon \hat{D}_i \to D_i$ such that $\hat{D} = \hat{D}_1 \amalg \hat{D}_2$ and $h^D = h_1^D \amalg_\iota h_2^D$. Via repeated application of Theorem 6 we get the commutative cube on the in (19)

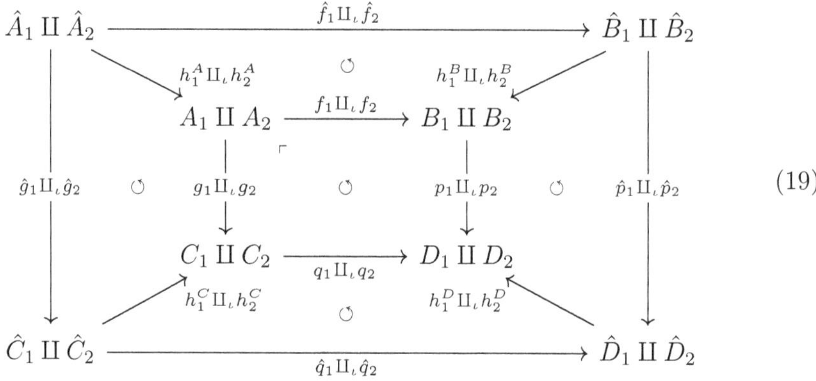

$$\tag{19}$$

that is essentially the *coproduct* of the cubes in (20). By the construction of the pullback in Theorem 6 the sides of the cubes in (20) are pullbacks and since the inner squares were assumed to be pushouts that are stable under pullback the outer squares are also pushouts.

$$\tag{20}$$

Finally by Theorem 7 then the outer square of (19) must also be a pushout. Therefore, the pushout on the right of (18) is stable under pullbacks as claimed. $\qquad\square$

Theorem 9. *Let $\mathcal{C}$ be an extensive category with pullbacks. If pushouts along monomorphisms exist, and there exists a set X of pushouts that are pullbacks and stable under pullbacks such that all pushouts along monomorphisms can be written as finite coproduct pushouts like in Theorem 7 (with possibly more than two components) of pushouts in X, then $\mathcal{C}$ is adhesive.*

Proof. By inductively applying Theorem 6 and Theorem 8 from pushouts in X we get that in $\mathcal{C}$ all pushouts along monomorphisms are pullbacks and stable under pullbacks. Therefore, as $\mathcal{C}$ was assumed to have pullbacks $\mathcal{C}$ is adhesive. $\square$

4   Higher-Order Graph Transformation: Spans and Points

In this section we take a closer look at the subcategory of spans and points over some category $\mathcal{C}$.

Definition 2. *Define category $\mathcal{D}_{sp} \subset \underline{Cat}$ with objects*

$$ob(\mathcal{D}_{sp}) := \{(\mathcal{I}_{n_s,n_p} \mid n_s, n_p \in \mathbb{N}_0\} \qquad (\mathcal{I}_{n_s,n_p} \text{ defined as in Sect. 1.3})$$

and morphisms $G\colon \mathcal{I}_{n_s^1,n_p^1} \to \mathcal{I}_{n_s^2,n_p^2}$ being functors induced by injective morphism of typed graphs over type graph $T := \bullet \leftarrow \bullet \to \bullet \, \bullet$. For a category $\mathcal{C}$ we define the category of spans and points over $\mathcal{C}$ as $\mathcal{SP}(\mathcal{C}) := Diag^{\mathcal{D}_{sp}}(\mathcal{C})$.

Remark 7. Note that $\mathcal{SP}\colon \underline{Cat} \to \underline{Cat}$ is in fact a functor, as any functor $H\colon \mathcal{C} \to \mathcal{E}$ immediately gives rise to a functor $\mathcal{SP}(\mathcal{C}) \to \mathcal{SP}(\mathcal{E})$.

Remark 8. It can be easily checked that the category $\mathcal{D}_{sp}$ in Definition 2 is closed under pushouts and pullbacks and therefore extensive as $\underline{Cat}$ is extensive.

Theorem 10. *Let $\mathcal{C}$ be an adhesive category, then $\mathcal{SP}(\mathcal{C})$ is also adhesive.*

Proof. As $\mathcal{C}$ and $\mathcal{D}_{sp}$ (as in Definition 2) have pullbacks $\mathcal{SP}(\mathcal{C})$ has pullbacks by Theorem 1. Because of the restriction on the shape of the functors in $\mathcal{D}_{sp}$, any morphism in $\mathcal{SP}(\mathcal{C})$ actually decomposes as a coproduct $\coprod_\iota$ of elements in $[\bullet \leftarrow \bullet \to \bullet, \mathcal{C}]$ and $[\bullet, \mathcal{C}]$.

Note that for a span $(\mathcal{I}_1, F_1) \xleftarrow{F} (\mathcal{I}_0, F_0) \xrightarrow{G} (\mathcal{I}_2, F_2)$ any parts of the index categories not in the image of F and G, can be seen as taking a *coproduct* of a span with surjective functors and spans of the form $(\mathcal{I}_1', F_1') \leftarrow (\emptyset, \emptyset \to \mathcal{C}) \to (\emptyset, \emptyset \to \mathcal{C})$ or $(\emptyset, \emptyset \to \mathcal{C}) \leftarrow (\emptyset, \emptyset \to \mathcal{C}) \to (\mathcal{I}_2', F_2')$ for some $(\mathcal{I}_i', F_i')$. It can be checked that for these spans pushouts exist and are pullbacks and stable under pullbacks.

We can see that pushouts along monomorphisms of spans with surjective functors can be written as *coproducts* over pushouts along monomorphisms in the aforementioned functor categories by Theorem 7, Theorem 6 and Theorem 5. Furthermore, as $\mathcal{C}$ is adhesive pushouts along monomorphisms exists in any functor categories into $\mathcal{C}$, and they are pullbacks and stable under pullbacks. Thus, we can now apply Theorem 9 with X given by the pushouts entirely in one of the functor categories $[\bullet, \mathcal{C}]$ or $[\bullet \leftarrow \bullet \to \bullet, \mathcal{C}]$ or with the initial object $(\emptyset, \emptyset \to \mathcal{C})$ as discussed above. Therefore, $\mathcal{SP}(\mathcal{C})$ is adhesive. $\square$

Remark 9. We did not need to require $\mathcal{C}$ to be (finite) cocomplete as the restriction to injective functors in the construction of $\mathcal{D}_{sp}$ ensures that all the Kan-extensions in pushouts (in X) will be trivial.

We can then repeatedly layer this construction to get rules of arbitrary high levels. Rules of lower levels naturally are always included, as we can simply consider a single object via a chain of functors $\bullet \to \bullet \to \cdots \to \mathcal{C}$. E.g. a first order rule $L \leftarrow K \to R$ naturally lifts to an equivalent second order rule $(\bullet \to L) \leftarrow (\bullet \to K) \to (\bullet \to R)$. A transformation system is then a collection of objects of possibly different levels. Replacement is done by picking any span in this collection, finding a match in the lower level contents of the collection while automatically *implicitly* lifting rules and objects if necessary and performing rewriting in the classical DPO way.

5   Outlook: Higher-Order Transformation with Variables

The author of [7] has argued for the increased abstraction and expressiveness gained from including variables in a rule-based system like graph transformation. In the following, we adapt that idea of graph transformation with variables to the context of higher-order transformations.

If we consider a category $\mathcal{I}$ as a graph with additional structure (i.e. the composition map) then we can interpret a diagram $\mathcal{I} \to \mathcal{C}$ as an attributed graph. Nodes (objects) have attributes in $ob(\mathcal{C})$ and edges (morphisms) are labelled in the type of morphisms in $\mathcal{C}$ between the labels of the tail and head of the edge. Leaving some attributes as variables and terms on these variables leads us to the notion of higher-order transformation with variables.

We can now borrow the language and procedure used by Hoffmann in [7] regarding graph transformation with attribute variables.

Definition 3. *1. Let $\mathcal{I}$ some index category. We call a functor $\underline{k} \colon \underline{\mathcal{I}} \to \mathcal{C}$ (the kernel) from a subcategory $\iota_{\mathcal{I}} \colon \underline{\mathcal{I}} \hookrightarrow \mathcal{I}$ and an assignment*

$$var_{ob} \colon \{X \in ob(\mathcal{I}) \mid X \notin ob(\underline{\mathcal{I}})\} \to \mathcal{X}_{ob}$$
$$var_{mor} \colon \{f \in \mathcal{I}(A,B) \mid A,B \in ob(\mathcal{I}), f \text{ not a morphism in } \underline{\mathcal{I}}\} \to \mathcal{X}_{mor}$$

a graph pattern. An instantiation of a pattern $(\mathcal{I}, \underline{\mathcal{I}}, \underline{k}, var)$ is a functor $k \colon \mathcal{I} \to \mathcal{C}$ extending $\underline{k}$ to $\mathcal{I}$; i.e. $\underline{k} = k \circ \iota$ in such a way that $k(A) = k(B)$ if $var_{ob}(A) = var_{ob}(B)$ and $k(f) = k(g)$ if $var_{mor}(f) = var_{mor}(g)$.

2. A rule scheme t is given by three patterns $(\mathcal{I}_i, \underline{\mathcal{I}}_i, \underline{k}_i, var_i)_{i \in \{L,K,R\}}$ together with functors $l \colon \mathcal{I}_K \to \mathcal{I}_L$ and $r \colon \mathcal{I}_K \to \mathcal{I}_R$ as well assignments

$$\beta^{var}(X) \in \mathcal{C}(\underline{k}_K(X), \underline{k}_L(l(X))) \qquad\qquad \text{if } X \in \underline{\mathcal{I}}_K \wedge l(X) \in \underline{\mathcal{I}}_L$$
$$\beta^{var}(X) \in \mathcal{X}_{nat} \qquad\qquad else$$

and γ^{var} with analogously defined codomain for $\underline{k}_R$.

3. *An instantiation of the rule scheme t is given by instantiations of its patterns as well as appropriate choices for the variables in β^{var} and γ^{var} to make them into natural transformations as required for morphisms of diagrams.*
4. *Rule application involves finding a kernel match from $(\underline{\mathcal{I}}_L, \underline{k}_L)$ into our context as usual that extends to a full match for some instantiation of $(\mathcal{I}_i, \underline{\mathcal{I}}_i, \underline{k}_i, var_i)_{i \in \{L,K,R\}}$ that is part of an instantiation of t (provided these even exist). Finally, the fully instantiated rule is applied for the full match.*

In some cases a functor m from $\mathcal{I}_L$ to an index category in our context together with a kernel match (call this a pre-morphism*) might be enough to present canonical choices for an instantiation of the rule by e.g. copying the functor into $\mathcal{C}$ at the destination of m.*

We now demonstrate the usefulness of higher-order (graph) transformations in general and specifically those with variables by rephrasing the known results of parallelization and parallelization with dedoubling in this context.

Example 1. Parallelization of two rules $p_i : L_i \leftarrow K_i \rightarrow R_i$ for $i \in \{1, 2\}$ can be viewed as a higher-order transformation rule $\hat{L} \leftarrow \hat{K} \rightarrow \hat{R}$ visualized as

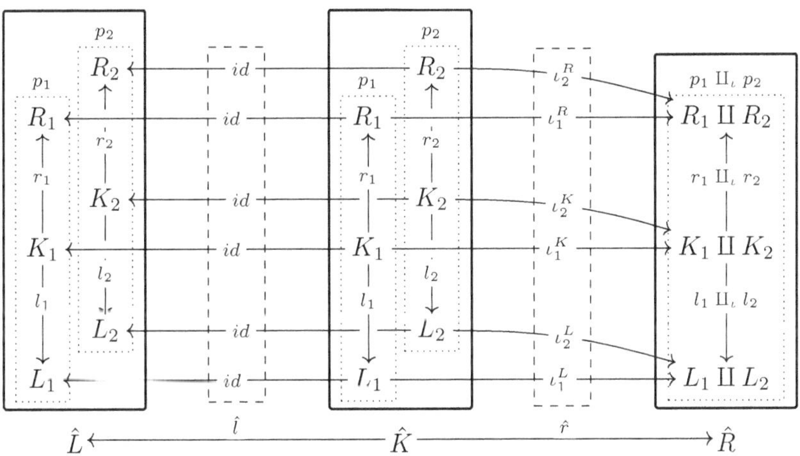

where $\hat{K} = \hat{L} := (\amalg_{i=1}^{2} (\bullet \leftarrow \bullet \rightarrow \bullet)_i, (\bullet \leftarrow \bullet \rightarrow \bullet)_i \mapsto p_i)$ and $\hat{R} = ((\bullet \leftarrow \bullet \rightarrow \bullet), (\bullet \leftarrow \bullet \rightarrow \bullet) \mapsto p_1 \amalg_\iota p_2)$.
We can choose to either directly use this rule for specific L_i, K_i and R_i or leave them as variables where the constituting maps of $\hat{r}$ and $\hat{l}$, the spans p_1 and p_2 in $\hat{K}$ and $p_1 \amalg_\iota p_2$ in $\hat{R}$ are generated as terms algebraically depending on the instantiation of p_i in $\hat{L}$ upon finding a *pre-morphism* $m \colon \hat{L} \rightarrow G$ into our context G. In this case a suitable activation condition should be used to prevent consolidation of all available rules as $\hat{R}$ and any other span are again candidates for a new *pre-morphism*.

Example 2. Parallelization with dedoubling of two rules p_1 and p_2 with respect to a common subrule p_0 has been studied in [17]. Let $p'_i \colon L'_i \leftarrow K'_i \rightarrow R'_i$ together with $p_0\colon L_0 \leftarrow K_0 \to R_0$ be a covering of $p_i\colon L_i \leftarrow K_i \to R_i$ via

$$L'_i \amalg L_0 \xleftarrow{\ l'_i \amalg_\iota l_0\ } K'_i \amalg K_0 \xrightarrow{\ r'_i \amalg_\iota r_0\ } R'_i \amalg R_0$$

with vertical maps $\lambda'_i \amalg \lambda^0_i$, $\kappa'_i \amalg \kappa^0_i$, $\rho'_i \amalg \rho^0_i$ (for $i \in \{1, 2\}$)

$$L_i \xleftarrow{\ l_i\ } K_i \xrightarrow{\ r_i\ } R_i$$

where the vertical arrows are epimorphisms and the squares pushouts. Then similar to the case of simple rule parallelization we can construct a concrete higher order rule $\hat{L} \leftarrow \hat{K} \to \hat{R}$ as depicted below.

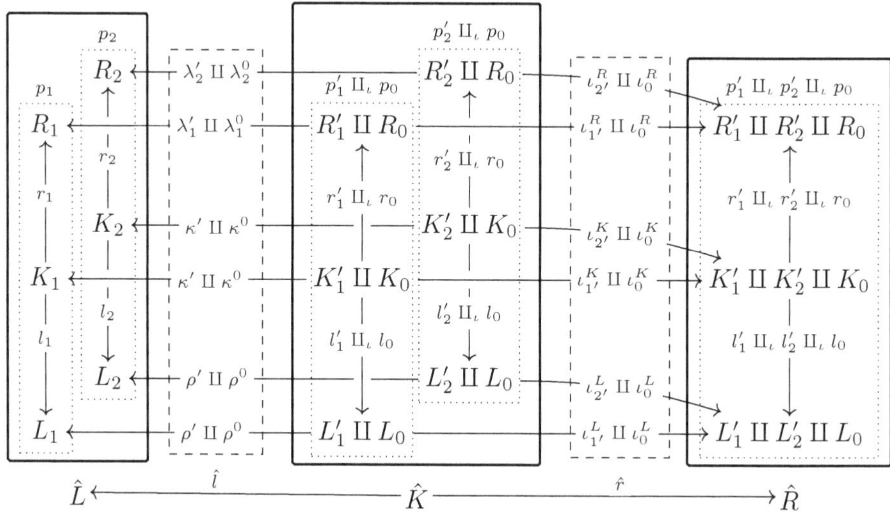

Unlike the example of parallelization, the rule for parallelization with dedoubling interpreted as a rule with variables is not *closed* (see [7]) i.e. rules p_0, p'_1 and p'_2 appear in $\hat{R}$ but not $\hat{L}$ and are not canonically determined from the rules p_1 and p_2. As such finding a pre-morphism is not sufficient to guarantee that rule application with some substitution is possible.

6   Conclusion and Future Work

With this paper we have provided a first step into the exploration of higher-order graph transformations as part of a rewriting system. Providing a clear view of how to construct them but also a proof to incorporate them into existing theory. Putting two or more spans into relation as is done in the examples in Sect. 5 was not possible with $T - Span$ rewriting. Furthermore, the changing of rules using these constructions was always positioned outside the formalism of graph transformations while we can include it as part of the rewriting system.

The main point of interest for further study is now to what degree the restrictions on $\mathcal{D}_{sp}$ in Definition 2 can be relaxed while still yielding an *adhesive* category and what tools can be used to help prove this. We hope to be able to at least include structures as shown in the examples below in a larger category $\mathcal{D}'$ on which to base the iterated construction and believe this should be possible using an argument similar to the one used in the proof of Theorem 10.

- Allowing more complex shapes brings with it the issue of assigning semantics to these structures. We can treat more complex structures as simply a form of hierarchical graph. In this case all structures except for spans would represent a form of data and only spans would be considered *executable*. This would open the possibility of activating and deactivating rules by attaching (respectively removing) extra structure to a span. Additionally, we could assign semantics to some (or all) of these other structures like some well established existing mechanisms; e.g.

  - positive or negative activation rules: $\quad P_1 \longleftarrow L \longleftarrow K \longrightarrow R$, $P_2 \longleftarrow$

  - probabilistic graph transformation rules: $\quad L \longleftarrow K \xrightarrow{p} R_1 \text{, } \xrightarrow{1-p} R_2$

  - sequencing of a set of graph transformation rules.

  The advantage of this kind of interpretation is that these mechanisms thereby become first-class members of our formalism and can therefore also be rewritten. So e.g. activation conditions could be added or removed, rewriting could be limited to rules with matching activation condition or additional variants for probabilistic rules could be added or removed.

  Note that allowing different functors between diagrams also inevitably requires allowing more complex diagrams, so that the construction remains closed under pullbacks and pushouts.

- Generating a rule via higher order rules can be used to perform complex transformations in one step while maintaining certain properties/correctness of the graph. This could be of help in attempts to use graph transformation techniques in model transformation like [18] where it is desirable for possibly making formal proofs of correctness easier. We believe this avenue of research to be future source for compelling examples for the usefulness of higher-order graph transformation.

- Because of the way we restricted the functors between diagrams in Definition 2, we think that a deeper investigation of typed attributed graphs could be a useful tool for classifying and analysing possible more complex choices for diagrams and functors as discussed above as well as maybe exploring behaviour of the resulting system like termination and confluence.

- It is well-known that Petri nets are not an adhesive category. However, as Petri nets are a well established fundamental model of concurrency and as a specification technique for distributed systems, it would be interesting to relate the approach of algebraic high-level net transformation systems to higher-order graph transformation.

Acknowledgements. We are grateful to the anonymous reviewers for their valuable comments that led to various improvements.

Disclosure of Interests. The authors have no competing interests to declare that are relevant to the content of this article.

Appendix

Proof (of Theorem 6). Since the ι_i^A are jointly epimorphic with

$$(p_1 \amalg_\iota p_2) \circ (f_1 \amalg_\iota f_2)\iota_1^A = \iota_i^D \circ p_i \circ f_i$$
$$= \iota_i^D \circ q_i \circ g_i$$
$$= (q_1 \amalg_\iota q_2) \circ (g_1 \amalg_\iota g_2)\iota_i^A$$

we indeed get a commutative square.

Now let $H \in ob(\mathcal{C})$, $f' \colon H \to B_1 \amalg B_2$ and $g' \colon H \to C_1 \amalg C_2$ such that $(p_1 \amalg_\iota p_2) \circ f' = (q_1 \amalg_\iota q_2) \circ g'$. As $\mathcal{C}$ is extensive we can construct two pullbacks as in the right diagram of (21) and H can actually be written as a coproduct $H = H_1 \amalg H_2$ and $f' = f_1' \amalg_\iota f_2'$.

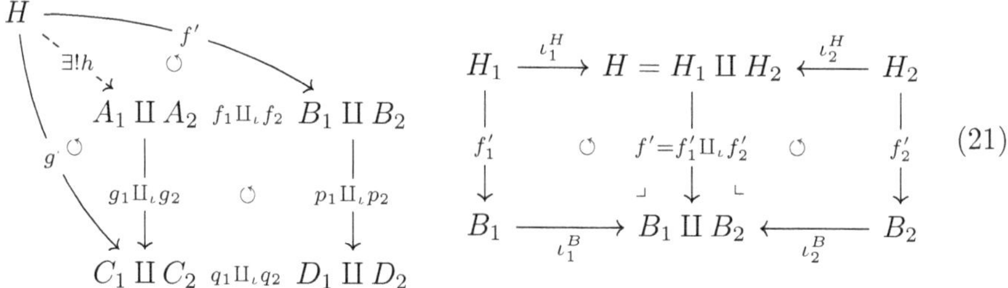

(21)

Now we get

$$\iota_i^D \circ (p_i \circ f_i') = (p_1 \amalg_\iota p_2) \circ (f_1' \amalg_\iota f_2') \circ \iota_i^H$$
$$= (q_1 \amalg_\iota q_2) \circ (g' \circ \iota_i^H)$$

for $i \in \{1,2\}$ and therefore as the rightmost square (and all others) of diagram (22) is a pullback we get unique maps $g_i' \colon H_i \to C_i$ such that $q_i \circ g_i' = p_i \circ f_i'$ and $\iota_i^C \circ g_i' = g' \circ \iota_i^H$. Because $\mathcal{C}$ is extensive the outer *square* of (22) must be a pullback and $g' = g_1' \amalg_\iota g_2'$.

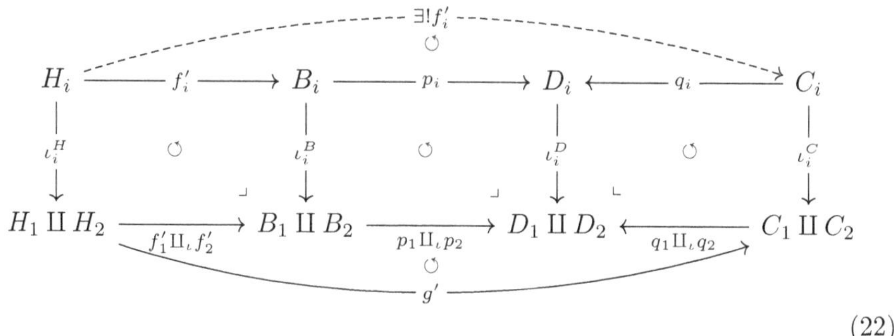

(22)

Then as the right diagrams of (16) were assumed to be pullbacks we get unique morphisms $h_i\colon H_i \to A_i$ such that $f_i' = f_i \circ h_i$ and $g_i' = g_i \circ h_i$. Thus, we get a unique $h = h_1 \amalg_\iota h_2\colon H_1 \amalg H_2 \to A_1 \amalg A_2$ with

$$
\begin{aligned}
(f_1 \amalg_\iota f_2) \circ (h_1 \amalg_\iota h_2) \circ \iota_i^H &= (f_1 \amalg_\iota f_2) \circ \iota_i^A \circ h_i \\
&= \iota_i^B \circ f_i \circ h_i \\
&= \iota_i^B \circ f_i' \\
&= (f_1' \amalg_\iota f_2') \circ \iota_i^H
\end{aligned}
$$

and therefore as the ι_i^H are jointly epimorphic we get $(f_1 \amalg_\iota f_2) \circ (h_1 \amalg_\iota h_2) = (f_1' \amalg_\iota f_2') = f'$. Analogously we get $(g_1 \amalg_\iota g_2) \circ (h_1 \amalg_\iota h_2) = (g_1' \amalg_\iota g_2') = g'$.

If we had any other $\hat{h}\colon H_1 \amalg H_2 \to A_1 \amalg A_2$ with $(f_1 \amalg_\iota f_2) \circ \hat{h} = f'$ and $(g_1 \amalg_\iota g_2) \circ \hat{h} = g'$ then $\iota_i^B \circ f_i' = f' \circ \iota_i^H = (f_1 \amalg_\iota f_2) \circ \hat{h} \circ \iota_i^H$. The right square in the diagram

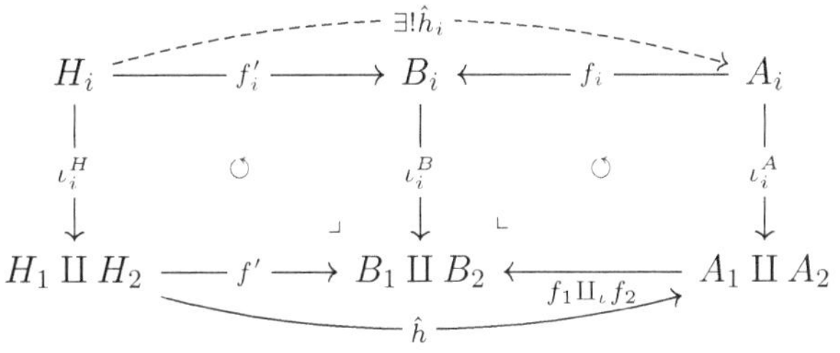

$$
\begin{array}{ccccc}
H_i & \xrightarrow{\ \ f_i'\ \ } & B_i & \xleftarrow{\ \ f_i\ \ } & A_i \\
\downarrow{\scriptstyle \iota_i^H} & \circlearrowright & \downarrow{\scriptstyle \iota_i^B} & \circlearrowright & \downarrow{\scriptstyle \iota_i^A} \\
H_1 \amalg H_2 & \xrightarrow{\ f'\ } & B_1 \amalg B_2 & \xleftarrow[f_1 \amalg_\iota f_2]{} & A_1 \amalg A_2
\end{array}
\qquad (23)
$$

with dashed arrow $\exists!\,\hat{h}_i$ above and $\hat{h}$ below.

is a pullback because of the extensiveness of $\mathcal{C}$ so we get unique $\hat{h}_i$ such that $f_i \circ \hat{h}_i = f_i'$ (and $\hat{h} \circ \iota_i^H = \iota_i^A \circ \hat{h}_i$) and consequently again by $\mathcal{C}$ being extensive $\hat{h} = \hat{h}_1 \amalg_\iota \hat{h}_2$. But the h_i already fulfil this property, so $h_i = \hat{h}_i$ and therefore $\hat{h} = \hat{h}_1 \amalg_\iota \hat{h}_2 = h_1 \amalg_\iota h_2 = h$. We can conclude that h is unique and therefore $B_1 \amalg B_2 \xleftarrow{f_1 \amalg_\iota f_2} A_1 \amalg A_2 \xrightarrow{g_1 \amalg_\iota g_2} C_1 \amalg C_2$ makes the diagram on the left of (16) a pullback a claimed $\qquad\square$

Proof (of Theorem 7). Since the ι_i^A are jointly epimorphic with

$$
\begin{aligned}
(p_1 \amalg_\iota p_2) \circ (f_1 \amalg_\iota f_2) \circ \iota_i^A &= \iota_i^D \circ p_i \circ f_i \\
&= \iota_i^D \circ q_i \circ g_i \\
&= (q_1 \amalg_\iota q_2) \circ (g_1 \amalg_\iota g_2) \circ \iota_i^A
\end{aligned}
$$

we indeed get a commutative square.

Now let $E \in ob(\mathcal{C})$, $p'\colon A_1 \amalg A_2 \to E$ and $q'\colon B_1 \amalg B_2 \to E$ such that $p' \circ (f_1 \amalg_\iota f_2) = q' \circ (g_1 \amalg_\iota g_2)$. Then

$$
\begin{aligned}
p' \circ \iota_i^B \circ f_i &= p' \circ (f_1 \amalg_\iota f_2) \circ \iota_i^A \\
&= q' \circ (g_1 \amalg_\iota g_2) \circ \iota_i^A \\
&= q' \circ \iota_i^C \circ g_i
\end{aligned}
$$

and therefore as the right diagram in (17) is a pushout we get a unique $k_i \colon D_i \to E$ such that $k_i \circ p_i = p' \circ \iota_i^B$ and $k_i \circ q_i = q' \circ \iota_i^C$.

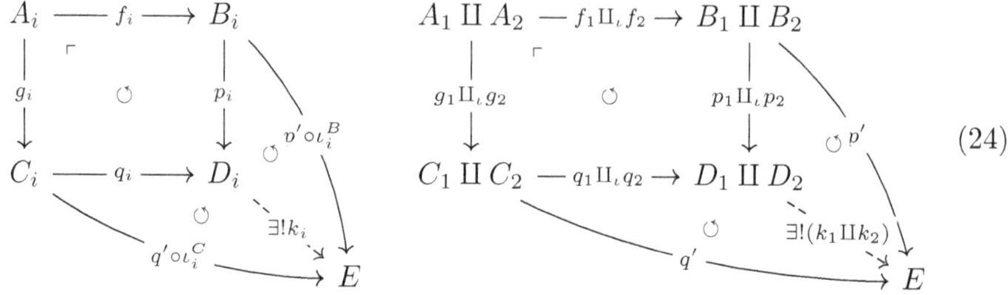

$$(24)$$

Then $k_1 \amalg k_2 \colon D_1 \amalg D_2 \to E$ with $(k_1 \amalg_\iota k_2) \circ (p_1 \amalg_\iota p_2) = p'$ as

$$(k_1 \amalg k_2) \circ (p_1 \amalg_\iota p_2) \circ \iota_i^B = (k_1 \amalg k_2) \circ \iota_i^D \circ p_i$$
$$= k_i \circ p_i$$
$$= p' \circ \iota_i^B$$

and the ι_i^B are jointly epimorphic. Similarly, we get $(k_1 \amalg k_2) \circ (q_1 \amalg_\iota q_2) = q'$. But this choice is unique as for any other $\hat{k} \colon D_1 \amalg D_2 \to E$ with $\hat{k} \circ (p_1 \amalg_\iota p_2) = p'$ and $\hat{k} \circ (q_1 \amalg_\iota q_2) = q'$ we get that $(\hat{k} \circ \iota_i^D) \circ p_i = \hat{k} \circ (p_1 \amalg_\iota p_2) \circ \iota_i^B = p' \circ \iota_i^B$ and $(\hat{k} \circ \iota_i^D) \circ q_i = \hat{k} \circ (q_1 \amalg_\iota q_2) \circ \iota_i^C = q' \circ \iota_i^C$. But the k_i fit uniquely into these equations by construction as a pushout, so $\hat{k} \circ \iota_i^D = k_i$ and therefore by the universal property of the coproduct $\hat{k} = k_1 \amalg k_2$. Thus, the square in the right diagram of (24) is a pushout as claimed. $\qquad\square$

References

1. Ehrig, H., Pfender, M., Schneider, H.J.: Graph-grammars: an algebraic approach. In: 14th Annual Symposium on Switching and Automata Theory, Iowa City, Iowa, USA, October 15-17, 1973, Proceedings. IEEE Computer Society, pp. 167–180 (1973). https://doi.org/10.1109/SWAT.1973.11
2. Ehrig, H., et al.: Fundamentals of Algebraic Graph Transformation. Monographs in Theoretical Computer Science. An EATCS Series. Springer (2006)
3. Ehrig, H., et al.: Graph and Model Transformation - General Framework and Applications. Monographs in Theoretical Computer Science. An EATCS Series. Springer (2015). https://doi.org/10.1007/978-3-662-47980-3
4. Ehrig, H., Kreowski, H.-J.: Parallelism of manipulations in multidimensional information structures. In: Proc. Mathematical Foundations of Computer Science. LNCS, vol. 45, pp. 284–293 (1976). https://doi.org/10.1007/3-540-07854-1_188
5. Kreowski, H.-J.: Manipulationen von Graphmanipulationen. Ph.D. thesis. Technische Universität Berlin (1978)
6. Ehrig, H., Padberg, J., Ribeiro, L.: Algebraic high-level nets: petri nets revisited. In: Recent Trends in Data Type Specification, 9th Workshop on Specification of Abstract Data Types Joint with the 4th COMPASS Workshop, Caldes de Malavella, Spain, October 26-30, 1992, Selected Papers. Ed. by Hartmut Ehrig. LNCS, pp. 188–206. Springer (1992). https://doi.org/10.1007/3-540-57867-6_11

7. Hoffmann, B.: Graph transformation with variables. In: Kreowski, H.-J., et al. (eds.) Formal Methods in Software and Systems Modeling: Essays Dedicated to Hartmut Ehrig on the Occasion of His 60th Birthday, pp. 101–115. Springer, Heidelberg (2005). ISBN: 978-3-540-31847-7. https://doi.org/10.1007/978-3-540-31847-7_6

8. Drewes, F., Hoffmann, B., Plump, D.: Hierarchical graph transformation. J. Comput. Syst. Sci. **64**(2), 249–283 (2002). ISSN: 0022-0000. https://doi.org/10.1006/jcss.2001.1790

9. Göttler, H.: Deriving productions from productions with an application to picasso's Œuvre. In: Handbook of Graph Grammars and Computing by Graph Transformation, pp. 459–484 (1999). https://doi.org/10.1142/9789812815149_0012

10. Parisi-Presicce, F.: On Modifying High Level Replacement Systems". Partially supported by the European Community under TMR GETGRATS and Esprit WG APPLIGRAPH. In: Electronic Notes in Theoretical Computer Science 44.4 (2001). UNIGRA 2001, Uniform Approaches to Graphical Process Specification Techniques (a Satellite Event of ETAPS 2001), pp. 16–27. ISSN: 1571-0661. https://doi.org/10.1016/S1571-0661(04)80940-X. https://www.sciencedirect.com/science/article/pii/S157106610480940X

11. Machado, R.: Higher-order graph rewriting systems. Ph.D. thesis. Universidade Federal do Rio Grande do Sul – Instituto de Informática (2012)

12. Machado, R., Ribeiro, L., Heckel, R.: Rule-based transformation of graph rewriting rules: towards higher-order graph grammars. Theor. Comput. Sci. **594**, 1–23 (2015). https://doi.org/10.1016/J.TCS.2015.01.034

13. Corradini, A., et al.: The category of typed graph grammars and its adjunction with categories of derivations. In: Cuny, J., et al. (eds.) Proceedings Fifth Intl. Workshop on Graph Grammars and Their Application to Comp. Sci. LNCS, vol. 1073, pp. 56–74. Springer (1996)

14. Schürr, A.: Specification of graph translators with triple graph grammars. In: Mayr, E.W., Schmidt, G., Tinhofer, G. (eds.) Graph-Theoretic Concepts in Computer Science, 20th International Workshop, WG '94, Herrsching, Germany, June 16-18, 1994, Proceedings. LNCS, vol. 903, pp. 151–163. Springer (1994). https://doi.org/10.1007/3-540-59071-4_45

15. Eilenberg, S., MacLane, S.: General theory of natural equivalences. Trans. Am. Math. Soc. **58**, 231–294 (1945). ISSN: 1088-6850. https://doi.org/10.1090/s0002-9947-1945-0013131-6. http://dx.doi.org/10.1090/S0002-9947-1945-0013131-6

16. Peschke, G., Tholen, W.: Diagrams, Fibrations, and the Decomposition of Colimits (2020). eprint: arXiv:2006.10890

17. Kreowski, H.-J., Lye, A.: Parallel rule application with doubling avoidance. In: Endrullis, J., Tichy, M. (eds.) Graph Transformation - 18th International Conference, ICGT 2025, Held as Part of STAF 2025, Koblenz, Germany, June 11-12, 2025, Proceedings, vol. 15720, pp. 44–62. LNCS. Springer (2025). https://doi.org/10.1007/978-3-031-94706-3_3

18. Friederichs, L., Lye, A.: Graph-transformational threat modeling. In: Endrullis, J., Tichy, M. (eds.) Graph Transformation - 18th International Conference, ICGT 2025, Held as Part of STAF 2025, Koblenz, Germany, June 11-12, 2025, Proceedings, vol. 15720, pp. 205–217. Springer (2025). https://doi.org/10.1007/978-3-031-94706-3_10

Parallel Transformations as Colimits

Thierry Boy de la Tour[✉]

CNRS and University Grenoble Alpes, LIG Lab., Grenoble, France
`thierry.boy-de-la-tour@imag.fr`

Abstract. Parallel transformations are easier to conceive as colimits in
a category of non rule-based transformations of the objects of a category
$\mathcal{C}$, thus eliminating the necessity of constructing a parallel rule. A category
of *replacements* in $\mathcal{C}$ is defined, and examples illustrate what can be
achieved by taking coproducts and other colimits in this category, and
different reasons why diagrams may not have colimits. A general result
is proved that characterizes the existence of colimits of replacements and
yields an algorithm to compute them, with minimal assumption on $\mathcal{C}$.

1 Introduction

One important issue in Graph Transformation is to identify the condition (called
independence) where two consecutive transformations can be performed simultaneously, by a unique *parallel* transformation that yields the same output from the
same input as the sequence. Since transformations are rule-based this requires
to find a suitable rule that generates the required parallel transformation on a
suitable matching.

But why should a parallel transformation be rule-based? It seems strange
that a new rule is required while we already have rules (and matchings) that
validate the given transformations. Furthermore, this new rule in itself does not
make the new transformation parallel. Even the fact that it yields the correct
output is not sufficient, since this may be true of many different transformations;
which is the parallel one?

The case is even worse when two transformations of a same graph overlap so
as not to be independent, since then there is no common result to be reached.
Amalgamation [21] offers a way of producing a rule and a matching for an overlap
transformation in the Double-Pushout (DPO) method, but it may not be a
correct DPO-transformation of the initial rules, hence it is not clear in what
sense it is admissible.

Hence it seems that producing a parallel or amalgamated rule, or any rule
at all, is not the safe way to perform parallelization correctly. Yet this seems
indispensable since rule-based graph transformations can only be considered
correct with respect to rules or rule systems.

The author has no competing interests to declare that are relevant to the content of
this article.

It therefore seems necessary to conceive transformations *per se*, without reference to rules, which leaves us with the problem of defining a correctness criterion. Assuming that a parallel transformation needs only be correct with respect to the parallelized transformations, we should be able to dispense completely with rules. What we need is to define the meaning of a transformation, independently of any rule, and how it may be preserved from transformation to transformation.

The core idea of the present paper is to understand the meaning of transformations as being defined by morphisms; the meaning (or structure) being what is preserved by (homo-) morphisms. Thus, in a category of transformations, the parallelization of t_1 and t_2 consists in finding a transformation t that preserves the structures of both t_1 and t_2, hence a cospan $t_1 \to t \leftarrow t_2$. And in order to get the minimal structure required by t_1 and t_2, and nothing more, then this cospan should be a coproduct of t_1 and t_2 (i.e., should be initial for such cospans). Besides, we may extend this notion to pushouts and other colimits, which should allow to share some common transformation whose structure may be present in both t_1 and t_2. This yields a simple and natural definition of (synchronous) parallelism.

A parallel transformation is a colimit of a diagram of transformations.

But this approach requires a category of transformations and much depends on its definition. In Sect. 2 a fairly general notion of transformations called *replacements* is proposed, their structure is explained and defined through morphisms called *subsumptions*. Section 3 illustrates the existence and scope of colimits of replacements through examples. Section 4 is devoted to computing colimits of particular diagrams of replacements, and Sect. 5 extends this result to general diagrams and provides a characterization for the existence of colimits. Related and future work are discussed in Sect. 6.

2   Replacements and Subsumptions

In order to parallelize transformations it is convenient to think of them as being composed of atomic actions that can be freely gathered. Most graph transformation approaches can be understood as replacements of a subgraph (determined by a matching of the left hand side of a rule) by another subgraph (the right hand side of the rule), similar to substitutions in terms. Thus atomic actions may simply be deletions and additions of individual items (vertices or edges, possibly labels...).

But there are different ways of deleting a subgraph, and more generally there is no standard tool in category theory that performs such an operation. However, there is generally an intermediate graph that is the result of this operation, together with a morphism towards the input (identifying the items of the input graph that are *not* removed). Addition of the right hand side to this intermediate graph is usually understood as a pushout. This is the convenient operation that allows to link the added subgraph to the intermediate graph and hence to the preserved items of the input graph.

If we abstract away the notions of rules and matchings, that are not identical in all approaches, we obtain a fairly general notion of replacement.

Definition 1. (replacements ϱ). *A replacement in $\mathcal{C}$ is a diagram[1] ϱ in $\mathcal{C}$ of the form*

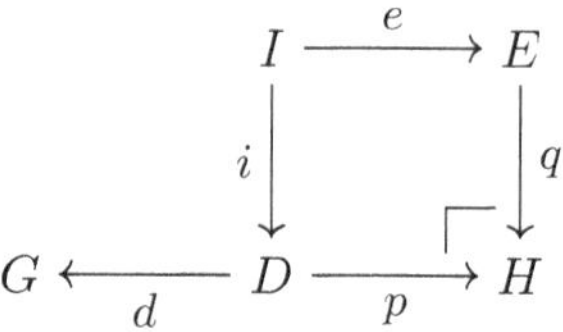

where the square is a pushout. G is the input, *D the* context, *I the* interface, *E the* extension *and H the* result *or* output *of the replacement. These $\mathcal{C}$-objects (and the $\mathcal{C}$-morphisms d, i...) depend on ϱ and are usually referred to as ϱG, ϱd... A replacement ϱ is* linear *if d is monic.*

In general we may refer to a replacement simply as a diagram

$$G \xleftarrow{d} D \xleftarrow{i} I \xrightarrow{e} E$$

leaving the result H implicit (but this is only possible if $D \xleftarrow{i} I \xrightarrow{e} E$ has a pushout).

Replacements also allow for duplications of parts of G, in which case the replacement is non-linear. An item x of a graph G can be duplicated as $x_1, \ldots, x_n$ in D, which is indicated by $d(x_1) = \cdots = d(x_n) = x$. Besides, the pushout with the extension allows for mergings of items of G, when e is not monic.

In order to define replacements as mathematical structures, we need a notion of morphism between them. We may understand this structure as a set of atomic actions, either deleting or adding items. In other words, we say that the structure (the atomic actions) of a replacement ϱ is preserved in ϱ' if *everything that is removed in ϱ is also removed in ϱ', and everything that is added in ϱ is also added in ϱ'.*

This is relevant in categories of graphs, but in a general category $\mathcal{C}$ there is no such thing as "items". The added items could be identified with the morphism e, and the fact that what is added by e is also added by e' ($= \varrho'e$) can be understood as a $\mathcal{C}^{\rightarrow}$-morphism from e to e'. But there is nothing in ϱ that can be identified with the removed items.

However, we can understand the condition *everything that is removed in ϱ is also removed in ϱ'* as meaning that *everything that is preserved in ϱ' is preserved in ϱ*, and hence as a $\mathcal{C}^{\rightarrow}$-morphism from d' to d. The problem is that if an item removed from G has no preimage in G', then it obviously cannot be removed from G'. For this reason we choose to ensure that $G = G'$, which suits our need of parallelizing transformations of the same object.

---

1 All finite diagrams in $\mathcal{C}$, i.e., functors from a finite category to $\mathcal{C}$, will be denoted by lowercase greek letters.

Definition 2. (subsumptions u, categories $\mathrm{Rpl}(\mathcal{C})$, functors Itf, Ext).
Given two replacements ϱ and ϱ' in $\mathcal{C}$, ϱ' is said to subsume ϱ if there exists a subsumption morphism $u : \varrho \to \varrho'$, that is a triple (u_1, u_2, u_3) of $\mathcal{C}$-morphisms such that

$$
\begin{array}{ccccccc}
G & \xleftarrow{\ d\ } & D & \xleftarrow{\ i\ } & I & \xrightarrow{\ e\ } & E \\
\Big\downarrow{\scriptstyle 1} & & \Big\uparrow{\scriptstyle u_1} & & \Big\downarrow{\scriptstyle u_2} & & \Big\downarrow{\scriptstyle u_3} \\
G' & \xleftarrow{\ d'\ } & D' & \xleftarrow{\ i'\ } & I' & \xrightarrow{\ e'\ } & E'
\end{array}
$$

commutes, where G denotes ϱG, G' denotes $\varrho' G$, etc. Let $u' : \varrho' \to \varrho''$ be a subsumption morphism composable with u, then it is obvious that their composite $u' \circ u := (u_1 \circ u'_1, u'_2 \circ u_2, u'_3 \circ u_3)$ is again a subsumption morphism, that this composition law is associative and that $1_\varrho := (1_D, 1_I, 1_E)$ is an identity subsumption morphism. The category of replacements in $\mathcal{C}$ and subsumption morphisms is denoted $\mathrm{Rpl}(\mathcal{C})$, and its full subcategory of linear replacements is denoted $\mathrm{Rpl}^*(\mathcal{C})$. For any $\mathcal{C}$-object G we write $\mathrm{Rpl}(G)$ (resp. $\mathrm{Rpl}^*(G)$) the full subcategory of (resp. linear) replacements with input G.

Let $\mathsf{Itf} : \mathrm{Rpl}(\mathcal{C}) \to \mathcal{C}$, $\mathsf{Ext} : \mathrm{Rpl}(\mathcal{C}) \to \mathcal{C}$ be the functors with $\mathsf{Itf}\varrho := \varrho I$, $\mathsf{Itf}u := u_2$, $\mathsf{Ext}\varrho := \varrho E$ and $\mathsf{Ext}u := u_3$.

In Definition 2, the commutation of the middle square means that the items added by ϱ are glued to the same items of G as the corresponding items added by ϱ'. This definition also has implications on the way items may be duplicated or merged, hence there is more to the structure of replacements than in the informal discussion above. It is also important to notice that subsumption do not induce any relationship between the results of the replacements.

3   Examples of Parallel Replacements

Suppose we have two replacements ϱ_1 and ϱ_2 with the same input G, we would like to define a replacement ϱ that embodies both replacements in one, that performs both replacements simultaneously. If the two replacements occur at disjoint places in G, this should certainly be possible: just remove everything that is removed either by ϱ_1 or ϱ_2, and then add everything that is added either by ϱ_1 or ϱ_2. We therefore require that ϱ subsumes both ϱ_1 and ϱ_2. And since we do not need anything else to be removed or added than what is removed or added in ϱ_1 or ϱ_2, the replacement ϱ should be subsumed by all replacements that subsume both ϱ_1 and ϱ_2. In other words, ϱ is the coproduct of ϱ_1 and ϱ_2.

If the replacements are not disjoint (whatever this may mean in absence of matchings), what could prevent these removals and additions? A simple example illustrates an important feature of replacements.

Example 1. In the category **Set**, for any x we consider the replacement ϱ_1 corresponding to the diagram

$$\{x\} \leftarrow \varnothing \leftarrow \varnothing \rightarrow \varnothing$$

(with result $\varnothing$) and the replacement ϱ_2 corresponding to

$$\{x\} \leftarrow \{x\} \leftarrow \{x\} \rightarrow \{x\}$$

(with result $\{x\}$). Assume there is a coproduct ϱ with diagram

$$\{x\} \leftarrow D \leftarrow I \rightarrow E$$

and subsumptions $u : \varrho_1 \rightarrow \varrho$ and $v : \varrho_2 \rightarrow \varrho$, then $u_1 : D \rightarrow \varnothing$ entails $D = \varnothing$ and thus $I = \varnothing$. But then $v_2 : \{x\} \rightarrow I$ is impossible.

The problem here is that we cannot simultaneously remove x, as required by ϱ_1, and use it as an interface as required by ϱ_2. The items of a context can be removed by another transformation only if they have no preimage in the interface, otherwise they are indispensable to preserve the added items and hence cannot be removed. This is a situation of conflict that is easily understood in terms of "items", but a general definition has to dispense with this notion (see Definition 7 in Sect. 5).

The next example shows that this still allows some amount of overlap.

Example 2. In Conway's Game of Life [14] there is an infinite 2-dimensional grid of cells each associated with a state, either dead or alive (pictured as □ and ■ respectively). In order to replace states by other states, we need to remove or add states and thus to have empty cells. This is easily represented by an "empty" state (pictured as □) that we define as being smaller than the other two. The category $\mathcal{C}$ of configurations is the set of functions from the grid to the set of states, ordered by the common extension of the order on states.

For the sake of simplicity we only consider a 3×3-grid and the transformations of the configuration ▦ according to the rules of the game. The top and bottom live cells die by isolation since they have only one neighbour, which yields the following two replacements (we omit the obvious results).

$$\varrho_1 = \boxed{} \leftarrow \boxed{} \leftarrow \boxed{} \rightarrow \boxed{} \qquad \varrho_2 = \boxed{} \leftarrow \boxed{} \leftarrow \boxed{} \rightarrow \boxed{}$$

The two middle left and right cells come to life by the birth rule since they have three neighbours.

$$\varrho_3 = \boxed{} \leftarrow \boxed{} \leftarrow \boxed{} \rightarrow \boxed{} \qquad \varrho_4 = \boxed{} \leftarrow \boxed{} \leftarrow \boxed{} \rightarrow \boxed{}$$

In these replacements the interface is the empty configuration (initial object of $\mathcal{C}$) since from one generation to the next no cell is protected from change. This means that there are no conflicts between these replacements. In terms of atomic actions they consist in "removing" one cell (change its state to □) and "adding" one cell (change □ to □ or ■). Note that such replacements, corresponding to the local applications of the cellular automata's rules, can easily be produced algorithmically but not by means of rules in an algebraic approach (in which case a different category must be used).

The reader can easily check that the replacement

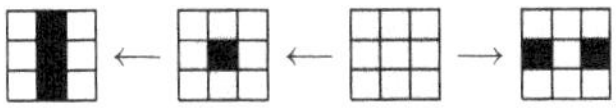

subsumes $\varrho_1, \ldots, \varrho_4$ and that its result is 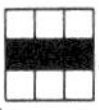. It is well known that this result cannot be obtained by sequential applications of the rules, in any order.

Conflicts are not the only obstacle to the existence of coproducts, an obvious problem arises depending on the properties of $\mathcal{C}$.

Example 3. With the category of Example 2, we consider two replacements (that have nothing to do with the Game of Life)

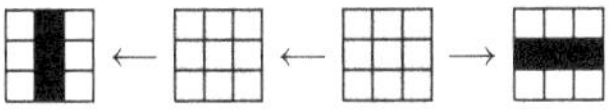 and 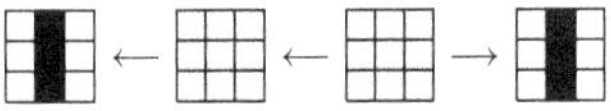

that clearly do not conflict. Yet they do not have a coproduct since their extensions 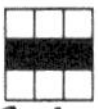 and 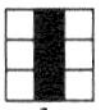 do not have a coproduct (or least upper bound) in $\mathcal{C}$. Note that $\mathcal{C}$ does not have pushouts either, and for example there is no replacement corresponding to the diagram

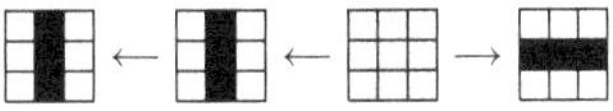

Hence the existence of colimits in Rpl(G) depend on their existence in $\mathcal{C}$ and also, as the reader has certainly guessed, on the existence of limits in $\mathcal{C}$.

A more subtle problem arises in case of ambiguity.

Example 4. In the category of directed graphs we consider the replacement ϱ_1 corresponding to the diagram

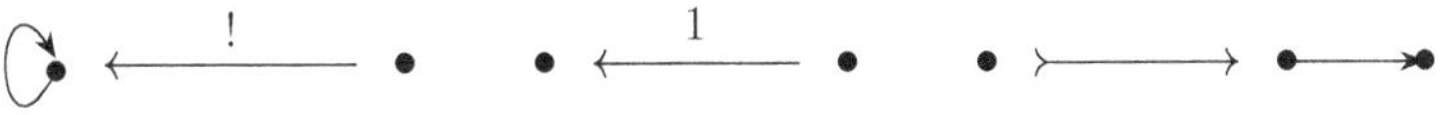

that deletes a loop, makes two copies of the vertex of the input, and adds an arrow beween them. We next consider the replacement ϱ_2

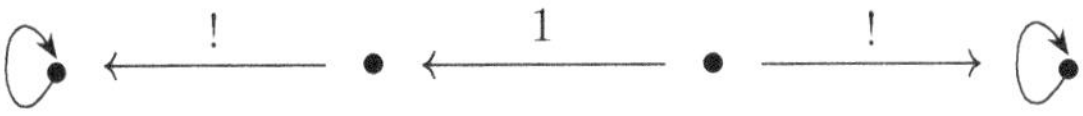

that deletes a loop and adds another one. There are two possible replacements that subsume both replacements:

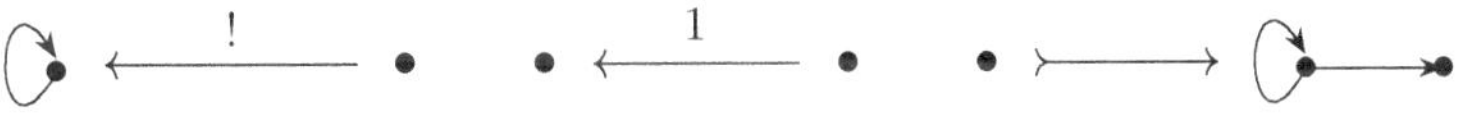

and

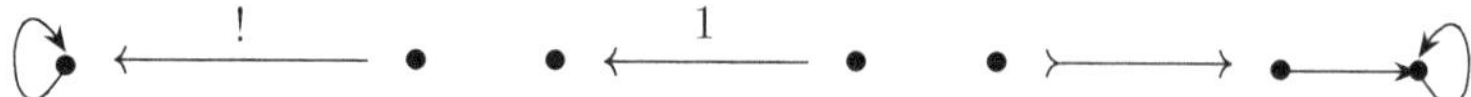

but none subsumes the other. They correspond to the two possible ways of applying the two replacements simultaneously.

The following example shows that parallelization can be enhanced by considering other colimits in $\mathrm{Rpl}(G)$ than just coproducts.

Example 5 (inspired by [13,20]). In the category of undirected graphs we consider replacements ϱ_1, ϱ_2 corresponding to the diagrams

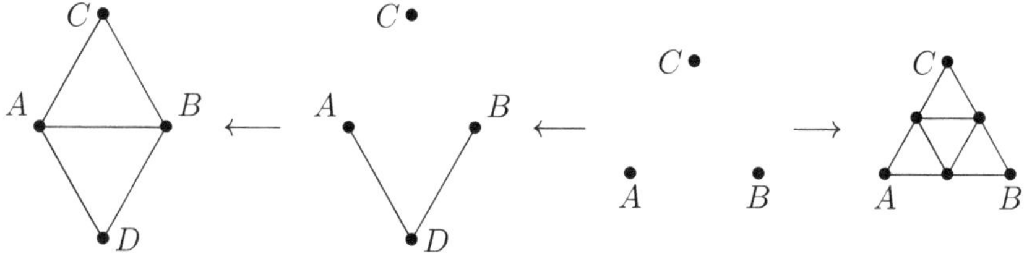

and

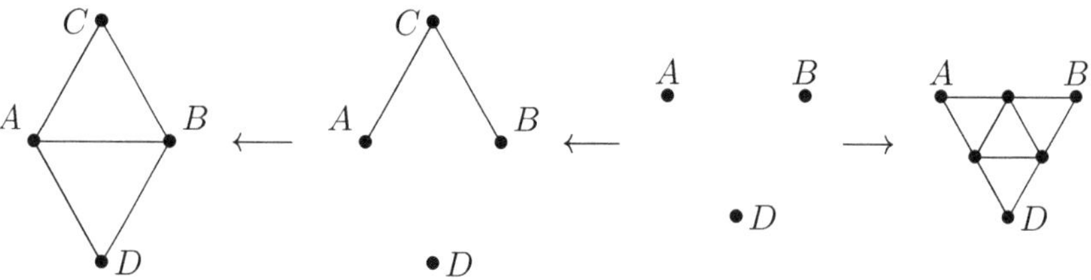

respectively, where the morphisms all preserve the named vertices. The coproduct γ of ϱ_1 and ϱ_2 is the replacement

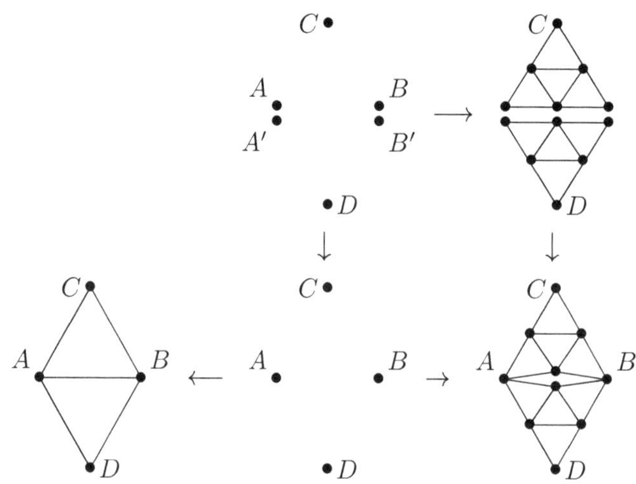

The reader can easily check that there are subsumptions $w_1 : \varrho_1 \to \gamma$ and $w_2 : \varrho_2 \to \gamma$. The atomic actions in γ are the disjoint union (coproduct in **Set**) of those in ϱ_1 and ϱ_2. But we may want to merge the two middle vertices between A and B into one, hence find a way to share the atomic actions consisting in adding one vertex and two edges common to ϱ_1 and ϱ_2. To do this, we need a replacement subsumed by both ϱ_1 and ϱ_2 and hence that corresponds to atomic actions that they have in common. This corresponds to the replacement ϱ with diagram

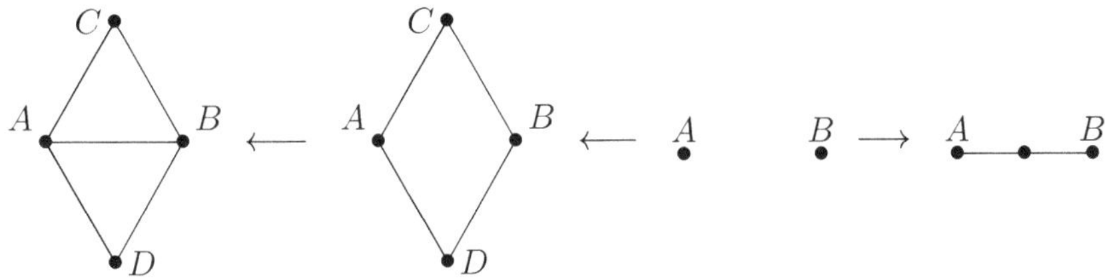

It is again easy to see that there are subsumptions $u_1 : \varrho \to \varrho_1$ and $u_2 : \varrho \to \varrho_2$. We can then merge the common parts of ϱ_1 and ϱ_2 in their parallel replacement by taking the pushout of $\varrho_1 \xleftarrow{u_1} \varrho \xrightarrow{u_2} \varrho_2$, that is the replacement π with diagram

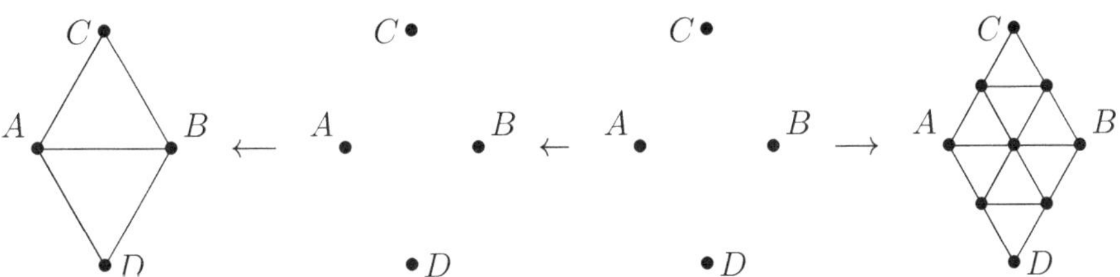

and the two obvious subsumptions $v_1 : \varrho_1 \to \pi$ and $v_2 : \varrho_2 \to \pi$ such that $v_1 \circ u_1 = v_2 \circ u_2$.

4 Diagrams with Fixed Contexts

We have seen in Example 2 that we cannot generally assume the category $\mathcal{C}$ to be cocomplete, hence colimits in $\mathrm{Rpl}(G)$ will explicitly depend on the existence of some colimits in $\mathcal{C}$. Another problem is that, in order to construct replacements, we need to find pushouts in $\mathcal{C}$ yet we cannot assume that $\mathcal{C}$ has pushouts. Instead we will rely on a weaker assumption.

Definition 3 (effective colimits). *For any small category $\mathcal{J}$, a category $\mathcal{C}$ has* effective $\mathcal{J}$-colimits *if for every diagram* $\mathsf{D} : \mathcal{J} \to \mathcal{C}$, *if there exists a natural sink[2] for* D *then* D *has a colimit. We write $j \in \mathcal{J}$ to indicate that j is a $\mathcal{J}$-object.*

---

[2] On natural sources and sinks, limits and colimits see [15, Sections 19, 20] or [1, Sections 10, 11].

From now on we assume that $\mathcal{C}$ *has effective $\mathcal{J}$-colimits for all $\mathcal{J}$* (hence in particular for pushouts), and $\mathcal{C}$ *has $\mathcal{J}$-limits for all non-empty $\mathcal{J}$*. It is easy to see that this is the case in Example 2, i.e. if there is an upper bound then there is a least upper bound, and there is always a greatest lower bound, except that there is no terminal object.

We first tackle the problem of colimits in a case where conflicts are obviously impossible, that is when all replacements remove exactly the same items, hence when they all have the same context. We assume a small category $\mathcal{J}$ and will consider the colimits of $\mathcal{J}$-indexed diagrams of replacements with input G.

Definition 4 (category $\mathrm{Rpl}(d)$). *For any $\mathcal{C}$-morphism $d : D \to G$, let $\mathrm{Rpl}(d)$ be the subcategory of $\mathrm{Rpl}(G)$ of replacements ϱ such that $\varrho d = d$ and subsumptions u such that $u_1 = 1_D$.*

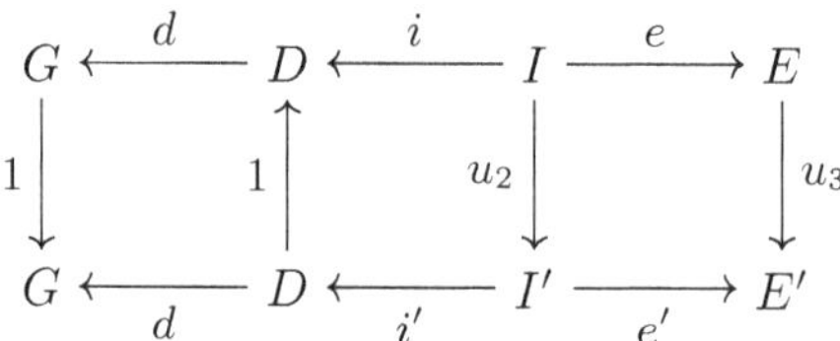

Lemma 1. *For every $\mathrm{Rpl}(d)$-morphism $u : \varrho \to \varrho'$ there exists a unique $\mathcal{C}$-morphism $h_u : \varrho H \to \varrho' H$ such that $h_u \circ \varrho p = \varrho' p$ and $h_u \circ \varrho q = \varrho' q \circ u_3$.*

Proof. Consider the diagram

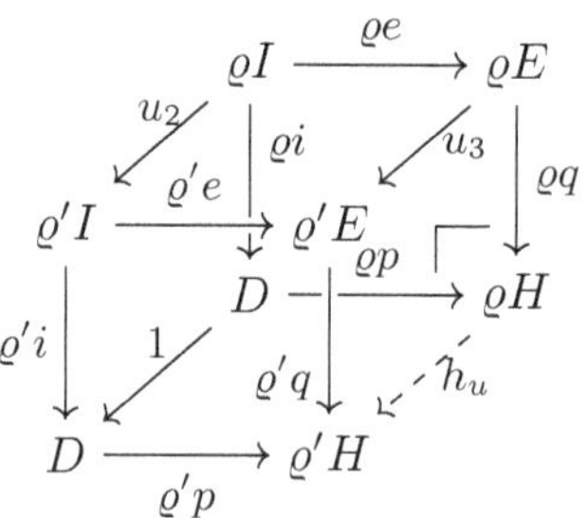

By the commutation of the top, left and front faces we get $\varrho' q \circ u_3 \circ \varrho e = \varrho' p \circ \varrho i$, and the conclusion follows since the back face is a pushout. $\qquad\square$

The correspondence from u to h_u preserves identities and products.

Corollary 1. $h_{1_\varrho} = 1_{\varrho H}$ *and* $h_{u' \circ u} = h_{u'} \circ h_u$ *for all* $u' : \varrho' \to \varrho''$.

Proof. $h_{1_\varrho} = 1_{\varrho H}$ is obvious by unicity, since $(1_\varrho)_3 = 1_{\varrho E}$. We have $h_{u'} \circ h_u \circ \varrho p = h_{u'} \circ \varrho' p = \varrho'' p$ and $h_{u'} \circ h_u \circ \varrho q = h_{u'} \circ \varrho' q \circ u_3 = \varrho'' q \circ (u' \circ u)_3$, hence by unicity $h_{u' \circ u} = h_{u'} \circ h_u$. $\qquad\square$

Hence there is a functor from $\mathrm{Rpl}(d)$ to $\mathcal{C}$ that yields the results of replacements. However, we will need not just the colimit of results but also a $\mathcal{C}$-morphism from D to this colimit. One possibility is to add the morphisms p to the diagram, hence an initial object to $\mathcal{J}$, but the easiest solution is to work in the coslice category $D\backslash\mathcal{C}$. This is possible since ϱp and $\varrho' p$ are $D\backslash\mathcal{C}$-objects and we can see h_u as a $D\backslash\mathcal{C}$-morphism from ϱp to $\varrho' p$.

Definition 5 (functor Res_d). *Let* $\mathsf{Res}_d : \mathrm{Rpl}(d) \to D\backslash\mathcal{C}$ *be the functor defined by* $\mathsf{Res}_d\varrho := \varrho p$ *and* $\mathsf{Res}_d u := h_u$ *for all* $\mathrm{Rpl}(d)$-*morphism* $u : \varrho \to \varrho'$.

We assume a diagram in $\mathrm{Rpl}(d)$, i.e., a functor $\mathsf{D}^{\cdot} : \mathcal{J} \to \mathrm{Rpl}(D)$.

Theorem 1. $\mathsf{D}^{\cdot}$ *has a colimit iff* $\mathsf{Itf} \circ \mathsf{D}^{\cdot}$, $\mathsf{Ext} \circ \mathsf{D}^{\cdot}$ *and* $\mathsf{Res}_d \circ \mathsf{D}^{\cdot}$ *have colimits.*

Proof. Sufficient Condition. Let $((x_j)_{j\in\mathcal{J}}, \vec{I})$, $((y_j)_{j\in\mathcal{J}}, \vec{E})$ and $((z_j)_{j\in\mathcal{J}}, \vec{p} : D \to \vec{H})$ be colimits of $\mathsf{Itf} \circ \mathsf{D}^{\cdot}$, $\mathsf{Ext} \circ \mathsf{D}^{\cdot}$ and $\mathsf{D}^{\cdot}f : \mathsf{D}^{\cdot}j \to \mathsf{D}^{\cdot}j'$ then the diagram

$$
\begin{array}{ccccccc}
G & \xleftarrow{\ \ d\ \ } & D & \xleftarrow{(\mathsf{D}^{\cdot}j)i} & (\mathsf{D}^{\cdot}j)I & \xrightarrow{(\mathsf{D}^{\cdot}j)e} & (\mathsf{D}^{\cdot}j)E \\
{\scriptstyle 1}\downarrow & & {\scriptstyle 1}\uparrow & & {\scriptstyle (\mathsf{D}^{\cdot}f)_2}\downarrow & & \downarrow{\scriptstyle (\mathsf{D}^{\cdot}f)_3} \\
G & \xleftarrow{\ \ d\ \ } & D & \xleftarrow{(\mathsf{D}^{\cdot}j')i} & (\mathsf{D}^{\cdot}j')I & \xrightarrow{(\mathsf{D}^{\cdot}j')e} & (\mathsf{D}^{\cdot}j')E
\end{array}
$$

commutes and we have $(\mathsf{D}^{\cdot}j')i \circ (\mathsf{D}^{\cdot}f)_2 = (\mathsf{D}^{\cdot}j)i$ and $(\mathsf{D}^{\cdot}j')e \circ (\mathsf{D}^{\cdot}f)_2 = (\mathsf{D}^{\cdot}f)_3 \circ (\mathsf{D}^{\cdot}j)e$, hence $(\mathsf{D}^{\cdot}j')i \circ (\mathsf{Itf} \circ \mathsf{D}^{\cdot})f = (\mathsf{D}^{\cdot}j)i$ and

$$y_{j'} \circ (\mathsf{D}^{\cdot}j')e \circ (\mathsf{Itf} \circ \mathsf{D}^{\cdot})f = y_{j'} \circ (\mathsf{Ext} \circ \mathsf{D}^{\cdot})f \circ (\mathsf{D}^{\cdot}j)e = y_j \circ (\mathsf{D}^{\cdot}j)e,$$

so that the sinks $(((\mathsf{D}^{\cdot}j)i)_{j\in\mathcal{J}}, D)$ and $((y_j \circ (\mathsf{D}^{\cdot}j)e)_{j\in\mathcal{J}}, \vec{E})$ are both natural for $\mathsf{Itf} \circ \mathsf{D}^{\cdot}$ and there exist a unique $\vec{i} : \vec{I} \to D$ and a unique $\vec{e} : \vec{I} \to \vec{E}$ such that $\vec{i} \circ x_j = (\mathsf{D}^{\cdot}j)i$ and $\vec{e} \circ x_j = y_j \circ (\mathsf{D}^{\cdot}j)e$ for all $j \in \mathcal{J}$. Similarly we have

$$
\begin{aligned}
z_{j'} \circ (\mathsf{D}^{\cdot}j')q \circ (\mathsf{Ext} \circ \mathsf{D}^{\cdot})f &= z_{j'} \circ (\mathsf{D}^{\cdot}j')q \circ (\mathsf{D}^{\cdot}f)_3 \\
&= z_{j'} \circ (\mathsf{Res}_d \circ \mathsf{D}^{\cdot})f \circ (\mathsf{D}^{\cdot}j)q \text{ by Lemma 1} \\
&= z_j \circ (\mathsf{D}^{\cdot}j)q
\end{aligned}
$$

so that $((z_j \circ (\mathsf{D}^{\cdot}j)q)_{j\in\mathcal{J}}, \vec{H})$ is a natural sink for $\mathsf{Ext} \circ \mathsf{D}^{\cdot}$ hence there exists a unique $\vec{q} : \vec{E} \to \vec{H}$ such that $\vec{q} \circ y_j = z_j \circ (\mathsf{D}^{\cdot}j)q$ for all j.

Now, we also see that

$$
\begin{aligned}
z_{j'} \circ (\mathsf{D}^{\cdot}j')(q \circ e) \circ (\mathsf{Itf} \circ \mathsf{D}^{\cdot})f &= z_{j'} \circ (\mathsf{D}^{\cdot}j')q \circ (\mathsf{Ext} \circ \mathsf{D}^{\cdot})f \circ (\mathsf{D}^{\cdot}j)e \\
&= z_j \circ (\mathsf{D}^{\cdot}j)(q \circ e)
\end{aligned}
$$

so that $((z_j \circ (\mathsf{D}^{\cdot}j)(q \circ e))_{j\in\mathcal{J}}, \vec{H})$ is natural for $\mathsf{Itf} \circ \mathsf{D}^{\cdot}$ hence there exists a unique $\vec{r} : \vec{I} \to \vec{H}$ such that $\vec{r} \circ x_j = z_j \circ (\mathsf{D}^{\cdot}j)(q \circ e)$ for all j. Since

$$\vec{q} \circ \vec{e} \circ x_j = \vec{q} \circ y_j \circ (\mathsf{D}^{\cdot}j)e = z_j \circ (\mathsf{D}^{\cdot}j)(q \circ e)$$

then $\vec{q} \circ \vec{e} = \vec{r}$, and since z_j is a $D\backslash\mathcal{C}$-morphism from $(\mathsf{Res}_d \circ \mathsf{D}^\cdot)j = (\mathsf{D}^\cdot j)p$ to $\vec{p}$ then

$$\vec{p} \circ \vec{i} \circ x_j = \vec{p} \circ (\mathsf{D}^\cdot j)i = z_j \circ (\mathsf{D}^\cdot j)(p \circ i) = z_j \circ (\mathsf{D}^\cdot j)(q \circ e)$$

hence $\vec{p} \circ \vec{i} = \vec{q} \circ \vec{e}$.

Let γ be the commuting diagram

$$
\begin{array}{ccc}
\vec{I} & \xrightarrow{\ \vec{e}\ } & \vec{E} \\
\downarrow{\scriptstyle \vec{i}} & & \downarrow{\scriptstyle \vec{q}} \\
 & & \\
G \xleftarrow{\ d\ } D & \xrightarrow{\ \vec{p}\ } & \vec{H}
\end{array}
$$

in $\mathcal{C}$. We now prove that this square is a pushout. Let $D \xrightarrow{p'} H' \xleftarrow{q'} \vec{E}$ be a cospan such that $p' \circ \vec{i} = q' \circ \vec{e}$, we thus have

$$p' \circ (\mathsf{D}^\cdot j)i = p' \circ \vec{i} \circ x_j = q' \circ \vec{e} \circ x_j = q' \circ y_j \circ (\mathsf{D}^\cdot j)e$$

and since $((\mathsf{D}^\cdot j)p, (\mathsf{D}^\cdot j)q)$ is a pushout of $((\mathsf{D}^\cdot j)i, (\mathsf{D}^\cdot j)e)$ then there exists a unique $\mathcal{C}$-morphism $h'_j : (\mathsf{D}^\cdot j)H \to H'$ such that $h'_j \circ (\mathsf{D}^\cdot j)q = q' \circ y_j$ and $h'_j \circ (\mathsf{D}^\cdot j)p = p'$ (i.e. $h'_j : (\mathsf{D}^\cdot j)p \to p'$ in $D\backslash\mathcal{C}$). For all $f : j \to j'$ and by Lemma 1 we have $h'_{j'} \circ (\mathsf{Res}_d \circ \mathsf{D}^\cdot)f \circ (\mathsf{D}^\cdot j)p = h'_{j'} \circ (\mathsf{D}^\cdot j')p = p'$ and

$$h'_{j'} \circ (\mathsf{Res}_d \circ \mathsf{D}^\cdot)f \circ (\mathsf{D}^\cdot j)q = h'_{j'} \circ (\mathsf{D}^\cdot j')q \circ (\mathsf{D}^\cdot f)_3 = q' \circ y_{j'} \circ (\mathsf{Ext} \circ \mathsf{D}^\cdot)f = q' \circ y_j$$

hence by unicity $h'_{j'} \circ (\mathsf{Res}_d \circ \mathsf{D}^\cdot)f = h'_j$, so that the sink $((h'_j)_{j \in \mathcal{J}}, p')$ is natural for $\mathsf{Res}_d \circ \mathsf{D}^\cdot$ and there exists a unique $D\backslash\mathcal{C}$-morphism $h' : \vec{p} \to p'$ such that $h' \circ z_j = h'_j$ for all j. In $\mathcal{C}$ we thus have a unique $h' : \vec{H} \to H'$ such that $h' \circ \vec{p} = p'$ and for all j

$$h' \circ \vec{q} \circ y_j = h' \circ z_j \circ (\mathsf{D}^\cdot j)q = h'_j \circ (\mathsf{D}^\cdot j)q = q' \circ y_j$$

hence $h' \circ \vec{q} = q'$ since $(y_j)_{j \in \mathcal{J}}$ is an epi-sink.

We have proved so far that γ is a replacement and that $(1_D, x_j, y_j)$ is a subsumption from $\mathsf{D}^\cdot j$ to γ for all j. For every $\mathcal{J}$-morphism $f : j \to j'$ we have

$$(1_D, x_{j'}, y_{j'}) \circ \mathsf{D}^\cdot f = (1_D, x_{j'} \circ (\mathsf{Itf} \circ \mathsf{D}^\cdot)f, y_{j'} \circ (\mathsf{Ext} \circ \mathsf{D}^\cdot)f) = (1_D, x_j, y_j)$$

hence $((1_D, x_j, y_j)_{j \in \mathcal{J}}, \gamma)$ is a natural sink for $\mathsf{D}^\cdot$, and there only remains to prove that it is a colimit of $\mathsf{D}^\cdot$.

Let $((u^j)_{j \in \mathcal{J}}, \varrho)$ be a natural sink for $\mathsf{D}^\cdot$, then obviously $((\mathsf{Itf}u^j)_{j \in \mathcal{J}}, \mathsf{Itf}\varrho)$ and $((\mathsf{Ext}u^j)_{J \in \mathcal{J}}, \mathsf{Ext}\varrho)$ are natural sinks for $\mathsf{Itf} \circ \mathsf{D}^\cdot$ and $\mathsf{Ext} \circ \mathsf{D}^\cdot$ respectively, hence there exist a unique $y : \vec{I} \to \varrho I$ and a unique $z : \vec{E} \to \varrho E$ such that $y \circ x_j = u_2^j$ and $z \circ y_j = u_3^j$, hence a unique $v := (1_D, y, z)$ such that $v \circ (1_D, x_j, y_j) = u^j$ for all j. Since $\varrho i \circ y \circ x_j = \varrho i \circ u_2^j = (\mathsf{D}^\cdot j)i$ then by unicity $\vec{i} = \varrho i \circ y$. Besides, we have

$$z \circ \vec{e} \circ x_j = z \circ y_j \circ (\mathsf{D}^\cdot j)e = u_3^j \circ (\mathsf{D}^\cdot j)e = \varrho e \circ u_2^j = \varrho e \circ y \circ x_j$$

for all j and since $(x_j)_{j \in \mathcal{J}}$ is an epi-sink then $z \circ \vec{e} = \varrho e \circ y$, and we have proved that v is a subsumption from γ to ϱ.

Necessary Condition. If $\mathsf{D}^{\cdot}$ has a colimit then $\mathsf{Itf} \circ \mathsf{D}^{\cdot}$, $\mathsf{Ext} \circ \mathsf{D}^{\cdot}$ and $\mathsf{Res}_d \circ \mathsf{D}^{\cdot}$ have natural sinks hence colimits. $\qquad\qquad\square$

Corollary 2. *If $\mathcal{C}$ has pushouts then $\mathsf{D}^{\cdot}$ has a colimit iff $\mathsf{Itf} \circ \mathsf{D}^{\cdot}$ and $\mathsf{Ext} \circ \mathsf{D}^{\cdot}$ have colimits.*

Proof. The colimit of $\mathsf{Res}_d \circ \mathsf{D}^{\cdot}$ is only used to construct $\vec{p}$, itself used to construct $\vec{q}$, hence we can dispense with this hypothesis by constructing $D \xrightarrow{\vec{p}} \vec{H} \xleftarrow{\vec{q}} \vec{E}$ as a pushout of $D \xleftarrow{\vec{i}} \vec{I} \xrightarrow{\vec{e}} \vec{E}$. $\qquad\qquad\square$

5 Coherence Systems and Colimits

We now consider the general case and assume a diagram $\mathsf{D} : \mathcal{J} \to \mathrm{Rpl}(G)$. In order to get a morphism d from the limit of the contexts to G we use the same trick as above and work in the slice category $\mathcal{C}\backslash G$. This is possible since for all $\mathcal{J}$-morphism $f : j \to j'$, $\mathsf{D}f$ is a subsumption and therefore its first component $(\mathsf{D}f)_1$ can be seen as a $\mathcal{C}\backslash G$-morphism from $(\mathsf{D}j')d$ to $(\mathsf{D}j)d$. Similarly, $(\mathsf{D}f)_2$ is a $\mathcal{C}\backslash G$-morphism from $(\mathsf{D}j)(d \circ i)$ to $(\mathsf{D}j')(d \circ i)$.

Definition 6 (functors Ctx, Itm, p_1, p_2). *Let $\mathsf{Ctx} : \mathrm{Rpl}(G) \to \mathcal{C}\backslash G$ be the contravariant functor such that $\mathsf{Ctx}\varrho := \varrho d$ and $\mathsf{Ctx}u := u_1$ for all subsumptions $u : \varrho \to \varrho'$, and $\mathsf{Itm} : \mathrm{Rpl}(G) \to \mathcal{C}\backslash G$ be the covariant functor such that $\mathsf{Itm}\varrho := \varrho(d \circ i)$ and $\mathsf{Itm}u := u_2$.*
Let $\mathsf{p}_1 : \mathcal{J}^{\mathrm{op}} \times \mathcal{J} \to \mathcal{J}^{\mathrm{op}}$ and $\mathsf{p}_2 : \mathcal{J}^{\mathrm{op}} \times \mathcal{J} \to \mathcal{J}$ be the canonical projections.

We need an algebraic way of expressing that there are no conflicts in D, i.e., that every item in G that has a preimage in $(\mathsf{D}k)I$ (by $(\mathsf{D}k)(d \circ i)$), for all $k \in \mathcal{J}$, is not removed by $\mathsf{D}j$ for any $j \neq k$, hence that it has a preimage in $(\mathsf{D}j)D$ by $(\mathsf{D}j)d$. This is guaranteed if we can find a $\mathcal{C}$-morphism $c_j^k : (\mathsf{D}k)I \to (\mathsf{D}j)D$ such that

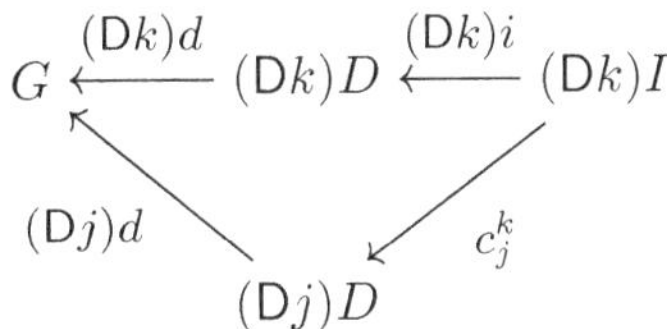

commutes, or equivalently a $\mathcal{C}\backslash G$-morphism c_j^k from $(\mathsf{D}k)(d \circ i) = (\mathsf{Itm} \circ \mathsf{D})k$ to $(\mathsf{D}j)d = (\mathsf{Ctx} \circ \mathsf{D})j$. It will be convenient to include the case $j = k$ with the trivial solution $c_k^k = (\mathsf{D}k)i$. We also need the commutation of c_j^k with the subsumptions present in the diagram D, by requiring naturality in j and k.

Definition 7 (coherence system c). *A coherence system for D is a natural transformation $c : \mathsf{Itm} \circ \mathsf{D} \circ \mathsf{p}_2 \dot\to \mathsf{Ctx} \circ \mathsf{D} \circ \mathsf{p}_1$ such that $c_k^k = (\mathsf{D}k)i$ for all $k \in \mathcal{J}$.*
D is coherent *if it admits a coherence system, otherwise it* has conflicts.

Hence for all $f : j \to j'$ and $g : k \to k'$ in $\mathcal{J}$ the diagram

$$
\begin{array}{ccc}
(\mathsf{D}k)(d \circ i) & \xrightarrow{\;c^k_{j'}\;} & (\mathsf{D}j')d \\
\downarrow{\scriptstyle (\mathsf{D}g)_2} & & \downarrow{\scriptstyle (\mathsf{D}f)_1} \\
(\mathsf{D}k')(d \circ i) & \xrightarrow[\;c^{k'}_{j}\;]{} & (\mathsf{D}j)d
\end{array}
$$

commutes in $\mathcal{C}\backslash G$.

Example 6. In Example 4 we see that there is exactly one morphism from $\varrho_1 I$ to $\varrho_2 D$, but two morphisms from $\varrho_2 I$ to $\varrho_1 D$. The commutation conditions being obvious, we get two coherence systems for the coproduct diagram $\{\varrho_1, \varrho_2\}$.

Coherence systems are closely related to natural sinks.

Definition 8. *The coherence system c associated to a sink $((u^j)_{j\in\mathcal{J}}, \varrho)$ is $c^k_j :=$ $u^j_1 \circ \varrho i \circ u^k_2$ for all $j, k \in \mathcal{J}$.*

Lemma 2. *The coherence system associated to any natural sink for D is a coherence system for D.*

Proof. Let $((u^j)_{j\in\mathcal{J}}, \varrho)$ be natural for D (so that $u^j : \mathsf{D}j \to \varrho$ and $u^j = u^{j'} \circ \mathsf{D}f$ for all $f : j \to j'$) and c its associated coherence system, since

$$(\mathsf{D}j)d \circ c^k_j = \varrho d \circ \varrho i \circ u^k_2 = \varrho(d \circ i) \circ u^k_2 = (\mathsf{D}k)(d \circ i),$$

then c^k_j can be seen as a $\mathcal{C}\backslash G$-morphism from $(\mathsf{D}k)(d \circ i)$ to $(\mathsf{D}j)d$. Since for all $f : j \to j'$ and $g : k \to k'$ in $\mathcal{J}$ we have

$$
\begin{aligned}
(\mathsf{D}f)_1 \circ c^k_{j'} &= (u^{j'} \circ \mathsf{D}f)_1 \circ \varrho i \circ u^k_2 = c^k_j, \\
c^{k'}_j \circ (\mathsf{D}g)_2 &= u^j_1 \circ \varrho i \circ (u^{k'} \circ (\mathsf{D}g))_2 = c^k_j
\end{aligned}
$$

and $c^k_k = (\mathsf{D}k)i$ (because $u^k : \mathsf{D}k \to \varrho$) then c is a coherence system for D. $\square$

Hence coherence appears as a necessary condition for D to have a colimit, but we can be more precise than this.

Corollary 3. *For every $u : \varrho \to \varrho'$, the coherence system associated to $((u \circ u^j)_{j\in\mathcal{J}}, \varrho')$ is the same as the coherence system associated to $((u^j)_{j\in\mathcal{J}}, \varrho)$.*

Proof. Trivial since $(u \circ u^j)_1 \circ \varrho' i \circ (u \circ u^k)_2 = u^j_1 \circ u_1 \circ \varrho' i \circ u_2 \circ u^k_2 = u^j_1 \circ \varrho i \circ u^k_2$. $\square$

In order to obtain a correspondence inverse to the one exposed in Lemma 2, we need the following restriction.

Definition 9. *A coherence system c for D is* effective *if there exists a natural sink for D whose associated coherence system is c. D is* strictly coherent *if it admits a unique effective coherence system.*

Theorem 2. *If D has a colimit then it is strictly coherent.*

Proof. Let c be any effective coherence system for D, then there is a natural sink for D whose coherence system is c, and since it factors through the colimit then by Corollary 3 c is the coherence system associated to the colimit of D. $\qquad\square$

We now show how a coherence system c can be used to reduce the problem of finding a colimit of D to that of finding a colimit of a diagram of replacements with the same context, and hence use Theorem 1. The common context is a limit of $\mathsf{Ctx} \circ \mathsf{D}$, that exists by the hypothesis on $\mathcal{C}$, and can be used since for every $k \in \mathcal{J}$, $((\mathsf{D}k)(d \circ i), (c_j^k)_{j \in \mathcal{J}})$ is a natural source for $\mathsf{Ctx} \circ \mathsf{D}$.

Definition 10 (functor $\mathsf{D}_c^{\cdot}$). *Given a coherence system c for D and a limit $(\overleftarrow{d}, (s_j)_{j \in \mathcal{J}})$ of $\mathsf{Ctx} \circ \mathsf{D}$, for all $k \in \mathcal{J}$ let $\mathsf{D}_c^{\cdot}k$ be the replacement with diagram*

$$G \xleftarrow{\;\overleftarrow{d}\;} \overleftarrow{D} \xleftarrow{\;i_k\;} (\mathsf{D}k)I \xrightarrow{\;(\mathsf{D}k)e\;} (\mathsf{D}k)E$$

where i_k is the unique $\mathcal{C}\backslash G$-morphism from $(\mathsf{D}k)(d \circ i)$ to $\overleftarrow{d}$ such that $s_j \circ i_k = c_j^k$ for all $j \in \mathcal{J}$. For all $\mathcal{J}$-morphisms $g : k \to k'$ let $\mathsf{D}_c^{\cdot}g := (1_{\overleftarrow{D}}, (\mathsf{D}g)_2, (\mathsf{D}g)_3)$.

Lemma 3. *$\mathsf{D}_c^{\cdot}$ is a functor from $\mathcal{J}$ to $\mathrm{Rpl}(\overleftarrow{d})$ such that $(s_k, 1_{(\mathsf{D}k)I}, 1_{(\mathsf{D}k)E}) : \mathsf{D}k \to \mathsf{D}_c^{\cdot}j$ for all $k \in \mathcal{J}$.*

Proof. We first prove that there exists a replacement $\mathsf{D}_c^{\cdot}k$, i.e., that the span of the given diagram has a pushout. Since

$$(\mathsf{D}k)p \circ s_k \circ i_k = (\mathsf{D}k)p \circ c_k^k = (\mathsf{D}k)p \circ (\mathsf{D}k)i = (\mathsf{D}k)q \circ (\mathsf{D}k)e$$

then $((\mathsf{D}k)p \circ s_k, (\mathsf{D}k)q, (\mathsf{D}k)H)$ is a natural sink for the span

$$\overleftarrow{D} \xleftarrow{\;i_k\;} (\mathsf{D}k)I \xrightarrow{\;(\mathsf{D}k)e\;} (\mathsf{D}k)E,$$

hence by our hypothesis on $\mathcal{C}$ it has a pushout.

We next see that $\mathsf{D}_c^{\cdot}g : \mathsf{D}_c^{\cdot}k \to \mathsf{D}_c^{\cdot}k'$ for all $g : k \to k'$ since in the diagram

$$
\begin{array}{ccccccc}
G & \xleftarrow{\;\overleftarrow{d}\;} & \overleftarrow{D} & \xleftarrow{\;i_k\;} & (\mathsf{D}k)I & \xrightarrow{\;(\mathsf{D}k)e\;} & (\mathsf{D}k)E \\
\downarrow{\scriptstyle 1} & & \uparrow{\scriptstyle 1} & & \downarrow{\scriptstyle (\mathsf{D}g)_2} & & \downarrow{\scriptstyle (\mathsf{D}g)_3} \\
G & \xleftarrow[\;\overleftarrow{d}\;]{} & \overleftarrow{D} & \xleftarrow[\;i_{k'}\;]{} & (\mathsf{D}k')I & \xrightarrow[\;(\mathsf{D}k')e\;]{} & (\mathsf{D}k')E
\end{array}
$$

the right square commutes because $\mathsf{D}g : \mathsf{D}k \to \mathsf{D}k'$ and the middle square commutes because for all j we have $s_j \circ i_k = c_j^k = c_j^{k'} \circ (\mathsf{D}g)_2 = s_j \circ i_{k'} \circ (\mathsf{D}g)_2$ and $(s_j)_{j \in \mathcal{J}}$ is a mono-source. It is obvious that $\mathsf{D}_c^{\cdot}1_k = 1_{\mathsf{D}_c^{\cdot}k}$ and that $\mathsf{D}_c^{\cdot}(g' \circ g) = \mathsf{D}_c^{\cdot}g' \circ \mathsf{D}_c^{\cdot}g$, hence $\mathsf{D}_c^{\cdot}$ is a functor.

For all k, $(s_k, 1_{(\mathsf{D}k)I}, 1_{(\mathsf{D}k)E})$ is a subsumption from $\mathsf{D}k$ to $\mathsf{D}_c^{\cdot}k$ since in the diagram

$$
\begin{array}{ccccccc}
G & \xleftarrow{\ (\mathsf{D}k)d\ } & (\mathsf{D}k)D & \xleftarrow{\ (\mathsf{D}k)i\ } & (\mathsf{D}k)I & \xrightarrow{\ (\mathsf{D}k)e\ } & (\mathsf{D}k)E \\
{\scriptstyle 1}\downarrow & & {\scriptstyle s_k}\uparrow & & \downarrow{\scriptstyle 1} & & \downarrow{\scriptstyle 1} \\
G & \xleftarrow{\ \overleftarrow{d}\ } & \overleftarrow{D} & \xleftarrow{\ i_k\ } & (\mathsf{D}k)I & \xrightarrow{\ (\mathsf{D}k)e\ } & (\mathsf{D}k)E
\end{array}
$$

the left square commutes because $s_k : \overleftarrow{d} \to (\mathsf{Ctx} \circ \mathsf{D})k$ in $\mathcal{C}\backslash G$, hence

$$(\mathsf{D}k)d \circ s_k = (\mathsf{Ctx} \circ \mathsf{D})k \circ s_k = \overleftarrow{d}$$

and the middle square commutes because $s_k \circ i_k = c_k^k = (\mathsf{D}k)i$. $\qquad\qquad \square$

Note that the result of the replacement $\mathsf{D}_c^{\cdot}k$ depends on the morphism $(\mathsf{D}_c^{\cdot}k)i = i_k$ and therefore on c. We now see how naturality of sinks can be preserved from $\mathsf{D}_c^{\cdot}$ to D.

Corollary 4. *If $((v^j)_{j \in \mathcal{J}}, \varrho)$ is a natural sink for $\mathsf{D}_c^{\cdot}$ then $((v^j \circ (s_j, 1, 1))_{j \in \mathcal{J}}, \varrho)$ is a natural sink for D whose associated coherence system is c.*

Proof. For all $f : j \to j'$, since $v_1^j = v_1^{j'} = 1_{\overleftarrow{D}}$ then

$$
\begin{aligned}
v^{j'} \circ (s_{j'}, 1, 1) \circ \mathsf{D}f &= ((\mathsf{D}f)_1 \circ s_{j'}, v_2^{j'} \circ (\mathsf{D}f)_2, v_3^{j'} \circ (\mathsf{D}f)_3) \\
&= ((\mathsf{Ctx} \circ \mathsf{D})f \circ s_{j'}, v_2^{j'} \circ (\mathsf{D}_c^{\cdot}f)_2, v_3^{j'} \circ (\mathsf{D}_c^{\cdot}f)_3) \\
&= (s_j, v_2^j, v_3^j) \\
&= v^j \circ (s_j, 1, 1).
\end{aligned}
$$

hence $((v^j \circ (s_j, 1, 1))_{j \in \mathcal{J}}, \varrho)$ is natural for D and its associated coherence system is $s_j \circ \varrho i \circ v_2^k = s_j \circ i_k = c_j^k$ since $v^k : \mathsf{D}_c^{\cdot}k \to \varrho$. $\qquad \square$

This entails that if $\mathsf{D}_c^{\cdot}$ has a colimit then c is effective. Hence by Theorem 1 only a lack of colimits in $\mathcal{C}$ may prevent a coherence system from being effective.

We now investigate the properties of the natural sink for D obtained from a colimit of $\mathsf{D}_c^{\cdot}$.

Lemma 4. *If $((u^j)_{j \in \mathcal{J}}, \varrho)$ is a natural sink for $\mathsf{D} : \mathcal{J} \to \mathrm{Rpl}(G)$, c is its coherence system and $((v^j)_{j \in \mathcal{J}}, \gamma_c)$ is a colimit of $\mathsf{D}_c^{\cdot}$ then there exists a unique $\mathcal{C}$-morphism $w : \gamma_c \to \varrho$ such that $w \circ v^k \circ (s_k, 1, 1) = u^k$ for all $k \in \mathcal{J}$.*

Proof. Since $(\mathsf{Ctx}\varrho, (\mathsf{Ctx}u^j)_{j\in\mathcal{J}})$ is a natural source for $\mathsf{Ctx} \circ \mathsf{D}$ there exists a unique $\mathcal{C}\backslash G$-morphism $s : \mathsf{Ctx}\varrho \to \overleftarrow{d}$ such that $s_j \circ s = \mathsf{Ctx}u^j = u_1^j$ for all j, so that in $\mathcal{C}$ we have $s \circ \overleftarrow{d} = \mathsf{Ctx}\varrho = \varrho d$. For every $j, k \in \mathcal{J}$ we have

$$s_j \circ s \circ \varrho i \circ u_2^k = u_1^j \circ \varrho i \circ u_2^k = c_j^k = s_j \circ i_k$$

by definition of $\mathsf{D}_c^{\cdot}k$, hence $s \circ \varrho i \circ u_2^k = i_k$ since $(s_j)_{j\in\mathcal{J}}$ is a mono-source, and therefore the diagram

$$
\begin{array}{ccccccc}
G & \xleftarrow{\ \overleftarrow{d}\ } & \overleftarrow{D} & \xleftarrow{\ i_k\ } & (\mathsf{D}k)I & \xrightarrow{\ (\mathsf{D}k)e\ } & (\mathsf{D}k)E \\
\downarrow{\scriptstyle 1} & & \uparrow{\scriptstyle s} & & \downarrow{\scriptstyle u_2^k} & & \downarrow{\scriptstyle u_3^k} \\
G & \xleftarrow[\ \varrho d\ ]{} & \varrho D & \xleftarrow[\ \varrho i\ ]{} & \varrho I & \xrightarrow[\ \varrho e\ ]{} & \varrho E
\end{array}
$$

commutes (also because $u^k : \mathsf{D}k \to \varrho$), hence $(s, u_2^k, u_3^k) : \mathsf{D}_c^{\cdot}k \to \varrho$. Besides we have for all $g : k \to k'$

$$(s, u_2^{k'}, u_3^{k'}) \circ \mathsf{D}_c^{\cdot}g = (s, u_2^{k'} \circ (\mathsf{D}_c^{\cdot}g)_2, u_3^{k'} \circ (\mathsf{D}_c^{\cdot}g)_3) = (s, u_2^k, u_3^k)$$

hence $((s, u_2^k, u_3^k)_{k\in\mathcal{J}}, \varrho)$ is a natural sink for $\mathsf{D}_c^{\cdot}$ and there exists a unique $w : \gamma_c \to \varrho$ such that $w \circ v^k = (s, u_2^k, u_3^k)$ for all k, so that $w \circ v^k \circ (s_k, 1, 1) = (s_k \circ s, u_2^k, u_3^k) = u^k$. $\qquad\square$

This means that this natural sink for D is initial for the natural sinks whose coherence system is c. We immediately deduce the colimit of strictly coherent diagrams, and the awaited characterization result.

Theorem 3. D *has a colimit iff* D *is strictly coherent with coherence system* c *and* $\mathsf{Itf} \circ \mathsf{D}$, $\mathsf{Ext} \circ \mathsf{D}$, $\mathsf{Res}_{\overleftarrow{d}} \circ \mathsf{D}_c^{\cdot}$ *have colimits.*

Proof. Sufficient Condition. Since $\mathsf{Itf} \circ \mathsf{D} = \mathsf{Itf} \circ \mathsf{D}_c^{\cdot}$ and $\mathsf{Ext} \circ \mathsf{D} = \mathsf{Ext} \cup \mathsf{D}_c^{\cdot}$ (by omitting the obvious inclusion functors) then by Theorem 1 there is a colimit $((v^j)_{j\in\mathcal{J}}, \gamma_c)$ of $\mathsf{D}_c^{\cdot}$. Any natural sink for D has coherence system c, and since $((v^k \circ (s_k, 1, 1))_{k\in\mathcal{J}}, \gamma_c)$ is a natural sink for D by Corollary 4, then it is a colimit of D by Lemma 4.
Necessary Condition. Obvious by Theorems 2 and 1. $\qquad\square$

Corollary 5. *If* $\mathcal{C}$ *has pushouts then* D *has a colimit iff* D *has a unique coherence system and* $\mathsf{Itf} \circ \mathsf{D}$, $\mathsf{Ext} \circ \mathsf{D}$ *have colimits.*

Proof. We first notice that if $\mathsf{Itf} \circ \mathsf{D}$ and $\mathsf{Ext} \circ \mathsf{D}$ have colimits then for any coherence system c for D, $\mathsf{D}_c^{\cdot}$ has a colimit by Corollary 2, hence c is effective by Corollary 4. Then the proof is the same as Theorem 3 only using Corollary 2 instead of Theorem 1. $\qquad\square$

We can therefore propose an algorithm for computing a colimit of D, provided that $\mathcal{J}$ and the sets $\mathcal{C}((\mathsf{D}k)I, (\mathsf{D}j)D)$ for all $j, k \in \mathcal{J}$ are finite.

1. Compute the set C of coherence systems for D. If C is empty then D has no colimit by Theorem 2.
2. Compute a limit $(\overleftarrow{d}, (s_j)_{j \in \mathcal{J}})$ of $\mathsf{Ctx} \circ \mathsf{D}$.
3. Compute the set Γ of colimits of $\mathsf{D}_c^{\cdot}$ for all $c \in C$ using Theorem 1 or Corollary 2, i.e., by computing the relevant colimits in $\mathcal{C}$ if possible.
4. If Γ is empty or has more than one element, then D has no colimit by Theorem 2.
5. If C has one element c and Γ has one element $((v^j)_{j \in \mathcal{J}}, \gamma_c)$ then $((v^j \circ (s_j, 1, 1))_{j \in \mathcal{J}}, \gamma_c)$ is a colimit of D by Theorem 3.
6. Otherwise Γ has one element $((v^j)_{j \in \mathcal{J}}, \gamma_c)$ of coherence system c and C as at least one element other than c, then $((v^k \circ (s_k, 1, 1))_{k \in \mathcal{J}}, \gamma_c)$ is a colimit of D iff all natural sinks for D have coherence system c.

In Step 4, if Γ is empty then we have been unable to find a colimit for $\mathsf{Itf} \circ \mathsf{D}$, $\mathsf{Ext} \circ \mathsf{D}$ or $\mathsf{Res}_{\overleftarrow{d}} \circ \mathsf{D}_c^{\cdot}$ for any $c \in C$. Since any effective coherence system must be in C, we conclude by Theorem 2 that D has no colimit.

If Γ has more than one element then we get more than one effective coherence system (by Corollary 4) and the conclusion is the same. From a pratical point of view, we may still use any natural sink for D computed from the elements of Γ. It could be selected either by hand or automatically by some criterion to be determined. One possibility is to distinguish in the non-linear contexts, among the copies of items of G, one that is considered as the original, and then consider only the coherence system that uses this original and not its copies.

When only linear replacements are involved there is at most one possible choice.

Theorem 4. *If* D $: \mathcal{J} \to \mathrm{Rpl}^*(G)$ *is coherent and* $\mathsf{Ctx} \circ \mathsf{D}$ *has a limit then* D *has a unique coherence system.*

Proof. Let $(\overleftarrow{d}, (s_j)_{j \in \mathcal{J}})$ be a limit of $\mathsf{Ctx} \circ \mathsf{D}$ and b, c two coherence systems for D. Since $(\mathsf{Ctx} \circ \mathsf{D})j$ is monic for all j then so are $s_j : \overleftarrow{d} \to (\mathsf{Ctx} \circ \mathsf{D})j$ and the limit $\overleftarrow{d}$. By coherence of b, c there exist unique $\mathcal{C} \backslash G$-morphisms $i_k : (\mathsf{D}k)(d \circ i) \to \overleftarrow{d}$ and $i'_k : (\mathsf{D}k)(d \circ i) \to \overleftarrow{d}$ such that $s_j \circ i_k = c_j^k$ and $s_j \circ i'_k = b_j^k$, hence $\overleftarrow{d} \circ i_k = (\mathsf{D}k)(d \circ i) = \overleftarrow{d} \circ i'_k$, so that $i_k = i'_k$ and therefore $c_j^k = b_j^k$. $\qquad\square$

Hence Step 6 cannot be reached if D is linear, nor if $\mathcal{C}$ has pushouts since then Γ and C have the same number of elements. Otherwise it may be reached and then we get a natural sink that cannot be guaranteed to be a colimit of D, unless D has a colimit. If D has a colimit of coherence system c and Step 6 is reached, then D has non-effective coherence systems (by Theorem 2) and a colimit of $\mathsf{D}_c^{\cdot}$ has been computed, hence a colimit of D is indeed obtained (Theorem 3).

The reader is invited to check that the examples of Sect. 3 can be obtained by this algorithm.

An interesting point is that to get an initial object (a colimit of the empty diagram) in $\mathrm{Rpl}(G)$ we need an initial object $\varnothing$ in $\mathcal{C}$, that exists by our hypothesis on $\mathcal{C}$, but no terminal object since 1_G is a terminal object of $\mathcal{C} \backslash G$. The initial replacement is

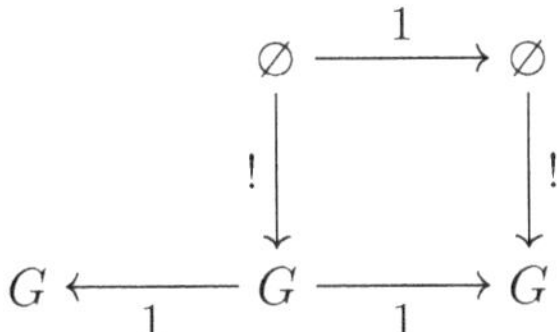

that removes/duplicates nothing and adds/merges nothing. Categories that have no terminal object (as in Example 2 and the category of monographs [6]) can be used since one is never needed for computing colimits in $\mathrm{Rpl}(G)$.

6   Related and Future Work

Parallel graph rewriting originated in [12] that introduced the notion of parallel independence. This problem has been systematically investigated in algebraic approaches to Graph Transformations, see [10] and the more recent contributions [7,17,19], and also in more general frameworks, see [2]. We easily see that the parallel independence diagram in the DPO approach

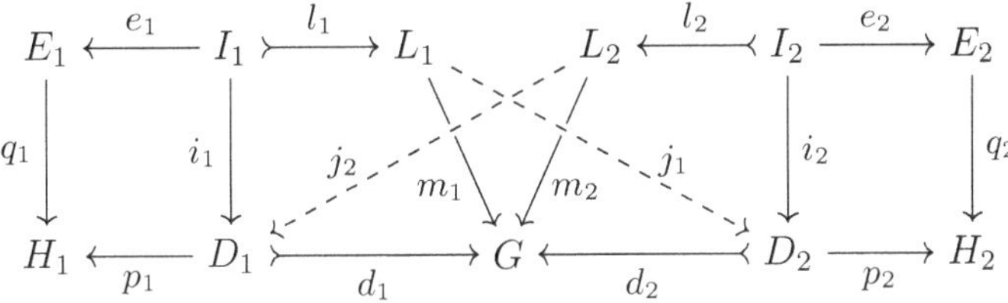

induces a coherence system $c_2^1 = j_1 \circ l_1$ and $c_1^2 = j_2 \circ l_2$, unique by Theorem 4, hence the two replacements have a coproduct replacement γ whose context is the pullback of $D_1 \xrightarrow{d_1} G \xleftarrow{d_2} D_2$, interface is the coproduct $I_1 + I_2$ and extension is $E_1 + E_2$. In the proof the Parallelism Theorem [11, Theorem 5.18] a parallel transformation of the parallel rule $L_1 + L_2 \xleftarrow{l_1+l_2} I_1 + I_2 \xrightarrow{e_1+e_2} E_1 + E_2$ is constructed, that happens to contain the coproduct γ. Thus independent parallelism appears as an instance of parallelism and parallel independence as a condition stronger than strict coherence (requiring that all c_j^k factorize through l_k) ensuring that γ can be obtained by applying the coproduct rule. Non independence is the impossibility of obtaining γ, neither by applying the coproduct rule nor by sequential application of the given rules (as in Example 2).

    Non independent parallelism has been considered in the Double-Pushout approach [21] where rules can be amalgamated by agreeing on common deletions and creations. Amalgamated rules can be seen as pushouts in a category of (span) rules, rather than coproducts as in independent parallelism, but the corresponding DPO-transformations are not known to be colimits in any category of DPO-transformations. In [16], a framework based on the algebraic Single-Pushout approach has been proposed where conflicts between parallel transformations are allowed but requires the user to solve them by providing the right control flow.

Graph transformations have also been used to model distributed systems through the Hyperedge Replacement approach, see [8,9]. The parallel replacement of individual hyperedges by rooted hypergraphs is a natural way of avoiding conflicts since overlaps are restricted to common nodes, but this supposes that at most one rule applies to every hyperedge. In [18] these nodes represent communication channels between hyperedges (representing processes), and a synchronization algebra is used to decide which hyperedges can be replaced simultaneously. By representing cells by hyperedges and neighborhoods by their nodes it is then possible to represent cellular automata on finite configurations (the Game of Life however requires 2^9 rules due to the lack of variables, see [18, Example 5.2]). This model is not formulated in algebraic terms, but it seems obvious that the replacement of an individual hyperedge could be seen as a replacement in a category $\mathcal{H}$ of rooted hypergraphs (with a single hyperedge in the interface), and that the simultaneous replacements of these hyperedges should be the multiple coproduct of these replacements in $\mathrm{Rpl}(\mathcal{H})$ (where i is a monomorphism).

The present work stems from [3] where an algorithmic framework is proposed for rule-based deterministic parallel transformations of graphs with sets of attributes. Replacements and effective coherence systems evolved from the algebraic approach in [4] extended in [5]. The idea of considering general colimits comes from the reconstruction step of Global Transformations [20].

The connection between rule-based transformations and replacements, and how to specify diagrams of replacements from rule systems, has been sketched in [5] and will be developed in a forthcoming paper.

Funding Information. This work has been partially funded by the French National Research Agency under project ANR-21-CE48-0011.

References

1. Adámek, J., Herrlich, H., Strecker, G.E.: Abstract and Concrete Categories - The Joy of Cats. Online Edition (2004). http://katmat.math.uni-bremen.de/acc/
2. Behr, N., Harmer, R., Krivine, J.: Fundamentals of compositional rewriting theory. J. Log. Algebraic Methods Program. **135**, 100893 (2023). https://doi.org/10.1016/J.JLAMP.2023.100893
3. Boy de la Tour, T., Echahed, R.: Parallel rewriting of attributed graphs. Theor. Comput. Sci. **848**, 106–132 (2020). https://doi.org/10.1016/j.tcs.2020.09.025
4. Boy de la Tour, T., Echahed, R.: Parallel coherent graph transformations. In: Roggenbach, M. (ed.) WADT 2020. LNCS, vol. 12669, pp. 75–97. Springer, Cham (2021). https://doi.org/10.1007/978-3-030-73785-6_5
5. Boy de la Tour, T.: Subsumptions of algebraic rewrite rules. In: Staton, S., Vasilakopoulou, C. (eds.) Proceedings of the Sixth International Conference on Applied Category Theory 2023. EPTCS, vol. 397, pp. 20–38. Open Publishing Association (2023). https://doi.org/10.4204/EPTCS.397.2
6. Boy de la Tour, T.: Algebraic properties and transformations of monographs. Theor. Comput. Sci. **1024**, 114939 (2025). https://doi.org/10.1016/j.tcs.2024.114939, https://www.sciencedirect.com/science/article/pii/S0304397524005565

7. Corradini, A., et al.: On the essence of parallel independence for the double-pushout and sesqui-pushout approaches. In: Heckel, R., Taentzer, G. (eds.) Graph Transformation, Specifications, and Nets - In Memory of Hartmut Ehrig. LNCS, vol. 10800, pp. 1–18. Springer (2018). https://doi.org/10.1007/978-3-319-75396-6_1

8. Degano, P., Montanari, U.: A model for distributed systems based on graph rewriting. J. ACM **34**(2), 411–449 (1987)

9. Drewes, F., Kreowski, H.J., Habel, A.: Hyperedge replacement graph grammars. In: Rozenberg, G. (ed.) Handbook of Graph Grammars and Computing by Graph Transformations, Volume 1: Foundations, pp. 95–162. World Scientific (1997). https://doi.org/10.1142/9789812384720_0002

10. Ehrig, H., Kreowski, H.J., Montanari, U., Rozenberg, G. (eds.): Handbook of Graph Grammars and Computing by Graph Transformation, Volume 3: Concurrency, Parallelism and Distribution. World Scientific (1999)

11. Ehrig, H., Ehrig, K., Prange, U., Taentzer, G.: Fundamentals of Algebraic Graph Transformation. MTCSAES, Springer, Heidelberg (2006). https://doi.org/10.1007/3-540-31188-2

12. Ehrig, H., Kreowski, H.: Parallelism of manipulations in multidimensional information structures. In: Mathematical Foundations of Computer Science. LNCS, vol. 45, pp. 284–293. Springer (1976). https://doi.org/10.1007/3-540-07854-1_188

13. Fernandez, A., Maignan, L., Spicher, A.: Cellular automata and kan extensions. In: Castillo-Ramirez, A., Guillon, P., Perrot, K. (eds.) 27th IFIP WG 1.5 International Workshop on Cellular Automata and Discrete Complex Systems, AUTOMATA 2021. OASIcs, vol. 90, pp. 7:1–7:12. Schloss Dagstuhl - Leibniz-Zentrum für Informatik (2021). https://doi.org/10.4230/OASIcs.AUTOMATA.2021.7

14. Gardner, M.: Mathematical games - the fantastic combinations of John Conway's new solitaire game "life". Sci. Am. **223**, 120–123 (1970)

15. Herrlich, H., Strecker, G.E.: Category Theory. Allyn and Bacon (1973)

16. Kniemeyer, O., Barczik, G., Hemmerling, R., Kurth, W.: Relational growth grammars - a parallel graph transformation approach with applications in biology and architecture. In: Third International Symposium AGTIVE, Revised Selected and Invited Papers, pp. 152–167 (2007). https://doi.org/10.1007/978-3-540-89020-1_12

17. Kreowski, H., Kuske, S., Lye, A.: A simple notion of parallel graph transformation and its perspectives. In: Graph Transformation, Specifications, and Nets - In Memory of Hartmut Ehrig. LNCS, vol. 10800, pp. 61–82. Springer (2018)

18. Lanese, I., Montanari, U.: Synchronization algebras with mobility for graph transformations. Electr. Notes Theor. Comput. Sci. **138**(1), 43–60 (2005). https://doi.org/10.1016/j.entcs.2005.05.004

19. Löwe, M.: Characterisation of parallel independence in AGREE-rewriting. In: 11th ICGT. LNCS, vol. 10887, pp. 118–133. Springer (2018)

20. Maignan, L., Spicher, A.: Global graph transformations. In: Plump, D. (ed.) Proceedings of the 6th International Workshop on Graph Computation Models. CEUR Workshop Proceedings, vol. 1403, pp. 34–49. CEUR-WS.org (2015). http://ceur-ws.org/Vol-1403/paper4.pdf

21. Taentzer, G.: Parallel high-level replacement systems. Theoret. Comput. Sci. **186**, 43–81 (1997)

Conflict Essences for Transformation Rules with Nested Application Conditions

Alexander Lauer[1]([⊠]) [iD], Jens Kosiol[1] [iD], Leen Lambers[2] [iD],
and Gabriele Taentzer[1] [iD]

[1] Philipps-Universität Marburg, Marburg, Germany
alexander.lauer@uni-marburg.de,
{kosiolje,taentzer}@mathematik.uni-marburg.de
[2] Brandenburg University of Technology Cottbus-Senftenberg, Cottbus, Germany
leen.lambers@b-tu.de

Abstract. *Conflict and dependency analysis* is an important static analysis tool that provides an overview of the potential interactions of (graph) transformation rules. This analysis is based on *critical pairs* and *initial conflicts*, which represent conflicting transformations in a minimal context. However, the crucial information about a conflicting transformation pair is contained in much smaller structures, called *disabling/conflict essences* in existing research. Recently, we introduced *disabling essences for rules with application conditions* which contain the information on how an application condition can be violated by another rule. In this paper, we extend the notion of disabling essences to support not only application conditions in *Alternating Quantifier Normal Form*, but also arbitrary nested conditions. We introduce *(symbolic) conflict essences* that are constructed from disabling essences and which capture the interaction between two rules. We show that a transformation pair is parallel dependent if and only if a symbolic conflict essence can be embedded into it and relate symbolic conflict essences to initial conflicts for transformation rules with application conditions. We present our results for adhesive HLR categories, which includes several types of graph-like structures.

Keywords: Graph transformation · Critical pair analysis · Static analysis · Adhesive HLR categories

1 Introduction

The algebraic approach to graph transformation [4,5] has a broad range of interesting applications, especially in software engineering [11]. *Transformation rules* specify how graphs can be modified by either deleting existing elements or creating new elements. In addition, rules may be equipped with a *nested application condition* to further model the situations in which a rule is allowed to be applied. When multiple rules are to be applied to the same graph, they can interact in the sense that one rule might prevent the application of the other by either deleting

B. Archibald and O. Semeráth (Eds.): ICGT 2026, LNCS 16624, pp. 88–108, 2026.
https://doi.org/10.1007/978-3-032-29730-3_5

elements that are used in the other transformation or by inserting or deleting elements so that the application condition is not satisfied anymore. Then one rule is said to cause a *conflict* for the other.

Statically analysing rules for these interactions plays an important role in applications such as feature interaction detection, model versioning, test case generation, and graph parsing (see [18] for an overview of such applications). Each of these analysis techniques provides an overview of all potential conflicts for a given rule set with different types of granularities. *Critical pairs* describe conflictual transformation pairs in a minimal context [7], whereas *initial conflicts* (a subset of the set of critical pairs of a rule pair) describe conflictual transformation pairs with minimal overlaps. Since critical pairs contain unnecessary information for many applications [18], research has been conducted to extract only the essential information about potential conflicts [3,14,16,18,21]. All notions developed for *plain* rules (i.e., those without application conditions) are closely related as shown at the top of Fig. 1.

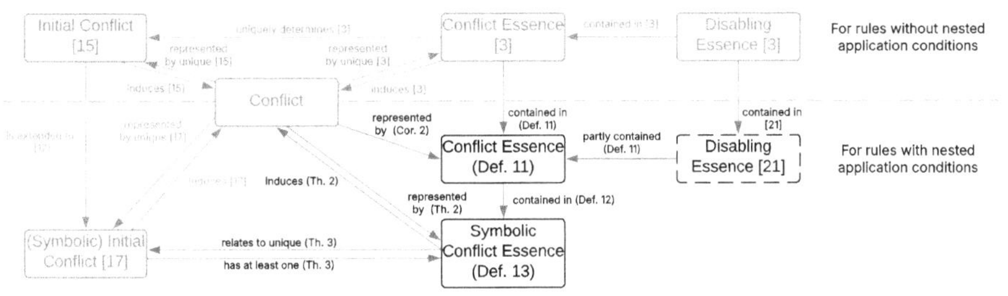

Fig. 1. Overview of concepts for conflicts between rules with and without nested application conditions (where square brackets contain literature references and round brackets refer to concepts and results of this paper).

Conflict reasons [14] or *conflict essences* [3] show the core information of a conflict, namely, the elements whose deletion leads to a conflict. Both approaches only consider plain rules. Since practical applications usually involve rules with conditions and these can be involved in conflicts, this is a significant gap in the research.

We have started to address this gap by introducing *disabling essences* for rules with application conditions in Alternating Quantifier Normal Form (ANF) [21]. These essences describe how a rule can prevent the application of another rule by either deleting its used elements or by violating its application condition. We showed that in each pair of conflicting transformations a disabling essence can be embedded. Conversely, an embedding of a disabling essence does not imply that the transformations are in conflict, which is a limitation of the theory. In this paper, we continue our work on disabling essences for rules with application conditions as follows: (1) We generalise our construction to support arbitrary nested application conditions. (2) We introduce *conflict essences* for rules with application conditions, which describe situations in which both transformations cause a conflict for the other. To achieve this, we present a construction for composing disabling essences and conflict essences. (3) We define *symbolic conflict essences*, which are *conflict essences* with additional application conditions that ensure they are only embeddable in conflictual transformation pairs. (4) We relate symbolic conflict essences to *initial conflicts* for rules with application conditions (see Fig. 1). Whereas contribution (1) is a rather straightforward extension of our work in [21], contributions (2)–(4) are results we did *not* already obtain for conditions in ANF there.

The paper is structured as follows: Sect. 2 presents related work on conflict analysis. Section 3 presents the example used throughout the paper. Section 4 presents the formal preliminaries, Sect. 5 introduces our generalised construction for disabling essences, Sect. 6 addresses conflict essences, and Sect. 7 introduces symbolic conflict essences and relates them to initial conflicts. A long version of this paper contains all proofs and additional examples [19].

2   Related Work

We have thoroughly discussed related work on the topic of this paper in [21]. Therefore, we here just focus on providing the immediate context of our work.

A *critical pair* is a pair of conflicting transformations in a minimal context and the set of all critical pairs gives an overview of all conflicts of a graph transformation system (*completeness*). Since critical pairs tend to be large objects, and even small transformation systems can induce large sets of critical pairs, two orthogonal research directions have been pursued: (1) reducing the number of critical pairs that must be computed while ensuring completeness and (2) identifying objects that contain the core information about conflicting transformations more compactly than critical pairs do. Both has been addressed first for *plain* rules and subsequently also for rules with application conditions. Regarding (1), it has been found that (under certain technical conditions) so-called *initial conflicts* are the smallest set of critical pairs that is still complete [15]; this also holds in the presence of application conditions (where initial conflicts then become *symbolic*) [17]. Regarding (2), i.e., computing the core information contained in a conflict, we [14] as well as Azzi et al. [3] introduced *(minimal) conflict reasons* and *conflict essences*, respectively, as suitable such objects and also showed their unique correspondence to initial transformations. Importantly, these works only treat plain rules. That is, a notion of conflict essences and clarification of their relation to initial conflicts is still missing in the presence of application conditions. We started work in this direction in [21], were we lift the notion of disabling essences of Azzi et al. to the setting of rules with application conditions. However, we only addressed application conditions in ANF and did not develop a composition of disabling essences to yield *conflict essences* (considering the conflicts caused by each of the two transformations for the other simultaneously) or relate them to initial conflicts – both of which we do in this paper for general application conditions.

3   Running Example

To illustrate our work, we will consider two refactoring methods [8]. Typically, a sequence of refactorings is required to achieve a larger system design improvement. Due to the potential of implicit conflicts and dependencies between refactorings, developers may have difficulties determining which refactorings to use and in what order. The identification of potential conflicts and dependencies can help developers in specifying correct refactorings.

Assuming graphs that model the class design of software systems, we consider Fig. 2 for two class model refactorings being specified as graph-based transformation rules. These rules are depicted in an integrated form (as used, e.g., in the model transformation tool Henshin [1]), with annotations specifying which graph elements are deleted, preserved, or created. The preserved and deleted elements form the Left-Hand Side (LHS) of a rule, and the preserved and created elements form the Right-Hand Side (RHS). Rule *decapsulateAttribute* removes the getter and setter methods for a given attribute, thus inverting the well-known encapsulate attribute refactoring. Rule *pullUpEncapsulatedAttribute* takes an attribute with its getter and setter methods and moves them to a superclass.

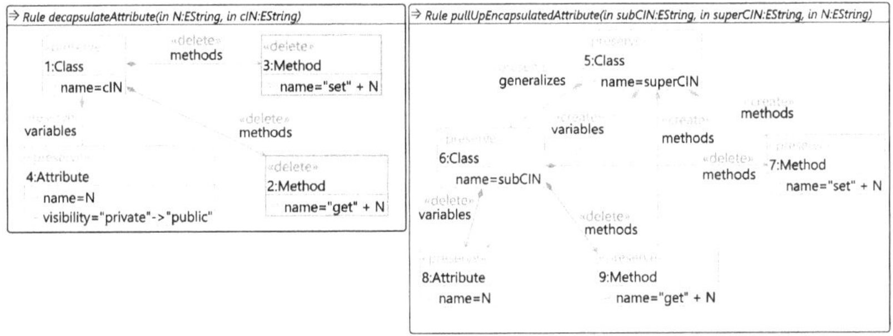

Fig. 2. Henshin rules of our running example

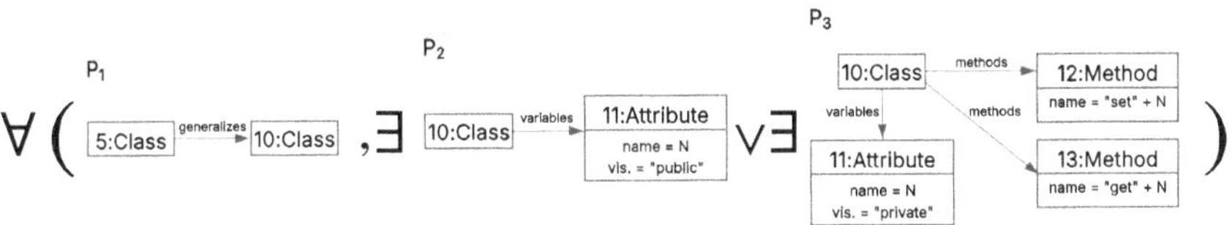

Fig. 3. Additional application condition for rule *pullUpEncapsulatedAttribute*

The rule *pullUpEncapsulatedAttribute* has an additional nested application condition that is depicted in Fig. 3. This condition specifies that all subclasses of 5:Class must also have a private attribute named N and corresponding getter and setter methods or a public attribute named N. In our presentation of the application condition, we omit morphisms and recurring parts of graphs.

4   Preliminaries

In this section, we present the preliminaries of our work. For reasons of space, we omit standard background information and technical details that are required for the proofs, but which are not necessary for understanding the main ideas of the paper. In particular, we assume familiarity with basic category theory (including the concept of adhesiveness) and the double-pushout approach to graph transformation [4,5,13]. A full introduction that covers all the necessary details can be found in [3]. Here, we recall *nested conditions* and concepts related to *parallel independence*.

Throughout our work, we make the following assumptions: we work in an adhesive HLR category $(\mathcal{C}, \mathcal{M})$ *with* all *pullbacks, initial pushouts over* $\mathcal{M}$*-morphisms, an* $\mathcal{M}$*-initial object* $\bot$*, whose outgoing arrows are denoted by* $!_A \colon \bot \hookrightarrow A$ *for any object* A*, initial transformations, binary coproducts, and a unique* $\mathcal{E}'$*-*$\mathcal{M}$ *factorization of cospans of morphisms.*

The semantics we assume for transformations in this paper is the double-pushout approach [5]. Thus, a *transformation* $t \colon G \Longrightarrow_{\rho,m} H$ comes with a span $G \overset{g}{\hookleftarrow} D \overset{h}{\hookrightarrow} H$ of $\mathcal{M}$-morphisms that has been computed via two pushouts for some transformation rule $\rho = (L \overset{l}{\longleftarrow} K \overset{r}{\longrightarrow} R, ac)$ and a match m of ρ in G (satisfying the application condition ac of ρ); G is the *input (graph)* of t, the *context (graph)* D is computed as a pushout complement (by deleting the elements specified by ρ from G), and H is computed as a pushout (by creating the elements specified by ρ on top of D). An *ac-disregarding transformation* is one for which the match does not need to satisfy the rule's application condition.

Nested Conditions. In the context of graph transformation, *nested conditions and constraints* have been developed as a suitable (graphical) formalism for expressing properties of graphs and graph homomorphisms. They have been shown to be expressively equivalent to first-order logic on graphs [10,23], but can be defined for arbitrary categories.

Definition 1 (Nested condition). *A* nested condition *over an object* P_0 *is defined recursively as follows:* **true** *is a condition over* P_0*, each Boolean combination of conditions over* P_0 *is a condition over* P_0*, and* $\exists\,(p_1 \colon P_0 \to P_1, d)$ *is a condition over* P_0 *if* d *is a condition over* P_1*. A morphism* $q \colon P_0 \to G$ *satisfies a condition* $c = \exists\,(p_1 \colon P_0 \to P_1, d)$*, denoted by* $q \models c$*, if there is an* $\mathcal{M}$*-morphism* $q_1 \colon P_1 \hookrightarrow G \in \mathcal{M}$ *so that* $q = q_1 \circ p_1$ *and* $q_1 \models d$*. Satisfaction for nested conditions composed by Boolean operators is defined as usual. We use the abbreviation* $\forall\,(p_0 \colon P_0 \to P_1, d) := \neg\exists\,(p_0 \colon P_0 \to P_1, \neg d)$*. The object* P_1 *in a condition of the form* $\exists\,(p_0 \colon P_0 \to P_1, d)$ *is called* existentially bound *and the object* P_1 *in a condition of the form* $\forall\,(p_0 \colon P_0 \to P_1, d)$ *is called* universally bound.

In this paper, we make the following assumptions about all conditions: (i) All morphisms appearing in a condition are $\mathcal{M}$-morphisms, except potentially those starting at the object P_0 over which the condition is defined (i.e., the condition is in $\mathcal{M}$-*normal form*); (ii) no isomorphisms appear in a condition; (iii) all negations are pushed inward as far as possible by eliminating double negations, replacing existential quantifiers with universal ones (and vice versa), and applying De Morgan's law (in this way, it is unambiguous whether an object is bound existentially or universally). *These assumptions do not restrict the expressivity of the considered conditions;* the desired presentation can be achieved by applying well-established equivalence rules [10, 22].

Conditions can be shifted along morphisms and left-translated along rules using operations called Shift and Left, respectively, in such a way that the semantics of the conditions are preserved [5, 10]. We will use these operations in the following without recalling their definitions.

Parallel Independence. Two *parallel independent* transformations do not interfere with each other. This concept is formally captured by the Local Church–Rosser theorem [4], which states that two such transformations can be applied in any order. We recall the definition of parallel independence and revisit the notion of a *disabling essence* [3] for analysing transformations that *conflict* with each other, i.e., those that are not parallel independent.

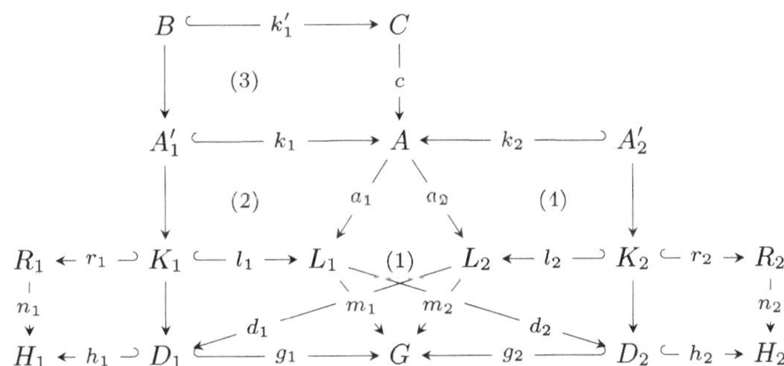

Fig. 4. Parallel independence and construction of disabling essence

Definition 2 (Parallel independence). *Given two rules* $\rho_j = (L_j \hookleftarrow K_j \hookrightarrow R_j, ac_j)$, *with* $j = 1, 2$, *two transformations* $(t_1, t_2) = (G \Longrightarrow_{\rho_1, m_1} H_1, G \Longrightarrow_{\rho_2, m_2} H_2)$ *are* parallel independent *if there are morphisms* $d_1 : L_2 \to D_1$ *and* $d_2 : L_1 \to D_2$ *to the contexts of* t_1 *and* t_2 *so that* $m_2 = g_1 \circ d_1$, $m_1 = g_2 \circ d_2$, $h_1 \circ d_1 \models ac_2$, *and* $h_2 \circ d_2 \models ac_1$ *(as shown in Fig. 4). If the morphism* d_1 *does not exist, or if* $h_1 \circ d_1 \not\models ac_2$, *we say that* t_1 *causes a conflict for* t_2. *We say that* t_1 *and* t_2 *are* parallel independent ac-disregarding *if both morphisms* d_j *exist.*

A transformation via a plain rule causes a conflict with another such transformation if it deletes items that the second transformation also requires. A *disabling essence* captures exactly this problematic structure and its occurrence in conflicting transformations. The construction can be introduced for arbitrary cospans of the LHSs of rules, leading to the notion of a *proto-essence*, whereas only matches for transformations lead to a *disabling essence*.

Definition 3 (Proto-/disabling essence [3]). *Given two plain rules $\rho_j = L_j \hookleftarrow K_j \hookrightarrow R_j$ and morphisms $m_j \colon L_j \to G$, with $j = 1, 2$, the proto-essence for (m_1, m_2) under l_1, denoted by $\mathrm{ess}_{l_1}(m_1, m_2)$, is defined as $(a_1 \circ c, a_2 \circ c)$, where the squares (1) and (2) in Fig. 4 are pullbacks and (3) is the initial pushout over k_1. C is called the* essence object. *A proto-essence $\mathrm{ess}_{l_1}(m_1, m_2)$ is a* disabling essence *if m_1 and m_2 are matches for transformations t_1 and t_2 as in Fig. 4; in that case, it is denoted as $\mathrm{ess}_{\mathrm{dbl}}(t_1, t_2)$ and called the* disabling essence *of (t_1, t_2).*

For ease of notation, we will sometimes drop the morphism c in proto-essences if it is not needed. Crucially, transformation t_1 causes a conflict for t_2 if and only if the disabling essence $\mathrm{ess}_{\mathrm{dbl}}(t_1, t_2)$ is not trivial, i.e., if it is not the pair of morphisms $(!_{L_1} \colon \bot \to L_1, !_{L_2} \colon \bot \to L_2)$ [3, Theorem 3.13].

Initial Conflicts. Starting with the notion of critical pairs, parallel (in)dependence of transformation pairs has been related to the kind of transformation pairs they *extend*, culminating in the concept of *initial conflicts* [14,17] and, for plain rules, the construction of initial conflicts from *conflict reasons* [3, Theorem 4.4]. In this paper, we continue this line of research to complete the picture for rules with application conditions. The following definitions briefly introduce the necessary concepts. For a detailed introduction to symbolic transformation pairs, the construction of the application conditions, and initial conflicts, we refer to [3,6,17].

Definition 4 (Extension of transformation. Initial transformation pair). *Given a transformation $t = G \Longrightarrow_{\rho,m} H$, an extension of t is a transformation $t' = G' \Longrightarrow_{\rho,m'} H'$ such that there is an extension morphism $f \colon G \to G'$ with $f \circ m = m'$ such that f is a match in G' for the transformation $t \colon G \hookleftarrow D \hookrightarrow H$ when considered as rule.*

Given a transformation pair (t_1, t_2), an initial transformation pair *for (t_1, t_2) is an ac-disregarding transformation pair (t_1^I, t_2^I) such that (i) there is a common extension morphism f^I from the transformation t_1^I to t_1 and from t_2^I to t_2 and (ii) the transformation pair (t_1^I, t_2^I) factors uniquely through any other transformation pair that (t_1, t_2) extends by a common extension morphism.*

Definition 5 (Symbolic transformation pair and initial conflict). *Given two rules ρ_1 and ρ_2, a symbolic transformation pair $stp_G = (tp_G, ac_G, ac_G^*)$ consists of a pair $tp_G \colon H_1 {}_{\rho_1, m_1} \!\!\Longleftarrow G \Longrightarrow_{\rho_2, m_2} H_2$ of ac-disregarding transformations and conditions ac_G, ac_G^* over G defined as $ac_G = \mathrm{Shift}(m_1, ac_1) \wedge \mathrm{Shift}(m_2, ac_2)$ and $ac_G^* = \neg(ac_{G,d_1}^* \wedge ac_{G,d_2}^*)$, where $ac_{G,d_1}^* = \mathrm{false}$ if d_1 does not exist and*

$$ac_{G,d_1}^* = \mathrm{Left}(G \hookleftarrow D_1 \hookrightarrow H_1, \mathrm{Shift}(h_1 \circ d_1, ac_2))$$

otherwise (analogously for ac^*_{G,d_2}).

An initial conflict *for two rules ρ_1 and ρ_2 is a symbolic transformation pair $stp_K = (tp_K, ac_K, ac^*_K)$ such that tp_K is (i) an initial transformation pair for itself and (ii) is* conflict-inducing, *i.e., it extends to at least one conflicting pair of transformations $H_1\ {}_{m_1,\rho_1} \Longleftarrow G \Longrightarrow_{m_2,\rho_2} H_2$.*

In the construction of symbolic transformation pairs, ac_G indicates when extending transformation pairs satisfy the rules' application conditions and ac^*_G indicates when an extending pair of transformations is in conflict. A transformation pair is in conflict if and only if an initial conflict $stp_K = (tp_K, ac_K, ac^*_K)$ extends to it and the extension morphism satisfies the condition $ac_K \wedge ac^*_K$. Given two rules, the initial conflict $(R_1 + L_2\ {}_{i_{L_1},\rho_1} \Longleftarrow L_1 + L_2 \Longrightarrow_{i_{L_2},\rho_2} L_1 + R_2, ac_{L_1+L_2}, ac^*_{L_1+L_2})$, where i_{L_1} and i_{L_2} are obtained by the universal property of the coproduct, plays an important role in Sect. 7 of this paper, as it is the only initial conflict that indicates a conflict caused solely by violations of the application conditions. We refer to it as the *symbolic initial conflict.*

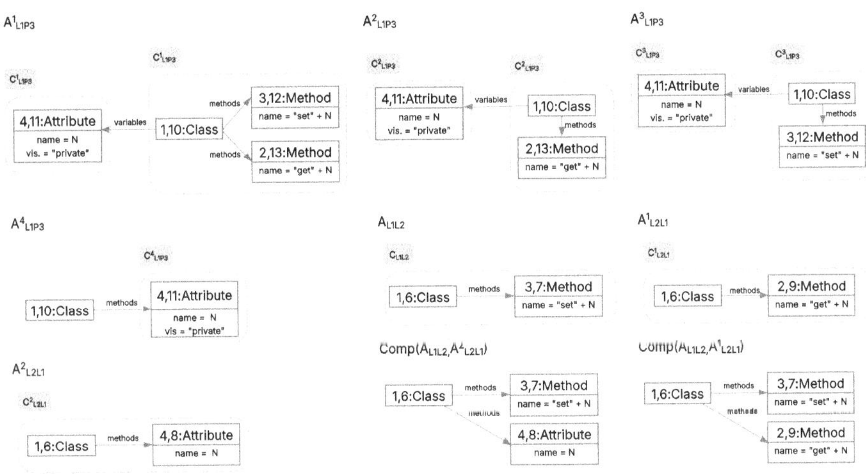

Fig. 5. Disabling essences of *decapsulateAttribute* and *pullUpEncapsulatedAttribute* and composed essences

5   Construction and Embedding of Disabling Essences

In this section, we extend the notion of *disabling essences* to cover arbitrary nested application conditions and develop a concept for embedding these into transformation pairs. To convey some intuition, we first continue our running example and then develop the formal details.

Example 1 (Disabling essences). Fig. 5 shows a selection of the disabling essences for the two rules in Fig. 2. The graphs with gray borders show how the LHSs and/or application condition graphs need to overlap in a pair of transformations for a conflict to potentially occur. The inner graphs with orange borders constitute the essence graphs, and the identifiers in the nodes indicate how the graphs are mapped to the LHSs and/or application condition graphs.

First, both rules can conflict with each other by matching to the same Methods and/or Attribute. The disabling essences A_{L1L2}, A^1_{L2L1}, and A^2_{L2L1} can be computed using the methods developed for plain rules in [3,14]. Importantly, when the two rules are matched as indicated by one of these essences, the resulting transformation pair is guaranteed to be conflicting.

Second, the *decapsulateAttribute* rule can conflict with the *pullUpEncapsulatedAttribute* rule by invalidating its application condition. To capture the core structure of these conflicts in a manner similar to that of classic disabling essences for plain rules, we expect results as displayed in the first and second row of Fig. 5 (cases A^1_{L1P3}–A^4_{L1P3}). The *decapsulateAttribute* rule can invalidate *pullUpEncapsulatedAttribute's* application condition by deleting an occurrence of P_3 in Fig. 3, for which there are different possibilities (e.g. deleting the getter or setter method, setting the visibility to public, or combinations thereof. While not possible in this example (given the semantics of the *decapsulateAttribute* rule), in principle *pullUpEncapsulatedAttribute's* application condition can also be invalidated by a rule creating an occurrence of the graph P_1 or deleting an occurrence of P_2. This occurs, for instance, with the rule *encapsulateAttribute*, the inverse of *decapsulateAttribute*, which switches the visibility of the attribute from public to private.

On closer inspection of the example, it becomes apparent that, in principle, disabling essences between rules and application conditions can be found through overlaps in the same way as disabling essences between plain rules. The central structural difference is that these overlaps are no longer restricted to the LHSs of the rules, but also involve the application condition graphs. Moreover, conflicts cannot only arise from the deletion of existentially bound graphs of the application condition (as illustrated above) but also from the creation of universally bound graphs: A further refactoring rule could invalidate applications of *pullUpEncapsulatedAttribute* by creating occurrences of P_1 (newly inserting inheriting classes). Importantly, (i) at points of bifurcation (like the disjunction in our example) all options have to be considered because each one can be the source of a conflict, and (ii) creating actions can also cause conflicts. Finally, the central semantic difference from the situation with plain rules is that matching a pair of rules as indicated by a disabling essence no longer guarantees a conflicting transformation pair. In our example, the deletion of an occurrence of P_3 may be compensated for by the presence of an occurrence of P_2, and vice versa. Moreover, even though it is semantically dubious in our specific example, there could be several occurrences of the graphs P_2 and P_3, such that deleting one of them would not invalidate the application condition.

In this section, we present the construction of disabling essences for rules with *arbitrary nested application conditions*. We started this work in [21], where we computed disabling essences for application conditions in ANF. This is a special case in which a condition is essentially a chain of morphisms (i.e., there are no points of bifurcation caused by conjunction or disjunction). The restriction in [21] mainly served to simplify the presentation. When conditions are in ANF, disabling essences can be computed using the construction developed in [2,3] for plain rules, which is then applied iteratively along the chain of morphisms that constitute the condition. For arbitrary conditions, whose morphisms form a tree structure (which we will introduce next; compare also [24]), the situation is slightly more involved. The construction must be applied iteratively along each path from the root to a leaf of the tree.

Definition 6 (Tree structure of a condition). *Given a condition c over an object P_0, the tree structure of c is a graph $\mathrm{Tr}(c) = (V_{\mathrm{Tr}(c)}, E_{\mathrm{Tr}(c)}, \mathrm{src}_{\mathrm{Tr}(c)}, \mathrm{tar}_{\mathrm{Tr}(c)})$ which is recursively constructed as follows: If $c = \bigodot_{i \in \mathcal{I}} Q(p_1^i : P_0 \to P_1^i, d_i)$ for some index set $\mathcal{I}$, $\odot \in \{\vee, \wedge\}$, and $Q \in \{\exists, \forall\}$, we set $V_{\mathrm{Tr}(c)} = \bigcup_{i \in \mathcal{I}} V_{\mathrm{Tr}(d_i)} \cup \{P_0\}$, $E_{\mathrm{Tr}(c)} = \bigcup_{i \in \mathcal{I}} (E_{\mathrm{Tr}(d_i)} \cup \{p_1^i\})$, $\mathrm{src}_{\mathrm{Tr}(c)} = \bigcup_{i \in \mathcal{I}} (\mathrm{src}_{\mathrm{Tr}(d_i)} \cup \{(p_1^i, P_0)\})$, and $\mathrm{tar}_{\mathrm{Tr}(c)} = \bigcup_{i \in \mathcal{I}} (\mathrm{tar}_{\mathrm{Tr}(d_i)} \cup \{(p_1^i, P_1^i)\})$. If $c = \mathbf{true}$ is a condition over P_i, we set $\mathrm{Tr}(\mathbf{true}) = (P_i, \emptyset, \emptyset, \emptyset)$, and $\mathrm{Tr}(c) = \mathrm{Tr}(c')$ if $c = \neg c'$. Each node of $\mathrm{Tr}(c)$ without outgoing edges is called a leaf, the set of all leaves is denoted by $\mathrm{Leaves}(\mathrm{Tr}(c))$.*

Example 2 (Tree structure). Fig. 3 shows the application condition of the *pullUpEncapsulatedAttribute* rule. The tree structure of this condition has four nodes starting with the LHS of the rule as root, which is embedded into graph P_1, which is again embedded into P_2 and into P_3, the two leaves of the tree.

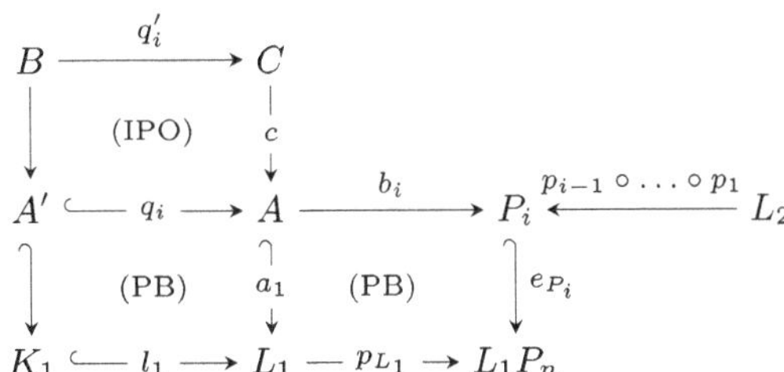

Fig. 6. Construction of proto-essences for rules with application conditions

Next, we define *proto-essences* for rules with application conditions; these are later filtered to obtain *disabling essences*. For their construction, we consider each path p in the tree structure of the second rule's application condition that starts at the root and ends at a leaf. For each overlap (cospan) between the LHS L_1 of the first rule and a leaf P_n, we iteratively calculate whether applying the rule can destroy an occurrence of a graph P_i contained within the path. We achieve this by applying the computation of proto-essences of plain rules to L_1 and P_i for all $i \leq n$. If such an object is found, a *proto-essence by deletion* has been identified. To account for the fact that the first rule might also invalidate the second rule's application condition by creating an occurrence of one of its objects P_i, we also define *proto-essences by insertion*. These are computed analogously to the ones by deletion, just using the RHS R_1 of the first rule instead of its LHS L_1.

Definition 7 (Proto-essence for rules with conditions). *Let two rules* $\rho_j = (L_j \xleftarrow{l_j} K_j \xrightarrow{r_j} R_j, ac_j)$, *with* $j = 1, 2$, *the tree-representation* $\mathrm{Tr}(ac_2)$ *of* ac_2, *an object* $P_n \in \mathrm{Leaves}(\mathrm{Tr}(ac_2)) \cup \{L_2\}$, *a path* $p_{L_2} = p_n \circ \ldots p_1$ *from* L_2 *to* P_n *in* $\mathrm{Tr}(ac_2)$, *and a cospan* $(e_{L_1} : L_1 \to L_1 P_n, e_{P_n} : P_n \hookrightarrow L_1 P_n) \in \mathcal{E}'$ *be given. The* proto-essence by deletion *of* e_{L_1} *and* e_{P_n} *at level* $1 \leq i \leq n$, *denoted as* $\mathrm{DPEss}^i(e_{L_1}, e_{P_n})$, *is defined as*

$$\mathrm{DPEss}^0(e_{L_1}, e_{P_n}) := \mathrm{ess}_{l_1}(e_{L_1}, e_{P_1} \circ p_1),$$

$$\mathrm{DPEss}^i(e_{L_1}, e_{P_n}) := \begin{cases} \mathrm{DPEss}^{i-1}(e_{L_1}, e_{P_n}) & \text{if } \mathrm{DPEss}^{i-1}(e_{L_1}, e_{P_n}) \neq (!_{L_1}, !_{P_{i-1}}) \\ \mathrm{ess}_{l_1}(e_{L_1}, e_{P_i}) & \text{if } \mathrm{DPEss}^{i-1}(e_{L_1}, e_{P_n}) = (!_{L_1}, !_{P_{i-1}}) \end{cases},$$

where $p_n \circ \ldots \circ p_{i+1}$ *is the path from* P_i *to* P_n *in* $\mathrm{Tr}(ac_2)$ *(and* P_i *is an object contained in the path from* L_2 *to* P_n*) and* $e_{P_i} := e_{P_n} \circ p_n \circ \ldots \circ p_{i+1}$ *(see Fig. 6). The* set of proto-essences by deletion *of* ρ_1 *in* ρ_2, *denoted by* $\mathrm{DPEss}(\rho_1, \rho_2)$, *is the set of all proto-essences by deletion at level* n *of morphism pairs* $(e_{L_1} : L_1 \to L_1 P_n, e_{P_n} : P_n \hookrightarrow L_1 P_n) \in \mathcal{E}'$ *of all leaves* P_n *contained in* $\mathrm{Tr}(ac_2)$.

The set of proto-essences by insertion, *denoted by* $\mathrm{IPEss}(\rho_1, \rho_2)$ *is defined as* $\mathrm{IPEss}(\rho_1, \rho_2) :- \mathrm{DPEss}(\rho_1^{-1}, \rho_2)$ *where we stop the recursion at* $i = 1$.

Example 3 (Construction of a proto-essence by deletion). In this example, we sketch the computation of a proto-essence by deletion between L_1 of *decapsulateAttribute* and the path L_2, p_1, P_1, p_3, P_3 in the application condition of *pullUpEncapsulatedAttribute*; a detailed version is provided in [19]. Figure 7 shows the crucial part of the computation, not displaying graphs that are already known or identical to other graphs displayed.

The construction starts with the overlap $L_1 P_3 = P_3$ of L_1 and P_3, to which P_3 is mapped via the identity morphism $e_{P_3} = id_{P_3}$ and L_1 by the morphism that is fixed by mapping 1:Class to 10:Class. It proceeds by computing the proto-essence by deletion at level 0, which is done by computing the pullback for L_1 and L_2 in $L_1 P_3$, resulting in A_0 (the empty graph), followed by computing the pullback of A_0 and K_1 in L_1, resulting in A_0' (also the empty graph). That A_0 and A_0' are isomorphic indicates that the proto-essence at this level will be trivial; we therefore continue to further levels, which are computed analogously. The computation at level 1 is done using P_1 instead of L_2, leading to isomorphic graphs A_1 and A_1', again indicative of a trivial proto-essence at this level. At level 2, we then use P_3 instead of L_2 and compute A_2 and A_2', which are not isomorphic. Because the proto-essences computed at lower levels were trivial, the

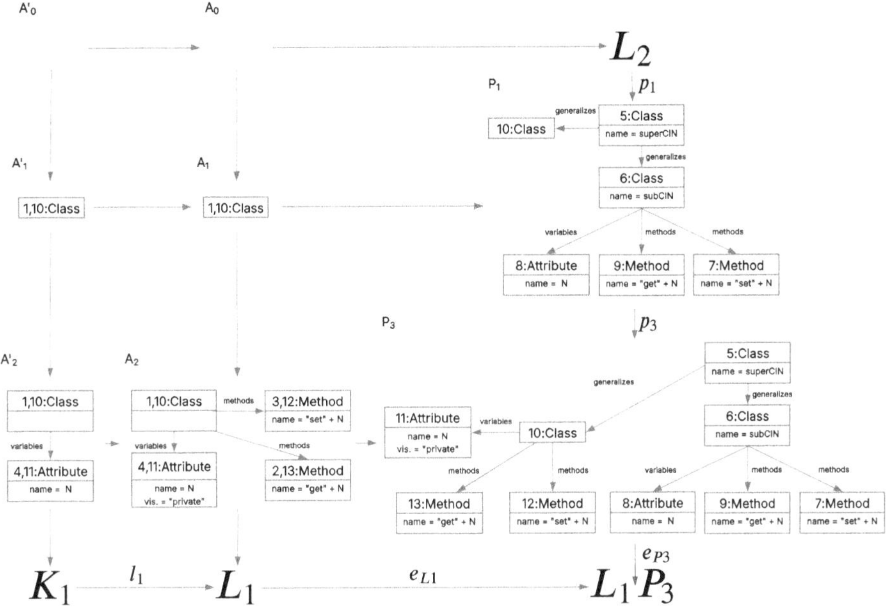

Fig. 7. Central extract of the construction of proto-essences by deletion of the rules *decapsulateAttribute* and *pullUpEncapsulatedAttribute*

proto-essence by deletion at level 2 turns out to be *the* proto-essence by deletion for the considered overlap $L_1 P_3$.

The actual essence graph is obtained by computing the initial pushout over the morphism from A_2' to A_2. It indicates as potential cause of a conflict that *decapsulateAttribute* simultaneously deletes the getter and setter methods and disables the attribute's visibility necessary for *pullUpEncapsulatedAttribute*'s application condition to be valid. It is displayed as $\mathsf{A}^1_{\mathsf{L1P3}}$ in Fig. 5.

To define *disabling essences*, we need a notion of *embeddability* for proto-essences. To be able to provide a single definition of *embeddability* that also covers the further kinds of essences we introduce in this paper, we first define *rule overlaps* (capturing the structure all essences have) and then define embeddings for rule overlaps.

Definition 8 (Rule overlap. Embedding of rule overlap). *Given two rules* $\rho_1 = (L_1 \xleftarrow{l_1} K_1 \xrightarrow{r_1} R_1, ac_1)$, $\rho_2 = (L_2 \xleftarrow{l_2} K_2 \xrightarrow{r_2} R_2, ac_2)$, *an overlap of* ρ_1 *and* ρ_2 *is a tuple* $ro = (b_j \colon A \to P_j, b_i \colon A \to P_i, p_{L_1} \colon L_1 \to P_j, p_{L_2} \colon L_2 \to P_i)$. *Here,* $P_j = L_1$ *and/or* $P_i = L_2$ *is allowed. A pair of morphisms* $(m_1^j \colon P_j \to G, m_2^i \colon P_j \to G)$ *is an embedding of* ro *in a transformation pair* $(t_1, t_2) = (G \Longrightarrow_{\rho_1, m_1} H_1, G \Longrightarrow_{\rho_2, m_2} H_2)$ *if* $m_1 = m_1^j \circ p_{L_1}$, $m_2 = m_2^i \circ p_{L_2}$ *and the square (1) in Fig. 8 is a pullback.*

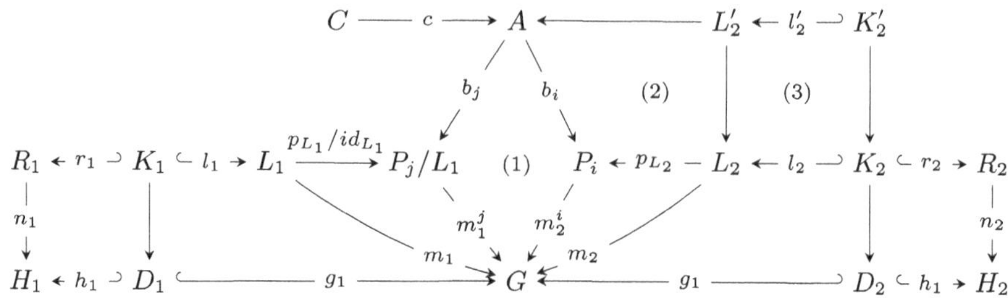

Fig. 8. Diagram for the embedding of rule overlaps and ac-conflicting disabling essences. Consider the alternatives P_j for the embedding of rule overlaps and L_1 (separated by "/") for ac-conflicting disabling essences

Disabling essences for rules with application conditions can now be defined analogously to [21]. For reasons of space, the exact construction will not be presented in this section, as it involves a somewhat lengthier construction to *shift* proto-essences by insertion so that both kinds of essences are defined as the same kinds of spans. Intuitively, the definition of disabling essences filters out proto-essences that can never indicate a conflict by requiring that a disabling essence (i) is non-trivial, (ii) can actually be embedded in a transformation pair, and (iii) indicates the creation of a universally bound object or the deletion of an existentially bound one (but not vice versa); this final requirement is well-defined if conditions are given as assumed here, i.e., if all negations are pushed inwards as far as possible. Importantly, given the more general definition of proto-essences here, the requirements for disabling essences remain identical to those presented in [21]. Moreover, each result presented in [21] directly transfers to our extended construction. We have included the concrete definition of *disabling essences* and re-proved the main results of [21] in the long version of this paper [19].

6 From Disabling Essences to Conflict Essences

The disabling essences constructed in the previous section are "asymmetric" in that they only indicate potential conflicts in one direction. Next, we introduce *conflict essences for rules with application conditions* that capture potential conflicts between rules in both directions simultaneously. These conflict essences are defined by composing the disabling essences for both directions.

When we start to compose disabling essences, i.e., when we consider the effects of both transformations on each other, some of the disabling essences that we previously computed become obsolete: A disabling essence $de = (b_1 \circ c \colon C \to L_1, b_i \circ c \colon C \to P_i) \in \mathrm{DEss}(\rho_1, \rho_2)$ indicates that the application of ρ_1 can prevent the application of ρ_2 by invalidating its application condition (by destroying an occurrence of P_i). However, when the roles are switched, the overlap used to compute de may instead produce a disabling essence $de' = (b_2 \circ c' \colon C \to L_2, b'_1 \circ c' \colon C' \to L_1) \in \mathrm{DEss}(\rho_2, \rho_1)$, which indicates that the application of ρ_2

can prevent the application of ρ_1 by destroying its match. In other words, when this disabling essence is embedded in a pair of transformations, the underlying ac-disregarding transformations are already in conflict. We introduce *ac-conflicting rule overlaps* which imply ac-disregarding parallel independence (i.e., neither transformation destroys the match of the other) when embedded in a transformation pair. Once again, we use *rule overlaps* to ensure that the definition can be applied to any kind of essence considered in this paper.

Definition 9 (Ac-conflicting rule overlap). *Given rules ρ_1 and ρ_2, a rule overlap ro of them is called* ac-conflicting *if there is an ac-disregarding parallel independent transformation pair (t_1, t_2) via ρ_1 and ρ_2 into which ro embeds.*

The following result shows that each transformation pair in which an ac-conflicting rule overlap is embedded is parallel independent ac-disregarding.

Proposition 1 (Disjoint sets of ac-conflicting and non-ac-conflicting rule overlaps). *If a rule overlap ro is* ac-conflicting, *then each transformation pair (t_1, t_2) such that ro is embeddable in (t_1, t_2) is parallel independent ac-disregarding. Moreover, if a non-ac-conflicting rule overlap is embeddable in a transformation pair (t_1, t_2), this pair is parallel dependent ac-disregarding.*

The following criterion can be used to decide whether a disabling essence $(b_1 \colon A \to L_1, b_j \colon A \to P_j)$ of a rule pair is ac-conflicting; we illustrate its use in the long version of our paper [19].

Proposition 2 (Ac-conflicting disabling essences). *Given rules ρ_1 and ρ_2, a disabling essence $ce = (b_1 \colon A \to L_1, b_i \colon A \to P_i, id_{L_1}, p_{L_2}) \in \mathrm{DEss}(\rho_1, \rho_2)$ is ac-conflicting if and only if the morphism l'_2, which is obtained by computing the pullbacks (2) and (3) shown in Fig. 8, is an isomorphism.*

We now develop a construction for composing rule overlaps (encompassing disabling essences) in such a way that composed overlaps can be embedded in a transformation pair if the individual overlaps are embedded in it, and vice versa.

Definition 10 (Composition of rule overlaps). *Given two rule overlaps*
$$ro = (P_i \xleftarrow{b_i} A \xrightarrow{b_j} P_j, e_{L_1}, e_{L_2}) \text{ and } ro' = (P'_i \xleftarrow{b'_i} A' \xrightarrow{b'_j} P'_j, e'_{L_1}, e'_{L_2}), \text{ the set of}$$
compositions of ro and ro', denoted by $\mathrm{Comp}(ro, ro')$, contains each rule overlap
$$(P^*_j \xleftarrow{b^*_j} A^* \xhookrightarrow{b^*_i} P^*_i, e_{P_j} \circ p_{L_1}, e_{P_i} \circ p_{L_2}) \text{ so that } (e_{P_j} \colon P_j \to P^*_j, e_{P'_j} \colon P'_j \to P^*_j),$$
$(e_{P_i} \colon P_i \to P^*_i, e_{P'_i} \colon P'_i \to P^*_i), (e_{P^*_j} \colon P^*_j \hookrightarrow K^*, e_{P^*_i} \colon P^*_j \hookrightarrow K^*) \in \mathcal{E}', e_{P_j} \circ p_{L_1} = e_{P'_j} \circ p'_{L_1}, e_{P_i} \circ p_{L_2} = e_{P'_i} \circ p'_{L_2}$, *the outer squares in the diagrams shown in Fig. 9 are pullbacks and b^*_j and b^*_i are obtained by computing the pullback (1).*

The following example briefly illustrates the result of composing rule overlaps; we illustrate a computation in detail in the long version of our paper [19].

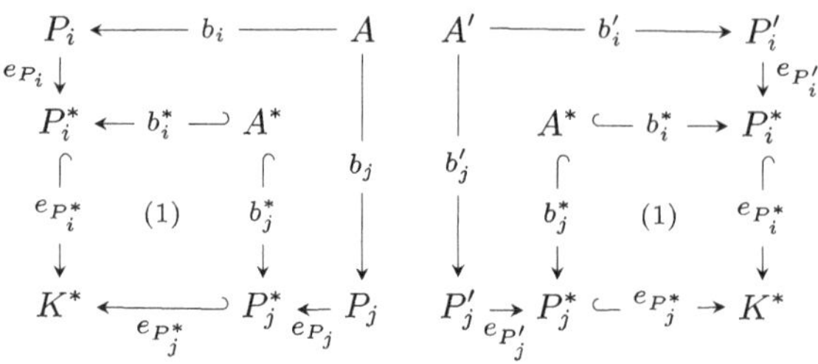

Fig. 9. Diagram for the composition of rule overlaps

Example 4 (Composed rule overlap).

The composed rule overlap $\mathsf{Comp}(A_{L1L2}, A^1_{L2L1})$ in Fig. 5 indicates that A_{L1L2} and A^1_{L2L1} can be embedded in the same transformation by identifying 1,6:Class. An occurrence of this composed overlap simultaneously indicates (i) that *decapsulateAttribute* causes a conflict with *pullUpEncapsulatedAttribute* by destroying 3,7:Method and (ii) that *pullUpEncapsulatedAttribute* causes a conflict with *decapsulateAttribute* by destroying the edge leading to 2,9: Method.

We show that the desired property of composed rule overlaps is satisfied, i.e., that a composed overlap is embedded in a transformation pair if and only if both of its constituent rule overlaps are also embedded in the pair.

Theorem 1 (Embedding of composed rule overlaps). *Given two rule overlaps ro and ro$'$ of two rules ρ_1, and ρ_2, if both rule overlaps ro and ro$'$ are embeddable in a transformation pair (t_1, t_2) via ρ_1 and ρ_2, then there is a composed overlap co $\in \mathrm{Comp}(ro, ro')$ that is also embeddable in (t_1, t_2). Conversely, if any composed overlap co $\in \mathrm{Comp}(ro, ro')$ is embedded in a transformation pair (t_1, t_2) via ρ_1 and ρ_2, then both ro and ro$'$ are also embedded in (t_1, t_2).*

A crucial observation is that if both rule overlaps are ac-conflicting, then so are all composed overlaps. This statement follows directly from the second part of Theorem 1. We will use this result later on when comparing conflict essences (which encompass composed disabling essences) with initial conflicts for rules with application conditions.

Corollary 1 (Inheritance of ac-conflicting rule overlaps). *Given two ac-conflicting rule overlaps ro and ro$'$ of rules ρ_1 and ρ_2, each composed overlap ce $\in \mathrm{Comp}(ro, ro')$ is ac-conflicting.*

We now define *conflict essences*, which provide an overview on how two transformations can cause a conflict for each other. To construct conflict essences, we compose rule overlaps, in which the first transformation causes a conflict with the second and the second transformation causes a conflict with the first. All disabling essences from Fig. 5 and, in particular, the composed rule overlap from Example 4 are conflict essences.

Definition 11 (Set of conflict essences).
Given two rules $\rho_j = (L_j \hookleftarrow K_j \hookrightarrow R_j, ac_j)$, with $j = 1, 2$, the set of conflict essences of ρ_1 and ρ_2, denoted by $\mathrm{CEss}(\rho_1, \rho_2)$, is recursively defined as follows:

1. *A disabling essence $de = (b_i \colon A \to P_i, b_j \colon A \to P_j) \in \mathrm{DEss}(\rho_1, \rho_2) \cup \mathrm{DEss}(\rho_2, \rho_1)$ is a conflict essence for ρ_1 and ρ_2 if and only if (i) de is ac-conflicting or (ii) $P_i = L_1$ and $P_j = L_2$.*
2. *If ce_1 and ce_2 are conflict essences so that both are either ac-conflicting or non-ac-conflicting, then every composed rule overlap $ce^* \in \mathrm{Comp}(ce_1, ce_2)$ is a conflict essence.*

The following corollary directly follows from the fact that, for each parallel dependent transformation pair, there is a disabling essence that embeds in it [21]. This is because the set of conflict essences contains each ac-conflicting disabling essence in both directions.

For ac-disregarding parallel dependent transformations, the claim follows from the fact that the set of conflict essences contains each conflict essence for plain rules, together with the results shown in [3].

Corollary 2 (Embedding of conflict essences). *Given a pair of parallel dependent transformations $(t_1, t_2) = (G \Longrightarrow_{\rho_1, m_1} H_1, G \Longrightarrow_{\rho_2, m_2} H_2)$ via rules ρ_1 and ρ_2, there is a conflict essence $ce \in \mathrm{CEss}(\rho_1, \rho_2)$ that is embeddable in (t_1, t_2).*

7 Symbolic Conflict Essences and Initial Conflicts

In this section, we introduce *symbolic conflict essences*, which consist of conflict essences accompanied by a nested condition. As with initial conflicts, the embedding morphisms of a conflict essence satisfy the corresponding condition if and only if the transformation pair is parallel dependent. This ensures that a *symbolic conflict essence* is embedded in a transformation pair if and only if the transformation pair is parallel dependent. Moreover, each embedded symbolic conflict essence indicates a location at which an occurrence of an application condition object is destroyed (or created), or a rule match is destroyed. We relate each symbolic conflict essence to a unique initial conflict. We then use the condition of the initial conflict to construct the condition of the conflict essence using the well-known shift operator for nested conditions [10].

To ensure that the condition of a *symbolic conflict essence* is satisfied if and only if the transformation pair is parallel dependent, both embedding morphisms of the conflict essence embedding must satisfy the corresponding condition. To achieve this, we introduce *cospan conditions*, which establish a way to restrict the satisfaction of conditions. Rather than using a single morphism, we will use a cospan on the first nesting level of the condition (whereas the condition itself is a nested condition as usual).

Definition 12 (cospan condition). *Given two objects P_0 and P_0', $cc = \exists(P_0 \xrightarrow{p_1} P_1 \xleftarrow{p_1'} P_0', d)$ is a* cospan condition *over P_0 and P_0' if d is a condition over P_1. Morever, every Boolean combination of cospan conditions over P_0 and P_0' is a cospan condition over P_0 and P_0'.*

Two morphisms $q\colon P_0 \to G$ and $q'\colon P_0' \to G$ satisfy the cospan condition cc, denoted by $(q, q') \models cc$, if there is a morphism $q_1\colon P_1 \to G$ so that $q_1 \models d$, $q = q_1 \circ p_1$ and $q' = q_1 \circ p_1'$.

Next, we introduce *symbolic conflict essences*. To relate each *conflict essence* to an initial conflict, we must consider two different cases: Either the conflict essence is ac-conflicting, or it is not. For a non-ac-conflicting conflict essence, there is no need of an additional condition to check for parallel dependence, since an embedding of a non-ac-conflicting conflict essence already shows (ac-disregarding) parallel dependence (Proposition 1). Therefore, the condition of ac-conflicting conflict essences is true.

If an ac-conflicting conflict essence is embeddable in a transformation pair, the pair is parallel independent and ac-disregarding (Proposition 1). This means that the symbolic initial conflict is also embeddable in this transformation pair [17, Lemma 4], and we can use the condition of the symbolic initial conflict to construct the condition for the conflict essence. If the symbolic initial conflict is embedded in a transformation pair, the transformation pair is parallel dependent ac-disregarding. Although each symbolic conflict essence uniquely corresponds to an initial conflict, the conflict essence is much more informative because it compactly encodes the root cause(s) of the conflicts present in the transformation pairs in which it is embedded.

Definition 13 (Symbolic conflict essence). *Given two rules $\rho_j = (L_j \hookleftarrow K_j \hookrightarrow R_j, ac_j)$, with $j = 1, 2$, and a conflict essence $ce = (b_i \circ c\colon C \to P_i, b_j \circ c\colon C \to P_j) \in \mathrm{DEss}(\rho_1, \rho_2)$, the pair (ce, ac_{ce}) is a symbolic conflict essence where*

$$ac_{ce} \coloneq \exists(P_i \xrightarrow{b_j'} D \xleftarrow{b_i'} P_j, \mathrm{Shift}(m^*, ac_{L_1+L_2} \wedge ac_{L_1+L_2}^*))$$

if ce is ac-conflicting, and $ac_{ce} \coloneq$ true otherwise.

The morphism b_j' is obtained by computing the pushout (1) in Fig. 10, $m^*\colon L_1 + L_2 \to D$ is the morphism obtained by the universal property of the coproduct $L_1 + L_2$ and $(R_1 + L_2 \underset{i_{L_1}, \rho_1}{\Longleftarrow} L_1 + L_2 \underset{i_{L_2}, \rho_2}{\Longrightarrow} L_1 + R_2, ac_{L_1+L_2}, ac_{L_1+L_2}^*)$ is the symbolic intitial conflict.

The set of symbolic conflict essences of the rules ρ_1 and ρ_2, denoted by $\mathrm{SCEss}(\rho_1, \rho_2)$, is defined as $\mathrm{SCEss}(\rho_1, \rho_2) \coloneq \{(ce, ac_{ce}) \mid ce \in \mathrm{CEss}(\rho_1, \rho_2)\}$.

Remark 1. The pushout (1) in Fig. 10 exists if the considered conflict essence is ac-conflicting because either b_i or b_j is an $\mathcal{M}$-morphism: If the essence is composed, both morphisms are $\mathcal{M}$-morphisms by construction (see Definition 10). Moreover, for disabling essences of the form $(b_1\colon A \to L_1, b_j\colon A \to P_j)$ where $P_j \neq L_2$, we have $b_1 \in \mathcal{M}$ by construction. Disabling essences of the form $(b_1\colon A \to L_1, b_j\colon A \to L_1)$ are also disabling essences for plain rules [21, Proposition 3], which directly implies that they are not ac-conflicting.

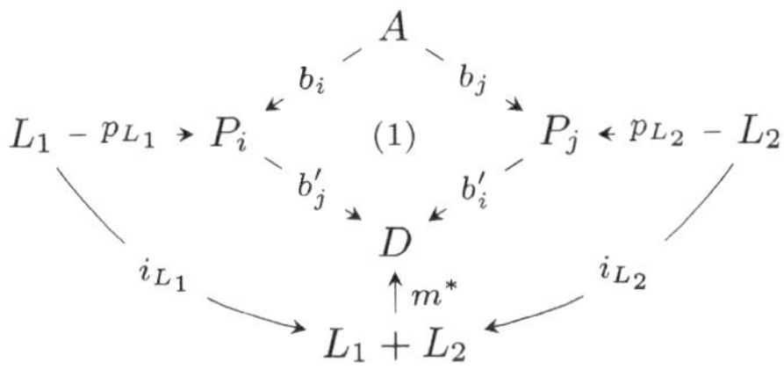

Fig. 10. Construction of symbolic conflict essences

The following example briefly illustrates symbolic conflict essences; we illustrate a symbolic conflict essence in detail in the long version of our paper [19].

Example 5 (Symbolic conflict essence). Together with a cospan condition ac_{ce}, each conflict essence shown in Fig. 5 forms a symbolic conflict essence. For $\mathsf{A}_{\mathsf{L1L2}}, \mathsf{A}^1_{\mathsf{L2L1}}, \mathsf{A}^2_{\mathsf{L2L1}}$, and the composed essences, which are not ac-conflicting, ac_{ce} is equal to true. For the remaining ones, ac_{ce} is non-trivial and ensures that (i) both rules satisfy their application conditions before the transformations and that (ii) the transformation pair is parallel dependent.

Because symbolic conflict essences consist of a conflict essence and a condition, we need to extend the notion of embeddability to also account for the condition: the embedding morphisms must satisfy it.

Definition 14 (Embeddability of symbolic conflict essences). *Given a pair of transformations $(t_1, t_2) = (G \Longrightarrow_{\rho_1, m_1} H_1, G \Longrightarrow_{\rho_2, m_2} H_2)$ via rules ρ_1 and ρ_2, a symbolic conflict essence $(ce, ac_{ce}) \in \mathrm{SCEss}(\rho_1, \rho_2)$ is embeddable in (t_1, t_2) if ce is embeddable in (t_1, t_2) via embedding morphisms m_1^j and m_2^i and $(m_1^j, m_2^i) \vdash ac_{ce}$.*

We can now establish the main results of this paper, namely that symbolic conflict essences play the same role for rules with application conditions that conflict essences do for plain rules (compare Fig. 1): They unambiguously indicate a transformation pair to be in conflict and correspond to (symbolic) initial conflicts.

Theorem 2 (Correctness of symbolic conflict essences). *Two transformations $(t_1, t_2) = (G \Longrightarrow_{\rho_1, m_1} H_1, G \Longrightarrow_{\rho_2, m_2} H_2)$ via rules ρ_1 and ρ_2 are parallel dependent if and only if a symbolic conflict essence $(ce, ac_{ce}) \in \mathrm{SCEss}(\rho_1, \rho_2)$ is embeddable in (t_1, t_2).*

Theorem 3 (Relation of symbolic conflict essences and initial conflicts). *For each symbolic conflict essence ce, there is a unique initial conflict so that the initial conflict is embeddable in a transformation pair via an extension diagram if ce is embeddable in the transformation pair. Moreover, when an initial conflict is embedded in a transformation pair, there is at least one symbolic conflict essence that is also embedded in this transformation pair.*

8   Conclusion

In this paper, we continue our work on providing techniques to statically analyse the interactions of (graph) transformation rules. Concretely, we introduce *conflict essences* for rules equipped with application conditions; these objects encapsulate the essential information about how two rule applications can cause a conflict with each other, potentially by invalidating one another's application condition. This closes an important gap because the construction was previously only available for plain rules (i.e., rules without application conditions). Our construction builds on the existing one, enabling us to lift the most important results from the "plain situation" to the case of application conditions. To achieve this, we construct *symbolic conflict essences* (which are conflict essences equipped with an application condition), which uniquely correspond to a *symbolic initial conflict* [17] and embed in a transformation pair if and only if that pair is conflicting.

For a conflicting transformation pair, the set of embedded symbolic conflict essences is not minimal, in the sense that each embedded symbolic conflict essence signals a spot that causes the conflict.

In the future, we plan to further investigate our composition operation. For example, we aim to identify the "maximal" ones that cannot be extended by additional spots. Moreover we intend to use this analysis to investigate the effects of rules on constraints to refine the graph repair approaches presented in [9,20] and to identify effective mutation orders in model-driven optimisation [12].

Acknowledgments. This work was partially funded by the German Research Foundation (DFG), project "Triple Graph Grammars (TGG) 3.0" and "Model-Driven Optimization in Software Engineering". The authors would like to thank the ICGT reviewers for their insightful comments.

References

1. Arendt, T., Biermann, E., Jurack, S., Krause, C., Taentzer, G.: Henshin: advanced concepts and tools for in-place EMF model transformations. In: Petriu, D.C., Rouquette, N., Haugen, Ø. (eds.) MODELS 2010. LNCS, vol. 6394, pp. 121–135. Springer, Heidelberg (2010). https://doi.org/10.1007/978-3-642-16145-2_9
2. Azzi, G.G., Corradini, A., Ribeiro, L.: On the essence and initiality of conflicts. In: Lambers, L., Weber, J. (eds.) ICGT 2018. LNCS, vol. 10887, pp. 99–117. Springer, Cham (2018). https://doi.org/10.1007/978-3-319-92991-0_7
3. Azzi, G.G., Corradini, A., Ribeiro, L.: On the essence and initiality of conflicts in $\mathcal{M}$-adhesive transformation systems. J. Log. Algebraic Methods Program. **109** (2019). https://doi.org/10.1016/J.JLAMP.2019.100482
4. Ehrig, H., Ehrig, K., Prange, U., Taentzer, G.: Fundamentals of Algebraic Graph Transformation. Monographs in Theoretical Computer Science. An EATCS Series. Springer, Heidelberg (2006). https://doi.org/10.1007/3-540-31188-2

5. Ehrig, H., Ermel, C., Golas, U., Hermann, F.: Graph and Model Transformation – General Framework and Applications. Monographs in Theoretical Computer Science. An EATCS Series. Springer, Heidelberg (2015). https://doi.org/10.1007/978-3-662-47980-3

6. Ehrig, H., Golas, U., Habel, A., Lambers, L., Orejas, F.: $\mathcal{M}$-adhesive transformation systems with nested application conditions. Part 2: embedding, critical pairs and local confluence. Fund. Informaticae **118**(1–2), 35–63 (2012). https://doi.org/10.3233/FI-2012-705

7. Ehrig, H., Habel, A., Padberg, J., Prange, U.: Adhesive high-level replacement categories and systems. In: Ehrig, H., Engels, G., Parisi-Presicce, F., Rozenberg, G. (eds.) ICGT 2004. LNCS, vol. 3256, pp. 144–160. Springer, Heidelberg (2004). https://doi.org/10.1007/978-3-540-30203-2_12

8. Fowler, M.: Refactoring: Improving the Design of Existing Code. Addison-Wesley Professional, Boston (2018)

9. Fritsche, L., Lauer, A., Kratz, M., Schürr, A., Taentzer, G.: Using weakest application conditions to rank graph transformations for graph repair. Log. Methods Comput. Sci. **22**(1) (2026). https://doi.org/10.46298/LMCS-22(1:10)2026

10. Habel, A., Pennemann, K.: Correctness of high-level transformation systems relative to nested conditions. Math. Struct. Comput. Sci. **19**(2), 245–296 (2009). https://doi.org/10.1017/S0960129508007202

11. Heckel, R., Taentzer, G.: Graph Transformation for Software Engineers - With Applications to Model-Based Development and Domain-Specific Language Engineering. Springer, Heidelberg (2020). https://doi.org/10.1007/978-3-030-43916-3

12. John, S., Kosiol, J., Lambers, L., Taentzer, G.: A graph-based framework for model-driven optimization facilitating impact analysis of mutation operator properties. Softw. Syst. Model. **22**(4), 1281–1318 (2023). https://doi.org/10.1007/S10270-022-01078-X

13. Lack, S., Sobocinski, P.: Adhesive and quasiadhesive categories. RAIRO Theor. Inf. Appl. **39**(3), 511–545 (2005). https://doi.org/10.1051/ITA:2005028

14. Lambers, L., Born, K., Kosiol, J., Strüber, D., Taentzer, G.: Granularity of conflicts and dependencies in graph transformation systems: a two-dimensional approach. J. Log. Algebraic Methods Program. **103**, 105–129 (2019). https://doi.org/10.1016/J.JLAMP.2018.11.004

15. Lambers, L., Born, K., Orejas, F., Strüber, D., Taentzer, G.: Initial conflicts and dependencies: critical pairs revisited. In: Heckel, R., Taentzer, G. (eds.) Graph Transformation, Specifications, and Nets. LNCS, vol. 10800, pp. 105–123. Springer, Cham (2018). https://doi.org/10.1007/978-3-319-75396-6_6

16. Lambers, L., Kosiol, J., Strüber, D., Taentzer, G.: Exploring conflict reasons for graph transformation systems. In: Guerra, E., Orejas, F. (eds.) ICGT 2019. LNCS, vol. 11629, pp. 75–92. Springer, Cham (2019). https://doi.org/10.1007/978-3-030-23611-3_5

17. Lambers, L., Orejas, F.: Transformation rules with nested application conditions: critical pairs, initial conflicts & minimality. Theor. Comput. Sci. **884**, 44–67 (2021). https://doi.org/10.1016/J.TCS.2021.07.023

18. Lambers, L., Strüber, D., Taentzer, G., Born, K., Huebert, J.: Multi-granular conflict and dependency analysis in software engineering based on graph transformation. In: Chaudron, M., Crnkovic, I., Chechik, M., Harman, M. (eds.) Proceedings of the 40th International Conference on Software Engineering, ICSE 2018, Gothenburg, Sweden, 27 May–03 June 2018, pp. 716–727. ACM (2018). https://doi.org/10.1145/3180155.3180258

19. Lauer, A., Kosiol, J., Lambers, L., Taentzer, G.: Conflict essences for transformation rules with nested application conditions – long version (2026). https://arxiv.org/abs/2605.04947
20. Lauer, A., Kosiol, J., Taentzer, G.: Empowering model repair: a rule-based approach to graph repair without side effects - extended version. Innov. Syst. Softw. Eng. **20**(4), 597–618 (2024). https://doi.org/10.1007/S11334-024-00587-W
21. Lauer, A., Kosiol, J., Taentzer, G.: Granular conflict analysis for transformation rules with application conditions. In: Endrullis, J., Tichy, M. (eds.) Graph Transformation – 18th International Conference, ICGT 2025, Held as Part of STAF 2025, Koblenz, Germany, 11–12 June 2025, Proceedings. Lecture Notes in Computer Science, vol. 15720, pp. 63–90. Springer, Heidelberg (2025). https://doi.org/10.1007/978-3-031-94706-3_4
22. Pennemann, K.: Development of correct graph transformation systems. Ph.D. thesis, University of Oldenburg, Germany (2009). https://nbn-resolving.org/urn:nbn:de:gbv:715-oops-9483
23. Rensink, A.: Representing first-order logic using graphs. In: Ehrig, H., Engels, G., Parisi-Presicce, F., Rozenberg, G. (eds.) ICGT 2004. LNCS, vol. 3256, pp. 319–335. Springer, Heidelberg (2004). https://doi.org/10.1007/978-3-540-30203-2_23
24. Rensink, A., Corradini, A.: On categories of nested conditions. In: Jansen, N., et al. (eds.) Principles of Verification: Cycling the Probabilistic Landscape – Essays Dedicated to Joost-Pieter Katoen on the Occasion of His 60th Birthday, Part I. Lecture Notes in Computer Science, vol. 15260, pp. 393–418. Springer, Heidelberg (2024). https://doi.org/10.1007/978-3-031-75783-9_16

Formalising and Verifying Graph Programs with Higher-Order Logic

Robert Söldner and Detlef Plump[✉]

University of York, York, UK
{rs2040,detlef.plump}@york.ac.uk

Abstract. We present an approach to verifying graph programs with higher-order logic, based on a formalisation of the graph programming language GP 2 in the HOL4 interactive theorem prover. The formalisation covers all language features, from labelled graphs and graph morphisms to rule schemata and their application, up to the full operational semantics. To prove programs correct, we use Hoare-style proof rules which have been verified with respect to the operational semantics. We introduce *track morphisms* of program executions as a new concept, to locate nodes and edges of the input graph in the output graph. Due to the power of higher-order logic, we can formalise track morphisms in HOL4 and use them in assertions. We demonstrate the use of our verification framework by a case study in which we prove the partial correctness of a program that computes the transitive closure of input graphs. The postcondition asserts not only that the result graph is transitive but also that it is a minimal extension of the input graph. The case study involves 50 mechanically verified theorems while the formalisation of GP 2 comprises approximately 20,000 lines of proof in 19 theories.

Keywords: Rule-based graph programming · GP 2 · Interactive theorem proving · HOL4 · Formalised operational semantics · Hoare-style proof rules · Track morphisms · Mechanical program verification

1 Introduction

Graph-structured data are ubiquitous, from pointer structures to program control-flow and call graphs, knowledge graphs, graph databases, model-driven software engineering, and biological networks. Rule-based graph transformation offers a visual formalism for computing with such data and underpins modelling languages, compiler optimisations, and domain-specific tools. As graph-manipulating code enters safety-critical and data-intensive domains, the correctness problem familiar from conventional programming becomes increasingly important: how do we prove that a given graph program meets its specification? In the context of imperative and functional programming, one approach to verification is the use of interactive theorem provers as witnessed by CompCert [9],

B. Archibald and O. Semeráth (Eds.): ICGT 2026, LNCS 16624, pp. 109–128, 2026.
https://doi.org/10.1007/978-3-032-29730-3_6

seL4 [8], and CakeML [1]. However, for rule-based graph programs, verification has so far remained almost exclusively a pen-and-paper activity.

The graph programming language GP 2 [3,14] is a rule-based experimental language with control constructs such as sequential composition, as-long-as-possible iteration, branching, and procedures. It comes with a formal semantics based on (an attributed version of) the double-pushout approach to graph transformation [6] and has been shown to be computationally complete [15].

Several verification calculi for GP 2 have been developed, using as assertions either first-order logic or monadic second-order logic on graphs [16–19,23,24]. These approaches come with weakest-precondition constructions, but none of them has been implemented yet.

In this paper we present, to the best of our knowledge, the first mechanised formalisation of a complete graph programming language in a theorem prover. Our development in HOL4 covers the full GP 2 language: from labelled graphs over morphisms and rule schemata up to attributed double-pushout graph transformation and GP 2's small-step operational semantics. In addition, we introduce a compositional program verification framework based on Hoare-style proof rules.

Specifically, this paper makes the following contributions:

- We formalise the complete GP 2 language in HOL4 and establish a Hoare-style verification framework covering sequential composition, consequence, conditional branching and as-long-as-possible iteration, among other constructs.
- We introduce track morphisms of program executions that allow to locate preserved nodes of input graphs in output graphs, and show how to extend these morphisms to injective graph morphisms that additionally track edges.
- We demonstrate our verification approach by proving the partial correctness of a GP 2 program computing the transitive closure of input graphs. While the program is short, the mechanised proof is of substantial size and involves 50 theorems.

2   Background

This section briefly introduces GP 2[1] and HOL4[2]. For more background on GP 2 we refer to [3,14] and for the HOL family to [11,20].

2.1   The Graph Programming Language GP 2

GP 2 programs transform input graphs by applying conditional rule schemata through attributed double-pushout graph transformation. We use the transitive closure program of Fig. 1 as a running example throughout this paper. The program applies the `link` rule schema as long as possible, which requires to find a match satisfying the application condition that there must be no edge from

---

node 1 to node 3. If a match is found, the rule adds an edge (labelled with the empty list) according to the rule and the match. This is repeated zero or more times until a match cannot be found anymore. Finding a match involves finding a node corresponding to node 1, then finding an outgoing edge to another node, corresponding to node 2, then finding an outgoing edge to yet another node, corresponding to node 3, and then checking the application condition.

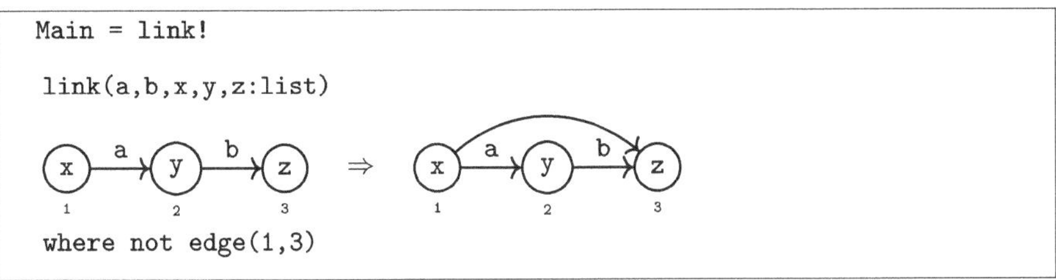

Fig. 1. GP 2 program `transitive-closure`.

GP 2 host graphs are directed and may have parallel edges and loops. Both nodes and edges are labelled with heterogeneous lists of integers and strings, organised in a small subtyping hierarchy. In addition, nodes and edges may be *marked* red, green, blue, grey (nodes only) or dashed (edges only). Our simple running example program does not require marks.

GP 2 provides several constructs for controlling the application of rules and procedures. The `transitive-closure` program uses only the loop construct $P!$ which executes the body P as long as possible, terminating when P fails and returning the graph on which the last iteration was entered.

When `link!` terminates, every pair of distinct nodes connected by a directed path in the input graph is connected by an edge in the output graph. Hence the output graph is the transitive closure of the input graph.

2.2   The Interactive Theorem Prover HOL4

HOL4 is an interactive theorem prover for higher-order logic following the LCF architecture: a small trusted kernel guarantees that every proof reduces to primitive inferences [20]. The logic extends Church's simply typed lambda calculus [2,4] with polymorphism: types include base types, function types, and polymorphic constructors (*e.g.* `'a list`, `('a,'b) fmap`). Quantifiers range over all types including functions and predicates, enabling assertions that quantify over morphisms, parameterised judgements, and polymorphic record types modelling graph structures.

Our formalisation uses `Datatype` (algebraic types for graphs, labels, terms), `Definition` (predicates, recursive functions), and `Inductive` definitions (operational semantics). The two central HOL4 standard-library theories we rely on are `finite_mapTheory` (finite maps for representing graphs) and `pred_setTheory` (predicate sets for node/edge sets).

3   Formalising GP 2 in HOL4

We now present our formalisation of GP 2 in HOL4. The development comprises approximately 20,000 lines of proof across ~20 theories and has been built with HOL4 master `f02a261b` (2025-11-27) using Poly/ML 5.9.1. The complete source code is available on GitHub.[3]

3.1   Graphs and Morphisms

Following our earlier Isabelle/HOL formalisation [21], graphs are represented as a polymorphic record with finite maps for the node set `G.V`, edge set `G.E`, source and target maps, label and mark maps, and a rootedness map `G.p`. The record is polymorphic in its node-label type `'l` and edge-mark type `'m`, instantiated for host graphs and rule graphs respectively (Sect. 3.2). The well-formedness predicate `wf_graph` requires finite node/edge sets, consistent source/target maps, and disjoint underlying identifiers.

A *premorphism* [5] is a pair of finite maps (one for nodes, one for edges) that preserve sources, targets and rootedness. A *morphism* is a premorphism that additionally preserves node and edge labels.

3.2   Labels and Types

The polymorphic label parameter `'l` of the graph record is instantiated with concrete label types for rule graphs and host graphs, respectively. Rule labels include constants (integers, strings, characters), list constructors (empty list and concatenation), variables, arithmetic and string operations, and degree expressions. Host labels are the ground fragment of rule labels: they are built exclusively from constants and list constructors, without variables or other operations. A host label is in *spine form* when it is an atom, the empty list, or a cons cell whose head is an atom and whose tail is in spine form. This canonical form is maintained as an invariant throughout label evaluation. Marks (`nodemark`, `edgemark`) instantiate the `'m` parameter. As mentioned in Sect. 2.1, rule marks additionally include a wildcard `any` for pattern matching. (We omit the mark definitions to save space).

Typing is defined as an inductive relation `label_typeof` over a variable context, a label, and a type drawn from the subtype hierarchy. Here is a representative rule:

$$\frac{\text{FLOOKUP } \mathit{vars} \ \ v \ = \text{SOME } \mathit{ty}}{\texttt{label\_typeof } (\mathit{vars},\texttt{label\_variable } v, \mathit{ty})} \ \text{Var}$$

We omit the remaining rules (arithmetic, concatenation, cons, degree expressions) for space reasons.

---

[3] https://github.com/UoYCS-plasma/gp2-hol. The repository includes the full GP 2 formalisation, the transitive-closure case-study proof of Sect. 6, and the `gp2convert` tool that translates GP 2 source code into HOL4 theory files.

A functional type checker `label_typeof_fun` is proved equivalent to the inductive relation, enabling computation inside proofs. Well-formedness of a host graph (`wf_hostgraph`) requires all labels to be in spine form; an analogous predicate `wf_rulegraph` constrains rule graphs to carry well-typed labels.

3.3 Attributed Double-Pushout Graph Transformation

A GP 2 rule schema comprises variable declarations, a left-hand graph and a right-hand graph (both well-formed), an interface consisting of unlabelled nodes only, and an optional application condition. Well-formedness (`wf_rule`) requires properties such as total labelling of left and right-hand graph, well-typing, restriction of RHS variables to those in the LHS, and well-formedness of the application condition.

Applying a rule requires first to instantiate the variables of the left-hand graph with values such that an injective graph morphism into the host graph exists. Subsequently, the application condition is evaluated and, if true, any expressions in the right-hand graph are evaluated. This yields an instance of the rule schema which is a rule in the double-pushout approach with relabelling [7]. This rule is then applied according to that approach and with the given match.

To keep the presentation simple, we ignore here so-called rooted rule schemata which allow to speed-up the matching process. See, for example, [3].

3.4 Operational Semantics and Track Morphisms

We follow GP 2's small-step operational semantics of Courtehoute and Plump [6]. Semantic inference rules (omitted here for lack of space) define a transition relation on *configurations*. These are either *running configurations* $\langle P, S \rangle$ consisting of a program P and a graph stack S, or *terminal configurations* of two kinds: just a single-entry graph stack S (denoting successful termination) or the element fail (denoting program failure). We write $[G]$ for the single-element stack whose only entry is graph G.

The *semantic function* $[\![P]\!]$ of a program P is then defined as follows:

$$[\![P]\!]\, G \;=\; \{X \mid \langle P, [G] \rangle \to_P^* X,\ X \text{ a terminal configuration}\}$$
$$\cup\; \{\bot \mid P \text{ can diverge from } G\},$$

where $\to_P^*$ denotes the reflexive-transitive closure of the small-step transition relation. Section 4 discusses the formalisation of the transition relation.

Similar to the track morphism in standard double-pushout graph transformation [13], every rule schema application transforming a graph G into a graph H induces a *track morphism* $tr\colon G \to H$: a partial, injective graph morphism that locates the preserved nodes (and unused edges) of G in H. We extend tr to a multi-step morphism $tr_{G_0 \to_P^* G_n}$ for every transition sequence transforming an input graph G_0 into an output graph G_n. We do this by making each stack entry in the configurations of [6] a pair $(G,\ tr_{G_0 \to_P^* G_i})$ whose second component is the track morphism from the initial graph G_0 to the current graph G_i.

Throughout, we highlight the new track-morphism component of a stack entry with a light grey background. By erasing the highlighted components one recovers the plain semantic inference rules of [6]. Only one inference rule changes non-trivially, namely the rule-set application $[\text{call}_1']$ which composes the single-step track $tr_{G \to_R H}$ with the multi-step track $tr_{G_0 \to_P^* G}$:

$$[\text{call}_1'] \quad \frac{(G,\ tr_{G_0 \to_P^* G}) = \text{top}(S) \qquad G \Rightarrow_R H}{\langle R, S \rangle \to \text{push}\big((H,\ tr_{G \to_R H} \circ tr_{G_0 \to_P^* G}),\ \text{pop}(S)\big)}$$

All other rules in [6] remain unchanged, the track component is threaded through without modification. The branching constructs `if_then_else` and `try_then_else` which discard the condition's graph also discard the associated track morphism. The HOL4 formalisation of this extended transition relation is discussed in Sect. 4.2.

4   Formalising the Operational Semantics

We now discuss the HOL4 formalisation of the operational semantics outlined in Sect. 3.4.

4.1   Rule Matching and Application

The function `apply_rule` implements rule application as a three-phase monadic pipeline: (1) `mk_assignment` replaces each LHS variable with its matched host value and merges the partial assignments; (2) `instantiate_rule` checks the application condition and evaluates all rule labels in the RHS to produce a concrete rule instance; (3) `apply_ruleinstance` feeds the instance and the match into the DPO construction (Sect. 3.3). The match is an injective premorphism satisfying the dangling condition (nodes to be deleted must not be incident with host graph edges outside the match).

$$
\begin{aligned}
\vdash\ &\texttt{wf\_rule}\ r \wedge \texttt{wf\_hostgraph}\ G\ \wedge \\
&\texttt{wf\_rulegraph\_labels}\ r.\texttt{lhs}\ \wedge \\
&\texttt{is\_prematch}\ r.\texttt{lhs}\ r.\texttt{inf}\ m\ G\ \wedge \\
&\texttt{apply\_rule}\ r\ m\ G = \texttt{SOME}\ h\ \Rightarrow \\
&\texttt{wf\_hostgraph}\ h
\end{aligned}
$$

This theorem connects the three phases: spine-form preservation, proved for variable instantiation and label evaluation, guarantees that the instantiated labels are well-formed, and the DPO results from Sect. 3.3 establish that the output graph is well-formed.

4.2   Program Execution

We formalise the configurations of Sect. 3.4 as follows. A HOL4 configuration pairs a state (`running t`, `final` or `failed`) with a stack of (hostgraph, morphism) frames, where the morphism is the track morphism $tr_{G_0 \to_P^* G}$ from the original input graph. The initial configuration is (`running P`, $[(G, id\_track\ G)]$).

The inductive `step` relation has 21 rules. On successful rule application, the per-step track is composed with the track morphism via `compose_morphism`. Sequential composition propagates steps through the first sub-term; as-long-as-possible iteration unfolds $P!$ to `try P then P! else skip`. Branching constructs push a saved frame onto the stack; `skip` and `fail` transition to `final` and `failed`, respectively.

Evaluation holds when the reflexive-transitive closure of `step` reaches a `final` configuration:

$$\vdash \texttt{evaluate}\ env\ G\ P\ (H, tr)\ \Longleftrightarrow$$
$$\exists S.\ \texttt{steps}\ env\ (\texttt{running}\ P, [(G, \texttt{id\_track}\ G)])$$
$$(\texttt{final}, S) \land \neg\texttt{can\_step}\ (\texttt{final}, S) \land$$
$$\exists rest.\ S = (H, tr) :: rest$$

Source-level programs preserve the stack length across evaluation, so the final stack has exactly one frame whose host graph is the output. Together with stack-length preservation, the step-level preservation of stack well-formedness yields well-formedness of the output graph:

$$\vdash \texttt{wf\_program}\ env\ \land\ \texttt{wf\_hostgraph}\ G\ \land$$
$$\texttt{evaluate}\ env\ G\ P\ (H, tr) \Rightarrow$$
$$\texttt{wf\_hostgraph}\ H$$

The step relation also preserves validity of the track morphism; we return to this in Sect. 5.3.

5   Program Verification Framework

With the operational semantics in place, we can develop a compositional framework for proving partial correctness of GP 2 programs. Subsection 5.1 explains what partial correctness means and what kind of assertions we are using. Subsection 5.2 presents some Hoare-style proof rules and explains in what sense they are sound. Subsection 5.3 discusses the formalisation of track morphisms.

5.1   Partial Correctness and Assertions

We adopt the notion of partial correctness from Poskitt and Plump [18]. A graph program t is *partially correct* with respect to a precondition P and postcondition Q, written $\models \{P\}\, t\, \{Q\}$, if for every host graph G with $G \models P$ and every graph

$H \in [\![t]\!]G$ we have $H \models Q$. Here $[\![t]\!]$ is the semantic function of t, so $[\![t]\!]G$ is the set of possible outcomes of running t on G (possibly including failure and/or divergence). Also, given a host graph X and an assertion A, $X \models A$ means that X satisfies A. Note that partial correctness makes no guarantees about program termination or the absence of failure.

From here on we use the convention that t denotes a program term, P the precondition and Q the postcondition. So the P used in Sect. 3.4 for programs re-appears as t in the verification framework.

In [18,24], assertions closed formulas of certain variants of monadic second-order logic. In our framework, assertions are higher-order logic formulas. HOL4 is based on classical higher-order logic in the tradition of Church's simple theory of types [2,4]: a typed lambda calculus extended with polymorphism, Hilbert choice, and quantifiers that range over every type, including function and predicate types.

Concretely, an assertion A is a HOL4 term either of type `hostgraph` $\to$ `bool` or of type `hostgraph` $\to$ `morphism` $\to$ `bool`. Equivalently, $A = \lambda G.\,\varphi(G)$ or $A = \lambda G\,m.\,\psi(G,m)$ for arbitrary higher-order logic formulas $\varphi(G)$ and $\psi(G,m)$ in which G (resp. G and m) may occur free. Thus, assertions may quantify over both graphs and morphisms.

Partial correctness is formalised by the predicate `WSPEC env P t Q`, asserting that whenever P holds for the input graph and t terminates successfully under env, Q holds for the output graph *and* the accumulated track morphism:

$$\vdash \texttt{WSPEC}\ env\ P\ t\ Q\ \iff$$

$$\texttt{wf\_program}\ env\ \wedge\ \texttt{no\_intermediate\_terms}\ t\ \wedge$$

$$\forall G\ og\ om\,.$$

$$\texttt{wf\_hostgraph}\ G\ \wedge\ P\ G\ \wedge$$

$$\texttt{steps}\ env\ (\texttt{running}\ t,[(G,\texttt{id\_track}\ G)])\ (\texttt{final},[(og,om)])\ \Rightarrow$$

$$Q\ og\ om$$

5.2   Hoare Rules and Their Soundness

We present a few Hoare-style proof rules which suffice to carry out the case study in Sect. 6. The call of a GP 2 rule-set $\mathcal{R}$ is our basic proof rule. The rule's premise requires that whenever a rule in $\mathcal{R}$ is applied to a host graph satisfying the precondition P, then the resulting graph satisfies the potscondition Q:

$$[\text{rscall}]\quad \frac{\models \{P\}\ \mathcal{R}\ \{Q\}}{\{P\}\ \mathcal{R}\ \{Q\}}$$

The corresponding HOL4 theorem is `WSPEC_rscall`.

The consequence rule allows to strengthen preconditions and to weaken post-conditions:

$$[\text{cons}] \quad \frac{P \Rightarrow P' \quad \{P'\}\, t\, \{Q'\} \quad Q' \Rightarrow Q}{\{P\}\, t\, \{Q\}}$$

For as-long-as-possible iteration of a rule set call, the following rule requires that an invariant I holds for the loop's body:

$$[\text{alap}] \quad \frac{\{I\}\, \mathcal{R}\, \{I\}}{\{I\}\, \mathcal{R}!\, \{I \wedge \neg\text{App}(\mathcal{R})\}}$$

Here $\neg\text{App}$ is an assertion expressing that $\mathcal{R}$ is not applicable to any graph resulting from the loop $\mathcal{R}!$. Note that I can be a predicate on (graph, morphism) pairs. The corresponding HOL4 theorem `WSPEC_alap` additionally quantifies its conclusion over an accumulated track m_0 so that the rule composes with an outer track when nested inside sequential composition.

We stress that each of the above proof rules is a HOL4 `Theorem`, not an `Axiom`: its statement has the shape *premises* $\Rightarrow$ `WSPEC env P t Q`, where `WSPEC` is the semantic predicate defined by `WSPEC_def`. Because `WSPEC` *is* the partial-correctness judgement $\models \{P\}\, t\, \{Q\}$ with respect to the operational semantics, any HOL4 theorem of this form is automatically sound; the `Proof` block is itself the soundness argument. We therefore do not need to prove a separate soundness meta-theorem of the form $\vdash \{P\}\, t\, \{Q\} \Rightarrow \models \{P\}\, t\, \{Q\}$: there is no independent syntactic judgement $\vdash$ to relate to $\models$, because every rule has been derived from the semantics. This is the shallow-embedding trade-off: rules are not inspectable as data, but they come with soundness by construction.

Verifying a program amounts to decomposing a top-level WSPEC judgement via the rules until every leaf is a rule-set call or a loop. Section 6 demonstrates this pattern.

5.3 Track Morphisms

We briefly return to the track morphisms defined in Subsect. 3.4 to show the formalisation in HOL4:

```
⊢ is_track_morphism G tr H  ⟺
    partial_dom_ran G tr H ∧
    partial_preserve_source G tr H ∧
    partial_preserve_target G tr H ∧
    INJ ((') tr.nodemap) (FDOM tr.nodemap) H.V ∧
    INJ ((') tr.edgemap) (FDOM tr.edgemap) H.E
```

As described in Sect. 3.4, the operational semantics composes these per-step tracks into a track morphism $tr_{G_0 \to_P^* G_n}$. Since the identity morphism is a valid

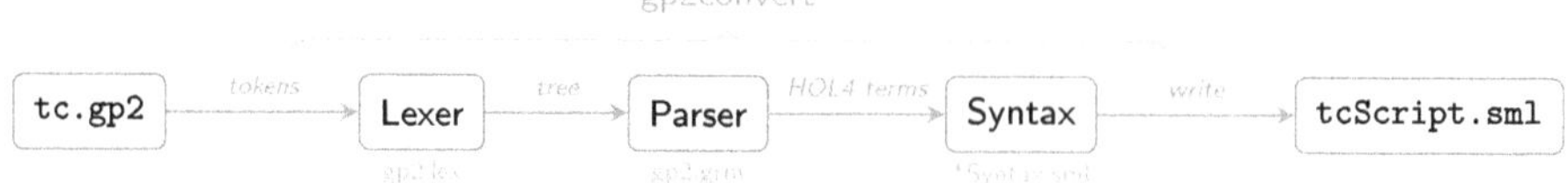

Fig. 2. The `gp2convert` pipeline. A GP 2 source file is lexed, parsed, translated into HOL4 terms, and written out as a theory file with definitions and proof obligations.

track morphism and composition preserves the track-morphism property, whenever a program evaluates from an input graph G to a result pair (H, tr), the track morphism is a valid track from G to H:

$$\vdash \texttt{wf\_program}\ env\ \wedge\ \texttt{wf\_hostgraph}\ G\ \wedge$$
$$\texttt{evaluate}\ env\ G\ P\ (H, tr) \implies$$
$$\texttt{is\_track\_morphism}\ G\ tr\ H$$

The morphism-aware ALAP rule `WSPEC_alap` used in Sect. 6) composes the per-iteration track at each step, combining the loop invariant with a property that must hold when the body fails.

6   Case Study: Transitive Closure

We now apply the verification framework of Sect. 5 to prove partial correctness of the transitive-closure program introduced in Section 2. Recall that the program consists of a single procedure, `Main = link!`, which applies the `link` rule as long as possible (see Fig. 1). Correctness means that whenever the program terminates, the output graph is the transitive closure of the input graph: every pair of distinct nodes connected by a directed path in the original graph is connected by an edge in the output graph, there is a total graph morphism from the input graph to the output graph that is bijective on nodes and injective on edges, and every edge not in the image of the morphism is justified by a path in the input graph. Figure 2 shows the `gp2convert` pipeline that translates the GP 2 source into HOL4 definitions, from which we derive the specification and proof.

6.1   Program and Specification

The program consists of a single procedure and a single rule. The `gp2convert` tool translates the source into a HOL4 definition of the procedure body:

$$\vdash \texttt{proc\_Main} =$$
$$\texttt{term\_alap (term\_rscall \{ruleid "link"\})}$$

The term `term_alap` encodes as-long-as-possible iteration, and `term_rscall` calls a rule set containing the single rule `ruleid "link"`. The program environment maps this identifier to the rule from Fig. 1:

```
⊢ program =
   <|proc := FEMPTY |++ [("Main",proc_Main)];
    rule :=
      FEMPTY |++ [(ruleid "link",rule_link)]|>
```

Before stating the correctness property, we define the two key concepts that occur in the postcondition.

Definition 1 (Transitive graph). A graph G is *transitive* if for all nodes $v, w \in V_G$ with $v \neq w$, if there is a directed path from v to w then there exists an edge from v to w.

Note that we require $v \neq w$ as otherwise each node in a transitive graph would have to have a self-loop.

Definition 2 (Minimal extension). A graph TC is a *minimal extension* of a graph G with respect to a total injective morphism $\overline{m}\colon G \to TC$ if:

(a) $\overline{m}_V$ is bijective;
(b) each edge e in TC that is not in the image of $\overline{m}_E$,
    (b1) connects two nodes $\overline{m}(v)$ and $\overline{m}(w)$ for some $v, w \in V_G$ such that there is a directed path from v to w in G, and
    (b2) has no parallel edges in TC, that is, there is no other edge e' in TC with the same source and target as e.

Since $\overline{m}$ is a graph morphism, it preserves sources and targets of edges, and labels of both nodes and edges. By the bijectivity of the node mapping, no nodes are added or removed when transforming G into TC. Condition (b1) requires that each new edge be justified by reachability in the original graph, and condition (b2) forbids new edges to have parallel edges, as otherwise the extension would not be minimal.

Using these definitions, we can concisely state the intended correctness property of the program `transitive-closure`.

Precondition. The input graph G_0 is a well-formed, unmarked, unrooted host graph.

Postcondition. The output graph TC is transitive and there exists a total injective extension $\overline{tr}_{G_0 \to^* TC}$ of the track morphism $tr_{G_0 \to^* TC}$ such that TC is a minimal extension of G_0 with respect to $\overline{tr}_{G_0 \to^* TC}$.

The predicate `extends_morphism` (defined below) connects the morphisms tr and $\overline{tr}$ by requiring that the latter agrees with tr on tr's domain of definition. The predicate `minimal_extension` (also defined below) combines two requirements: $\overline{tr}$ must be a total injective graph morphism (`is_inj_morphism`) and TC must be a minimal extension of G with respect to $\overline{tr}$. The next subsection defines the extension of tr to $\overline{tr}$.

6.2   Total Extension of the Track Morphism

To keep GP 2's rule format simple, rule applications temporarily delete all matched edges and possibly re-create them by the DPO construction. As a consequence, track morphisms are undefined on host graph edges that are matched in any rule applications. However, the `link` rule of the program `transitive-closure` re-creates both of its edges in a unique way, allowing us to extend the partial track morphism to a total injective graph morphism.

We define the total extension inductively. The base case is the identity $\overline{tr}_{G_0 \to^* G_0} = \mathrm{id}_{G_0}$. For a rule application $G \Rightarrow_{\texttt{link}} H$ with match m and current extension $\overline{tr}_{G_0 \to^* G}$, the updated extension $\overline{tr}_{G_0 \to^* H}$ agrees with $\overline{tr}_{G_0 \to^* G}$ on nodes and maps each edge $e \in E_{G_0}$ as follows:

$$
\overline{tr}_{G_0 \to^* H}(e) = \begin{cases} e' & \text{if } \overline{tr}_{G_0 \to^* G}(e) \in m(\text{LHS}), \text{ where } e' \text{ is} \\ & \text{the unique RHS edge replacing } \overline{tr}_{G_0 \to^* G}(e), \\ tr_{G \to H}(\overline{tr}_{G_0 \to^* G}(e)) & \text{otherwise (edge is not matched).} \end{cases}
$$

The extension is proved to exist as part of `link_preserves_invariant` (witness `link_new_track_bar` in the repository).

6.3   Formalising the Specification

We formalise the precondition and postcondition in HOL4. The notion of minimal extension (Definition 2) is captured by the ternary relation `minimal_extension`:

$$
\begin{aligned}
\vdash\ &\texttt{minimal\_extension}\ G_0\ \textit{track\_bar}\ TC\ \Longleftrightarrow \\
&\texttt{is\_inj\_morphism}\ G_0\ \textit{track\_bar}\ TC\ \wedge \\
&\texttt{BIJ}\ ((\text{'})\ \textit{track\_bar}.\texttt{nodemap})\ G_0.\text{V}\ TC.\text{V}\ \wedge \\
&\texttt{edge\_path\_justified}\ G_0\ \textit{track\_bar}\ TC\ \wedge \\
&\texttt{parallel\_free\_extension}\ \textit{track\_bar}\ TC
\end{aligned}
$$

The top-level predicate `is_transitive_closure_tracked` combines transitivity and minimal extension:

$$
\begin{aligned}
\vdash\ &\texttt{is\_transitive\_closure\_tracked}\ G_0\ \textit{track\_bar}\ TC\ \Longleftrightarrow \\
&\texttt{is\_transitive}\ TC\ \wedge \\
&\texttt{minimal\_extension}\ G_0\ \textit{track\_bar}\ TC
\end{aligned}
$$

The predicate `extends_morphism` requires that $\overline{tr}$ extends the track morphism tr to a total morphism such that both morphisms have the same node mapping and agree on every edge in tr's domain of definition:

$$
\begin{aligned}
\vdash\ &\texttt{extends\_morphism}\ \textit{track}\ \textit{track\_bar}\ \Longleftrightarrow \\
&\textit{track\_bar}.\texttt{nodemap} = \textit{track}.\texttt{nodemap}\ \wedge \\
&\forall e.\ \ e \in \texttt{FDOM}\ \textit{track}.\texttt{edgemap}\ \Longrightarrow \\
&\quad \textit{track}.\texttt{edgemap}\ \text{'}\ e = \textit{track\_bar}.\texttt{edgemap}\ \text{'}\ e
\end{aligned}
$$

Transitivity (Definition 1) is formalised as:

$$\vdash \texttt{is\_transitive}\ G \iff$$
$$\forall v\ w\,.$$
$$v \in G.\mathrm{V}\ \wedge\ w \in G.\mathrm{V}\ \wedge\ v \neq w\ \wedge$$
$$\texttt{reachable\_in}\ G\ v\ w \implies$$
$$\texttt{has\_edge}\ G\ v\ w$$

The top-level correctness theorem is a WSPEC judgement:

$$\vdash \texttt{WSPEC program}$$
$$(\lambda\,G\,.$$
$$G = G_0\ \wedge\ \texttt{wf\_hostgraph}\ G_0\ \wedge$$
$$\texttt{unmarked\_hostgraph}\ G_0\ \wedge$$
$$\texttt{unrooted\_hostgraph}\ G_0)$$
$$(\texttt{term\_proc}\ \text{``Main''})$$
$$(\lambda\,TC\ track\,.$$
$$\exists track\_bar\,.$$
$$\texttt{is\_transitive\_closure\_tracked}\ G_0$$
$$track\_bar\ TC\ \wedge$$
$$\texttt{extends\_morphism}\ track\ track\_bar)$$

The postcondition requires (1) the existence of the total morphism $\overline{tr}$ extending the track morphism and (2) that the output graph is transitive and a minimal extension of the input graph. The proof decomposes into a loop invariant (Sect. 6.4), transitivity upon termination (Sect. 6.5), and preservation of the minimal extension property (Sect. 6.6).

6.4 Loop Invariant

The proof of `transitive_closure_correct` proceeds by instantiating the morphism-aware ALAP rule `WSPEC_alap` from Sect. 5.3 with a loop invariant that captures two concerns:

Loop invariant. After every iteration of `link!`, writing m for the track morphism $tr_{G_0 \to^* H}$ accumulated so far, the current graph H satisfies:

1. *Structural properties:* H is a well-formed, unmarked, unrooted host graph.
2. *Minimal extension:* H is a minimal extension of the input graph G_0 with respect to a total morphism $\overline{m}$ that extends the morphism m.

The proof maintains two parallel invariants. The *base invariant* tracks the morphism m using the weaker property `minimally_extends`, which requires m to be a partial and injective graph morphism with bijective node mapping, and every edge not in the image of m to be justified by a directed path in the input graph:

$$\vdash \texttt{tc\_loop\_invariant}\ G_0\ H\ m\ \Longleftrightarrow$$
$$\texttt{wf\_hostgraph}\ H\ \wedge\ \texttt{minimally\_extends}\ G_0\ m\ H\ \wedge$$
$$\texttt{unmarked\_hostgraph}\ H\ \wedge\ \texttt{unrooted\_hostgraph}\ H$$

The *augmented invariant* addresses the total morphism $\overline{tr}$ by using `minimal_extension`, strengthening the base invariant by requiring a total injective morphism with bijective node mapping:

$$\vdash \texttt{tc\_loop\_invariant\_total}\ G_0\ G\ \mathit{track\_bar}\ \Longleftrightarrow$$
$$\texttt{wf\_hostgraph}\ G\ \wedge\ \texttt{unmarked\_hostgraph}\ G\ \wedge$$
$$\texttt{unrooted\_hostgraph}\ G\ \wedge$$
$$\texttt{minimal\_extension}\ G_0\ \mathit{track\_bar}\ G$$

The two invariants are connected by `extends_morphism`: the total morphism and tr share the node mapping and agree on every edge in tr's domain of definition.

The precondition together with the identity morphism establishes the augmented invariant:

$$\vdash \texttt{wf\_hostgraph}\ G_0\ \wedge\ \texttt{unmarked\_hostgraph}\ G_0\ \wedge$$
$$\texttt{unrooted\_hostgraph}\ G_0\ \Longrightarrow$$
$$\texttt{tc\_loop\_invariant\_total}\ G_0\ G_0\ (\texttt{id\_track}\ G_0)$$

The ALAP rule `WSPEC_alap`, parameterised by an invariant Q on (graph, morphism) pairs and a termination property R, has three main premises: (P1) P preserves Q on successful runs, i.e. $\{Q\}\,P\,\{Q\}$, with the postcondition composed through the per-iteration track morphism; (P2) when P fails from a Q-satisfying graph G with morphism m, $R\,G\,m$ holds; and (P3) $Q\,G\,m$ implies that m maps nodes (resp. edges) of G into G's own nodes (resp. edges). The two small-step side conditions of Sect. 5.2 (atomic body failure, no top-level `break`) are vacuous for the rule-set body `link` and discharged in a single step each.

We instantiate `WSPEC_alap` with

$$Q\ =\ \lambda\,G\,m.\,\texttt{tc\_loop\_invariant}\ \texttt{G0}\ \texttt{G}\ \texttt{m}\ \wedge$$
$$\exists\,\overline{track}.\,\texttt{tc\_loop\_invariant\_total}\ \texttt{G0}\ G\ \overline{track}\ \wedge$$
$$\texttt{extends\_morphism}\ m\ \overline{track},$$
$$R\ =\ \lambda\,G\,m.\,\texttt{is\_transitive}\ \texttt{G}.$$

Premise (P1) is established operationally: for every iteration from a Q-satisfying graph, the body either succeeds with both invariants preserved (via morphism composition) or fails atomically:

$$\vdash \texttt{wf\_hostgraph } G_0 \;\wedge\; \texttt{tc\_loop\_invariant } G_0 \; G \; m_0 \;\wedge$$

$$\texttt{tc\_loop\_invariant\_total } G_0 \; G \; track\_bar \;\wedge$$

$$\texttt{extends\_morphism } m_0 \; track\_bar \;\wedge$$

$$\texttt{steps program}$$

$$\texttt{(running (term\_rscall \{ruleid ``link''\}),}$$

$$\texttt{[(}G\texttt{,id\_track }G\texttt{)]) } c \;\wedge\; \neg\texttt{can\_step } c \implies$$

$$(\exists H \; mH.$$

$$c = \texttt{(final,[(}H\texttt{,}mH\texttt{)])} \;\wedge$$

$$\texttt{tc\_loop\_invariant } G_0 \; H$$

$$\texttt{(compose\_morphism } mH \; m_0\texttt{)} \;\wedge$$

$$\exists track\_bar'.$$

$$\texttt{tc\_loop\_invariant\_total } G_0 \; H \; track\_bar' \;\wedge$$

$$\texttt{extends\_morphism (compose\_morphism } mH \; m_0\texttt{)}$$

$$track\_bar'\texttt{)} \;\vee$$

$$c = \texttt{(failed,[(}G\texttt{,id\_track }G\texttt{)])}$$

The successful branch yields the body's WSPEC judgement directly, while the atomic-failure branch discharges the corresponding side condition. The success-preservation argument relies on `link_preserves_total` (Sect. 6.6).

Premise (P2) requires transitivity upon failure (Sect. 6.5). Premise (P3) requires that the track morphism maps into the current graph, which the base invariant guarantees.

Once the loop terminates, the ALAP rule combines the augmented invariant with transitivity. The following theorem converts this conjunction into the top-level postcondition:

$$\vdash \texttt{tc\_loop\_invariant\_total } G_0 \; TC \; track\_bar \;\wedge$$

$$\texttt{is\_transitive } TC \implies$$

$$\texttt{is\_transitive\_closure\_tracked } G_0 \; track\_bar \; TC$$

Together with the procedure rule and identity-track simplification, this completes the proof of `transitive_closure_correct`, apart from two obligations developed next: transitivity upon termination (Sect. 6.5) and preservation of the augmented invariant (Sect. 6.6).

6.5   Proving Transitivity

We now prove premise (P2) of the ALAP rule (Sect. 6.4): whenever the body `link` fails from a Q-satisfying graph, the current graph is transitive. Since `link!` exits exactly on body failure, this is also what guarantees transitivity at loop termination. The main step is to move from the operational semantics, which talks about rule-set call failure, to a purely graph-theoretic argument.

We introduce the predicate `link_can_apply`, which holds when three distinct nodes form a two-step path whose shortcut edge is absent. The following equivalence connects the operational and graph-theoretic views:

$$\vdash \texttt{wf\_hostgraph}\ G \Rightarrow$$
$$((\exists\, G'\ m'\,.$$
$$\texttt{step program}$$
$$(\texttt{running (term\_rscall \{ruleid "link"\})},$$
$$[(G, \texttt{id\_track}\ G)])\ (\texttt{final}, [(G', m')])) \iff$$
$$\texttt{link\_can\_apply}\ G)$$

Operational failure of the `link` rule-set call is equivalent to $\neg\,\texttt{link\_can\_apply G}$. This allows us to reason entirely within graph theory for the remainder of this subsection.

The central lemma shows that `link` can be applied to each two-edge path in the graph whose shortcut edge is missing:

$$\vdash \texttt{wf\_hostgraph}\ G\ \wedge\ \texttt{unmarked\_hostgraph}\ G\ \wedge$$
$$\texttt{unrooted\_hostgraph}\ G\ \wedge$$
$$(\exists\, v\ u\ w\,.$$
$$v \in G.V\ \wedge\ u \in G.V\ \wedge\ w \in G.V\ \wedge\ v \neq w\ \wedge$$
$$\texttt{has\_edge}\ G\ v\ u\ \wedge\ \texttt{has\_edge}\ G\ u\ w\ \wedge$$
$$\neg\texttt{has\_edge}\ G\ v\ w) \Rightarrow$$
$$\texttt{link\_can\_apply}\ G$$

Equivalently, when the rule cannot fire ($\neg\,\texttt{link\_can\_apply G}$), every two-step path already has a shortcut edge (the *2-step closure property*). The proof constructs a concrete prematch and verifies all conditions. We then prove `is_transitive` by induction on path length: the inductive step decomposes the path into a two-step prefix, applies the 2-step closure property to obtain a shortcut edge, and invokes the induction hypothesis on the shorter path.

Combining   the   equivalence between operational failure and $\neg\,\texttt{link\_can\_apply}$ with the inductive argument yields:

$$\texttt{wf\_hostgraph}\ G\ \wedge\ \texttt{unmarked\_hostgraph}\ G\ \wedge$$
$$\texttt{unrooted\_hostgraph}\ G\ \wedge$$
$$\neg(\exists\, G'\ m'\,.$$
$$\texttt{step program}$$
$$(\texttt{running (term\_rscall \{ruleid "link"\})},$$
$$[(G, \texttt{id\_track}\ G)])\ (\texttt{final},\ [(G', m')])) \Rightarrow$$
$$\texttt{is\_transitive}\ G$$

This discharges premise (P2) of the ALAP instantiation from Sect. 6.4.

6.6   Proving Minimal Extension

We now prove premise (P1) of the ALAP rule (Sect. 6.4): each successful application of `link` preserves the augmented loop invariant. The theorem `link_preserves_total` states that after a rule application, there exists an updated total morphism $\overline{tr}'$ satisfying `tc_loop_invariant_total` and extending the composed track morphism.

Well-formedness follows from `wf_dpo` (Sect. 3.3); the unmarked and unrooted properties are preserved because the `link` rule introduces only unmarked, unrooted elements. Since `link` preserves all nodes, the track morphism is bijective on nodes, and the composition of bijections establishes the node condition.

Every non-image edge must connect nodes reachable in G_0. The following lemma establishes reachable preimages for every RHS edge:

$$\vdash \texttt{wf\_hostgraph}\ G_0\ \wedge\ \texttt{wf\_hostgraph}\ G\ \wedge$$

$$\texttt{minimally\_extends}\ G_0\ m\ G\ \wedge$$

$$\texttt{is\_match}\ lhs'\ \texttt{rule\_link.inf}\ m''\ G\ \wedge$$

$$\texttt{instantiate\_rulegraph rule\_link.lhs}\ \textit{assign}\ m''$$

$$G =$$

$$\texttt{SOME}\ lhs'\ \wedge$$

$$\texttt{instantiate\_rulegraph rule\_link.rhs}\ \textit{assign}\ m''$$

$$G =$$

$$\texttt{SOME}\ rhs'\ \wedge\ x \in rhs'.\text{E}\ \implies$$

$$\exists v_0\ w_0\ .$$

$$v_0 \in G_0.\text{V}\ \wedge\ w_0 \in G_0.\text{V}\ \wedge$$

$$m.\texttt{nodemap}\ \text{'}\ v_0 = m''.\texttt{nodemap}\ \text{'}\ (rhs'.\text{s}\ \text{'}\ x)\ \wedge$$

$$m.\texttt{nodemap}\ \text{'}\ w_0 = m''.\texttt{nodemap}\ \text{'}\ (rhs'.\text{t}\ \text{'}\ x)\ \wedge$$

$$\texttt{reachable\_in}\ G_0\ v_0\ w_0$$

The shortcut edge is justified because the matched edges have reachable preimages by the induction hypothesis, composing via `reachable_in_trans`. The updated edge map remains injective and preserves sources and targets because `link` only adds edges, so every original edge survives. Together with the structural properties, this establishes `link_preserves_total`.

7   Related Work

Previous work on verifying GP 2 programs includes the Hoare-style proof calculi of Poskitt and Plump [18] and Wulandari and Plump [24], which use variants of monadic second-order logic as assertion languages. Both frameworks come with weakest-precondition constructions, but neither approach has been implemented yet.

Our earlier work with Isabelle/HOL [21] mechanises the double-pushout approach to graph transformation and focuses on proving two classical results of DPO theory. The track morphism of DPO derivations has been introduced in [13]. In the current paper, we extend this concept to transition sequences in the semantics of graph programs with attributed rules. We make the track morphism of a program available in assertions so that specifications can refer to the input/output relation of individual graph elements.

Strecker [22] provides an Isabelle/HOL framework for proving invariants of individual graph-transformation rules (in an ad-hoc formalism), without extending the framework to a full graph programming language.

Noschinski [12] presents a general graph-theory library for Isabelle whose path and reachability infrastructure is similar in spirit to the path theory we build on top of our graph records.

Broadly, the current paper also falls into the area of mechanised semantics for programming languages and systems. For example, CompCert [9] and CakeML [1,10] verify a C compiler and an ML compiler, respectively, and seL4 [8] verifies an operating-system kernel written in C. Our work is narrower in scope but shares the shallow-embedding methodology: a semantic predicate (here WSPEC) is defined directly in the prover's logic and serves as both the specification target and the object of the derived proof rules.

8   Conclusion

We have presented the first mechanised formalisation of a complete graph programming language in a theorem prover, covering the full GP 2 language including attributed DPO graph transformation and the operational semantics.

On top of the formalisation, we have established a compositional verification framework based on Hoare-style proof rules, and we have demonstrated it with a case study proving the partial correctness of a transitive-closure program in 50 mechanically verified theorems. The postcondition expresses transitivity and a minimal extension of the input graph via the new concept of a track morphism.

HOL's expressive power lets us quantify over morphisms and specify the trace of individual graph elements throughout entire execution sequences. The underlying framework (operational semantics, DPO construction, track morphisms, Hoare-style calculus) is reusable in further case studies.

In future work, we plan to pursue three directions: (1) verifying programs such as graph colouring and shortest-path algorithms, which will exercise the loop rule on compound bodies and motivate a standard lemma library for discharging the side conditions mechanically; (2) partial proof automation by generating assertions such as loop invariants from annotated programs; and (3) deriving an executable GP 2 semantics inside HOL4 for comparison against the existing C implementation, exploiting the fast computation primitive introduced in [1].

Acknowledgements. We are grateful for the comments of two anonymous reviewers which helped to improve the presentation of this paper.

Disclosure of Interests. The authors have no competing interests to declare that are relevant to the content of this article.

References

1. Abrahamsson, O., Myreen, M.O., Norrish, M., Kanabar, H., Pohjola, J.Å.: Fast, verified computation for HOL ITPs. J. Autom. Reason. **69**(1), 7 (2025). https://doi.org/10.1007/s10817-025-09719-8
2. Barendregt, H.P., Dekkers, W., Statman, R.: Lambda Calculus with Types. Perspectives in Logic. Cambridge University Press (2013). https://doi.org/10.1017/CBO9781139032636
3. Campbell, G., Courtehoute, B., Plump, D.: Fast rule-based graph programs. Sci. Comput. Program. **214**, 102727 (2022). https://doi.org/10.1016/j.scico.2021.102727. 32 pages
4. Church, A.: A formulation of the simple theory of types. J. Symb. Log. **5**, 56–68 (1940)
5. Courtehoute, B.: Time and space complexity of rule-based graph programs. Ph.D. thesis, University of York (2023)
6. Courtehoute, B., Plump, D.: A small-step operational semantics for GP 2. In: Graph Computation Models (GCM 2021), Revised Selected Papers. Electronic Proceedings in Theoretical Computer Science, vol. 350, pp. 89–110. Open Publishing Association (2021). https://doi.org/10.4204/EPTCS.350.6
7. Habel, A., Plump, D.: Relabelling in graph transformation. In: Corradini, A., Ehrig, H., Kreowski, H.-J., Rozenberg, G. (eds.) ICGT 2002. LNCS, vol. 2505, pp. 135–147. Springer, Heidelberg (2002). https://doi.org/10.1007/3-540-45832-8_12
8. Klein, G., et al.: seL4: formal verification of an OS kernel. In: Proceedings of the ACM SIGOPS 22nd Symposium on Operating Systems Principles (SOSP 2009), pp. 207–220. ACM (2009). https://doi.org/10.1145/1629575.1629596
9. Leroy, X.: Formal verification of a realistic compiler. Commun. ACM **52**(7), 107–115 (2009). https://doi.org/10.1145/1538788.1538814
10. Myreen, M.O., Carneiro, M.: GOL in GOL in HOL: verified circuits in Conway's Game of Life. In: 16th International Conference on Interactive Theorem Proving (ITP 2025). Leibniz International Proceedings in Informatics (LIPIcs), vol. 352, pp. 25:1–25:18. Schloss Dagstuhl – Leibniz-Zentrum für Informatik (2025). https://doi.org/10.4230/LIPIcs.ITP.2025.25
11. Nipkow, T., Klein, G.: Concrete Semantics with Isabelle/HOL. Springer (2014). https://doi.org/10.1007/978-3-319-10542-0
12. Noschinski, L.: A graph library for Isabelle. Math. Comput. Sci. **9**(1), 23–39 (2014). https://doi.org/10.1007/s11786-014-0183-z
13. Plump, D.: Hypergraph rewriting: critical pairs and undecidability of confluence. In: Term Graph Rewriting: Theory and Practice, chap. 15, pp. 201–213. Wiley (1993). https://www-users.york.ac.uk/~djp10/Papers/wiley.93.pdf
14. Plump, D.: The design of GP 2. In: Proceedings of Workshop on Reduction Strategies in Rewriting and Programming (WRS 2011). Electronic Proceedings in Theoretical Computer Science, vol. 82, pp. 1–16. Open Publishing Association (2012). https://doi.org/10.4204/EPTCS.82.1

15. Plump, D.: From imperative to rule-based graph programs. J. Log. Algebraic Methods Program. **88**, 154–173 (2017). https://doi.org/10.1016/j.jlamp.2016.12.001
16. Poskitt, C.M., Plump, D.: Hoare-style verification of graph programs. Fund. Inform. **118**(1–2), 135–175 (2012). https://doi.org/10.3233/FI-2012-708
17. Poskitt, C.M., Plump, D.: Verifying total correctness of graph programs. In: Graph Computation Models (GCM 2012), Revised Selected Papers. Electronic Communications of the EASST, vol. 61. Berlin Universities Publishing (2013). https://doi.org/10.14279/tuj.eceasst.61.827
18. Poskitt, C.M., Plump, D.: Verifying monadic second-order properties of graph programs. In: Giese, H., König, B. (eds.) ICGT 2014. LNCS, vol. 8571, pp. 33–48. Springer, Cham (2014). https://doi.org/10.1007/978-3-319-09108-2_3
19. Poskitt, C.M., Plump, D.: Monadic second-order incorrectness logic for GP 2. J. Logical Algebraic Methods Program. **130**, 100825 (2023). https://doi.org/10.1016/j.jlamp.2022.100825
20. Slind, K., Norrish, M.: A brief overview of HOL4. In: Mohamed, O.A., Muñoz, C., Tahar, S. (eds.) TPHOLs 2008. LNCS, vol. 5170, pp. 28–32. Springer, Heidelberg (2008). https://doi.org/10.1007/978-3-540-71067-7_6
21. Söldner, R., Plump, D.: Formalising the double-pushout approach to graph transformation. Logical Methods Comput. Sci. **19**(4), 1–42 (2023). https://doi.org/10.46298/lmcs-19(4:20)2023
22. Strecker, M.: Interactive and automated proofs for graph transformations. Math. Struct. Comput. Sci. **28**(8), 1333–1362 (2018). https://doi.org/10.1017/S096012951800021X
23. Wulandari, G., Plump, D.: Verifying graph programs with first-order logic. In: Graph Computation Models (GCM 2020), Revised Selected Papers. Electronic Proceedings in Theoretical Computer Science, vol. 330, pp. 181–200. Open Publishing Association (2020). https://doi.org/10.4204/EPTCS.330.11
24. Wulandari, G.S., Plump, D.: Verifying graph programs with monadic second-order logic. In: Gadducci, F., Kehrer, T. (eds.) ICGT 2021. LNCS, vol. 12741, pp. 240–261. Springer, Cham (2021). https://doi.org/10.1007/978-3-030-78946-6_13

Approximately Compatible Graph Predicates
Verifying Program Termination Using Graph Grammars

Alexander Ferber[1], Ira Fesefeldt[1,2], Thomas Noll[1]($\boxtimes$), and Emmett Rayes[1]

[1] RWTH Aachen University, Aachen, Germany
ira.fesefeldt@uni-due.de, noll@cs.rwth-aachen.de
[2] University of Duisburg-Essen, Duisburg, Germany

Abstract. We present a novel technique to verify termination of imperative programs supporting heap-manipulating operations and especially dynamic data structures. The latter can have many shapes and forms, going beyond simple lists or simple binary trees. In such cases, state-of-the-art termination checkers often fail. An approach to handle various data structures involving user input is called for to complete the landscape of termination verification.

We use hyperedge-replacement graph grammars to guide abstraction of data structures. An edge labelled with a nonterminal symbol represents here an abstraction of an entire data structure with various endpoints from which we can access the data structure. Using this abstraction, we construct an abstract transition system for the given program. This transition system can already be checked for various properties such as the absence of null-pointer exceptions. By looking for loops in the transition system, we can further analyse whether all execution of the program are terminating. We pick one state for each loop (called the critical state) and verify that every path starting from this state and returning to it has a ranking function, thus enabling a termination proof. For this, we further annotate the grammar by rules that specify how to adjust the variant leading to the ranking function.

Keywords: Hyperedge-Replacement Grammars · Termination · Static Program Analysis

1 Introduction

We propose a novel technique for proving termination of heap-manipulating programs involving complex data structures. A *heap* is a memory addressed by locations which is used in programming for implementing data structures. A common problem is to analyse programs using data structures going beyond simple linked lists. One solution is to model the shape of the data structure as a user-defined *hyperedge-replacement grammar* and to use this formalisation to guide the abstraction by means of *symbolic execution* of programs [1,15]. Here,

B. Archibald and O. Semeráth (Eds.): ICGT 2026, LNCS 16624, pp. 129–148, 2026.
https://doi.org/10.1007/978-3-032-29730-3_7

hyperedges with nonterminal symbols represent a *language of heaps*. Each hyperedge labelled by a nonterminal symbol can be replaced by any derived graph to obtain a more concretised (but possibly still abstract) graph representation of the heap. This allows the generation of an *abstracted transition system*.

The details of this approach haven bee laid out in [1,15]. In a nutshell, the user has to give both an application program operating on the heap and a hyperedge-replacement grammar specifying the set of heap data structures maintained by the program. Next, the abstract transition system is generated by means of symbolic execution of the program on abstract graphs (possibly) containing nonterminals. An abstract transition is performed by taking such a graph, expanding the nonterminals that have to be concretised to apply the pointer operation, and abstracting again by applying hyperedge-replacement rules backwards (cf. Fig. 4a on page 18).

We use this hyperedge-replacement based approach and enrich it with an analysis capable of proving the termination of a program on all input graphs satisfying a given precondition, which is modelled as an abstract graph. In order to prove termination, a user has to give, in addition to the grammar from above, *transformation rules* that are *compatible* with a certain predicate indexed by natural numbers. These predicates usually represent size quantities of the data structure. In order to enable the analysis of the program on a set of inputs, we introduce a symbolic version of natural numbers with variables, and we annotate nonterminal edges in the abstract transition system with these symbolic natural numbers. The predicates mentioned before then yield a filtration on the hypergraphs in the transition system. Using techniques from *dataflow analysis* [21], we can analyse the change of the index values of these predicates during one loop iteration. A negative change gives rise to a *ranking function* and thus concludes our termination proof.

Related Work. There is a zoo of different termination tools for heap-manipulating programs (e.g. [3–5,12,16,20]). One particular related approach implements the termination analysis by Rowe and Brotherston [22]. The corresponding tool employs *separation logic with inductive predicates* and exhaustively searches for a termination proof using Hoare-like proof rules. The connection to our work becomes clear when considering the possibility to transform (a fragment of) separation logic with inductive predicates to hyperedge-replacement grammars and vice versa [7]. In contrast to their work, we do not have to exhaustively search proofs but can directly generate an abstract transition system and the corresponding data-flow analysis.

Our framework is inspired by work on *compatible predicates* in hyperedge-replacement grammars [14]. These predicates are *indexed* by a finite set of indices and require the existence of a (computable) *helper predicate* on the rules of the grammar. It is then required that a graph derived from the grammar satisfies the desired predicate if and only if one can prove the soundness iteratively using the helper predicate. Using a filter theorem, one can use compatible predicates to decide various questions about the grammar and the compatible predicate such as deciding whether every graph in the language of the grammar satisfies the predicate. These predicates have also been extended to compatible functions [8, page 136]. Our work uses an adaptation of compatible predicates. However, we do not require the proof guarantee of a helper predicate. Instead, we employ functions that yield an overapproximation of the predicate (i.e. a greater natural number) both for derivations and reverse derivations. Moreover, as we consider predicates indexed by natural numbers, we allow infinite sets of indices.

Overview. In this paper, we will first introduce in Sect. 2 hyperedge-replacement grammars as a generation mechanism for languages of graphs. With this formalism at hand, we proceed by introducing approximately compatible graph predicates as our first major contribution in Sect. 3. Our second main contribution is the application of approximately compatible graph predicates to program termination analysis, which we detail out in Sect. 4. In Sect. 5, we demonstrate our implementation of the termination analysis on an example using In-Trees and finally conclude in Sect. 6.

2 Hyperedge-Replacement Grammars

Hypergraphs are graphs where edges may be *hyperedges*, that is, edges connecting an arbitrary number of vertices (not necessarily two). We label these hyperedges and require that two hyperedges with the same label connect the same number of vertices, which is called their *rank*. Moreover, our hypergraphs come with a sequence of *external vertices*, used to further differentiate vertices under isomorphism.

Definition 1 (Hypergraph). *Let Σ be a set of labels and* arity: $\Sigma \to \mathbb{N}$ *an arity function. The tuple $H = (V_H, E_H, att_H, label_H, ext_H)$ is a labelled hypergraph over Σ where*

- V_H *is a finite set of vertices over some universe of vertices,*
- E_H *is a finite set of hyperedges over some universe of hyperedges,*
- $att_H : E_H \to V_H^*$ *maps every hyperedge to a sequence of attached vertices,*
- $label_H : E_H \to \Sigma$ *labels every hyperedge $e \in E_H$ such that* $arity(label_H(e)) = |att_H(e)|$, *and*
- $ext_H \in V_H^*$ *is a sequence of external vertices.*

We define $\mathcal{H}_S$ as the set of all hypergraphs over the symbols $S \subseteq \Sigma$. $\triangle$

We will also use the notation E_H^S for the subset of E_H that contains exactly the hyperedges with labels in S.

To define a starting hypergraph for derivations using graph grammars, we often assume a hypergraph only containing one hyperedge with a certain label. This hypergraph is called a *handle*.

Definition 2 (Handle). *The handle of a symbol $a \in \Sigma$ is the hypergraph $a^\bullet$ with $V_{a^\bullet} = \{v_1 \ldots v_{arity(a)}\}, E_{a^\bullet} = \{e_a\}, att_{a^\bullet} = v_1 \ldots v_{arity(a)}, label_{a^\bullet} = a$ and $ext_{a^\bullet} = \varepsilon$, where $v_1, \ldots, v_{arity(a)}$ are pairwise distinct.* $\triangle$

Hyperedge-replacement grammars [13] are equipped with a set of *nonterminal labels* N, a set of *terminal labels* T, and *production rules* that guide derivations. We assume that N and T are disjoint and together form the set of possible labels for hyperedges.

Definition 3 (Hyperedge-Replacement Grammar). $G = (N, T, P)$ *is a hyperedge-replacement grammar over* $\Sigma = N \cup T$ *where* N *and* T *are the sets of nonterminal and terminal symbols, respectively, and* $P \subseteq N \times \mathcal{H}_\Sigma$ *are productions such that* $\forall (A, H) \in P.\ |ext_H| = arity(A)$. *We define* HRG_Σ *as the set of all hyperedge-replacement grammars over* Σ. $\triangle$

Assuming that the number of external vertices ext_H on the right-hand side of a production rule corresponds to the rank of the symbol on the left-hand side guarantees that a hyperedge with nonterminal labels will always have the same number of attached vertices.

We use hyperedges with terminal labels to model program constructs such as selectors and variables, and hyperedges with nonterminal labels to denote the language of all heaps representing a data structure. In this sense, we interpret hyperedges with nonterminal labels as a representation of a data structure by its language.

In the following definition, we use the symbol $\uplus$ to express that the vertices and hyperedges of hypergraphs H and R need to be disjoint. This can easily be achieved by renaming them in R. To this extent, whenever we consider *equality between graphs* we mean here *equality up to isomorphism between these graphs*.

Definition 4 (Hyperedge Replacement). *Let* $H, R \in \mathcal{H}_\Sigma$ *and* $\xi \in E_H$. *We call* $H[\xi \to R]$ *the replacement of* ξ *by* R *in* H *and define it by its components:*

- $V_{H[\xi \to R]} = V_H \uplus (V_R \setminus [ext_R])$
- $E_{H[\xi \to R]} = (E_H \setminus \{\xi\}) \uplus E_R$
- $att_{H[\xi \to R]}(e)(m) = \begin{cases} att_H(e)(m) & \textit{if } e \in E_H \\ att_R(e)(m) & \textit{if } e \in E_R \wedge att_R(e)(m) \notin [ext_R] \\ att_H(\xi)(m') & \textit{if } e \in E_R \wedge att_R(e)(m) = ext_R(m') \end{cases}$
- $label_{H[\xi \to R]}(e) = \begin{cases} label_H(e) & \textit{if } e \in E_H \\ label_R(e) & \textit{if } e \in E_R \end{cases}$
- $ext_{H[\xi \to R]} = ext_H$

where $\cdot(m)$ *refers to the m-th element of a sequence and* $[\cdot]$ *denotes the set of all its elements.* $\triangle$

Before wrapping up this section by introducing the language of hyperedge-replacement grammars, let us consider a little example.

Example 1. We define the grammar $G = (N, T, P)$ with $N = \{List\}$, $T = \{next\}$ where $arity(List) = arity(next) = 2$ and P as

$$List \to \quad \boxed{1} \xrightarrow{\ next\ } \boxed{2} \quad (1) \quad \bigg| \quad \boxed{1} \xrightarrow{\ next\ } \circ \overset{1}{\underline{\quad}} \fbox{$List$} \overset{2}{\underline{\quad}} \boxed{2} \quad (2)$$

Let $(List, H_1), (List, H_2)$ be these production rules respectively. We can now replace the hyperedge in the handle $List^\bullet$ first by H_2 (see below left) and then the new remaining hyperedge by H_1 (see below right):

We use this replacement operation to first define derivations in hyperedge-replacement grammars. The generated language consists of all terminal graphs derived from a certain starting hypergraph.

Note here that since the handle has no external vertices, the results of the replacements also do not have external vertices. External vertices are only used to match a graph with the edge that is replaced.

We use this replacement operation to first define derivations in hyperedge-replacement grammars. The generated language consists of all terminal graphs derived from a certain starting hypergraph.

Definition 5 (Derivations and Language).

– *For $G = (N, T, P) \in HRG_\Sigma$, $(A, R) = p \in P$, $H, H' \in \mathcal{H}_\Sigma$ and $\xi \in E_H$ with $label_H(\xi) = A$, H forward derives H' by p applied to ξ, written as $H \Rightarrow_{(\xi,p)} H'$, if and only if $H[\xi \to R] = H'$. We write $H \Rightarrow H'$ (or sometimes $H \Rightarrow_G H'$) for $\exists \xi.\ \exists p.\ H \Rightarrow_{(\xi,p)} H'$ and $\Rightarrow^*$ for the reflexive and transitive closure of $\Rightarrow$.*
– *The language of $G = (N, T, P)$ with respect to H is defined as the set $L_G(H) = \{H_T \in \mathcal{H}_T \mid H \Rightarrow^* H_T\}$.* $\triangle$

Since hyperedge-replacement grammars are *context-free* (see [13]), a hyperedge with a nonterminal label in H is associated to a sub-graph for every hypergraph in the language $L_G(H)$. We call this connection a *joint-embedding*. Joint-embeddings are unique up to isomorphism. Since we also consider equality up to isomorphism, we will thus assume uniqueness of joint-embeddings.

Definition 6 (Joint-Embedding). *Let $H, H' \in \mathcal{H}_\Sigma$ be two hypergraphs with $E_H = \{e_1, \dots e_m\}$, $H \Rightarrow^* H'$ and $H[e_1 \to R_1] \dots [e_m \to R_m] = H'$. For a hyperedge $e_i \in E_H$, the joint-embedding of e_i in H' is $H'(e_i) = R_i$.* $\triangle$

3   Approximately Compatible Graph Predicates

Our next goal is to define predicates that can be used with hyperedge-replacement grammars to analyse the *change* of *quantitative properties* of data structures. To achieve this, we use an abstract domain that allows us to track a decreasing change. As such, we use indexed graph predicates where the indices range over the integers. Furthermore, as a ranking argument requires a well-founded domain, we will require that the set of graphs described by the predicate is empty for negative index values.

Indeed, we could choose different domains such as lexicographically-ordered tuples. For reasons of clarity and since our implementation only uses integers, we will stick to the domain of integers and refer to [10] for a more general examination of the domain.

Firstly, we require an abstract domain which represents a sum of variables and a constant. Indeed, if starting with only one variable, it is easy to keep track of changes by observing the constant. For suprema and infima to always exist (thus forming a complete lattice), we will use here integers enriched with top and bottom symbols, which we call the extended integers $\mathbb{Z}^\infty$.

Definition 7 (Symbolic Integers and their Evaluation). *Let Var be a set of variables. The set $\mathbb{Z}^\infty_{sym} = 2^{Var} \times \mathbb{Z}^\infty$ is called symbolic integers. The partial order on this set is given by $(V, i) \sqsubseteq (V', i') \Leftrightarrow V \subseteq V' \wedge i \leq i'$, and we let $(V, i) \sqsubset (V', i')$ iff $(V, i) \sqsubseteq (V', i')$ and $(V, i) \neq (V', i')$. We write x instead of $(\{x\}, 0)$ and i instead of $(\emptyset, i)$. An evaluation is a map $\nu \colon \mathbb{Z}^\infty_{sym} \to \mathbb{Z}^\infty$ with $\nu(V, i) = i + \sum_{x \in V} \nu(x) = i + \sum_{x \in V} \nu((\{x\}, 0))$. The set of all evaluations is denoted by $\mathcal{V}$.* △

Every hyperedge with nonterminal label is assigned one index. The semantics of assigning a hyperedge e in the hypergraph H an index is that we filter the language $L_G(H)$ such that the joint embeddings of e satisfy the index assigned to e with respect to a given predicate. We will introduce this formally later in Definition 12.

The variables Var are used to assign initial values to indices. Since we start with a graph of arbitrary size, we assign a variable this size and compute a relative change. This is why we require variables to track initial size values.

Definition 8 (Assign Domain). *Let E^N be a set of hyperedges with nonterminal labels in N. We call the mapping $idx \colon E^N \to \mathbb{Z}^\infty_{sym}$ an index assignment of hyperedges and denote with Assign the set of all such assignments, with $\dot{\sqsubseteq}$ the pointwise order on assignments, with $\dot{\bigsqcup}$ the least upper bound on assignments, and for evaluation ν with $\nu(idx)$ the pointwise application of ν on idx.* △

Finally, we have all ingredients to introduce approximately compatible predicates. These are inspired by the compatible predicates used for reasoning about decidability of certain properties of hyperedge-replacement grammars [13, p. 128–141]. A predicate is compatible if the index set is finite and there is a computable helper predicate for each right-hand side of a production such that instead of proving the property on the initial graph, we can also prove it on every possible single derivation using the helper predicate. This can then be used to derive decision procedures to check certain properties on graph languages defined by hyperedge-replacement grammars.

However, we (1) do not require a finite index set and (2) do not require semantic equivalence between the helper predicate and the predicate in question. Instead, we require (a) a partial order over the indices and (b) functions that map indices in either direction of a derivation. That is, if we have a derivation $A^\bullet \Rightarrow R$, we want to have a function taking an index for $A^\bullet$ and transforming it to indices for every nonterminal edge in R. Moreover, we also like to have the reverse, that is, a function taking indices for every edge in R and transforming them to an index for $A^\bullet$. All of these transformations should be language inclusive, i.e. we may only be less restrictive, not more restrictive.

Definition 9 (Approximately Compatible Predicates). *Let* $(N, T, P) \in$ *HRG_Σ be a grammar and $Q \colon \mathbb{Z}^\infty \to 2^{\mathcal{H}_T}$ be an indexed graph predicate.*

- *We call $(F_p)_{p \in P}$ with $F_p \colon \mathbb{Z}^\infty_{sym} \to Assign$ approximately compatible forward derivation rules of Q for G if for all $A^\bullet \Rightarrow_{(\xi, p)} R \Rightarrow^* H_T \in \mathcal{H}_T$, $\nu \in \mathcal{V}$ and $\sigma \in \mathbb{Z}^\infty_{sym}$ we have*

$$H_T \in Q(\nu(\sigma)) \Rightarrow \forall e \in E_R^N .\ H_T(e) \in Q(\nu(F_p(\sigma)(e))).$$

- *We call $(B_p)_{p \in P}$ with $B_p \colon Assign \to \mathbb{Z}^\infty_{sym}$ approximately compatible backwards derivation rules of Q for G if for all $A^\bullet \Rightarrow_{(\xi, p)} R \Rightarrow^* H_T \in \mathcal{H}_T$ with $E_R^N = \{e_1, \ldots e_m\}$, $\nu \in \mathcal{V}$ and $idx \in Assign$ we have*

$$\left(\forall e_j \in E_R^N .\ H_T(e_j) \in Q(idx(e)) \right) \Rightarrow H_T \in Q(\nu(B_p(idx))).$$

$$\triangle$$

We assume all of $(F_p)_{p \in P}$ and $(B_p)_{p \in P}$ to be computable mappings.

Example 2. We consider again the grammar from Example 1 where we enumerate the rules from left to right as 1 and 2:

$$List \to \quad \textcircled{1} \xrightarrow{\ next\ } \textcircled{2} \quad (1) \quad \Big| \quad \textcircled{1} \xrightarrow{\ next\ } \circ \xrightarrow{1} \boxed{List} \xrightarrow{2} \textcircled{2} \quad (2)$$

We define $\mathsf{LE\text{-}EDGES} \colon \mathbb{Z}^\infty \to 2^{\mathcal{H}_T}$ such that $\mathsf{LE\text{-}EDGES}(i)$ is the set of hypergraphs with at most i hyperedges (such that $\mathsf{LE\text{-}EDGES}(i) = \emptyset$ for $i < 0$). We proceed by defining the approximately compatible derivation rules where e is the hyperedge with label $List$ in the replacement:

$$
\begin{aligned}
F_1(s, i) &= \emptyset \\
F_2(s, i)(e) &= (s, i - 1) \\
B_1(idx) &= (0, 1) \\
B_2(idx) &= (s, i + 1) \text{ where } idx(e) = (s, i)
\end{aligned}
$$

Note here that for production rule 1, there is no hyperedge with nonterminal labels on the right-hand side. Thus, the forward rule maps to the empty assignment whereas the backward rule does not use the assignment. For production rule 2, the approximately compatible derivation rules respectively decrease and increase the number of edges.

4   Analysis of Program Termination

We now move on towards a termination analysis framework for pointer programs using approximately compatible predicates. We assume that a suitable operational semantics dealing with program locations and terminal hypergraphs is already given for the pointer program [15]. Modelling the heap of pointer programs as graphs has tradition and is also useful in our application. That is, a *concrete graph transition system* $(S, \to_c)$ consists of the states $S = Loc \times \mathcal{H}_T$ and the transition relation $\to_c$. Every state's first entry is from a universe of program locations Loc and its second entry is a hypergraph from $\mathcal{H}_T$.

Example 3. Consider the hypergraphs G_i with

$$G_1 = \quad \bigcirc \xrightarrow{\text{next}} \bigcirc\!-\!\boxed{\text{null}} \qquad G_2 = \quad \bigcirc \xrightarrow{\text{next}} \bigcirc \xrightarrow{\text{next}} \bigcirc\!-\!\boxed{\text{null}} \quad \cdots$$

and the hypergraph G_0 with

$$\bigcirc\!-\!\boxed{\text{null}}$$

where the hyperdge with label `null` is labelling the null pointer object. The following are concrete graph transition systems TS_i (for all $i \geq 0$):

$$(1, G_i) \xrightarrow{f} (1, G_{i-1}) \xrightarrow{f} \cdots \xrightarrow{f} (1, G_2) \xrightarrow{f} (1, G_1) \xrightarrow{f} (0, G_0)$$

Here, the function f removes the first vertex in the list.

For the abstract semantics, we want every transition to consist of three operations. First, we may apply *derivations forward* on the hypergraph, then we may *change* the hypergraph on a sub-graph only containing *hyperedges with terminal symbols* and, finally, we may apply *derivations backward* on the result. These operations constitute the core part of symbolic execution of pointer programs (as visualised by the grey area in Fig. 4a on page 18). Indeed, there has been manifold work on such abstract semantics [1,9,15,17]. Here, we will not formally introduce semantics for a specific programming language but only describe the framework.

Definition 10 (Abstract HRG Transition System). *Let $G = (N, T, P) \in HRG_\Sigma$ be a grammar and F be a set of operations on $\mathcal{H}_\Sigma$. We call an F-labelled transition system $(\mathbb{S}, \rightarrow)$ with $\mathbb{S} \subseteq Loc \times \mathcal{H}_\Sigma$ an abstract HRG transition system if every transition $(l, H) \xrightarrow{f} (l', H')$ can be decomposed into $H \Rightarrow_G^* H_m$, $f(H_m) = H'_m$ and $H'_m \Leftarrow_G^* H'$ where $f \in F$.* △*

A first inspection may suggest that by this definition, concrete transition systems need to be deterministic. This is not the case. Although we enforce a function on the transitions, we can have multiple functions attached to different transitions. The nondeterminism then chooses one function.

Definition 11 (Abstraction of a Concrete Transition System). *We call the transition system $(\mathbb{S}_c, \rightarrow_c)$ a concrete transition system of the abstract HRG transition system $(\mathbb{S}_a, \rightarrow_a)$ with respect to $G = (N, T, P)$ if there exists an abstraction function $\alpha \colon \mathbb{S}_c \rightarrow \mathbb{S}_a$ such that for any $\alpha(l, H_c) = (l, H_a)$ we have that $H_c \in L_G(H_a)$ and for any $(l, H_c) \xrightarrow{f}_c (l', H'_c)$ we have that $(l, H_a) \xrightarrow{f}_a (l', H'_a)$ and $\alpha(l', H'_c) = (l', H'_a)$.* △

Example 4. Consider the abstract hypergraph G_a as

$$\bigcirc \xrightarrow{1} \boxed{List} \xrightarrow{2} \bigcirc\!-\!\boxed{\text{null}}$$

and the abstract HRG transition system TS_a as

$$\begin{array}{c} f \\ \curvearrowright \\ (1, G_a) \xrightarrow{\ f\ } (0, G_0). \end{array}$$

TS_a is an abstract HRG transition system for all TS_i from Example 3. For this, consider that G_a is an abstraction of every G_i using Example 1. The transformation consists of removing one vertex from G_i. Thus we get

$$G_a \Rightarrow G_i, f(G_i) = G_{i-1}, G_{i-1} \Leftarrow G_a,$$

and analogous for the other transitions.

The abstraction of a transition system [2] is often derived by using an abstract interpretation [6]. We will not go further into details and instead concentrate on checking whether an abstract transition system enables a non-terminating concrete transition system.

For doing so, we leverage dataflow analysis techniques [21, Chapter 2]. These use transfer functions to let abstract data flow over an already existing transition system. This gives rise to an equation system involving these transfer functions. Computing the smallest solution to the equation system is desirable in our setting. Unfortunately, this is not possible and thus we compute any solution. We will not go further in detail how to guarantee computability of a solution and refer to [10, 19] for details. Instead we settle by defining the equation system and proving its soundness.

Definition 12 (Assign Filter). *Let $G \in HRG_\Sigma$ be a grammar. The filtration of a hypergraph $H \in \mathcal{H}_\Sigma$ with respect to an indexed predicate $Q\colon \mathbb{Z}^\infty \to 2^{\mathcal{H}_T}$, an assignment $idx \in Assign$ and evaluation $\nu \in \mathcal{V}$ is*

$$L_G(H) \cap Q_\nu(idx) = \{H_T \in L_G(H) \mid \forall e \in E_H^N.\ H_T(e) \in Q(\nu(idx(e)))\}.$$

△

Example 5. Consider the grammar from Example 1 and the predicate LE-EDGES from Example 2. The filtration of the hypergraph $L_G(G_a) \cap \mathsf{LE\text{-}EDGES}_\nu(idx)$ with $\nu(idx(e)) = 3$, where e is the only hyperedge in G_a, yields the set of all hypergraphs $\{G_3, G_2, G_1\}$. Note that G_0 is not included, as this graph is not derivable from G_a.

Transfer functions use the approximation rules from Definition 9 to derive indices that are language-inclusive under assign filters (see Definitions 8 and 12) for a derivation in both directions and lift them to the setting of assignments. Here, the three basic types of transfer functions correspond to the three kinds of operations given in Definition 10: concretisation by forward derivation, application of a pointer operation, and abstraction by backward derivation.

Definition 13 (Transfer Functions). *Let $G \in HRG_\Sigma$ be a grammar with forward approximately compatible rules $(F_p)_{p \in P}$ and backward approximately compatible rules $(B_p)_{p \in P}$ for an indexed predicate Q, and let $\nu \in \mathcal{V}$ be an evaluation.*

- *The transfer function of $H \Rightarrow_{(\xi,(A,R))} H'$ is defined by*

$$\psi_{(\xi,(A,R))}(idx) = \lambda e. \begin{cases} idx(e) & \text{if } e \in E_{H'} \setminus E_R \\ F_{(A,R)}(idx)(e) & \text{if } e \in E_R \\ \bot & \text{else.} \end{cases}$$

- *The transfer function for $f \in F$ is a function $\varphi_f(idx) = idx'$ with*

$$H_T \in L_G(H) \cap Q_\nu(idx) \Rightarrow f(H_T) \in L_G(f(H)) \cap Q_\nu(idx').$$

- *The transfer function of $H \Leftarrow_{(\xi,(A,R))} H'$ is defined by*

$$\rho_{(\xi,(A,R))}(idx) = \lambda e. \begin{cases} idx(e) & \text{if } e \in E_{H'} \setminus \{\xi\} \\ B_{(A,R)}(idx) & \text{if } e = \xi \\ \bot & \text{else.} \end{cases}$$

- *The transfer function of $(l, H) \rightarrow_a (l', H')$ with the attached operations $H = H_0 \Rightarrow_{r_1} \ldots \Rightarrow_{r_n} H_n$, $f(H_n) = H_0'$ and $H_0' \Leftarrow_{r_1'} \ldots \Leftarrow_{r_m'} H_m' = H'$ is given by the composition of the previous functions:*

$$\varphi_{(l,H),(l',H')} = \rho_{r_m'} \circ \cdots \circ \rho_{r_1'} \circ \varphi_f \circ \psi_{r_n} \circ \cdots \circ \psi_{r_1}$$

$$\triangle$$

According to the previous definition, we postulate the existence of a transfer function φ_f. This is only a mild requirement. In fact, we required that f can only manipulate hyperedges with terminal labels. But since we assign indices only to hyperedges with nonterminal labels, φ_f will usually be the identity.

It is now left to prove that the previous definition soundly overapproximates indices for every hyperedge labelled by a nonterminal symbol.

Theorem 1 (Soundness of Transfer Functions). *For a transition $(l, H) \rightarrow_a (l', H')$ with the attached operations $H = H_0 \Rightarrow_{r_1} \ldots \Rightarrow_{r_n} H_n$, $f(H_n) = H_0'$ and $H_0' \Leftarrow_{r_1'} \ldots \Leftarrow_{r_m'} H_m' = H'$ and given transfer function φ_f, we have*

$$H_T \in L_G(H) \cap Q_\nu(idx)$$
$$\Rightarrow f(H_T) \in L_G(H') \cap Q_\nu(\varphi_{(l,H),(l',H')}(idx))$$

Proof. We have $H_T \in L_G(H) \cap Q_\nu(idx)$ and by Definition 12 we have $\forall e \in E_H^N.\ H_T(e) \in Q(\nu(idx(e)))$. We now prove by induction over $i \leq n$ that $\forall e \in E_{H_i}^N.\ H_T(e) \in Q(\nu(\psi_{r_i} \circ \cdots \circ \psi_{r_1}(idx)(e)))$.

Case 1 $(i = 0)$. We immediately have $\forall e \in E_H^N.\ H_T(e) \in Q(\nu(idx(e)))$.

Case 2 ($i > 0$). By the induction hypothesis we have $\forall e \in E^N_{H_{i-1}}$. $H_T(e) \in Q(\nu(\psi_{r_{i-1}} \circ \cdots \circ \psi_{r_1}(idx)(e)))$. Now let $r_i = (\xi, (A, R))$ and we have:

Case 2.1 ($e \in E_{H_{i-1}} \setminus E_R$). Then immediately we have $H_T(e) \in Q(\nu(\psi_{r_i} \circ \psi_{r_{i-1}} \circ \cdots \circ \psi_{r_1}(idx)(e)))$.

Case 2.2 ($e \in E_R$). By Definition 9 and since we have $H_T(\xi) \in Q(\nu(\psi_{r_{i-1}} \circ \cdots \circ \psi_{r_1}(idx)(\xi)))$, we also have $H_T(e) \in Q(\nu(F_{(A,R)} \circ \psi_{r_{i-1}} \circ \cdots \circ \psi_{r_1}(idx)(e)))$, and thus, by Definition 13, $H_T(e) \in Q(\nu(\psi_{r_i} \circ \psi_{r_{i-1}} \circ \cdots \circ \psi_{r_1}(idx)(e)))$.

Therefore we have $H_T \in L_G(H_n) \cap Q_\nu(\psi_{r_n} \circ \cdots \circ \psi_{r_1}(idx))$. By Definition 13 we now also have that $f(H_T) \in L_G(f(H_n)) \cap Q_\nu(\varphi_f \circ \psi_{r_n} \circ \cdots \circ \psi_{r_1}(idx))$.

Lastly we prove by induction over $j \leq m$ that $f(H_T) \in L_G(H'_j) \cap Q_\nu(\rho_{r'_j} \circ \cdots \circ \rho_{r'_1} \varphi_f \circ \psi_{r_n} \circ \cdots \circ \psi_{r_1}(idx))$.

Case 1 ($j = 0$). By replacing $f(H_n)$ with H'_0, we immediately have $f(H_T) \in L_G(H'_0) \cap Q_\nu(\varphi_f \circ \psi_{r_n} \circ \cdots \circ \psi_{r_1}(idx))$.

Case 2 ($j > 0$). By the induction hypothesis we have $\forall e \in E^N_{H'_{j-1}}$. $f(H_T)(e) \in Q(\nu(\rho_{r'_{j-1}} \circ \cdots \circ \rho_{r'_1} \circ \varphi_f \circ \psi_{r_n} \circ \cdots \circ \psi_{r_1}(idx)(e)))$. Now let $r'_i = (\xi, (A, R))$ and we have:

Case 2.1 ($e \in E_{H_{j-1}} \setminus \{\xi\}$) Then immediately we have $H_T(e) \in Q(\nu(\rho_{r'_j} \circ \rho_{r'_{j-1}} \circ \cdots \circ \rho_{r'_1} \circ \varphi_f \circ \psi_{r_n} \circ \cdots \circ \psi_{r_1}(idx)(e)))$.

Case 2.2 ($e = \xi$). By Definition 9, since we have $E^N_R \subseteq E^N_{H_{j-1}}$ and we have $\forall e \in E^N_{H_{j-1}}$. $H_T(e) \in Q(\nu(\psi_{r_{j-1}} \circ \cdots \circ \psi_{r_1}(idx)(e)))$ we also have $H_T(\xi) \in Q(\nu(B_{(A,R)} \circ \psi_{r_{j-1}} \circ \cdots \circ \psi_{r_1}(idx)(\xi)))$, thus we have by Definition 13 that $H_T(\xi) \in Q(\nu(\psi_{r_j} \circ \psi_{r_{j-1}} \circ \cdots \circ \psi_{r_1}(idx)(\xi)))$.

Lastly, we also have that $H_T \in L_G(H') \cap Q_\nu(\varphi_{(l,H),(l',H')}(idx))$.   ⊔

The equation system of the transfer functions φ requires *monotonicity* to enable a solution. We can guarantee this by requiring that the property Q is monotone. Since we will use the equation system for termination analysis, we also require that strictly decreasing chains are *terminating*. In our settings, this means that strictly decreasing chains lead to an index i with $Q(i) = \emptyset$. Lastly, we want to be able to always instantiate our equation system to a certain transition system. That is, we want values that are satisfied by the starting hypergraph of the concrete transition system. We call the property that these always exists *always satisfiable*.

Definition 14 (Indexed Predicate Properties). *Let $Q \colon \mathbb{Z}^\infty \to 2^{\mathcal{H}_T}$ be an indexed predicate. We call Q*

- *monotone if for $i \leq j$ we have $Q(i) \subseteq Q(j)$,*
- *terminating if for $i < 0$ we have $Q(i) = \emptyset$, and*
- *always satisfiable for $G = (N, T, P) \in HRG_\Sigma$ if for $A \in N$ and $H_T \in L_G(A^\bullet)$ there exists i with $H_T \in Q(i)$.*   △

Example 6. Let us reconsider the predicate LE-EDGES from Example 2. We will show all three properties from Definition 14.

- LE-EDGES is monotone as if $i \leq j$ every graph $H \in$ LE-EDGES(i) also has at most j edges and thus $H \in$ LE-EDGES(j).
- LE-EDGES is terminating as no graph can have a negative number of hyperedges.
- LE-EDGES is always satisfiable for any G as any graph has a certain number of hyperedges.

Monotonicity of the transfer functions allows us to define an equation system over the transfer functions whose solution overapproximates assignments for every hypergraph. This equation system is solvable by the dataflow analysis framework, which guarantees the existence of the solution of the equation system and on top allows usage of algorithms to compute this solution.

Definition 15 (Dataflow Equation System). *The dataflow equation system* $\Phi^{\hat{s}} : \mathbb{S} \to \mathcal{I}_\alpha$ *for an abstract HRG transition system* $(\mathbb{S}, \to)$, *a monotone indexed predicate* Q *and some state* $\hat{s}$ *is defined as*

$$\Phi^{\hat{s}}(s) = \begin{cases} \lambda e.\ (\{v_e\}, 0) & \textit{if } s = \hat{s} \\ \bigsqcup \{\varphi_{s',s}(\Phi^{\hat{s}}(s')) \mid s' \to_a s\} & \textit{else} \end{cases}$$

where v_e *are variable indices as given in Definition 7.* △

Example 7. We set up the equation system for the abstract transition system (cf. Example 4)

$$(1, G_a) \xrightarrow{f} (0, G_0).$$

for LE-EDGES and the initial state $(1, G_a)$, since it is the only one in a cycle:

$$\Phi^{(1,G_a)}((1, G_a)) = \lambda e.\ (\{v_e\}, 0)$$

$$\Phi^{(1,G_a)}((0, G_0)) = \bigsqcup \{\varphi_{(1,G_a),(0,G_0)}(\Phi^{(1,G_a)}((1, G_a)))\}.$$

We have

$$\bigsqcup \{\varphi_{(1,G_a),(0,G_0)}(\Phi^{(1,G_a)}((1, G_a)))\} = \bigsqcup \{\rho_1 \circ \varphi_f(\lambda e.\ (\{v_e\}, 0))\}$$

since we forward derive once using rule 1 to get the end of the list, and remove the first element with f to obtain G_0. No further backwards derivations are required. The derivation removes the only hyperedge with non-terminal label, so we are left with the empty assign function, i.e. $\Phi^{(1,G_a)}((0, G_0)) = \emptyset$.

Now the steps going back to the original state $(1, G_a)$ are taken with the supremum, and we obtain a value that is decreasing:

$$\dot{\bigsqcup}\{\varphi_{(1,G_a),(1,G_1)}(\Phi^{(1,G_a)}((1,G_a)))\} = \dot{\bigsqcup}\{\rho_2 \circ \varphi_f(\lambda e.\ (\{v_e\}, 0))\}.$$

We take one forward derivation by rule 2, manipulate the list and apply no backwards derivation. The first step reduces the size of the hyperedge with label *List* by one (compare Example 2) and the function f only removes one vertex and selector edge. Together, we have that $\dot{\bigsqcup}\{\rho_2 \circ \varphi_f(\lambda e.\ (\{v_e\}, 0))\} = \lambda e.\ (\{v_e\}, -1)$, for which the value at least one vertex is smaller than $(\{v_e\}, 0)$. Next we see how we can use this intuition to prove termination using Theorem 2.

Definition 15 overapproximates the values of all paths. We have shown in Theorem 1 that the value of every path is soundly approximating the size of the graph and by classic results from dataflow analysis, we also have that this equation system overapproximates the values for every path (cf. [21, pp. 74–82]).

Our termination analysis works for every solution of the equation system in Definition 15, but the least solution will give the best results.

The last step is to prove that the solution to the equation system of Definition 15 is actually useful. For this, we will show that checking whether the value at state $\hat{s}$ decreases when following any path starting from $\hat{s}$ and returning to $\hat{s}$ without entering $\hat{s}$ in between helps to prove the non-existence of infinite paths. The required condition that the path does not enter $\hat{s}$ except for the first and the last position can be interpreted as a loop iteration in the underlying program.

Theorem 2 (Termination using Equation System). *Let $(l, H) = s \in \mathbb{S}_a$ be a state of an abstract HRG transition system $(\mathbb{S}_a, \rightarrow_a)$, let Φ^s be a solution of the equation system from Definition 15, and let Q be a terminating and always satisfiable predicate. If for some $e \in E_H$ we have $\bigsqcup\{\psi_{s',s}(\Phi^s(s')) \mid s' \rightarrow_a s\}(e) \sqsubseteq \Phi^s(s)(e)$, then for any concrete transition system $(\mathbb{S}_c, \rightarrow_c)$ of $(\mathbb{S}, \rightarrow)$ there is no path in $(\mathbb{S}_c, \rightarrow_c)$ containing infinitely many states $s_1 \ldots$ with $\alpha(s_i) = s$.*

Lemma 1 (Soundness over Paths). *Let $\Phi^{\hat{s}}$ be a solution of the equation system from Definition 15 for a monotonic predicate Q and the abstract HRG transition system $(\mathbb{S}_a, \rightarrow_a)$. For a path $s_0 \ldots s_n$ in a concrete transition system $(States_c, \rightarrow_c)$ with $s_i = (l_i, H_i)$ and $\alpha(s_i) = (l_i, H_i^a)$*

1. *such that $\alpha(s_0) = \hat{s}$, $\forall i \in \{1 \ldots n\}.\ \alpha(s_i) \neq \hat{s}$ we have*

$$H_0 \in L_G(H_0^a) \cap Q_\nu(\Phi_{\hat{s}}(\alpha(s_0))) \Rightarrow H_n \in L_G(H_n^a) \cap Q_\nu(\Phi_s(\alpha(s_n))).$$

2. *such that $\alpha(s_0) = \alpha(s_n) = \hat{s}$, $\forall n > i > 0.\ \alpha(s_i) \neq \hat{s}$ and with the shortened index assignment $\bigsqcup\{\varphi_{s',\hat{s}}(\Phi^{\hat{s}}(s')) \mid s' \rightarrow_a \hat{s}\} = idx$ we have*

$$H_0 \in L_G(H_0^a) \cap Q_\nu(\Phi_{\hat{s}}(\alpha(s_0)) \Rightarrow H_n \in L_G(H_n^a) \cap Q_\nu(idx).$$

Proof. 1. By induction over n. For $n = 0$ the claim holds immediately. For $n > 0$ we assume that the claim holds for $s_0 \ldots s_{n-1}$. We have $H_{n-1} \in L_G(H_{n-1}^a) \cap Q_\nu(\Phi^{\hat{s}}(\alpha(s_{n-1})))$ by the induction hypothesis, thus we also have $H_n = f(H_{n-1}) \in L_G(H_n^a) \cap Q_\nu(\varphi_{\alpha(s_{n-1}),\alpha(s_n)}(\Phi^{\hat{s}}(\alpha(s_{n-1}))))$ using Theorem 1. Since $\varphi_{\alpha(s_{n-1}),\alpha(s_n)}(\Phi^{\hat{s}}(\alpha(s_{n-1}))) \sqsubseteq \bigsqcup\{\varphi_{s',\alpha(s_n)}(\Phi^{\hat{s}}(s')) \mid s' \to_a \alpha(s_n)\} = \Phi^{\hat{s}}(\alpha(s_n))$ and Q is monotone, we also have $H_n \in L_G(H_n^a) \cap Q_\nu(\Phi^{\hat{s}}(\alpha(s_n)))$.
2. Using the previous result and using the idea from the induction step we have with $\bigsqcup\{\varphi_{s',s_n}(\Phi^{\hat{s}}(s')) \mid s' \to_a s_n\} = idx$ that $H_n \in L_G(H_n^a) \cap Q_\nu(idx)$. $\qquad\square$

Proof (of Theorem 2). For a contradiction, we assume that there is a path in $(\mathbb{S}_c, \to_c)$ such that infinitely many states $s_1 \ldots$ with $\alpha(s_j) = s$ exist. Without loss of generality we assume that every other state s' in the path does not have such an abstraction, i.e. $\alpha(s') \neq s$.

Let $s_j = (l, H_j)$ and $s = (l, H)$. Since Q is always satisfiable we have that there is some i_0 with $H_0(e) \in Q(i_0)$. Due to Lemma 1, $H_j(e) \in Q(i_j)$ with $\nu(v_e) = i_j$ and $\bigsqcup\{\varphi_{s',s}(\Phi^{\hat{s}}(s')) \mid s' \to_a s\}(e) = is$ we have also have that $\nu(is) = i_{j+1}$ and $H_{j+1}(e) \in Q(i_{j+1})$.

Since $\bigsqcup\{\varphi_{s',s}(\Phi^{\hat{s}}(s')) \mid s' \to_a s\}(e) = (v, i) \sqsubseteq \Phi^{\hat{s}}(s)(e)$ we have $v = \emptyset, i \leq 0$ or $v = \{v_e\}, i < 0$. In the first case, we have $Q(\nu(\emptyset, i)) = \emptyset$ since Q is terminating, which is a contradiction to $H_1(e) \in Q(i_1)$. In the second case, we have that $i_j = \nu(v_e) > i + \nu(v_e) = \nu(\{v_e\}, i) = i_{j+1}$. Therefore we have an infinite, strictly descending chain and therefore there exists $i_j < 0$, and thus we again have $Q(i_j) = \emptyset$, which is a contradiction to $H_j(e) \in Q(i_j)$. $\qquad\square$

5   Implementation

We implemented our method in the Attestor tool[1]. Attestor generates the abstract HRG transition system as described in Definition 10 by means of an abstract interpretation on the bytecode of a given Java program (see Fig. 4a). Our extension of Attestor uses this transition system, reads additional definitions for approximately compatible predicates and computes a solution of the equation system as in Definition 15 for each critical state $\hat{s}$ in the program. Using Theorem 2, we can finally conclude that the associated critical state $\hat{s}$ is only abstracting concrete states s_c for which all outgoing paths are finite. We select a set of critical states by finding nodes that cover each loop in the program. By checking this for each element in the set of critical states, we can conclude that the concrete transition system only contains finite paths and thus the program is terminating.

The solution of the equation system in Definition 15 is found using the Worklist algorithm [21]. We identify a set of critical states by computing all simple cycles in the abstract transition system using Johnson's algorithm [18]. We then greedily select a set of states such that every simple cycle contains at least one node. Doing this greedily may not result in a minimal set of critical states. This

---

[1] https://github.com/moves-rwth/attestor.

algorithm may result in an exponential runtime due to the necessity to compute all simple cycles. We may instead select states based on their command, e.g. since we analyse Java Bytecode, we could select all jump commands. This prevents the possible exponential runtime, but may increase the number of equations to solve.

We do not attempt to verify termination of integer loops as we lack good support for integers (but see [9] for a first approach). Moreover, due to the possibility of hand-crafting abstractions for data structures, our approach is especially suited for situations involving non-standard data structures. One such data structure we will consider in this section are In-Trees. In an In-Tree, every object has one selector pointing to the parent object. The roots are objects where the parent pointer leads to null (alternatively null itself in case of the empty In-Tree). Leaf objects are those objects which do not have a parent pointer pointing to them. We study here a simple traversal of an In-Tree, starting from a leaf and ending in the root. The Java definition of the data structure is given in Fig. 1a, and the traversal algorithm is shown in Fig. 1b.

```
class  InTree{
      InTree p;
}
```

```
static public void
      traverse(InTree tree){
      while(tree.p != null) {
            tree = tree.p;
      }
}
```

(a) Class definition for In-Trees   (b) Method definition for the traversal

Fig. 1. Java Implementation of the In-Tree data structure and traversal method

We abstract In-Trees by a graph grammar consisting of the terminal selector label p and the nonterminal label IT. The terminal selector must match the pointer name of the data structure. The nonterminal can be arbitrary. Our grammar allows replacing an edge with label IT by one of six graphs. We depict the possible replacements in Fig. 2.

The first rule describes the situation that the current object has a parent pointer directly to the root and there are no (further abstracted) sibling objects. The second rule allows us to derive that the current object has a parent pointer that is not pointing to the root, but has an In-Tree connection to the root. The third rule allows us to derive a graph where the current object is directly connected to the root, but the root may have more children objects. The fourth rule describes the situation where the current object has a parent pointer to an object that is not the root object, but whose parent may have further children. The next two rules are mainly to ensure finiteness of the abstract transition system. We allow abstracting an object that is between the leaf and the root and connected by two IT edges. The last rule lets us abstract the edges labelled

144   A. Ferber et al.

IT between a parent object and two children, where one of the children is the new non-abstracted child.

$$G = (N, T, P) \text{ with } T = \{p\}, N = \{IT\} \text{ and } P:$$

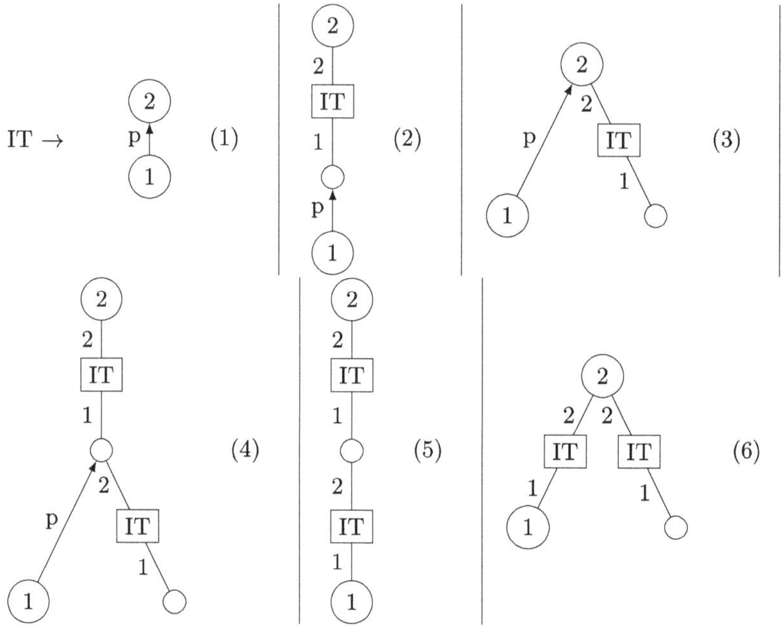

Fig. 2. Grammar for In-Tree data structures

This allows to derive any possible In-Tree and enables unique abstractions by applying rules backwards. The desired property here is called backwards confluence, and its decidability was discussed in [11]. It turns out that the given grammar is indeed backwards-confluent. However, the method is even sound for non-backwards-confluent grammars.

In order to check for termination, we also need to annotate the grammar with indices according to some approximately compatible predicate. This predicate is the number of selector edges p between the two objects that are attached to the edge IT in the terminal graph represented by IT. This predicate is obviously monotone, terminating and always satisfiable. For this we now define rules for every production rule in the grammar:

1. $F_1(s, i) = \emptyset, B_1(idx) = (0, 1)$,
2. $F_2(s, i)(e) = (s, i - 1), B_2(idx) = (s, i + 1)$ where $idx(e) = (s, i)$,
3. $F_3(s, i)(e) = (0, \infty), B_3(idx) = (0, 1)$,
4. $F_4(s, i)(e) = \begin{cases} (s, i - 1) & \text{if } e \text{ is connected to the external node 2} \\ (0, \infty) & \text{else,} \end{cases}$

   $B_4(idx) = (s, i+1)$ where $idx(e) = (s, i)$ and e is connected to the external node 2,

5. $F_5(s, i)(e) = (s, i-1), B_5(idx) = (s \cup s', i + i')$ where $idx(e) = (s, i)$ and $idx(e') = (s', i')$ for the two nonterminal edges,

6. $F_6(s, i)(e) = \begin{cases} (s, i) & \text{if } e \text{ connected to the external node 1} \\ (0, \infty) & \text{else, and} \end{cases}$

   $B_6(idx) = (s, i)$ where $idx(e) = (s, i)$ and e is connected to external node 1.

The initial heap which we use as parameter for the method is depicted in Fig. 3. This heap consists of an In-Tree where exactly one leaf is referenced by the input variable `tree`. The root's pointer `p` is pointing to null, which we left out for brevity. We note that Java would garbage collect most parts of the tree in a real program run. However, we can create a list storing all leaves (or potentially all objects) and define an abstraction for this as well. This would avoid garbage collection of the objects. For our purpose to demonstrate the applicability of the approach, we ignore garbage collection by the Java runtime system, but possibly remove unreachable objects during the analysis as they can be abstracted away anyway.

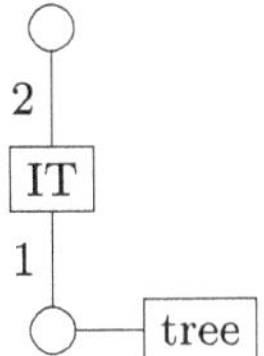

Fig. 3. The initial heap for the In-Tree traversal

We note that standard termination checkers like AProVE [12] are not able to verify termination in this example, as they do not support user-defined abstractions and as the built-in abstractions are not sufficient to handle In-Trees. We also tried to verify termination using cyclic proofs as described in [22] using a separation-logic representation of the graph grammar. The related tool implementation was however unable to find a termination proof in the standard time-out span of 20 s. Our implementation, however, is able to prove the termination of this program in around 3 s. It also generates the abstract transition system for which we provide a screen shot in Fig. 4b. One can see that we have one critical state, namely state 1. By verifying that every concrete transition path does not visit state 1 infinitely often, no such path can be infinite. The results of our analysis show that indeed state 1 only occurs on terminating paths and thus every concrete transition system is finite.

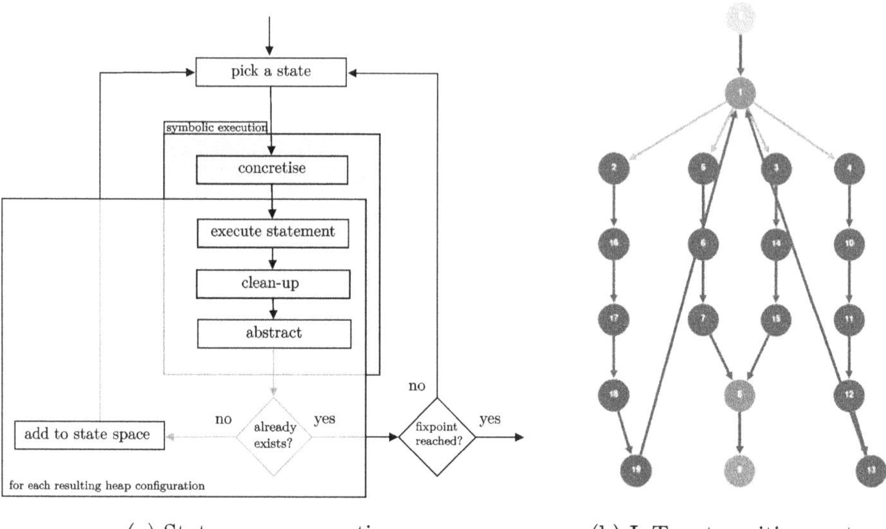

(a) State-space generation   (b) InTree transition system

Fig. 4. Generation of abstract transition system in Attestor

6 Conclusion

We presented a method to automatically generate termination proofs based on abstract transition systems that are constructed using graph grammars. To achieve this, we refined the concept of compatible predicates into approximately compatible predicates, which allow us to handle forward derivations and backward derivations separately, resembling the symmetry in Galois connections as they are used for abstract interpretation. Setting up a data-flow analysis on the abstract transition system finally allows us to compute variant properties on the transition system, which ultimately generates a termination proof. We implemented the technique and saw that in certain cases where we use specialised data structures like In-Trees, our method is able to prove termination where other state-of-the-art tools fail. We thus advocate for an integrated approach where software components are verified using different techniques, and the results obtained are combined. Our approach can thus be a valuable extension to such a framework in cases where specialised data structures are required.

Acknowledgments. We would like the (anonymous) reviewers for their valuable comments.

Disclosure of Interests. The authors have no competing interests to declare that are relevant to the content of this article.

References

1. Arndt, H., Jansen, C., Katoen, J.-P., Matheja, C., Noll, T.: Let this graph be your witness! In: Chockler, H., Weissenbacher, G. (eds.) CAV 2018. LNCS, vol. 10982, pp. 3–11. Springer, Cham (2018). https://doi.org/10.1007/978-3-319-96142-2_1
2. Baier, C., Katoen, J.P.: Principles of Model Checking. The MIT Press (2008)
3. Beyer, D., Henzinger, T.A., Theoduloz, G.: Program analysis with dynamic precision adjustment. In: 2008 23rd IEEE/ACM International Conference on Automated Software Engineering, pp. 29–38 (2008). https://doi.org/10.1109/ASE.2008.13
4. Chalupa, M., et al.: Symbiotic 7: integration of predator and more. In: TACAS 2020. LNCS, vol. 12079, pp. 413–417. Springer, Cham (2020). https://doi.org/10.1007/978-3-030-45237-7_31
5. Chen, H.Y., David, C., Kroening, D., Schrammel, P., Wachter, B.: Bit-precise procedure-modular termination analysis. ACM Trans. Program. Lang. Syst. **40**(1) (2017). https://doi.org/10.1145/3121136
6. Cousot, P., Cousot, R.: Abstract interpretation frameworks. J. Log. Comput. **2**(4), 511–547 (1992). https://doi.org/10.1093/logcom/2.4.511
7. Dodds, M.: From separation logic to hyperedge replacement and back. In: Ehrig, H., Heckel, R., Rozenberg, G., Taentzer, G. (eds.) ICGT 2008. LNCS, vol. 5214, pp. 484–486. Springer, Heidelberg (2008). https://doi.org/10.1007/978-3-540-87405-8_40
8. Drewes, F., Kreowski, H.J., Habel, A.: Hyperedge Replacement Graph Grammars, pp. 95–162. World Scientific (1997). https://doi.org/10.1142/9789812384720_0002
9. Ferber, A.: Combining integer programs and graph grammars: theory and implementation in Attestor. Bachelor's thesis, RWTH Aachen University, Aachen, Germany (2023). https://doi.org/10.18154/RWTH-2024-00784
10. Fesefeldt, I.: Proving Termination of Pointer Programs on Top of Symbolic Execution. Master's thesis, RWTH Aachen University, Aachen, Germany (2019). https://doi.org/10.18154/RWTH-2020-04970
11. Fesefeldt, I., Matheja, C., Noll, T., Schulte, J.: Automated checking and completion of backward confluence for hyperedge replacement grammars. In: Gadducci, F., Kehrer, T. (eds.) ICGT 2021. LNCS, vol. 12741, pp. 283–293. Springer, Cham (2021). https://doi.org/10.1007/978-3-030-78946-6_15
12. Giesl, J., et al.: Analyzing program termination and complexity automatically with APROVE. J. Autom. Reason. **58**(1), 3–31 (2016). https://doi.org/10.1007/s10817-016-9388-y
13. Habel, A.: Hyperedge Replacement: Grammars and Languages, 1st edn. Springer (1992). https://doi.org/10.1007/BFb0013875
14. Habel, A., Kreowski, H.J., Vogler, W.: Metatheorems for decision problems on hyperedge replacement graph languages. Acta Informatica **26**(7), 657–677 (1989). https://doi.org/10.1007/bf00288976
15. Heinen, J., Jansen, C., Katoen, J.-P., Noll, T.: Juggrnaut: using graph grammars for abstracting unbounded heap structures. Formal Methods Syst. Des. **47**(2), 159–203 (2015). https://doi.org/10.1007/s10703-015-0236-1
16. Heizmann, M., Hoenicke, J., Podelski, A.: Software model checking for people who love automata. In: Sharygina, N., Veith, H. (eds.) CAV 2013. LNCS, vol. 8044, pp. 36–52. Springer, Heidelberg (2013). https://doi.org/10.1007/978-3-642-39799-8_2
17. Jansen, C.: Static Analysis of Pointer Programs - Linking Graph Grammars and Separation Logic. Ph.D. thesis, RWTH Aachen University (2017). https://doi.org/10.18154/RWTH-2017-09657

18. Johnson, D.B.: Finding all the elementary circuits of a directed graph. SIAM J. Comput. **4**(1), 77–84 (1975). https://doi.org/10.1137/0204007
19. Khalifa, M.: Termination analysis of procedural pointer programs modelled by graph grammars. Master thesis, RWTH Aachen University, Aachen, Germany (2022). https://doi.org/10.18154/RWTH-2022-09096
20. Le, T.C., Gherghina, C., Hobor, A., Chin, W.-N.: A resource-based logic for termination and non-termination proofs. In: Merz, S., Pang, J. (eds.) ICFEM 2014. LNCS, vol. 8829, pp. 267–283. Springer, Cham (2014). https://doi.org/10.1007/978-3-319-11737-9_18
21. Nielson, F., Nielson, H.R., Hankin, C.: Principles of Program Analysis, 2nd edn. Springer (2005)
22. Rowe, R.N.S., Brotherston, J.: Automatic cyclic termination proofs for recursive procedures in separation logic. In: Proceedings of the 6th ACM SIGPLAN Conference on Certified Programs and Proofs, CPP 2017, pp. 53–65. Association for Computing Machinery (2017). https://doi.org/10.1145/3018610.3018623

CGACell: A Cellular Automata-Based Graph Transformation Framework for Neural Pooling

Doru Constantin$^{(\boxtimes)}$ and Costel Bălcău

National University of Science and Technology POLITEHNICA Bucharest, Piteşti University Centre, Piteşti, Romania
`{doru.constantin0804,costel.balcau}@upb.ro`

Abstract. Pooling in convolutional neural networks is usually introduced as a numerical aggregation operator, while its structural effect on feature maps is often left implicit. This paper studies pooling from a graph-transformation perspective. We present CGACELL, a framework in which a convolutional feature map is represented as a labeled grid graph, a deterministic cellular rule updates node states locally, and pooling is defined as the induced subgraph selected by the evolved state configuration. The main contribution is formal: pooling is described as the composition of *local state evolution* and *structural reduction*. To remove ambiguity, the paper defines explicitly the graph neighborhood, the ordered local interface used to instantiate Rule 110 on a grid graph, the local transition cases of Rule 110, and the boundary convention. The paper also distinguishes between framework-level properties of deterministic local-rule graph transformations on finite labeled graphs and properties specific to the Rule 110 grid-graph realization considered here. We establish well-definedness, determinism, eventual periodicity on finite graphs, induced-subgraph semantics, monotonic node reduction under repeated pooling, and total complexity $O(t|V| + |E|)$ for t cellular iterations. Since standard CNN pipelines require tensor-shaped outputs, the paper also studies a tensor-compatible experimental realization inspired by the formal framework. An experimental study on MNIST, Fashion-MNIST, and CIFAR-10 indicates that this realization remains operationally viable and does not show an evident degradation relative to max and average pooling in the reported setting.

Keywords: Graph transformation · Cellular automata · Neural pooling · Induced subgraph · Deterministic local rules

1 Introduction

Graph transformation provides a formal language for describing systems whose states are discrete structures and whose evolution is determined by local rewriting steps [1–4]. In this perspective, the relevant mathematical object is not

B. Archibald and O. Semeráth (Eds.): ICGT 2026, LNCS 16624, pp. 149–165, 2026.
https://doi.org/10.1007/978-3-032-29730-3_8

merely a numerical array but a finite structure together with explicitly defined local and global transformation semantics. This viewpoint is central in the graph transformation community, where the meaning of an operation is tied to the structure it acts on and to the way local rules induce global evolution. In parallel, graph-based viewpoints have become increasingly relevant in machine learning, where images, feature maps, and relational data may be represented as structured domains over which information is propagated and aggregated [10–14]. A convolutional feature map, in particular, admits a natural graph representation: spatial positions may be regarded as nodes, adjacency as the edge relation, and activations as node labels. Despite this structural interpretation, pooling in convolutional networks is usually described numerically. Max pooling and average pooling reduce spatial resolution by applying fixed-window operators to arrays [22,23]. Their structural effect is therefore implicit rather than formulated as a transformation of a labeled graph. This differs from the graph-learning literature, where hierarchical reduction of graph structure has been studied extensively [15–21]. Even in that setting, however, pooling is often introduced as an optimization, assignment, or node-selection mechanism rather than as an explicit graph transformation with a clearly identified structural output.

Cellular automata provide a complementary local-rule formalism. Their global behavior results from synchronous deterministic updates based on bounded local contexts [7]. Among elementary cellular automata, Rule 110 is of particular interest because of its nontrivial dynamics and computational universality [8,9]. In the present paper, Rule 110 is used as a concrete, classical, and nontrivial local rule through which the graph-transformation framework can be specified completely. The contribution is therefore not the choice of Rule 110 by itself, but the explicit graph-transformation semantics obtained from a fully defined local-rule instance.

This paper develops CGACELL, a cellular-automata-based graph transformation framework for pooling. The central idea is to describe pooling as the composition of two transformations:

1. a deterministic local state evolution on a labeled graph, and
2. an induced-subgraph reduction that retains exactly the nodes whose evolved state equals 1.

Under this interpretation, pooling receives an explicit structural semantics.

The contribution is primarily formal rather than empirical. The aim is not to claim that CGACELL is universally preferable to standard pooling operators, but to provide a mathematically explicit graph-transformation account of pooling and to show that this account can also be realized constructively. The graph-transformation relevance is therefore direct: the paper identifies the transformed object, the local transformation mechanism, the induced global semantics, and the structural nature of the output. In other words, the paper is not merely "deep learning with graph terminology"; it reformulates a common neural-network operation as a transformation over a finite labeled graph. Two concerns naturally arise in a graph-transformation venue.

The first is *novelty*. The contribution does not lie merely in using Rule 110 or in renaming a reduction mechanism in graph-theoretic language. Rather, the novelty lies in describing pooling as a two-stage graph transformation with explicit local transition semantics, explicit ordered interfaces, and an induced-subgraph output. This gives a structural account of a neural-network operation that is often described only procedurally.

The second is *scope and generality*. To avoid overstatement, the paper distinguishes three layers:

- *framework-level properties*, which hold for deterministic local-rule evolution on finite labeled graphs;
- *instantiation-specific choices*, which here correspond to the Rule 110 realization on labeled grid graphs via a horizontal ordered interface;
- *experimental realization choices*, such as thresholding policy, optimizer settings, and the tensor-compatible reduction used in the CNN experiments.

This separation is helpful because it shows which conclusions are generic and which belong specifically to the realization studied in the paper.

The main contributions are as follows:

C1. Pooling is formalized as a graph transformation composed of local state evolution and induced-subgraph reduction.
C2. The graph neighborhood, the ordered interface used to instantiate Rule 110 on grid graphs, the local transition cases of Rule 110, and the boundary convention are defined explicitly.
C3. The paper establishes well-definedness, determinism, eventual periodicity on finite graphs, induced-subgraph semantics, monotonic node reduction under repeated pooling, and total complexity $O(t|V| + |E|)$ for t iterations.
C4. A constructive algorithm is provided for the formal graph transformation.
C5. A small worked example is given to make explicit the passage from labeled grid graph to evolved state pattern and induced subgraph.
C6. A tensor-compatible experimental realization inspired by the formal framework is specified in detail and evaluated on MNIST, Fashion-MNIST, and CIFAR-10.
C7. The approach is positioned relative to earlier ECA-based pooling [24] and earlier work connecting graph rewriting and graph neural networks [25].

The remainder of the paper is organized as follows. Section 2 introduces the formal ingredients. Section 3 defines CGACELL and the concrete Rule 110 realization. Section 4 establishes the theoretical properties. Section 5 gives the constructive algorithm. Section 6 reports the experimental study and makes explicit the relation between the formal framework and the tensor-compatible realization used in practice. Section 7 discusses related work. Section 8 concludes.

2   Preliminaries

We first introduce the graph-theoretic and cellular notions used throughout the paper. The key point is to distinguish clearly between the *unordered* graph neighborhood and the *ordered* local interface required by an elementary cellular automaton.

Definition 1 (Labeled Graph). *A labeled graph is a triple $G = (V, E, \ell)$ where V is a finite node set, $E \subseteq \{\{u, v\} \mid u, v \in V,\ u \neq v\}$ is an undirected edge set, and $\ell : V \to L$ assigns to each node a label from a set L.*

For a node $v \in V$, its graph neighborhood is $N_G(v) = \{u \in V \mid \{u, v\} \in E\}$. Thus the neighborhood function has type $N_G : V \to \mathcal{P}(V)$. A graph $H = (V_H, E_H, \ell_H)$ is an *induced subgraph* of $G = (V, E, \ell)$ if $V_H \subseteq V$, $\ell_H = \ell|_{V_H}$, and $E_H = \{\{u, v\} \in E \mid u, v \in V_H\}$.

Definition 2 (Two-Dimensional Grid Graph). *For integers $m, n \geq 1$, the $m \times n$ grid graph is $G_{m,n} = (V, E)$ with $V = \{(i, j) \mid 1 \leq i \leq m,\ 1 \leq j \leq n\}$ and $\{(i, j), (k, \ell)\} \in E \iff |i - k| + |j - \ell| = 1$.*

This is the graph model used for feature maps in the present paper. Nodes correspond to spatial positions and edges encode unit horizontal or vertical adjacency. The graph is finite whenever the feature map is finite, which is the only case relevant here. We consider a binary state space $S = \{0, 1\}$ and a state assignment $\sigma : V \to S$. The label function and the state function serve different purposes: labels retain feature information, whereas states drive the local cellular dynamics that ultimately determine the structural reduction. To instantiate an elementary cellular automaton on a grid graph, one must extract an *ordered* interface from the graph, because the graph neighborhood itself is unordered and therefore cannot directly serve as input to a one-dimensional cellular rule.

Definition 3 (Ordered Local Interface on a Grid Graph). *Let $G_{m,n} = (V, E)$ be a grid graph. For $v = (i, j) \in V$, define* $\text{left}(v) = \begin{cases} (i, j - 1), & j > 1, \\ \bot, & j = 1, \end{cases}$

and $\text{right}(v) = \begin{cases} (i, j + 1), & j < n, \\ \bot, & j = n. \end{cases}$ *The horizontal ordered interface at v is* $\pi_G(v) = \big(\text{left}(v), v, \text{right}(v)\big).$

The symbol $\bot$ denotes a formal boundary placeholder. To evaluate states on this interface, a padding state $p \in S$ is fixed and $\widehat{\sigma}(x) = \begin{cases} \sigma(x), & x \in V, \\ p, & x = \bot. \end{cases}$ Unless stated otherwise, the paper uses $p = 0$. This convention resolves the interface ambiguity explicitly. The graph itself remains two-dimensional, but the local update acts on a precisely defined one-dimensional ordered projection extracted from the graph. Other interface extractors are possible, but the present work studies this one because it is concrete, simple, and natural for convolutional feature maps. Rule 110 is the elementary binary cellular rule defined by $111 \mapsto 0$, $110 \mapsto 1$, $101 \mapsto 1$, $100 \mapsto 0$, $011 \mapsto 1$, $010 \mapsto 1$, $001 \mapsto 1$, $000 \mapsto 0$. Equivalently, Rule 110 defines a local map $f_{110} : S^3 \to S$. On a grid graph, the update is applied to the ordered interface: $\sigma_{t+1}(v) = f_{110}\big(\widehat{\sigma}_t(\text{left}(v)), \sigma_t(v), \widehat{\sigma}_t(\text{right}(v))\big)$.

3   CGACELL **Framework**

We now define CGACELL as a graph-transformation framework built from two components: deterministic local state evolution and induced-subgraph reduction. Let $G = (V, E, \ell)$ be a labeled grid graph representing a feature map. A *cellular graph configuration* is a pair (G, σ), where $\sigma : V \to S$ is a binary state assignment. The initial configuration is obtained from the labels through a discretization map $\phi : L \to S,$ $\sigma_0(v) = \phi(\ell(v))$. At the formal level, ϕ is any fixed map from labels to binary states. At the experimental level, the tensor-compatible realization uses an analogous local binarization principle, implemented by thresholding normalized activations within each pooling window. The concrete Rule 110 realization is specified by the eight local transition cases shown in Table 1. Equivalently, these cases may be written as $r_{abc} : (a, b, c) \mapsto f_{110}(a, b, c)$, for $a, b, c \in S$.

Table 1. Local transition table induced by Rule 110 on the ordered interface $\pi_G(v) = (\text{left}(v), v, \text{right}(v))$.

111	110	101	100	011	010	001	000
0	1	1	0	1	1	1	0

Definition 4 (Cellular Transformation Operator). *Let G be a labeled grid graph. The* cellular transformation operator *is $T_G : (G, \sigma_t) \mapsto (G, \sigma_{t+1})$, where for every node $v \in V$,*

$$\sigma_{t+1}(v) = f_{110}\big(\widehat{\sigma}_t(\text{left}(v)), \sigma_t(v), \widehat{\sigma}_t(\text{right}(v))\big) \tag{1}$$

The graph structure is unchanged during this phase; only node states evolve. The use of synchronous updates is essential: all values of σ_{t+1} are computed from σ_t, never from partially updated states. After the state-evolution phase, the structural reduction is defined by retaining exactly the nodes whose final state equals 1.

Definition 5 (Pooling Operator). *Given a cellular graph configuration (G, σ) with $G = (V, E, \ell)$, define $V_\sigma = \{v \in V \mid \sigma(v) = 1\}$. The* pooled graph *is the induced subgraph $P(G, \sigma) = G[V_\sigma] = (V_\sigma, E_\sigma, \ell|_{V_\sigma})$, where $E_\sigma = \{\{u, v\} \in E \mid u, v \in V_\sigma\}$.*

Therefore CGACELL pooling is the composition $G \xRightarrow{\phi} (G, \sigma_0) \xRightarrow{T_G^t} (G, \sigma_t) \xRightarrow{P} G'$, where $t \geq 0$ is the chosen number of cellular iterations. This decomposition is the core structural content of the paper. The first stage is a deterministic local transformation of states. The second stage is a graph reduction obtained by taking the induced subgraph on a state-defined vertex set. This separation makes the semantics explicit and avoids conflating local evolution with structural reduction. The pooled output is, in general, not a regular grid. It is an induced subgraph of the original grid graph, and therefore its size and shape depend on the final state pattern. This differs fundamentally from standard image pooling, which always returns another array of predetermined geometry. If a downstream architecture requires tensor-shaped outputs, an additional re-embedding step may be introduced, but such a step is external to the present formal core. More generally, the framework does not depend specifically on Rule 110. One may consider any deterministic local rule $f : S^k \to S$ together with an interface extractor assigning to each node an ordered k-tuple of local positions. In the present paper, the specific choices are:

- the binary state space $S = \{0, 1\}$;
- the Rule 110 local map f_{110};
- the horizontal interface extractor on grid graphs;
- the concrete discretization and experimental settings.

This flexibility is important for the scope of the framework. The present paper analyzes one fully specified instance in detail, while the same overall graph-transformation pattern can accommodate other local rules, other ordered interfaces, and other graph classes (Fig. 1).

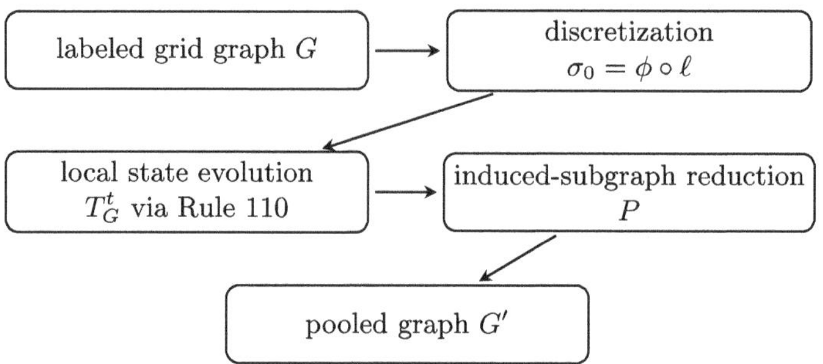

Fig. 1. Conceptual flow of the formal CGACELL framework: labeled-grid representation, state discretization, deterministic local evolution, and induced-subgraph reduction.

A Small Worked Example

To make the formal construction fully explicit, consider the 3×3 grid graph with nodes (i, j) for $1 \leq i, j \leq 3$. Suppose the discretization map has already produced the initial state assignment $\sigma_0 = \begin{bmatrix} 1 & 0 & 1 \\ 0 & 1 & 0 \\ 1 & 1 & 0 \end{bmatrix}$ read row by row as states attached to the corresponding grid positions, and suppose the padding state is $p = 0$. Using the horizontal ordered interface, the node $(2, 2)$ has interface $\pi_G((2, 2)) =$

$((2,1),(2,2),(2,3))$, so its input triple is $(0,1,0)$ and Rule 110 gives $\sigma_1(2,2) = 1$. The boundary node $(1,1)$ has interface $\pi_G((1,1)) = (\bot,(1,1),(1,2))$, so its input triple is $(0,1,0)$ and again $\sigma_1(1,1) = 1$. The node $(3,3)$ has interface $\pi_G((3,3)) = ((3,2),(3,3),\bot)$, so its input triple is $(1,0,0)$ and Rule 110 gives $\sigma_1(3,3) = 0$.

Proceeding in the same way for all nodes yields $\sigma_1 = \begin{bmatrix} 1 & 1 & 1 \\ 1 & 1 & 0 \\ 1 & 1 & 0 \end{bmatrix}$ after one iteration. Each row evolves independently under the horizontal interface with zero boundary padding, so the one-step update can be checked row by row. The retained vertex set is therefore $V' = \{(i,j) \mid \sigma_1(i,j) = 1\}$, that is, all nodes except $(2,3)$ and $(3,3)$. The pooled graph is the induced subgraph on this retained set. Thus, in this example, the formal pooling output is not another regular 3×3 grid, but the induced subgraph obtained by deleting the two state-0 nodes and all incident edges. This small example illustrates explicitly the passage from labeled grid graph to evolved state pattern and then to structural reduction.

4 Theoretical Properties

This section records the basic structural properties of the framework. The goal is not to claim deep rule-specific meta-theorems for Rule 110, but to establish clearly the formal status of the construction introduced in Sect. 3. We therefore separate the central structural facts from simpler consequences of finiteness and determinism.

Theorem 1 (Well-Defined Deterministic Transformation). *Let $G = (V, E, \ell)$ be a labeled grid graph, let $p \in S$ be a fixed padding state, and let $\phi : L \to S$ be a discretization map. For every integer $t \geq 0$, the configuration σ_t generated by repeated application of (1) is uniquely determined by G, ϕ, and p.*

Consequently, the transformation $G \xRightarrow{\phi} (G, \sigma_0) \xRightarrow{T_G^t} (G, \sigma_t) \xRightarrow{P} P(G, \sigma_t)$ is well defined and deterministic.

Proof. The initial state assignment is $\sigma_0 = \phi \circ \ell$, so σ_0 is uniquely determined by ℓ and ϕ. Assume that σ_t is known. For each node $v \in V$, the ordered interface $\pi_G(v) = \big(\mathrm{left}(v), v, \mathrm{right}(v)\big)$ is uniquely determined by the position of v in the grid. The padding convention determines the values assigned to boundary placeholders. Hence the triple $\big(\widehat{\sigma}_t(\mathrm{left}(v)), \sigma_t(v), \widehat{\sigma}_t(\mathrm{right}(v))\big)$ is uniquely determined. Since $f_{110} : S^3 \to S$ is a function, the value $\sigma_{t+1}(v) = f_{110}\big(\widehat{\sigma}_t(\mathrm{left}(v)), \sigma_t(v), \widehat{\sigma}_t(\mathrm{right}(v))\big)$ is uniquely determined for every $v \in V$. Therefore σ_{t+1} is uniquely determined by σ_t. By induction on t, every configuration σ_t is uniquely determined. Finally, by the definition of the pooling operator, the retained node set $V_{\sigma_t} = \{v \in V \mid \sigma_t(v) = 1\}$ is uniquely determined by σ_t, and so are the restricted edge set and label function. Hence $P(G, \sigma_t)$ is uniquely determined. Therefore the whole transformation is well defined and deterministic.

Proposition 1 (Finite Configuration Space). *If $|V| = n$ and $S = \{0,1\}$, then the set of all state assignments $\sigma : V \to S$ has cardinality 2^n.*

Proof. Each of the n nodes can independently take one of the two values in $S = \{0,1\}$. Therefore the total number of state assignments is 2^n.

Proposition 2 (Eventual Periodicity). *Let $G = (V, E, \ell)$ be a finite labeled grid graph. Then the sequence $\sigma_0, \sigma_1, \sigma_2, \ldots$ generated by repeated application of T_G is eventually periodic.*

Proof. By the previous proposition, the set S^V of all state assignments on V is finite. The update rule induces a deterministic function $F : S^V \to S^V$, $\quad F(\sigma_t) = \sigma_{t+1}$. A deterministic trajectory in a finite set must eventually revisit a previous state. Thus there exist integers $i < j$ such that $\sigma_i = \sigma_j$. Applying F repeatedly yields $\sigma_{i+k} = \sigma_{j+k}$ for all $k \geq 0$. Hence the sequence is eventually periodic.

Proposition 3 (Locality of the Update). *For every node $v \in V$, the updated value $\sigma_{t+1}(v)$ depends only on the ordered interface $\pi_G(v)$ and the padding convention. In particular, it is independent of all state values outside $\{\text{left}(v), v, \text{right}(v)\} \cap V$.*

Proof. By definition, $\sigma_{t+1}(v) = f_{110}\big(\hat{\sigma}_t(\text{left}(v)), \sigma_t(v), \hat{\sigma}_t(\text{right}(v))\big)$. Only the left interface value, the current node value, and the right interface value appear in this expression, together with the fixed padding convention. Therefore no other node state can influence $\sigma_{t+1}(v)$.

Theorem 2 (Pooling Produces an Induced Subgraph). *Let $G = (V, E, \ell)$ be a labeled grid graph and let $\sigma : V \to S$ be any state assignment. Then the pooled graph $P(G, \sigma)$ is an induced subgraph of G. More precisely, if $P(G, \sigma) = (V', E', \ell')$, then $V' = \{v \in V \mid \sigma(v) = 1\}, E' = \{\{u,v\} \in E \mid u, v \in V'\}, \ell' = \ell|_{V'}$.*

Proof. By the definition of the pooling operator, the retained node set is $V' = \{v \in V \mid \sigma(v) = 1\}$. The edge set is obtained by restricting the original edge set to pairs of retained nodes: $E' = \{\{u,v\} \in E \mid u, v \in V'\}$. The label function is restricted to the retained node set: $\ell' = \ell|_{V'}$. These are precisely the defining conditions of the induced subgraph of G on vertex set V'.

Corollary 1 (Monotonic Node Reduction Under Repeated Pooling). *Let $G_{i+1} = P(G_i, \sigma^{(i)})$ for a sequence of pooling steps, where each $\sigma^{(i)} : V(G_i) \to S$ is a state assignment on the current graph G_i. Then $|V(G_{i+1})| \leq |V(G_i)|$ for all i.*

Proof. By definition of the pooling operator, $V(G_{i+1}) = \{v \in V(G_i) \mid \sigma^{(i)}(v) = 1\}$. Hence $V(G_{i+1}) \subseteq V(G_i)$. Taking cardinalities yields $|V(G_{i+1})| \leq |V(G_i)|$.

Theorem 3 (Total Complexity for t Iterations). *Let $G = (V, E, \ell)$ be a labeled grid graph and let $t \geq 0$. Computing $(G, \sigma_t) = T_G^t(G, \sigma_0)$ and then constructing the pooled graph $P(G, \sigma_t)$ takes time $O(t|V| + |E|)$. For a two-dimensional grid graph, where $|E| = O(|V|)$, this simplifies to $O((t+1)|V|)$.*

Proof. One synchronous Rule 110 update computes one new state for each node. Since the ordered interface has constant size, each node update takes constant time. Hence one iteration costs $O(|V|)$, and t iterations cost $O(t|V|)$. To construct the pooled graph after the evolution phase, one scans the nodes once to determine $V' = \{v \in V \mid \sigma_t(v) = 1\}$, which costs $O(|V|)$, and one scans the edge set once to retain exactly those edges whose endpoints both belong to V', which costs $O(|E|)$. Restricting the label function to V' adds at most linear overhead in $|V|$. Therefore the total cost is $O(t|V|) + O(|V| + |E|) = O(t|V| + |E|)$. For a grid graph, each node has degree at most four, so $|E| = O(|V|)$. Substituting this yields $O(t|V| + |E|) = O((t + 1)|V|)$.

Remark 1 (Scope of the Formal Results). The results above separate naturally into two groups. Well-definedness, eventual periodicity, monotonic node reduction, and the complexity bound rely on finiteness, determinism, and constant-size local interfaces. By contrast, the specific choice of Rule 110 and of the horizontal ordered interface determines the concrete update behavior studied in this paper on labeled grid graphs. Thus the framework-level statements do not claim special dynamical properties of Rule 110 itself; rather, they establish the formal status of the graph-transformation construction introduced here.

5   Algorithmic Realization

The theoretical construction introduced in Sect. 3 is not merely definitional: it admits a direct, explicit, and fully constructive algorithmic realization. This section clarifies how the abstract components—discretization, deterministic local evolution, and induced-subgraph reduction—translate into an operational procedure. The algorithm serves two purposes. First, it demonstrates that the proposed semantics is implementable without additional assumptions or approximations. Second, it provides a concrete reference for reproducibility and for future extensions to other local rules or graph classes.

The CGACell framework decomposes pooling into three conceptually distinct phases: (i) discretization, which maps feature labels to binary states and initializes the cellular configuration; (ii) iterative local state evolution, which applies the deterministic local rule synchronously across the graph; and (iii) induced-subgraph construction, which extracts the structural output by retaining exactly the nodes whose final state equals 1. This decomposition is not an implementation choice but follows directly from the formal semantics $G \overset{\phi}{\Longrightarrow} (G, \sigma_0) \overset{T_G^t}{\Longrightarrow} (G, \sigma_t) \overset{P}{\Longrightarrow} G'$. Algorithm 1 is therefore a faithful operationalization of the framework.

Algorithm 1 implements the formal semantics exactly: the discretization map ϕ initializes the state configuration; the synchronous update rule T_G evolves the configuration deterministically; and the operator P constructs the induced subgraph on the retained nodes. No heuristic, approximation, or learned component is introduced. The output graph G' is precisely the object defined in the framework. From an implementation perspective, the procedure is straightforward on

---

Algorithm 1. CGACELL Pooling on a Labeled Grid Graph

Require: labeled grid graph $G = (V, E, \ell)$, discretization map ϕ, padding state p, iteration count t
Ensure: pooled graph G'
1: $\sigma_0(v) \leftarrow \phi(\ell(v))$ for all $v \in V$
2: **for** $k = 0$ to $t - 1$ **do**
3:      **for all** $v \in V$ **do**
4:          $a \leftarrow \widehat{\sigma_k}(\text{left}(v))$
5:          $b \leftarrow \sigma_k(v)$
6:          $c \leftarrow \widehat{\sigma_k}(\text{right}(v))$
7:          $\sigma_{k+1}(v) \leftarrow f_{110}(a, b, c)$
8:      **end for**
9: **end for**
10: $V' \leftarrow \{v \in V \mid \sigma_t(v) = 1\}$
11: $E' \leftarrow \{\{u, v\} \in E \mid u, v \in V'\}$
12: $\ell' \leftarrow \ell|_{V'}$
13: **return** $G' = (V', E', \ell')$

---

grid-structured data. The ordered interface is derived directly from row and column indices, the Rule 110 transition can be implemented as a constant-time lookup table of size 8, and synchronous updates require only two state arrays. Memory usage is linear in $|V|$, and no dynamic graph rewriting is needed during the evolution phase. These properties show that the framework is not only mathematically well-defined but also computationally lightweight. As established in Sect. 4, the total running time is $O(t|V| + |E|)$, which reduces to $O((t + 1)|V|)$ on grid graphs. This linear-time behavior is comparable to standard convolutional operations and significantly cheaper than many learned or optimization-based pooling mechanisms used in graph neural networks. Beyond its practical role, the algorithmic realization reinforces the graph-transformation semantics of the framework. It shows that the global structural effect of pooling arises from repeated local deterministic rewriting, consistent with the principles of graph transformation. It makes explicit the separation between state evolution and structural reduction, a distinction often implicit in neural-network practice. Finally, it provides a concrete witness that the proposed semantics is constructive, reproducible, and independent of neural-network machinery. In this sense, the algorithm is not merely an implementation detail but an integral part of the contribution.

6 Experimental Evaluation

The purpose of this section is to show that the proposed formalization is operationally meaningful and can be integrated into a practical convolutional pipeline. The experiments address two questions:

1. whether the proposed pooling mechanism can be used in a standard image-classification setting;

2. whether the explicit structural interpretation is accompanied by an evident empirical degradation relative to max pooling and average pooling.

The experimental section is therefore intended to demonstrate feasibility and comparative behavior, not to support a claim of universal superiority.

Formal Framework Versus Experimental Realization. A central point must be stated explicitly. The formal framework defined in Sects. 3–5 outputs an induced subgraph. Standard CNN pipelines, however, require tensor-shaped intermediate outputs. For this reason, the experiments do not directly use the graph object $P(G, \sigma_t)$ as the next network input. Instead, they use a *tensor-compatible realization inspired by the formal framework.* Concretely, each local 2×2 window is treated as a small ordered state configuration, transformed by a one-step Rule 110 update after binarization, and then reduced to a scalar by normalized summation. Thus the experiments evaluate a tensor-compatible surrogate realization of the formal idea, not the direct use of the induced-subgraph object inside a standard CNN backbone. The experimental operator should therefore be interpreted as a tensor-compatible local realization inspired by the formal graph-transformation framework, rather than as a direct execution of the induced-subgraph output inside a conventional CNN stack.

Software and Hardware. The experimental study was conducted in Python. The models were implemented and trained in PyTorch 2.10.0, while NumPy, SciPy, and scikit-learn were used for numerical processing and evaluation. Matplotlib was used for figure generation. The experiments were run on a system equipped with an AMD Ryzen 7 PRO 8700G processor (8 cores, 16 threads), AMD Radeon 780M integrated graphics, 32 GB RAM, 512 GB SSD, and Microsoft Windows 11 Pro.

Datasets. The evaluation used three benchmark datasets: MNIST, Fashion-MNIST, and CIFAR-10. MNIST and Fashion-MNIST contain grayscale images of size 28×28, whereas CIFAR-10 contains RGB images of size 32×32. These datasets were selected because they are standard benchmarks for convolutional architectures and cover both grayscale and color image classification.

Splits, Preprocessing, and Augmentation. The data splits used in the implementation were as follows.

- For MNIST, the original training set of 60,000 images was split into 50,000 training images and 10,000 validation images; the standard test set of 10,000 images was kept unchanged.
- For Fashion-MNIST, the same protocol was used: 50,000 training images, 10,000 validation images, and the original 10,000-image test set.
- For CIFAR-10, the original training set of 50,000 images was split into 40,000 training images and 10,000 validation images; the standard 10,000-image test set was kept unchanged.

For MNIST and Fashion-MNIST, preprocessing consisted of conversion to tensors. For CIFAR-10, training-time augmentation consisted of random horizontal flipping and random cropping to 32×32 with padding 4, followed by channel-wise normalization; validation and test data used only tensor conversion and normalization.

Backbone Architecture. Feature maps produced by convolutional layers were interpreted conceptually as labeled grid graphs, while the actual CNN implementation used a tensor-compatible local realization inspired by this graph view. Conventional pooling layers were replaced by the selected pooling operator, while the remaining network architecture was kept unchanged across compared methods. All compared models used the same baseline convolutional architecture:

- a first convolutional block with 64 filters of size 3×3, followed by the selected pooling operator;
- a second convolutional block with 128 filters of size 3×3, followed by the selected pooling operator;
- a fully connected layer with 256 units;
- a final linear classification layer producing class logits.

This architectural constraint is important because it isolates the influence of the pooling mechanism from unrelated changes in depth or model capacity.

Optimization Protocol. All models were trained with the same optimization protocol. Stochastic Gradient Descent (SGD) was used together with cross-entropy loss. The learning rate was fixed to 0.01, the momentum coefficient to 0.9, and the weight decay coefficient to 5×10^{-4}. The mini-batch size was 64 for MNIST, Fashion-MNIST, and CIFAR-10. A ReduceLROnPlateau scheduler was used, monitored on validation F_1-macro, with multiplicative factor 0.5 and patience 3. Early stopping was also used, again monitored on validation F_1-macro, with patience 10 and minimum improvement threshold 10^{-4}. In the implementation template, the full training mode uses dataset-specific epoch limits: 30 epochs for MNIST, 40 epochs for Fashion-MNIST, and 100 epochs for CIFAR-10. A shorter debug mode exists only for sanity checks and was not intended as the basis for the final reported comparisons.

Tensor-Compatible CGACELL Realization Used in the Experiments. In the formal framework, t denotes the number of cellular iterations. In the tensor-compatible experimental realization, the corresponding local Rule 110 step count was fixed to 1 throughout the reported experiments. The CNN experiments use a tensor-compatible transform–reduce operator inspired by the formal framework. For each local 2×2 window:

1. the window is flattened into a vector $\mathbf{z} \in \mathbb{R}^4$;
2. a local threshold τ is computed as the arithmetic mean of the four entries;
3. a binary state vector $\mathbf{z}_b = \mathbf{1}[\mathbf{z} \geq \tau]$ is formed;
4. Rule 110 is applied synchronously for exactly one step, with zero padding at the sequence boundaries;

5. the transformed binary sequence is reduced to a scalar by normalized summation, i.e. by dividing the sum of the transformed binary states by the window cardinality.

Hence the experimental realization uses: threshold mode: local mean, Rule 110 steps: 1 and boundary convention: zero padding. These values were kept fixed across the reported comparisons.

Multi-run Protocol. The reported classification accuracies are averages over 12 independent runs with fixed pseudo-random seeds. The repeated-run protocol was used to reduce sensitivity to stochastic training variation and to obtain more stable estimates of the observed behavior. This unified setup is important for two reasons. First, it ensures comparative fairness across pooling variants. Second, it responds directly to the reviewer expectation that all practically relevant experimental parameters should be stated explicitly. To clarify the semantic difference between CGACELL and standard pooling, consider the illustrative 4×4 activation patch shown in Fig. 2. Under standard 2×2 stride-2 pooling, max pooling and average pooling return another regular 2×2 array, with one value per window. By contrast, the tensor-compatible CGACELL-inspired realization first binarizes each local window, evolves the binary states by Rule 110 on the ordered sequence extracted from that window, and then reduces the transformed state vector to a scalar. The formal framework behind this realization is graph-transformational; the experimental output, however, is deliberately kept tensor-shaped.

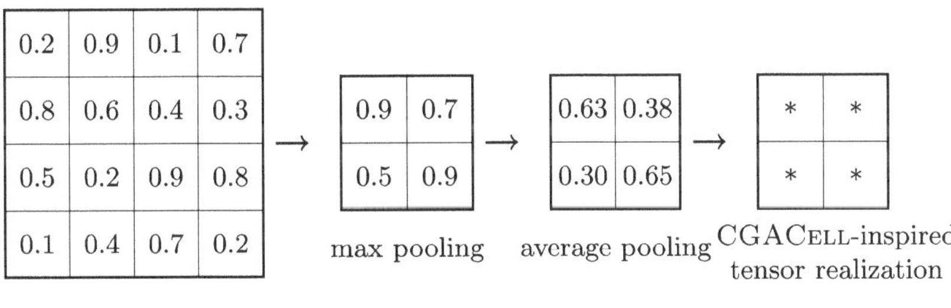

Fig. 2. Illustrative difference between pooling operators.

The example is not intended as a substitute for the formal definition; rather, it clarifies the distinction between the graph-transformational semantics of the framework and the tensor-compatible realization used in the CNN experiments. To quantify the reduction effect, we report different quantities depending on the semantic type of the operator.

– For max pooling and average pooling, we report the *effective regular-grid reduction factor*, i.e. the ratio induced by mapping the input feature map to a smaller regular output grid under fixed 2×2 stride-2 pooling.

– For the formal CGACELL framework, the natural structural quantity is the *retention ratio* $\rho = \frac{|V'|}{|V|}$, where V is the original node set and V' is the retained node set of the induced subgraph.

These are related but not identical notions. They are reported together only to compare reduction behavior, not to claim that the operators produce the same type of structural object. For CGACELL, the reported structural retention ratios were computed from the retained-node criterion induced by the corresponding evolved binary state patterns and then averaged at dataset level; they do not describe the tensor output shape of the surrogate realization. Table 2 characterizes reduction behavior at the level of structural semantics; it should not be interpreted as reporting identical output objects across all operators. These values show that standard fixed-window pooling produces a predetermined regular-grid reduction factor, whereas CGACELL yields a structural retention quantity that depends on the evolved local state configuration. In this sense, CGACELL behaves as an adaptive structural filter rather than a purely geometric downsampling mechanism. Table 3 reports classification accuracy averaged over 12 runs. The reported values are test accuracies averaged over the 12 runs described above. The results indicate that the tensor-compatible CGACELL-inspired realization can be used in the tested configuration without an evident degradation relative to max pooling and average pooling on the considered datasets. In the current tables, it yields slightly higher values on the three benchmarks. This observation should nevertheless be interpreted cautiously. The role of the experimental section is to show that the graph-transformational semantics is compatible with practically comparable behavior, not to support a general claim of superiority across architectures or datasets. From the standpoint of computational effort, max pooling and average pooling perform a single fixed aggregation per window. The tensor-compatible CGACELL-inspired realization adds local transform–reduce operations based on thresholding, one Rule 110 step, and scalar reduction. The overhead remains controlled and arises from repeated local operations rather than from global optimization. Overall, the experiments support three conclusions. First, the proposed mechanism can be inserted into a standard convolutional pipeline in a concrete and reproducible way. Second, the graph-transformational semantics corresponds to an implementable family of realizations with explicit parameters. Third, on the benchmarks considered, the method remains operationally viable and yields results comparable to those obtained with standard pooling operators. At the same time, the present study has limits. In its current formal form, the output after pooling is graph-shaped rather than necessarily tensor-shaped. This makes the method particularly natural in graph-based or hybrid settings, whereas tensor-only downstream architectures may require an additional re-embedding step. A further limitation is that the experiments focus on standard image benchmarks and one concrete realization of the framework. They demonstrate feasibility, but they do not exhaust the design space of possible local rules, interface extractors, thresholding policies, or downstream architectures.

Table 2. Reported reduction-related quantities for structurally different pooling operators. For max and average pooling the reported quantity is the effective regular-grid reduction factor. For CGACELL the reported quantity is the structural retention ratio $\rho = |V'|/|V|$.

Operator	Reported quantity	MNIST	Fashion-MNIST	CIFAR-10	Mean
Max pooling	effective reduction factor	0.50	0.50	0.50	0.50
Average pooling	effective reduction factor	0.50	0.50	0.50	0.50
CGACELL	structural retention ratio	0.44	0.47	0.52	0.48

Table 3. Classification accuracy (%) averaged over 12 runs.

Pooling method	MNIST	Fashion-MNIST	CIFAR-10	Mean
Max pooling	98.7	92.4	84.3	91.8
Average pooling	98.3	91.7	83.5	91.2
CGACELL-inspired realization	98.9	92.8	85.0	92.2

7   Related Work

Graph transformation systems provide a mature formal framework for rule-based changes of graph structure [1–6]. In the present paper, the graph-transformation viewpoint is used in a direct and explicit sense: the paper identifies a finite graph object, a deterministic local state transformation on that object, and a global structural reduction defined as an induced-subgraph construction. The objective is not to develop a full DPO/SPO meta-theory for the whole neural-learning pipeline, but to expose pooling itself as a structural graph transformation on a finite labeled graph. The graph-learning literature contains many pooling methods for irregular domains, including differentiable assignment-based pooling [15], top-k/selection-based pooling [16,17], and spectral or cut-based variants [18,20]. Surveys such as [21] illustrate the breadth of this area. In comparison, the contribution here is not a new learned pooling criterion, but an explicit structural formulation of reduction. The closest pooling-related antecedent to the present work is the earlier ECA110-based study [24]. That work focused primarily on empirical comparison among pooling strategies inspired by ECA110 in convolutional architectures. The present paper has a different goal: it develops a graph-transformation formulation of pooling as a composition of local cellular evolution and induced-subgraph construction, and it distinguishes clearly between this formal semantics and the tensor-compatible realization used in standard CNN experiments. The relation between graph rewriting and graph neural networks was also discussed in [25]. That work argues that graph rewriting can serve as a semantic foundation for graph neural networks and illustrates the idea on a message-passing-style case study. The present paper is narrower in scope and concentrates specifically on pooling, showing how a deterministic local rule can induce a structurally interpretable reduction on labeled grid graphs. Finally, cellular automata are a classical model of discrete local computation [7]. Rule 110 is notable because of its nontrivial dynamics and universality [8,9]. In the present context, Rule 110 is used as a concrete instance of a deterministic local rule, not as a sufficient argument for novelty by itself.

8   Conclusion

This paper presented CGACELL, a cellular-automata-based graph transformation framework for neural pooling. The main contribution is formal: pooling is described as a composition of deterministic local state evolution and structural reduction by induced subgraph. In this form, pooling receives an explicit structural semantics. The revised presentation clarifies four points. First, the framework-level properties do not depend specifically on Rule 110, but on deterministic local evolution over a finite configuration space. Second, the instance studied here is concrete and fully specified: Rule 110 on labeled grid graphs through a horizontal ordered interface with explicit padding. Third, the experimental section does not silently identify the formal induced-subgraph output with the tensor-shaped output required in a standard CNN, but instead studies a tensor-compatible realization inspired by the formal framework. Fourth, all practically relevant experimental parameters have been stated explicitly. The theoretical analysis shows that the transformation is well defined and deterministic, that the configuration space is finite and eventually periodic, that pooling yields an induced subgraph, and that after t iterations the total cost is $O(t|V| + |E|)$. The experiments indicate that the tensor-compatible realization derived from this idea can be used in practice while maintaining behavior comparable to max pooling and average pooling on the considered datasets. Natural extensions include the study of other local rules, other interface extractors, variants for irregular graphs, and re-embedding strategies that map the pooled graph back to a regular tensor representation when such a representation is required by downstream layers. Another direction is to investigate whether specific local rules induce structural biases that are useful for particular learning tasks.

Disclosure of Interests. The authors have no competing interests to declare that are relevant to the content of this article.

References

1. Corradini, A., Montanari, U., Rossi, F., Ehrig, H., Heckel, R.: Algebraic approaches to graph transformation. Part I: basic concepts and double pushout approach. In: Rozenberg, G. (ed.) Handbook of Graph Grammars and Computing by Graph Transformation. World Scientific (1997)
2. Ehrig, H., et al.: Algebraic approaches to graph transformation. Part II: single pushout approach and comparison with double pushout approach. In: Rozenberg, G. (ed.) Handbook of Graph Grammars and Computing by Graph Transformation. World Scientific (1997)

3. Ehrig, H., Ehrig, K., Prange, U., Taentzer, G.: Fundamentals of Algebraic Graph Transformation. Springer (2006)
4. Heckel, R.: Graph transformation in a nutshell. Electron. Notes Theor. Comput. Sci. **148**(1), 187–198 (2006)
5. Ehrig, H., Taentzer, G. (eds.): Graph Transformations: Theory and Applications. LNCS, vol. 2505. Springer (2002)
6. Löwe, M.: Graph rewriting in span-categories. In: Graph Transformations and Model-Driven Engineering. LNCS. Springer (2010)
7. Wolfram, S.: Statistical mechanics of cellular automata. Rev. Mod. Phys. **55**, 601–644 (1983)
8. Cook, M.: Universality in elementary cellular automata. Complex Syst. **15**(1), 1–40 (2004)
9. Wolfram, S.: A New Kind of Science. Wolfram Media (2002)
10. Kipf, T.N., Welling, M.: Semi-supervised classification with graph convolutional networks. In: Proceedings of ICLR (2017)
11. Defferrard, M., Bresson, X., Vandergheynst, P.: Convolutional Neural Networks on Graphs with Fast Localized Spectral Filtering. Advances in Neural Information Processing Systems (2016)
12. Hamilton, W.L., Ying, R., Leskovec, J.: Inductive representation learning on large graphs. In: Advances in Neural Information Processing Systems (2017)
13. Veličković, P., Cucurull, G., Casanova, A., Romero, A., Liò, P., Bengio, Y.: Graph attention networks. In: Proceedings of ICLR (2018)
14. Zhou, J., et al.: Graph neural networks: a review of methods and applications. AI Open **1**, 57–81 (2020)
15. Ying, R., You, J., Morris, C., Ren, X., Hamilton, W.L., Leskovec, J.: Hierarchical graph representation learning with differentiable pooling. In: Advances in Neural Information Processing Systems (2018)
16. Gao, H., Ji, S.: Graph U-nets. In: Proceedings of ICML (2019)
17. Lee, J., Lee, I., Kang, J.: Self-attention graph pooling. In: Proceedings of ICML (2019)
18. Ma, Y., Wang, S., Aggarwal, C.C., Tang, J.: Graph convolutional networks with EigenPooling. In: Proceedings of KDD (2019)
19. Cangea, C., Veličković, P., Jovanović, N., Kipf, T., Liò, P.: Towards Sparse Hierarchical Graph Classifiers. arXiv preprint arXiv:1811.01287 (2018)
20. Bianchi, F.M., Grattarola, D., Alippi, C.: Spectral clustering with graph neural networks for graph pooling. In: Proceedings of ICML (2020)
21. Li, Z.P., et al.: Graph pooling for graph-level representation learning: a survey. Artif. Intell. Rev. (2024)
22. LeCun, Y., Bottou, L., Bengio, Y., Haffner, P.: Gradient-based learning applied to document recognition. Proc. IEEE **86**(11), 2278–2324 (1998)
23. Krizhevsky, A., Sutskever, I., Hinton, G.E.: ImageNet classification with deep convolutional neural networks. In: Advances in Neural Information Processing Systems (2012)
24. Constantin, D., Bălcău, C.: ECA110-pooling: a comparative analysis of pooling strategies in convolutional neural networks. Big Data Cogn. Comput. **9**(12), 306 (2025)
25. Machowczyk, A., Heckel, R.: Graph Rewriting for Graph Neural Networks. arXiv preprint arXiv:2305.18632 (2023)

From Graph Rewriting to Markov Automata: Mass-Action Semantics for Stochastic and Probabilistic Systems

Reiko Heckel[(✉)] [ID] and Neel Vinod Lad

School of Computing and Mathematical Sciences, University of Leicester, Leicester, UK
`rh122@le.ac.uk`

Abstract. We present a unified semantics for Markov graph rewriting, combining stochastic behaviour and probabilistic rule selection. Timed rules are interpreted under per-match exponential race semantics, while immediate rules are organised into families whose outcomes are resolved by dynamic weight normalisation. Under maximal progress, the resulting operational semantics induces a Markov automaton that integrates nondeterminism, discrete probabilistic branching, and continuous-time stochastic evolution.

We show that the framework conservatively extends both stochastic graph rewriting, yielding continuous-time Markov chains, and probabilistic graph rewriting, yielding Markov decision processes. We establish expressiveness by showing that every finite Markov automaton can be encoded as a Markov graph rewriting system. This positions Markov graph rewriting as a native structural modelling language for quantitative verification based on Markov automata, while preserving compatibility with established graph rewriting techniques.

Keywords: stochastic graph rewriting · probabilistic graph rewriting · Markov automata

1 Introduction

Graph rewriting provides a structural formalism for modelling dynamic systems. Typed graphs capture system configurations and transformation rules describe local structure evolution [11,16]. Over the past decades, graph rewriting has been successfully applied to modelling software architectures, distributed systems, biological networks, and reconfigurable infrastructures [11].

Many such systems exhibit quantitative behaviour. Some evolve in continuous time under stochastic race semantics, as in chemical reaction systems or reliability models [10]. Here, mass-action semantics assigns quantitative behaviour

---

N. V. Lad—Independent Researcher.

B. Archibald and O. Semeráth (Eds.): ICGT 2026, LNCS 16624, pp. 166–183, 2026.
https://doi.org/10.1007/978-3-032-29730-3_9

to individual rule occurrences (matches) and derives global dynamics by aggregation. In stochastic settings, each enabled match contributes an independent exponential race, and overall rates sum over matches, following classical kinetics [7]. Other approaches involve discrete probabilistic branching, representing alternative outcomes, failures, or randomised decisions [13]. While stochastic and probabilistic graph rewriting have been studied independently [10,13], there is no unified approach integrating both aspects nor applying a mass action interpretation to the probabilistic setting.

This paper develops such an approach, extending graph rewriting systems with two types of quantitative annotations: timed rules equipped with exponential rate expressions, and immediate rules organised into families with weight expressions. Timed rules are interpreted under per-match exponential race semantics, realising mass-action behaviour [10]. Immediate rules resolve probabilistic branching by dynamically normalising weights over all enabled occurrences in a state, following the line of work on probabilistic graph transformation mapping to Markov Decision Processes (MDP) [13]. A maximal progress convention gives priority to immediate transitions over timed ones.

The resulting operational semantics induces a Markov automaton, which naturally combines nondeterminism, discrete probabilistic branching, and continuous-time stochastic evolution. In contrast to CTMC-based approaches (stochastic GT), nondeterministic rule application is preserved [10]. In contrast to MDP-style probabilistic graph rewriting, continuous-time behaviour is captured explicitly [13]. The choice of Markov automata thus provides the minimal semantic structure required to accommodate both quantitative aspects simultaneously.

The framework is conservative over established semantics. If only timed rules are present, the semantics collapses to stochastic graph rewriting and yields a continuous-time Markov chain [10]. If only immediate probabilistic rules are present, it yields a Markov decision process corresponding to probabilistic graph rewriting [13]. Moreover, every finite Markov automaton can be encoded as a Markov graph rewriting system, establishing completeness.

The semantics is designed to be tool-compatible. State spaces generated by existing graph rewriting engines, including those supporting control and application conditions, can be analysed by exporting the labelled transition system to an explicit Markov automaton representation [1,6]. A correctness result ensures that this export preserves behaviour.

Next, we discuss the relevant design choices before introducing the formal framework of Markov graph rewriting while presenting a running example to illustrate mass-action and maximal progress. Then we develop the Markov automaton semantics and prove the main results. Finally, we discuss implications and future directions.

2   Design Choices and Alternatives

The framework presented here is the result of a sequence of explicit design choices. We summarise the main alternatives and justify the selected options.

Semantic Domain. Possible semantic targets include continuous-time Markov chains (CTMCs), continuous-time Markov decision processes (CTMDPs), stochastic games, and Markov automata. CTMCs are insufficient, because they do not support nondeterminism. CTMDPs combine nondeterminism and stochastic time but do not natively support instantaneous probabilistic branching with maximal progress (as required to model vanishing phases cleanly); see, e.g., standard CTMDP reachability analyses [2,15]. Stochastic games add an explicit adversarial interpretation (multiple players/strategies) that is not required for rule-based system evolution [3]. Markov automata provide the minimal semantic structure that simultaneously supports nondeterministic choice, discrete probabilistic branching, and continuous-time stochastic behaviour, together with a standard maximal progress convention (vanishing vs. Markovian states) [4,18]. They therefore form a natural semantic domain for graph rewriting systems combining probabilistic and stochastic rules.

Timed Versus Immediate Rules. An alternative would be to associate both rates and probabilities with a single rule. Separating timed and immediate rules yields a clearer semantics and aligns directly with the two transition types of Markov automata [4]. Immediate rules represent resolution of discrete choices without time elapse, while timed rules represent stochastic delay governed by exponential distributions.

Per-match Race Semantics. Timed behaviour could be defined per rule or per match. The per-match interpretation follows the mass-action principle used in stochastic graph rewriting and related reaction-style modelling, where enabled matches race and their rates sum to the state exit rate [10]. It ensures compositionality with respect to graph structure and allows the modeller to control aggregate rates by controlling the number of enabled matches [10].

Probabilistic Choice by Weights. Instead of fixed probabilities, immediate rules are annotated with weights that are normalised dynamically in each state. This supports state-dependent probabilistic behaviour and mirrors mass-action counting on the stochastic side. Probabilities are therefore derived, not primitive, and depend on the number and parameters of enabled occurrences, as in probabilistic graph transformation approaches based on MDP-style resolution [13].

Families and Nondeterminism. Immediate rules are grouped into families. Within a family, probabilistic choice is resolved by weight normalisation; between families, choice is nondeterministic. This separation preserves nondeterminism explicitly in the model and corresponds to the structure of Markov automata, where schedulers resolve nondeterministic choices between enabled probabilistic transitions [4].

Maximal Progress. Immediate transitions are given priority over timed transitions. This avoids ambiguity about interleaving of probabilistic resolution and time elapsed and is standard in the interpretation of Markov automata (vanishing states suppress Markovian timing) [4,18]. Alternative semantics without maximal progress would require additional modelling choices (e.g., explicit time-passage steps in vanishing phases) and complicate tool interoperability.

Control, NACs, and Application Conditions. Rather than integrating control constructs into the semantic core, they are treated uniformly as constraints on enabledness, following standard GT practice for application conditions such as NACs [5]. This allows existing graph rewriting tools such as Groove [6] with control, priorities, or NACs to be used unchanged for state-space generation.

Well-Formedness. Immediate transitions may induce vanishing states. Instead of resolving these during semantics definition (e.g., by on-the-fly elimination), we impose a semantic well-formedness condition. This excludes vanishing divergence (no reachable bottom SCC consisting solely of immediate steps), which is the standard technical condition ensuring that maximal-progress MA semantics yields a well-defined stochastic model [4].

3   Markov Graph Rewrite Systems

Based on the discussion above we are now ready to define our notion of graph rewriting integrating stochastic and probabilistic behaviours with mass-action semantics.

Let TG be a fixed type graph, and $\mathbf{Graph}_{TG}$ denote the class of typed, attributed instance graphs over TG. A *state graph* is an element $G \in \mathbf{Graph}_{TG}$. A *graph rewrite rule* is given abstractly as $r : L_r \Rightarrow R_r$ with parameters X_r, interpreted according to a chosen approach (e.g., DPO or SPO), possibly equipped with application conditions, and subject to external control.

An *occurrence* of a rule r in a state G is a triple $e = (r, m, \sigma)$ where $m : L_r \to G$ is a match and σ is a valuation of the rule's parameters X_r. If the occurrence is enabled (i.e., it satisfies the application and control conditions), its application yields a successor graph $H = \mathsf{apply}(r, m, \sigma)$.

Definition 1 (Markov GRS). *A* Markov graph rewriting system *is a tuple* $\mathcal{G} = (TG, G_0, \mathcal{R}_M, \mathcal{R}_P, \mathsf{rew}_S, \mathsf{rew}_T, \mathsf{lab})$ *where*

- *TG is a type graph and G_0 the initial graph;*
- *$\mathcal{R}_M$ is a finite set of* timed rules*;*
- *$\mathcal{R}_P$ is a finite set of* immediate probabilistic rules*;*
- *$\mathsf{rew}_S : S \to \mathbb{R}$ is a state reward function;*
- *$\mathsf{rew}_T : T \to \mathbb{R}$ is a transition reward function;*
- *$\mathsf{lab} : S \to \mathcal{P}(AP)$ is a state labelling function defined by graph patterns.*

Each timed rule $r \in \mathcal{R}_M$ consists of

- *a base transformation rule $L_r \Rightarrow R_r$;*
- *a rate expression $\lambda_r(X_r)$ over the rule parameters which, when instantiated, yields a positive real value $\lambda_r(\sigma) \in \mathbb{R}_{\geq 0}$.*

For each enabled occurrence $e = (r, m, \sigma)$ in a state G, the occurrence rate is $\lambda(e) = \lambda_r(\sigma)$.

Each immediate probabilistic rule $r \in \mathcal{R}_P$ consists of:

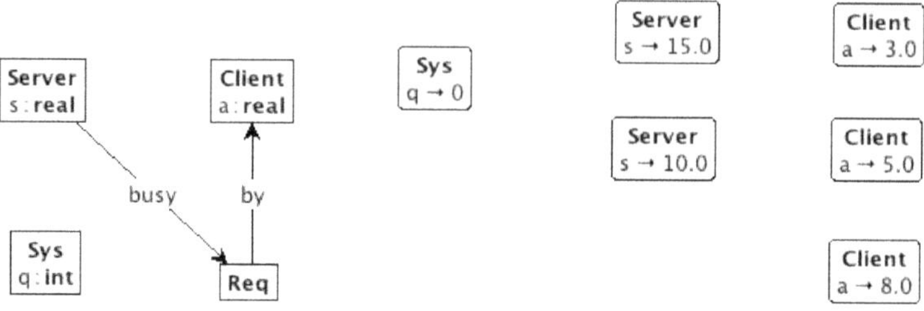

Fig. 1. Type graph TG and start graph G with 2 idle servers, 3 clients and no requests.

- *a base transformation rule $L_r \Rightarrow R_r$;*
- *a family identifier $f(r)$;*
- *a response identifier $\rho(r)$;*
- *a weight expression $w_r(X_r)$ over the rule parameters which, when instantiated, yields a positive real value $w_r(\sigma) \in \mathbb{R}_{>0}$.*

For each enabled occurrence $e = (r, m, \sigma)$ in a state G, its weight is $w(e) = w_r(\sigma)$.   △

Atomic propositions AP are used inside temporal logic formulas to express basic state properties. They are included here for completeness but we do not make use of them in our example. In a graph rewriting context, such state properties are often expressed by graph patterns or rules' left-hand sides. For example, we could use rule *complete* in Fig. 2 below to define a property *busy* that is satisfied in a state if it contains a busy server.

4   A Running Example

We illustrate the concepts using a simple but expressive model of request handling in a client-server system. The example is intentionally minimal, but it shows the essential semantic features: mass-action dependence of both rates and probabilities on the number of matches, maximal progress, and the interaction between stochastic and probabilistic rules. Rewards will be illustrated in Example 1 based on the generated transition system, rate and weight calculations in Example 2.

The type graph in the left of Fig. 1 has four node types: *Sys*, *Client*, *Server*, and *Req*. A distinguished node of type *Sys* maintains a queue attribute q recording the number of pending requests. Each *Client* node carries an attribute a representing an arrival rate parameter. Each *Server* node carries a service parameter s representing its speed. Requests are represented as nodes of type *Req* referencing their initiating clients using edges of type *by*. An *busy* edge indicates that a server is processing a request, otherwise it is considered idle.

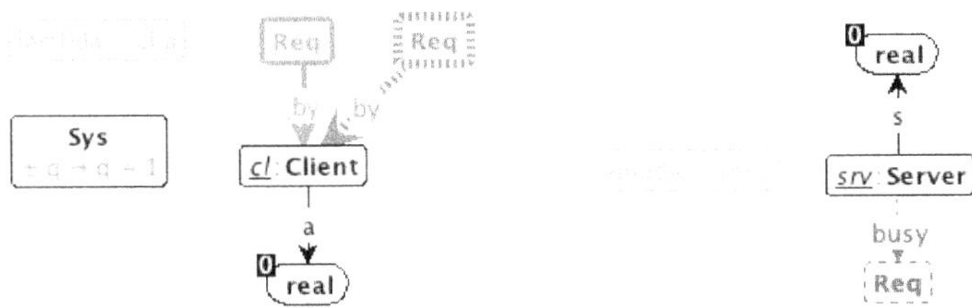

Fig. 2. Timed rules *arrive* (one match per client without pending request) and *complete* (one match per busy server). Rate expressions *lambda* in the yellow top left comment nodes are based on client arrival rate a and server speed s. We use Groove [6] notation showing rules as integrated rule graphs, distinguishing reader elements in solid grey, creators in bold green, erasers in dashed blue and embargoes in dotted red lines and borders. (Color figure online)

The initial graph in the right of Fig. 1 consists of one *Sys* node with $q = 0$, a fixed set of *Client* nodes, and a fixed set of *Server* nodes, all idle. No requests are present.

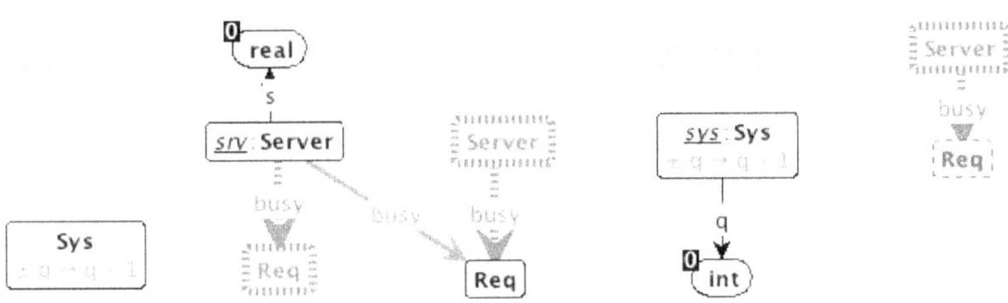

Fig. 3. Immediate probabilistic rule family Resp: *dispatch* (one match per pair of idle server and pending request) and *drop* (one match per pending request). Weight expressions w in comment nodes based on server speed s and system queue length s.

Arrival and Completion. In the rules shown in Fig. 2, incoming requests are generated by a timed rule *arrive*. For each match of a *Client* node, the rule creates a fresh *Req* node, links it to the *Client* node, and increments q. A client is only allowed one request at a time, so a negative application condition checks that it has no existing requests.

The rate $\lambda_{arrive} = a$ of each occurrence equals the arrival rate attribute a of the matched client, hence, if n clients are present with attributes $a_1, \ldots, a_n$, the total arrival rate is

$$\Lambda_{arrive}(G) = \sum_{i=1}^{n} a_i,$$

illustrating per-match exponential race semantics. The overall arrival intensity therefore scales with the number of matches.

Processing completion is captured by a timed rule *complete*, one occurrence per busy server. The rate $\lambda_{complete} = s$ of each occurrence equals the speed attribute of the server. Again, the total completion rate is obtained by summing over matches, realising mass-action behaviour on the stochastic side.

Responses. In the rules shown in Fig. 3, whenever at least one request is pending ($q > 0$), the immediate rule family *Resp* becomes enabled and, by maximal progress, time cannot elapse thus all timed rules are disabled. Note that *Resp* is the only rule family in this model, because timed rules are not organised in families. Since *Resp* is the only family, there is no nondeterminism in this example: If a rule in *Resp* is enabled, there is a probabilistic choice between all its enabled rules while all the timed rules are suppressed; if no rule from *Resp* is enabled, we have a race between the enabled timed rules.

Family *Resp* comprises two rules: *dispatch*, which assigns a request to an idle server, and *drop*, which discards a request.

Each enabled match contributes a strictly positive weight. For *dispatch*, the weight equals the speed of the matched server: $w_{dispatch} = s$. For *drop*, the weight is the current queue length: $w_{drop} = q$. For k_i idle servers with speeds $s_1, \ldots, s_{k_i}$ and x pending requests, the number of matches for *dispatch* equals $x \cdot k_i$, while *drop* has x matches.

Since weights are accumulated over enabled occurrences in the family, the total weight contributed by *drop* is

$$W_{drop}(G) = x \cdot q = x^2$$

assuming invariant $q = x$, and the total weight contributed by *dispatch* is

$$W_{dispatch}(G) = x \cdot \sum_{j=1}^{k_i} s_j,$$

because each idle server contributes a match when paired with any of the x requests. Then the probability is

$$\Pr_G(dispatch) = \frac{W_{dispatch}(G)}{W_{drop}(G) + W_{dispatch}(G)} = \frac{x \cdot \sum_{j=1}^{k_i} s_j}{x \cdot (x + \sum_{j=1}^{k_i} s_j)} = \frac{\sum_{j=1}^{k_i} s_j}{x + \sum_{j=1}^{k_i} s_j}.$$

This illustrates *mass action* for probabilistic choice: the derived probabilities depend on the number of enabled matches and on state-dependent weights. That means, $W_{dispatch}(G)$ increases with the number and speed of available servers and decreases with the number of requests in the queue.

Maximal Progress. By construction, if $q > 0$, the family *Resp* is enabled. Under maximal progress, timed rules are suppressed in such states. In Groove [6] this is realised by setting priorities for immediate rules higher than for timed rules. Thus time can elapse only in states without pending requests. Operationally, executions alternate between timed phases (where arrivals and completions race) and vanishing phases (where response rules resolve instantaneously).

Discussion. The example highlights three design principles. First, rates and probabilities are derived from the number of matches, not attached globally to rules. Second, stochastic and probabilistic aspects are treated symmetrically, both following a mass-action intuition. Third, maximal progress cleanly separates probabilistic resolution from time evolution, aligning the operational interpretation with that of Markov automata.

Despite its simplicity, the example induces a non-trivial Markov automaton whose quantitative behaviour varies systematically with the number of sources, the number and speed of servers, and the queue length. In the next section, we will formalise this intuition.

5   Markov Automaton Semantics

We recall the standard definition of *Markov automata* (MA), which combine continuous-time Markovian transitions with instantaneous probabilistic branching under a maximal-progress convention.

Definition 2 (Markov automaton). *A* Markov automaton *is a tuple*

$$\mathcal{M} = (S, \Rightarrow, \xrightarrow{\lambda}, \mathsf{rew}_S, \mathsf{rew}_T, \mathsf{lab})$$

where:

- S *is a countable set of states;*
- $\Rightarrow \subseteq S \times \mathcal{D}(S)$ *is a set of* immediate probabilistic transitions, *where* $\mathcal{D}(S)$ *denotes the set of discrete probability distributions over* S*;*
- $\xrightarrow{\lambda} \subseteq S \times \mathbb{R}_{>0} \times S$ *is a set of* Markovian transitions *labelled with rates* λ *(exponential residence-time parameters);*
- $\mathsf{rew}_S : S \to \mathbb{R}_{\geq 0}$ *is a state-reward rate (accrued per time unit spent in a state);*
- $\mathsf{rew}_T : (\Rightarrow \cup \xrightarrow{\lambda}) \to \mathbb{R}_{\geq 0}$ *is a transition reward (awarded instantaneously when a transition is taken);*
- $\mathsf{lab} : S \to \mathcal{P}(AP)$ *assigns to each state the set of atomic propositions it satisfies.*

A state s is vanishing *if it has at least one outgoing immediate transition ($\exists \mu.\; s \Rightarrow \mu$); otherwise it is* Markovian *(or* waiting*). Under the standard* max*imal* progress *convention, time may elapse only in Markovian states: if s is vanishing, Markovian transitions $s \xrightarrow{\lambda} s'$ do not exist, so only immediate probabilistic transitions can be taken.*   △

Note that probabilistic transitions are expressed as a relation between states and probability distributions over states, $\Rightarrow \subseteq S \times \mathcal{D}(S)$. This captures both nondeterminism (the choice between different distributions because $\Rightarrow$ is a relation) and, once a distribution is chosen, the probabilistic choice defined by this distribution.

Markov automata generalise CTMCs (only $\overset{\lambda}{\dashrightarrow}$), MDPs (only $\Rightarrow$ plus nondeterminism), and CTMDPs (nondeterminism over Markovian transitions), while additionally supporting instantaneous probabilistic branching with maximal progress [4,18].

Now we are ready to define the Markov automaton induced by a Markov graph rewriting system. For a graph G, we write

- $E_M(G)$ for the set of enabled timed occurrences in G;
- $E_P(G)$ for the set of enabled immediate occurrences in G.

For a family F, let $E_{P,F}(G) = \{e \in E_P(G) \mid f(\text{rule}(e)) = F\}$ be the set of *enabled immediate occurrences in G from rules in F*. The *set of enabled families in G is* $\mathsf{Fam}(G) = \{F \mid E_{P,F}(G) \neq \emptyset\}$.

Construction 1 (Markov Automaton Semantics). *From a Markov graph rewriting system $\mathcal{G}$, we construct a Markov automaton*

$$\mathcal{M}(\mathcal{G}) = (S, \Rightarrow, \overset{\lambda}{\dashrightarrow}, \text{rew}_S, \text{rew}_T, \text{lab})$$

where S is the set of state graphs reachable from G_0 by repeated application of enabled occurrences, with timed and immediate transitions defined as follows.

If $\mathsf{Fam}(G) \neq \emptyset$, there are no timed transitions from G. For each enabled family $F \in \mathsf{Fam}(G)$, define a probability distribution $\mu_{G,F}$ over successor states by

$$\mu_{G,F}(H) = \sum_{\substack{e \in E_{P,F}(G) \\ \text{apply}(e)=H}} \frac{w(e)}{\sum_{e' \in E_{P,F}(G)} w(e')}.$$

This yields an immediate probabilistic transition

$$G \Rightarrow_F \mu_{G,F}.$$

If several families are enabled, the choice of family is nondeterministic.

If $\mathsf{Fam}(G) = \emptyset$, then for each enabled timed occurrence $e \in E_M(G)$ with successor H, include a timed transition

$$G \xrightarrow{\lambda(e)} H.$$

Timed occurrences follow a per-match exponential race semantics: *the residence time in G is exponentially distributed with parameter $\sum_{e \in E_M(G)} \lambda(e)$.*
State rewards and transition rewards are interpreted as follows:

- $\text{rew}_S(G)$ *accrues per unit time spent in state G and therefore only contributes during timed residence;*
- $\text{rew}_T(e)$ *is awarded instantaneously when occurrence e fires, for both immediate and timed transitions.*

Immediate transitions consume zero time and therefore do not accumulate state reward. Atomic propositions can be defined by graph pattern predicates.
The labelling function $\text{lab}(G)$ yields the set of propositions satisfied by G. $\triangle$

The induced semantics combines three forms of behaviour in a uniform way: *nondeterministic choice* between enabled rule families, *probabilistic choice* resolved by weight-based normalisation within a family, and *stochastic time* governed by exponential rates and per-match race semantics.

Under maximal progress, immediate probabilistic transitions have priority over timed transitions. This corresponds exactly to the standard interpretation of *Markov automata*, where states with enabled immediate transitions are *vanishing*, and time may elapse only in states without such transitions.

If all immediate probabilistic rules are removed, the semantics collapses to a continuous-time Markov chain generated by stochastic graph rewriting with mass-action race semantics. If all timed rules are removed, the semantics yields a purely probabilistic, nondeterministic transition system, corresponding to probabilistic graph transformation models and Markov decision processes.

A bottom strongly connected component (BSCC) is a set of states that are mutually reachable and have no outgoing transition to a different SCC—a trap that once entered, the system cannot leave. A reachable BSCC of *immediate* transitions represents *vanishing divergence*: the system can execute an infinite number of zero-time steps and thus never let time elapse. In Markov-automaton semantics this can make time-bounded and reward-based measures ill-defined (e.g., residence time remains 0 while transitions accumulate), and it breaks the intended maximal-progress interpretation of vanishing states [4, 18].

Condition 1 (Well-Formedness). *A Markov GRS is well-formed if, in the induced Markov automaton, the subgraph consisting only of immediate transitions contains no BSCC. Equivalently, with probability 1, every execution performs only finitely many immediate steps before reaching a state in which time may elapse or termination occurs.* △

To check this condition we can construct the directed graph of reachable states using only immediate transitions; compute SCCs, identify bottom SCCs (no outgoing edge to another SCC). Since, by construction, our directed graph only contains reachable states, any such SCC is reachable from the initial state [4]. Such an analysis could be performed after state-space generation and before export to a model checker for Markov automata such as Storm [12] or Modest [9].

Example 1 (well-formedness and rewards). Applying this to our running example, the transition system (generated from a start graph with 1 server and 2 clients) is shown in Fig. 4. Here, every state with $q = x > 0$ enables *Resp*, hence is *vanishing*. Maximal progress implies that no timed transition (neither *arrive* nor *complete*) may occur while $q > 0$. Thus executions alternate between timed phases (when $q = 0$) and immediate bursts that reduce q until time may elapse again. Since each immediate step reduces q by 1, vanishing divergence is excluded.

We define rewards using state properties and transition labels. For every state $s \in S$ where none of the servers is busy, let the reward rate $\mathsf{rew}_S(s) = 1$ and 0

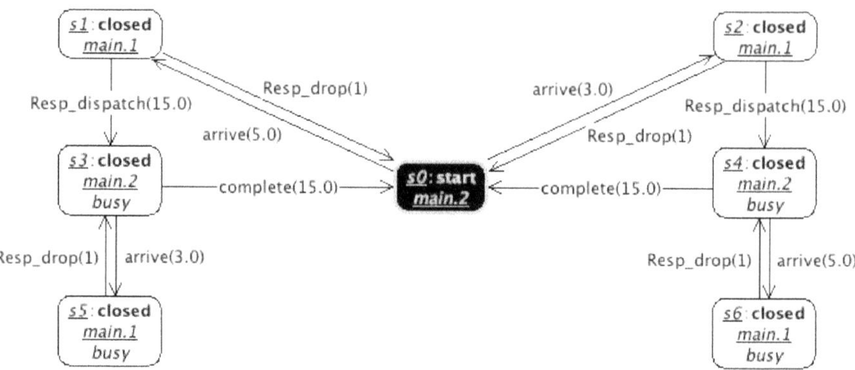

Fig. 4. LTS for start graph with 1 server and 2 clients: states $s0, s3, s4$ are Markovian with outgoing timed transitions *arrive, complete* while $s1, s2, s5, s6$ are vanishing states with transitions *Resp_arrive, Resp_complete*.

otherwise. The actual reward will depend on the time spent in s. We can detect if a state has a busy server by means of the graph condition *busy* below, which defines the state property of the same name shown in the LTS in Fig. 4.

$$\boxed{\text{Server}}\!-\!\text{busy}\!\twoheadrightarrow\!\boxed{\text{Req}}$$

Transitions are rewarded if they represent the serving of requests, e.g., $\mathsf{rew}_T(complete) = 10$. Then, for each set of timed trajectories through the Markov automaton, an analysis tool can calculate the total (or expected) reward. The sequence

$$s0[15] \xrightarrow{arrive} s2 \xrightarrow{dispatch} s4[3] \xrightarrow{complete} s0[12]$$

first spends 15 units of time in $s0$, then 3 in $s4$ and finally 12 units in $s0$ again. It would receive a total reward of $15 + 3 + 12 + 10 = 40$ because $s2$ is an immediate state and $s4$ has a busy server, and for each unit spent in $s0$ we earn a reward of 1, plus the transition reward of 10 for *complete*.   △

The same rule set illustrates other semantic choices. If timed semantics were *per-rule* rather than per-match, then $\Lambda_{arrive}(G)$ would not scale with the number of clients, eliminating mass-action semantics. If immediate choices used *fixed probabilities* rather than weight normalisation over occurrences, then adding idle servers or changing their speeds would no longer affect $\Pr_G(dispatch)$, weakening the connection between graph structure and behaviour.

If maximal progress were dropped, timed transitions could interleave with immediate response resolution. In particular, arrivals could occur while $q > 0$, potentially increasing queue length during responses and changing performance and loss probabilities. Finally, enabling multiple immediate families would introduce explicit nondeterminism at vanishing states: a scheduler could choose which family resolves first, affecting quantitative properties.

6   Properties of Markov Graph Rewriting

Next we explore the consequences of our semantic choices for the relation of Markov GRS with other stochastic and probabilistic forms of graph rewriting, Markov automata, and modular tool support.

Theorem 1 (Conservative Extension of Existing GR Semantics). *Let $\mathcal{G}$ be a Markov GRS.*

1. *If $\mathcal{R}_P = \emptyset$, then the induced Markov automaton $\mathcal{M}(\mathcal{G})$ is a continuous-time Markov chain whose transition rates coincide with the standard stochastic graph rewriting semantics based on per-match exponential race.*
2. *If $\mathcal{R}_M = \emptyset$, then $\mathcal{M}(\mathcal{G})$ is a purely probabilistic and nondeterministic transition system, equivalent to a Markov decision process induced by probabilistic graph rewriting.*
3. *In the general case, $\mathcal{M}(\mathcal{G})$ is a Markov automaton that conservatively extends both semantics.*

Proof (sketch). For (1), with $\mathcal{R}_P = \emptyset$, every reachable state satisfies $\mathsf{Fam}(G) = \emptyset$, hence only timed transitions are enabled. Each enabled occurrence contributes an exponential transition with its rate, and the per-match race property yields the usual CTMC semantics.

For (2), with $\mathcal{R}_M = \emptyset$, time never elapses. Each enabled family induces a probability distribution over successor states, and the nondeterministic choice between families yields an MDP semantics.

The general case follows by combining both constructions under maximal progress, which is precisely the defining structure of Markov automata. $\square$

The next result shows that the framework is not merely compatible with Markov automata but *complete* with respect to them.

Theorem 2 (Expressiveness: Encoding of Finite Markov Automata). *For every finite Markov automaton*

$$\mathcal{M} = (S, \Rightarrow, \xrightarrow{\lambda}, \mathsf{rew}_S, \mathsf{rew}_T, \mathsf{lab}),$$

there exists a Markov GRS $\mathcal{G}$ such that the induced Markov automaton $\mathcal{M}(\mathcal{G})$ is behaviourally equivalent to $\mathcal{M}$, up to isomorphism of states and preservation of labels and rewards.

Proof (sketch). Let $\mathcal{M}$ be finite. Construct a type graph containing a distinguished node type State with an attribute id ranging over identifiers for states in S. Represent each MA state $s \in S$ by an instance graph G_s containing exactly one State node with $\mathsf{id} = s$.

For each Markovian transition $s \xrightarrow{\lambda} s'$, introduce a timed rule $r_{s,s'} \in \mathcal{R}_M$ that rewrites $\mathsf{State}(s)$ to $\mathsf{State}(s')$ with rate λ. For each immediate probabilistic transition $s \Rightarrow \mu$, introduce a family F_s of immediate rules. For each successor s'

with $\mu(s') > 0$, add a rule $r_{s,s'} \in \mathcal{R}_P$ rewriting $\mathsf{State}(s)$ to $\mathsf{State}(s')$ with weight $w_{s,s'} = \mu(s')$.

Nondeterministic choice between multiple immediate transitions in $\mathcal{M}$ is realised by assigning different families. Maximal progress ensures that immediate transitions suppress timed transitions exactly as in $\mathcal{M}$. State rewards, transition rewards, and state labels are transferred directly via rew_S, rew_T, and lab.

By construction, the reachable state graphs correspond one-to-one with S, and the induced transitions coincide with those of $\mathcal{M}$. $\qquad\qquad\square$

Combined with the conservative extension theorem, this places Markov GRS as a unifying front-end for rule-based stochastic and probabilistic system modelling. More pragmatically, it is important to be able to use existing tools for state space generation and analysis, as stated by the modular construction below.

Construction 2 (LTS to Explicit Markov Automaton Export). *Given a finite state laballed transition system with space S generated by an existing graph rewriting tool, with labels identifying rule classes, families and parameters, the corresponding explicit Markov automaton can be constructed as follows:*

1. *For each state $G \in S$, compute the sets $E_M(G)$, $E_P(G)$, and $\mathsf{Fam}(G)$ from the labels of outgoing transitions.*
2. *If $\mathsf{Fam}(G) \neq \emptyset$, then for each $F \in \mathsf{Fam}(G)$:*
   (a) *compute the total family weight $W_{G,F} = \sum_{e \in E_{P,F}(G)} w(e)$;*
   (b) *for each successor H, compute $\mu_{G,F}(H)$ by aggregating the normalised weights of occurrences leading to H;*
   (c) *emit an immediate probabilistic transition $G \Rightarrow_F \mu_{G,F}$.*
3. *If $\mathsf{Fam}(G) = \emptyset$, then for each $e \in E_M(G)$ with successor H, emit a Markovian transition $G \xrightarrow{\lambda(e)} H$.*
4. *Attach state rewards, transition rewards, and state labels according to rew_S, rew_T, and lab.*
5. *Check the well-formedness condition (absence of reachable vanishing bottom strongly connected components) before exporting the model.* $\qquad\triangle$

This construction decouples state-space generation from stochastic analysis. Existing graph rewriting tools can be used to generate the labelled transition system, while the explicit Markov automaton representation can be exported to model checkers for Markov automata such as Storm [12] or Modest [9].

Example 2 (rates and weights). In our LTS in Fig. 4, transitions are labelled by rule names which, for immediate rules, contain the family name (e.g. *Resp_dispatch*). This allows us to distinguish timed from immediate rules and to identify their family. Rule priorities ensure that immediate and timed rules do not compete. Rule parameters represent the values from which rates and weights are calculated. E.g., for *dispatch*(15) we have $w_{dispatch} = srv.s = 15$ based on the weight expression and the parameter definition for that rule in Fig. 3.

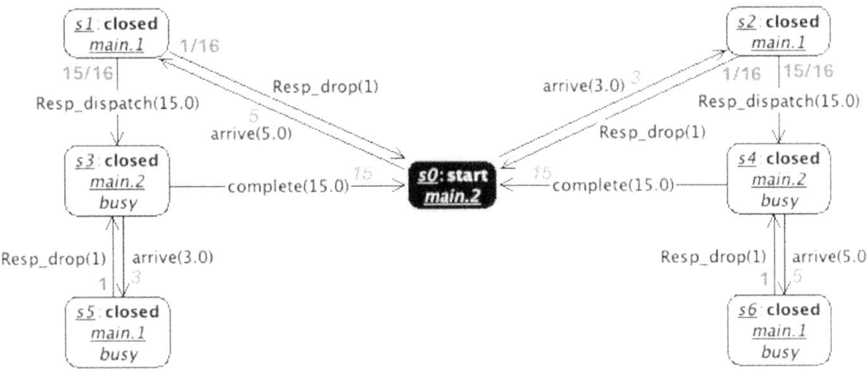

Fig. 5. Markov automaton derived from the LTS in Fig. 4: bold blue fractions are probabilities induced by the weights; rates are shown in red italics font. (Color figure online)

The Markov automaton derived from the LTS is shown in Fig. 5. Rates are copied verbatim from the labels of the LTS but weight normalisation within the *Resp* family of immediate transitions leads to state-dependent probabilities for the *drop* and *dispatch* transitions.   △

The final correctness result justifies the two-stage approach to generating the Markov automaton.

Theorem 3 (Correctness of Explicit MA Construction). *Let $\mathcal{G}$ be a well-formed Markov GRS and $\mathcal{M}(\mathcal{G})$ its induced Markov automaton as defined above. Let $\mathcal{M}_{\mathrm{exp}}(\mathcal{G})$ be the explicit Markov automaton constructed from the LTS by the LTS-to-MA export.*

Then $\mathcal{M}(\mathcal{G})$ and $\mathcal{M}_{\mathrm{exp}}(\mathcal{G})$ are behaviourally equivalent, i.e. they are bisimilar with respect to:

- *probabilistic branching,*
- *Markovian transition rates,*
- *state labelling and reward structures.*

Proof (sketch). Both constructions are based on the same set of reachable graph states and the same sets of enabled rule occurrences.

Immediate probabilistic transitions coincide because, in both cases, each enabled family induces a probability distribution obtained by normalising the weights of enabled occurrences leading to the same successor state.

Timed transitions coincide because both constructions associate exactly one Markovian transition per enabled timed occurrence, with identical exponential rate, and rely on the same per-match race semantics.

Maximal progress ensures that immediate transitions suppress timed transitions in exactly the same states in both models. Rewards and labels are attached identically by construction.   □

7   Related Work

We position our work in the context of graph transformation (GT) formalisms that incorporate stochastic, timed, and probabilistic behaviours, with or without mass-action semantics and maximal progress. Table 1 summarises the key approaches, distinguishing:

- Stochastic: Probability distributions over delays (e.g., exponential races).
- Timed: Fixed delays or time bounds (e.g., real-time constraints).
- Probabilistic: Probability distributions over outgoing transitions (e.g., weighted choices).
- Mass Action: Rates/probabilities scale with the number of matches (per-match semantics).
- Maximal Progress: Immediate transitions suppress timed ones.
- Nondeterminism: Scheduler-resolved choice between enabled transitions.

Stochastic Graph Transformation (SGT). Stochastic graph transformation systems extend GT with exponential race semantics, where each match contributes a rate, and the global exit rate is the sum of all enabled matches [10]. This yields a CTMC, with mass-action behaviour (rates scale with match multiplicity). SGTS have been applied to reliability modelling and performance analysis [10].

Probabilistic Graph Transformation (PGT). Probabilistic GT associates probabilities with rules sharing the same left-hand side. That means, probabilities are independent of the state so there is no need for dynamic normalisation over enabled matches [13]. They map to Markov Decision Processes (MDPs), where nondeterminism is resolved by a scheduler, and probabilistic transitions. PGT supports probabilistic branching but lacks explicit timing.

Timed Graph Transformation (TGT). Timed GT introduces fixed delays or time bounds via clock attributes, guards, and invariants [8]. Unlike stochastic GT, TGT models deterministic timing (e.g., real-time systems) and nondeterministic choice between alternative rule applications rather than a race.

Probabilistic Timed Graph Transformation (PTGT). PTGT integrates probabilistic choices and timed behaviour [14,19]. As in PGT, rules are assigned probabilities and they are equipped with clock attributes and time constraints to control delays. Stochastic TGT [17] adds stochastic variables, e.g., to model the time of failure, but do not inherently support stochastic time mass-action semantics.

Markov Graph Rewriting. Our approach unifies stochastic and probabilistic (weight-based) mass action with maximal progress and nondeterminism. This yields a Markov automaton semantics, conservatively extending SGT (CTMC) and PGT (MDP).

Table 1. Comparison of GT and Petri net formalisms with stochastic, timed, and probabilistic behaviours.

Framework	Stoch	Timed	Prob	Mass	Max Prog	Nondet
Stochastic GT [10]	✓	–	–	✓	–	–
Probabilistic GT [13]	–	–	✓	–	–	✓
Timed GT [8]	–	✓	–	–	–	✓
Probabilistic Timed GT [14,17]	(✓)	✓	✓	–	–	✓
Markov GRS (this work)	✓	–	✓	✓	✓	✓

8 Conclusion

We introduced Markov graph rewriting, a unified quantitative semantics for graph transformation systems that combines continuous-time, mass-action stochastic evolution with instantaneous, state-dependent probabilistic branching. Timed rules follow a per-match exponential race, while immediate rules are organised into families whose outcomes are derived by dynamic weight normalisation, with maximal progress separating probabilistic resolution from the elapse of time. We showed that the semantics is a conservative extension of established stochastic (CTMC) and probabilistic (MDP) graph rewriting. We established expressiveness by encoding every finite Markov automaton as a Markov GRS, and justified a practical tool architecture via a correctness theorem: exporting an LTS generated by existing graph rewriting engines to an explicit Markov automaton preserves rates, probabilities, labels, and rewards up to behavioural equivalence.

Future work aims at realising this tool chain end-to-end: enriching state-space generators with occurrence data, implementing the LTS to MA export (including reward/label compilation and automatic well-formedness checks), and connecting to Markov-automata model checkers for quantitative verification. We plan to investigate real-world applications and evaluate scalability and expressiveness.

Acknowledgements. GPT-5 was used for background research and LaTeX typesetting.

References

1. Arendt, T., Biermann, E., Jurack, S., Krause, C., Taentzer, G.: Henshin: advanced concepts and tools for in-place EMF model transformations. In: Petriu, D.C., Rouquette, N., Haugen, Ø. (eds.) MODELS 2010. LNCS, vol. 6394, pp. 121–135. Springer, Heidelberg (2010). https://doi.org/10.1007/978-3-642-16145-2_9
2. Baier, C., Hermanns, H., Katoen, J.P., Haverkort, B.R.: Efficient computation of time-bounded reachability probabilities in uniform continuous-time Markov decision processes. Theor. Comput. Sci. **345**(1), 2–26 (2005). https://www.sciencedirect.com/science/article/pii/S030439750500383X. Tools and Algorithms for the Construction and Analysis of Systems (TACAS 2004)
3. Condon, A.: The complexity of stochastic games. Inf. Comput. **96**(2), 203–224 (1992). https://www.sciencedirect.com/science/article/pii/089054019290048K
4. Deng, Y., Hennessy, M.: On the semantics of Markov automata. Inf. Comput. **222**, 139–168 (2013). https://www.sciencedirect.com/science/article/pii/S0890540112001514. 38th International Colloquium on Automata, Languages and Programming (ICALP 2011)
5. Ehrig, H., Ehrig, K., Prange, U., Taentzer, G.: Fundamentals of Algebraic Graph Transformation. Monographs in Theoretical Computer Science. An EATCS Series. Springer (2006). https://d-nb.info/978015258/04
6. Ghamarian, A.H., de Mol, M., Rensink, A., Zambon, E., Zimakova, M.: Modelling and analysis using GROOVE. STTT **14**(1), 15–40 (2012). https://doi.org/10.1007/s10009-011-0186-x
7. Gillespie, D.T.: Exact stochastic simulation of coupled chemical reactions. J. Phys. Chem. **81**(25), 2340–2361 (1977). https://doi.org/10.1021/j100540a008
8. Gyapay, S., Heckel, R., Varró, D.: Graph transformation with time: causality and logical clocks. In: Corradini, A., Ehrig, H., Kreowski, H.J., Rozenberg, G. (eds.) Graph Transformation, pp. 120–134. Springer, Heidelberg (2002). https://api.semanticscholar.org/CorpusID:5469215
9. Hartmanns, A., Hermanns, H.: A modest Markov automata tutorial. In: Krötzsch, M., Stepanova, D. (eds.) Reasoning Web. Explainable Artificial Intelligence. LNCS, vol. 11810, pp. 250–276. Springer, Cham (2019). https://doi.org/10.1007/978-3-030-31423-1_8
10. Heckel, R., Lajios, G., Menge, S.: Stochastic graph transformation systems. Fundam. Inform. **74**(1), 63–84 (2006). http://content.iospress.com/articles/fundamenta-informaticae/fi74-1-04
11. Heckel, R., Taentzer, G.: Graph Transformation for Software Engineers - With Applications to Model-Based Development and Domain-Specific Language Engineering. Springer (2020). https://doi.org/10.1007/978-3-030-43916-3
12. Hensel, C., Junges, S., Katoen, J., Quatmann, T., Volk, M.: The probabilistic model checker Storm. Int. J. Softw. Tools Technol. Transf. **24**(4), 589–610 (2022). https://doi.org/10.1007/s10009-021-00633-z
13. Krause, C., Giese, H.: Probabilistic graph transformation systems. In: Ehrig, H., Engels, G., Kreowski, H.-J., Rozenberg, G. (eds.) ICGT 2012. LNCS, vol. 7562, pp. 311–325. Springer, Heidelberg (2012). https://doi.org/10.1007/978-3-642-33654-6_21
14. Maximova, M., Giese, H., Krause, C.: Probabilistic timed graph transformation systems. J. Logical Algebraic Methods Program. **101**, 110–131 (2018). https://www.sciencedirect.com/science/article/pii/S2352220817302365

15. Neuhäußer, M.R., Zhang, L.: Time-bounded reachability probabilities in continuous-time Markov decision processes. In: 7th International Conference on Quantitative Evaluation of Systems, QEST 2010, Williamsburg, Virginia, USA, 15–18 September 2010, pp. 209–218 (2010). https://ieeexplore.ieee.org/document/5600386
16. Rozenberg, G. (ed.): Handbook of Graph Grammars and Computing by Graph Transformation.: Vol. 1: Foundations, vol. 1. World Scientific, Singapore (1997). https://scispace.com/pdf/handbook-of-graph-grammars-and-computing-by-graph-2rwjem0eoo.pdf
17. Schneider, S., Maximova, M., Giese, H.: Stochastic timed graph transformation systems. In: Boronat, A., Fraser, G. (eds.) Fundamental Approaches to Software Engineering - 28th International Conference, FASE 2025, Held as Part of the International Joint Conferences on Theory and Practice of Software, ETAPS 2025, Hamilton, ON, Canada, 3–8 May 2025, Proceedings. Lecture Notes in Computer Science, pp. 188–213. Springer (2025). https://doi.org/10.1007/978-3-031-90900-9_10
18. Timmer, M., Katoen, J.-P., van de Pol, J., Stoelinga, M.I.A.: Efficient modelling and generation of Markov automata. In: Koutny, M., Ulidowski, I. (eds.) CONCUR 2012. LNCS, vol. 7454, pp. 364–379. Springer, Heidelberg (2012). https://doi.org/10.1007/978-3-642-32940-1_26
19. Zöllner, C., Barkowsky, M., Maximova, M., Schneider, M., Giese, H.: A simulator for probabilistic timed graph transformation systems with complex large-scale topologies. In: Gadducci, F., Kehrer, T. (eds.) ICGT 2020. LNCS, vol. 12150, pp. 325–334. Springer, Cham (2020). https://doi.org/10.1007/978-3-030-51372-6_20

Tool and Vision Papers

GHL: An Extensible C++ Library for Flexible and Performant Graph Pattern Matching and Rewriting

Tunaberk Almaci[1], Corey Lammie[2], Hadjer Benmeziane[2],
Clément Fournier[3], Orhun Görkem[2], Irem Boybat[2],
and William Andrew Simon[2(✉)]

[1] ETH Zürich, 8092 Zürich, Switzerland
[2] IBM Rüschlikon, 8803 Rüschlikon, Switzerland
william.simon1@ibm.com
[3] TU Dresden, 01069 Dresden, Germany

Abstract. Graph pattern matching and replacement are foundational techniques spanning domains from cheminformatics to deep learning. Existing graph libraries, however, often expose a trade-off between performance and flexibility: general-purpose libraries incur substantial overhead and rarely offer integrated replacement support, while domain-specific infrastructures lack generality. In this paper, we introduce the Graph Hook Library (GHL), a modular and extensible C++ architecture with Python bindings for high-performance graph pattern matching and rewriting. GHL exposes explicit hooks, architectural extension points that enable fine-grained specialization of match-and-replace behavior. This structure supports rapid adaptation to diverse application domains without compromising efficiency. GHL source code is available at https://github.com/IBM/graph-hook-library. Benchmarking shows that GHL performs subgraph matching 2.3x/100x/207x faster than the general-purpose libraries iGraph/NetworkX/Graph-tool.

Keywords: Graph pattern matching and replacement · Open source library · Benchmarking

1 Introduction

Graphs serve as a universal data model in diverse domains including cheminformatics [13], biochemical data [5], social network analysis [21], graph databases [17], and machine learning [15]. Representing a system as a graph captures semantic and relational attributes while abstracting away domain-specific details, enabling a wide range of analysis and optimization techniques. Pattern matching and replacement [27] are pervasive requirements across these domains. Pattern matching (hereafter referred to as SI) seeks subgraphs in a target graph that are isomorphic to a pattern, requiring a solution to the NP-complete subgraph isomorphism (SI) problem [10]. Pattern replacement

© The Author(s), under exclusive license to Springer Nature Switzerland AG 2026
B. Archibald and O. Semeráth (Eds.): ICGT 2026, LNCS 16624, pp. 187–198, 2026.
https://doi.org/10.1007/978-3-032-29730-3_10

(hereafter referred to as SR) seeks to replace matched subgraphs in a domain-specific manner while maintaining graph integrity. The combination of expensive search and domain-specific rewriting underscores the challenge of delivering a generic, efficient pattern matching and replacement library [28]. General-purpose libraries support pattern matching but lack a comprehensive framework for pattern replacement, which is essential for applications beyond static analysis. On the other hand, domain-specific libraries provide efficient solutions tailored to specific use cases but offer limited flexibility outside their scope.

In response to these limitations, we present the Graph Hook Library (GHL), a general-purpose graph library built on the Boost Graph Library (BGL) [20]. GHL extends BGL with faster subgraph matching and introduces customizable **hooks** that govern how a subgraph is matched, modified, and reinserted. The library is highly performant and easily extensible to domain-specific workloads. The main contributions of GHL are:

- an open-source, general-purpose graph library built on BGL, exposed as a header-only C++ package with Python bindings;
- integration of the high-performance VF3 isomorphism algorithm into BGL, delivering faster matching than existing general-purpose libraries; and
- a hook-based subgraph matching/replacement framework that lets users inject domain-specific predicates, specialization, and reconnection logic without explicit recompilation, enabling complex match-and-rewrite workflows.

We validate GHL's performance via a systematic comparison against popular general-purpose graph libraries (iGraph, Graph-tool, NetworkX) on the SI benchmark dataset [22], demonstrating speedups of 2.3x/100x/207x, respectively. We further demonstrate GHL's applicability in two domain-specific settings: DNN pattern matching and replacement, and molecule filtering and highlighting. We compare against state-of-the-art domain-specific graph libraries, demonstrating competitive or superior performance. Our aim is not to supplant specialized tools but to show how GHL enables rapid application of graph algorithms in domains lacking mature domain-specific graph libraries.

2   Related Work

Graph libraries may be categorized into two camps, general-purpose and domain-specific, each fulfilling a purpose but also incurring drawbacks.

2.1   General-Purpose Graph Libraries

Popular open-source, general-purpose graph libraries provide support for subgraph isomorphism on generic graph structures. Three popular libraries, iGraph [9], NetworkX [11], and Graph-Tool [19], available in flavors of Python and C++, vary in terms of features and performance. These libraries are useful as comparison points against GHL, as they utilize similar algorithms (VF2) and working environments (Python/C++). Critically, however, these libraries do not natively support SR operations, restricting their utility to static analysis and requiring users to implement custom SR logic.

In contrast, a large number of grammars and tools have been developed to study and implement graph transformations. For a variety of reasons, these systems are not well suited to the use case envisioned for GHL.

Many existing approaches are designed as standalone transformation environments rather than composable software components. For example, GP2 [3] expects a host graph and rule set as input and compiles them into optimized C code, which is efficient for executing transformations but challenging to integrate into larger applications. Similarly, tools such as GROOVE [6] and AGG [24] are designed as self-contained systems for exploration and analysis of graph transformations, while eMoflon [1] and Henshin [23] are tightly coupled to Eclipse-based modeling environments. GrGen.NET [14] holds greatest similarity to GHL, with its combination of declarative/imperative operating paradigm and object-oriented approach, however written in C# rather than C++/Python.

Qualitatively, prior approaches are typically designed as standalone tools, which limits their composability and makes it difficult to integrate them into existing software pipelines. In contrast, GHL is a high-performance graph transformation library built on top of the Boost Graph Library, designed for seamless integration into domain-specific C++ and Python applications while retaining flexibility and performance.

2.2 Domain-Specific Graph Libraries

In application domains where graphs play a central role, domain-specific tools have been developed that often support SI/SR functionalities. Examples such as RDKit [16] (cheminformatics), BioNetGen [4] (bioinformatics), Neo4j [26] (data management), and PyTorch FX [2] (deep learning) are but a few examples.

While highly efficient within their specific domains, tight coupling with their use cases makes these libraries unsuitable for cross-domain reuse.

In contrast to both current generic and domain-specific libraries, GHL provides performant and domain-agnostic SI/SR functionality, enabling researchers to quickly leverage SI/SR features on top of already-available BGL graph algorithms, without the need to develop domain-specific libraries.

3 Graph Hook Library Representation and Extensibility

Figure 1 presents a simplified UML graph of the GHL library. As its foundation, GHL builds on BGL's C++ graph representation and traversal framework ❶. BGL provides a generic interface to graph data structures and algorithms which is extended by this infrastructure with additional components to support SI/SR on generic patterns. The GHL library can be installed via `pip` for use in a Python project with a Python API exposed by the `pybind11` library ❷, or pulled and incorporated into a C++ project directly as a header-only add-on. The GHL pipeline ❸ applies a series of functions which result in a default SI/SR behavior

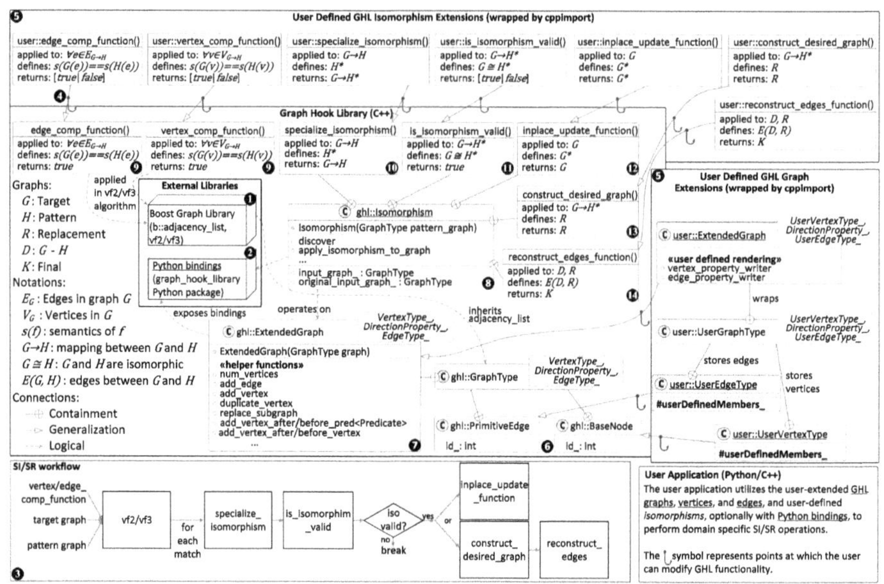

Fig. 1. Simplified UML graph highlighting important aspects of the GHL library. Inset displays the workflow to accomplish SI/SR functionality.

of a double pushout rewrite, with the left and right hand sides being identical; in other words, the graph is unmodified. To specialize GHL, users extend the C++ code and Python API via hooks ❹ that specialize key functionality to domain needs. These hooks come in the form of classes that can be inherited and extended, and functions which are overridden with user-defined criteria. In short, these hooks enable the user to define:

- node and edge semantics and visualization rules,
- criteria for semantic equivalence between target and pattern nodes/edges,
- programmatic expansion of an isomorphism to surrounding graph elements,
- validity of an isomorphism based on pattern-global criteria,
- arbitrary replacement graphs, and
- programmatic glue logic between target and replacement graphs.

These specializations are defined outside of GHL core ❺ code and are implemented via the `cppimport` [25] Python library, whose file-tracking enables transparent recompilation of C++ code into an importable Python package. We illustrate GHL's functionality via a simple example where we search for candidate cities arranged in a triangular structure to construct an expressway hub. Figure 2 serves as a visual representation of the process.

3.1   GHL BaseNode and Primitive Edge

Graph representation in GHL is built around two fundamental abstractions: `BaseNode` and `PrimitiveEdge` ❻. These classes provide the minimal structures

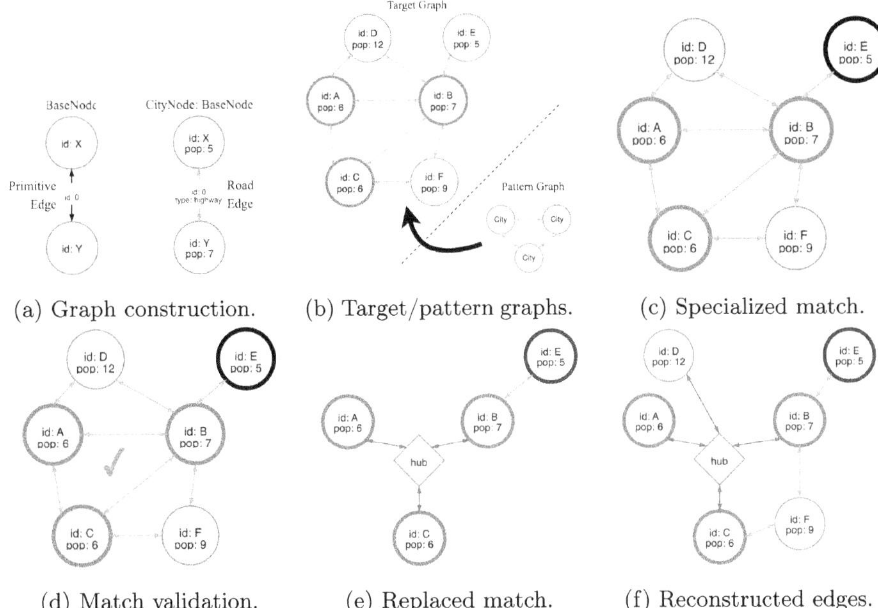

(a) Graph construction.   (b) Target/pattern graphs.   (c) Specialized match.

(d) Match validation.   (e) Replaced match.   (f) Reconstructed edges.

Fig. 2. Depiction of SI/SR pipeline. (a) Extending BaseNode and PrimitiveEdge types with additional properties. (b) Target and pattern graphs. Pattern defines three cities in a triangular structure connected with highways (orange). Matching subgraph A-B-C of the target graph is shown with bold outline. (c) The matched subgraph is extended to include the city E. (d) The match is validated based on aggregate population of involved cities. (e) New substructure to replace the matched subgraph. (f) The replacement subgraph is reconnected via expressways (red) with the rest of the graph, with reconnection dependent on city population. (Color figure online)

necessary to represent and manipulate graphs while remaining extensible for specific use cases. Users employ these classes to define custom node and edge types with domain-specific attributes or behaviors such as computational costs, type annotations, or semantic information, and use them inside custom SI/SR strategies. Figure 2(a) illustrates this extensibility: nodes are enriched with city-population data, while edges are annotated with road types. The separation of minimal base structures from user-defined extensions allows GHL to provide both a lightweight foundation and the flexibility to support diverse applications.

3.2 ExtendedGraph Type

ExtendedGraph ❼ is the base class of GHL. It contains a `GraphType graph` member that inherits the BGL directed or undirected `adjacency_list` graph representation. `ExtendedGraph` simplifies BGL's heavily templated API via intuitive graph manipulation functions, callable from C++ and exposed via the Python API. It also serves as a hook class, extendable like the node and edge classes. In particular, it hosts `vertex_property_writer` and `edge_property_writer`, which govern rendering when `write_graph` is called and can be specialized for domain-specific output. `ExtendedGraph` further exposes the graph to the other core mechanism of GHL, the `Isomorphism` class.

4 SI/SR Implementation via the Isomorphism Class

The core SI/SR functionality of GHL is implemented via the `Isomorphism` class ❽. Like the `BaseNode` and `PrimitiveEdge` classes, this class implements a series of customizable hooks with overridable default implementations, as detailed in the following sections and illustrated in Fig. 2.

4.1 Structural SI with VF2/VF3

The first step in the SI/SR process is identifying possible subgraphs that necessarily match the pattern graph structure and optionally match according to defined semantic rules. Structural matching can be accomplished via the VF2 algorithm prepackaged in the BGL. However, we found that this implementation was severely underperformant in comparison to the generic graph libraries and algorithms. We therefore implemented the more modern VF3 [7] algorithm in the style of BGL to accelerate SI. The VF3 implementation will be submitted for integration into the BGL post-publication.

4.2 Semantic SI with Vertex/Edge Predicates

Structural matches found by VF2/VF3 may then be optionally filtered based on semantic features. `vertex_comp_function` and `edge_comp_function` ❾ act as filtering predicates to define semantic equivalence between pattern and target graph vertices and edges. This design decouples the definition of a pattern from its matching criteria, offering users the ability to reuse existing matching predicates with different patterns or vice versa. We note that the signatures of these functions are already provided in BGL; GHL extends their functionality by exposing them to the user in the same manner as the rest of its hooks.

In our example, `vertex_comp_function` requires vertices to be cities with a population of no more than 8, while `edge_comp_function` requires edges between vertices to be highways. As illustrated in Fig. 2(b), the subgraph induced by cities **A-B-C** is identified by the SI mechanism as a candidate for replacement. Notice that the cities **A-B-D** and **B-C-F** also satisfy the pattern topology to be matched, but are rejected as cities **D** and **F**, with populations 12 and 9, violate the `vertex_comp_function` evaluation.

4.3 Specializing Isomorphisms

Before SR, GHL provides two unique hooks to refine matches. After an isomorphic subgraph is found, the user-defined `specialize_isomorphism` ❿ method is called. This method allows users to programmatically modify the matched subgraph by expanding or eliminating matched nodes. For instance, users might want to expand the match to a chain of identical nodes, or include surrounding nodes that meet certain criteria. In our setting, we extend the identified isomorphisms by including peripheral cities that are connected to any city in the triangle via exactly one road. In the target graph (Fig. 2(b)), city **E** is incorporated into the extended isomorphism for the **A-B-C** subgraph, while cities **D** and **F** are excluded from the extension. This hook enables a single base isomorphism to capture unique pattern variants that would otherwise require multiple isomorphism passes.

Following this, the `is_isomorphism_valid` ⓫ method is invoked to validate the specialized subgraphs. This additional functionality gives users a break point to enforce custom constraints that go beyond the initial matching criteria; e.g. rejecting a mapping if certain global conditions are not met. For cities, we require that the accumulated population of cities included in the extended subgraph exceed the threshold of 20, validated in the case of **A-B-C-E** with an aggregate population of 24. Note that the `is_isomorphism_valid` function filters isomorphisms based on global properties of the extended subgraph, assessing conditions that cannot be captured by either the `vertex_comp_function` or the `edge_comp_function` alone.

4.4   SR Replacement or In-Place Modification

Once a valid subgraph match has been identified, GHL handles the task of replacing that subgraph with a new substructure specified by the user. This transformation is orchestrated via one of two methods, `inplace_update_function` ⓬ or `construct_desired_graph` ⓭.

The `inplace_update_function` is a straightforward method for changing the target graph without modifying its structure. It does not add or remove nodes or edges, rather allowing the user to edit them in-place before returning the target graph structurally unchanged.

The second SR method, `construct_desired_graph`, allows the user to programmatically define the replacement subgraph in the context of the original graph. The replacement subgraph can be arbitrarily different from the matched subgraph, as the user's implementation of `construct_desired_graph` may add new vertices or edges, omit some of those from the original subgraph, or alter metadata and properties of the graph. This flexibility is crucial for applying complex rewrite rules in different domains. For our example, we introduce a new expressway hub and connect the cities **A, B**, and **C** directly to this hub via expressway edges, removing the original highways (Fig. 2(e)).

Connecting the Replacement Subgraph. After a new subgraph is constructed, any edges present in the rest of the target graph that were incident on the removed subgraph need to be attached to the appropriate points in the new subgraph. GHL offers a default strategy: all external edges that were incoming to the old subgraph are now connected to all root vertices of the new subgraph, and all external edges that were outgoing from the old subgraph are connected to all leaf vertices of the new subgraph.

In many cases, the default edge reconnection is sufficient. However, complex SR processes may require specialized edge reconstruction, e.g. distributing incoming edges among several entry points in the new subgraph or rerouting outgoing edges based on new vertex roles. In such cases, users can override the `reconstruct_edges_function` ⓮ to implement a different reconnection strategy. In our example, we employ a custom `reconstruct_edges_function` which constructs a direct expressway connection from an adjacent city to the expressway hub if the city has a population greater than 10, while removing previous connections. As a result, in Fig. 2(f), the city **D** is directly connected to the hub while old edges connecting city **D** to cities **A** and **B** are removed. Edges connecting city **F** to cities **B** and **C** are restored unmodified, as city **F** does not qualify for an expressway connection to the hub.

5   Benchmarking Performance and Generalizability

We assessed the performance and generalizability of GHL via several general and domain-specific benchmarks. In the interest of brevity, we only briefly highlight the main results in this section; however, we encourage the reader to refer to the GHL source code [1] for a more thorough analysis of our experimental results.

5.1   Evaluation of VF3 Algorithm Implementation

We evaluated the implementation of the VF3 algorithm in GHL against BGL's VF2 implementation, using the publicly available SI dataset [22]. GHL's VF3 implementation operates with mean/median latencies 1.7x/16x lower than BGL's VF2, with a lower latency in 96% of cases.

We also evaluated the performance of GHL's SI operation with respect to iGraph, Graph-tool, and NetworkX, on the SI dataset. When averaging speedup across all target-pattern pairs, GHL outperforms iGraph/Graph-tool/NetworkX by 2.3x/100x/207x. Beyond speed, iGraph, NetworkX, and Graph-tool do not support SR primitives.

5.2   Application to Neural Network and Cheminformatics Domains

Finally, we assessed GHL's generalizability to domain-specific tasks by applying it to SI/SR problems in neural networks and cheminformatics.

Domain A: Subgraph Replacement in Neural Network Graphs
Within the domain of neural networks, we studied the application of three common transformations, comparing against popular libraries Apache TVM [8] and PyTorch FX [2]. Figure 3 shows the results of our experiments on ResNet [12] architectures of increasing depth.

---

[1] https://github.com/IBM/graph-hook-library

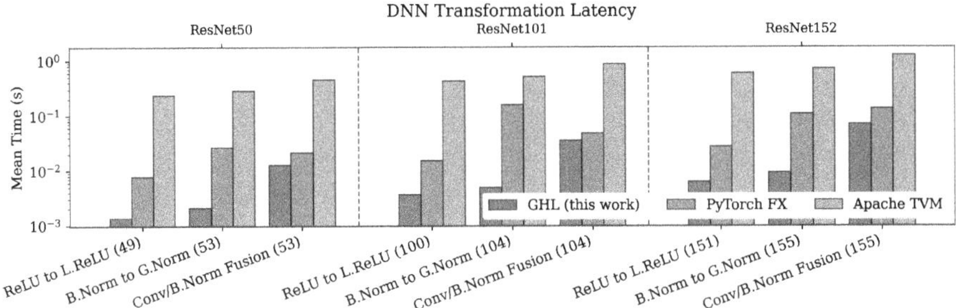

Fig. 3. Comparison of the runtime for three transformations on three ResNet depths. Time in seconds, y-axis on a logarithmic scale. On average, GHL outperforms PyTorch FX/Apache TVM by 8x/87x.

GHL successfully identified and replaced the target subgraphs in all deep learning models, achieving performance that consistently surpassed domain-specific frameworks. This improvement is attributable to its efficient subgraph matching implementation and its lightweight SR mechanism. Furthermore, these results demonstrate that GHL's domain-agnostic design does not come at the cost of efficiency, enabling optimizations that are competitive with, and in many cases superior to, domain-specific systems.

Domain B: Molecular Substructure Highlighting/Filtering

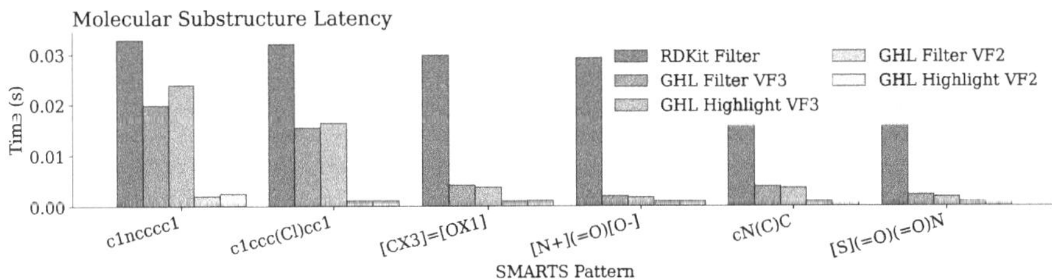

Fig. 4. Latency results for RDKit, VF2, and VF3 molecular filtering and highlighting. GHL demonstrates competitive performance relative to RDKit.

We also specialized GHL for the cheminformatics domain by performing simple molecular substructure, representation, and filtering, comparing against the popular RDKit library [16]. Figure 4 illustrates the results over the 6 benchmarked substructures for the VF3 and VF2 SI implementations. The results demonstrate an interesting property in contrast to the above evaluations, as the VF2 implementation significantly outperforms VF3 across all tests. This may be attributed to the fact that the graphs under study are significantly smaller and less densely connected in comparison to those of the SI benchmarks and the ResNet DNNs, consisting of only on average 22.8 atoms. VF3 features that make it effective on large, densely connected graphs, such as its complex look-ahead rules, may reduce its effectiveness on small, sparse graphs [18]. Fortunately, GHL makes choosing between the algorithms simple, finding in both cases identical matches to RDKit with competitive performance. The intent here is not to convince users of RDKit to switch to GHL; rather, it is to demonstrate the adaptability of GHL to domain-specific scenarios and encourage researchers in fields without tailored graph libraries to explore how graph theory and algorithms can be quickly and efficiently applied via GHL.

6   Conclusions and Future Directions

In this paper, we introduced GHL, an extensible, open-source C++ library with Python bindings enabling efficient and flexible SI/SR functionality. GHL integrates a high-performance SI algorithm with an extensible hook-based design, allowing users to implement custom logic for SI/SR tasks. Through its domain-agnostic design, GHL supports complex transformations that are not possible in existing general-purpose libraries or narrowly scoped domain-specific frameworks. Performance and generalizability evaluations indicate that GHL outperforms general-purpose libraries for SI tasks and is easily generalizable and performant across neural network and cheminformatics domains. We emphasize that our goal in developing GHL is not to convince users of existing libraries to switch to GHL; rather, it is to demonstrate the adaptability of GHL to domain-specific scenarios and encourage researchers in fields without tailored graph libraries to explore how graph theory and graph transformation algorithms can be quickly and efficiently applied via GHL.

In the process of using GHL for our primary research goals, we will continue to improve the library's feature set and performance. Two avenues of development under consideration are (1) the integration of GHL's VF3 algorithm into BGL and (2) integration with Graph-tool to benefit from features from both tools, as both libraries are built on BGL.

Acknowledgments. We thank Abu Sebastian of the IBM AI Compute Frontiers group for supporting the development of this tool.

Conflict of Interest. The authors have no competing interests to declare that are relevant to the content of this article.

References

1. Anjorin, A., Lauder, M., Patzina, S., Schürr, A.: Emoflon: leveraging emf and professional case tools. In: GI-Jahrestagung (2011)
2. Ansel, J., et al.: PyTorch 2: faster machine learning through dynamic python bytecode transformation and graph compilation. In: 29th ACM International Conference on Architectural Support for Programming Languages and Operating Systems, Volume 2 (ASPLOS 2024) (2024)

3. Bak, C.: GP 2: efficient implementation of a graph programming language (2015)
4. Blinov, M.L., Faeder, J.R., Goldstein, B., Hlavacek, W.S.: Bionetgen: software for rule-based modeling of signal transduction based on the interactions of molecular domains. Bioinformatics (2004)
5. Bonnici, V., Giugno, R., Pulvirenti, A., Shasha, D., Ferro, A.: A subgraph isomorphism algorithm and its application to biochemical data. BMC Bioinf. (2013)
6. Bracchiglione, J., et al.: Graphical representation of overlap for OVErviews: GROOVE tool. Res. Synthesis Methods (2022)
7. Carletti, V., Foggia, P., Saggese, A., Vento, M.: Challenging the time complexity of exact subgraph isomorphism for huge and dense graphs with vf3. IEEE Trans. Pattern Anal. Mach. Intell. (2018)
8. Chen, T., et al.: Tvm: an automated end-to-end optimizing compiler for deep learning. In: Proceedings of the 13th USENIX Conference on Operating Systems Design and Implementation (2018)
9. Csardi, G., Nepusz, T.: The igraph software package for complex network research. InterJ. (2005)
10. Garey, M.R., Johnson, D.S.: Computers and Intractability; A Guide to the Theory of NP-Completeness. W. H. Freeman & Co. (1990)
11. Hagberg, A.A., Schult, D.A., Swart, P., Hagberg, J.: Exploring network structure, dynamics, and function using networkx. In: Proceedings of the Python in Science Conference (2008)
12. He, K., Zhang, X., Ren, S., Sun, J.: Deep residual learning for image recognition. In: Proceedings of the IEEE Conference on Computer Vision and Pattern Recognition (2016)
13. Huber, W., Carey, V.J., Long, L., Falcon, S., Gentleman, R.: Graphs in molecular biology. BMC Bioinf. (2007)
14. Jakumeit, E., Buchwald, S., Kroll, M.: Grgen.net. Int. J. Softw. Tools Technol. Transf. (2010)
15. Jia, Z., Padon, O., Thomas, J., Warszawski, T., Zaharia, M., Aiken, A.: Taso: optimizing deep learning computation with automatic generation of graph substitutions. In: Proceedings of the 27th ACM Symposium on Operating Systems Principles (2019)
16. Landrum, G.: Rdkit: open-source cheminformatics. https://www.rdkit.org
17. McCreesh, C., Prosser, P., Solnon, C., Trimble, J.: When subgraph isomorphism is really hard, and why this matters for graph databases. J. Artif. Intell. Res. (2018)
18. Lanese, I., Montanari, U.: Synchronization algebras with mobility for graph transformations. Electr. Notes Theor. Comput. Sci. **138**(1), 43–60 (2005). https://doi.org/10.1016/j.entcs.2005.05.004
19. Peixoto, T.P.: The graph-tool python library. figshare (2014)
20. Siek, J.G., Lee, L.Q., Lumsdaine, A.: The boost graph library - user guide and reference manual. In: C++ In-Depth Series (2001)
21. Snijders, T.A.B., Pattison, P.E., Robins, G.L., Handcock, M.S.: New specifications for exponential random graph models. Soc. Methodol. (2006)
22. Solnon, C.: Benchmarks for the subgraph isomorphism problem. https://perso.liris.cnrs.fr/christine.solnon/SIP.html (2017). Accessed 9 Sep 2025
23. Strüber, D., et al.: Henshin: a usability-focused framework for emf model transformation development. In: Graph Transformation (2017)
24. Taentzer, G.: AGG: a graph transformation environment for modeling and validation of software. In: Applications of Graph Transformations with Industrial Relevance (2004)

25. Thompson, B.: cppimport. https://github.com/tbenthompson/cppimport
26. Webber, J.: A programmatic introduction to neo4j. In: Proceedings of the 3rd Annual Conference on Systems, Programming, and Applications: Software for Humanity (2012)
27. Yan, J., Yin, X.C., Lin, W., Deng, C., Zha, H., Yang, X.: A short survey of recent advances in graph matching. In: Proceedings of the 2016 ACM on International Conference on Multimedia Retrieval. ICMR 2016 (2016)
28. Zundorf, A.: Graph pattern matching in progres. In: Cuny, J., Ehrig, H., Engels, G., Rozenberg, G. (eds.) Graph Grammars and Their Application to Computer Science (1996)

EVOLVEGDB: Model-Driven Graph Schema Transformation

Dominique Hausler[1]([envelope]) [ORCID], Torben Eckwert[2]([envelope]) [ORCID], Meike Klettke[1] [ORCID],
Michael Guckert[2] [ORCID], and Gabriele Taentzer[3] [ORCID]

[1] University of Regensburg, Data Engineering Group, Bajuwarenstrasse 4,
93053 Regensburg, Germany
{dominique.hausler,meike.klettke}@ur.de
[2] KITE - University of Applied Sciences Mittelhessen, Wiesenstraße 7,
35390 Gießen, Germany
{torben.eckwert,michael.guckert}@mnd.thm.de
[3] Philipps-University Marburg, Biegenstraße 10, 35037 Marburg, Germany
taentzer@mathematik.uni-marburg.de

Abstract. Modern software development cycles require continuous evolution of databases and database schemas. Although graph databases are often considered as schemaless, they have an implicit schema that evolves over time. Schema changes in graph databases are often implicit and undocumented, so migrating between different schema versions can be costly, error-prone, and may lead to data quality problems. Therefore, comparing different database versions provides valuable insights for traceability and reproducibility. We introduce EVOLVEGDB, a semi-automated tool to make graph schema transformation explicit by reconstructing the evolutionary process between two schema versions. The tool extracts implicit schemas as graph models and analyses differences between the source and the target models. To remain independent of specific graph database technologies, EVOLVEGDB builds on Graph Query Language (GQL), the ISO standard for graph databases. It then derives candidate graph transformations and guides users through an interactive review process to validate or refine the inferred transformations. The final result is a Graph Evolution Operation (GEO) language script to migrate the source graph data that does not yet conform to the specified target schema. An initial evaluation of three evolution scenarios showed promising results, indicating high accuracy and low manual input.

Keywords: Model-driven engineering · Schema transformation · Schema evolution · Schema extraction · Graph database

1 Introduction

In the context of agile software development, reacting adequately to changing requirements involves the necessary yet challenging task of evolving the schemas

---

D. Hausler and T. Eckwert—Joined first authorship.

© The Author(s), under exclusive license to Springer Nature Switzerland AG 2026
B. Archibald and O. Semeráth (Eds.): ICGT 2026, LNCS 16624, pp. 199–210, 2026.
https://doi.org/10.1007/978-3-032-29730-3_11

of underlying databases. While schema evolution is commonly associated with relational databases and SQL scripts, NoSQL databases present additional challenges due to their schemaless nature. In this paper, we extend our EvolveDB tool [14], which supports migrating relational data from a source to a target schema by generating an SQL migration script, to graph databases, specifically property graphs. Graph schema transformation aims to convert a source schema into a target schema. The identified changes are described using the well-known operations `add, rename, delete, copy, move, split, and merge`, as well as the graph-specific `transform` operation, which describes the conversion of a node into an edge, and vice versa [21].

Graph databases commonly evolve continuously in modern development cycles. Although graph databases are often described as schemaless, they have an implicit schema that evolves over time. As schema changes are often undocumented, migrating between different schema versions can be error-prone and may result in problems with data quality. Therefore, comparing different database versions can provide valuable insights for traceability and reproducibility.

Model-driven engineering (MDE) raises the level of abstraction by treating models as primary artifacts and ensures transparency, which is becoming an increasingly important counter to black-box AI approaches. Our tool EvolveGDB conducts graph schema transformation in an MDE manner and is applicable to any property graph database, as our metamodel is based on the ISO GQL standard [22]. Migration operations are identified by comparing conceptualised graph schemas at a meta level, specified in the Geo evolution language.

Problem Description. Although graph databases allow data to be inserted directly without a predefined schema, they do have an implicit schema. Schema changes frequently occur to align the current schema with newly emerging requirements, such as the introduction of new features. During development, two versions of a graph database often emerge: a source version before evolution and a target version after evolution. As the evolution process is often not documented, these changes may be unknown and lead to data quality problems. Consequently, they need to be reconstructed. Currently, there are no tools for semi-automated graph data migration.

Contribution. To this end, database engineers benefit from our EvolveGDB tool to make schema changes explicit. The tool automatically identifies schema modifications between two versions and translates them into statements of the Geo graph evolution language [21]. Users benefit from an intuitive description of how each operation affects the schema, as well as all the necessary data migration operations to ensure conformity with the target schema. These Geo statements then form the basis of the knowledge base, which is used to detect recurring patterns and best practices. In this paper, building on our previous work [19], we improved the tooling to make it more intuitive and usable in practice. We also updated the terminology of Geo to align with the naming used in our metamodel and extended GEO to express data modifications in addition to the previously supported schema changes.

2 Related Work

In this section, we present related work on *graph schemas, schema extraction, schema evolution, schema transformation*, and *model-driven engineering*.

Graph Schema. To describe the implicit schema of graph databases, the schema description language PG-Schema is used in [3], whereas in [18], the schema is made explicit using description logic. [4] extends PG-Schema by constraints, while [9] presents work on triggers. [31] focuses on the role of schema constraints for query optimisation, whereas [29] ensures data quality via constraints. Integrity constraints were addressed in [26]. In addition, [17] proposes regular path constraints to quantify inconsistency. *Overall, previous work emphasises the need to derive both schemas and constraints from semi-structured graph data.*

Schema Extraction, Mapping and Matching. Schema extraction is a prerequisite for schema transformation. NoSQL databases offer additional flexibility by being schemaless and storing an implicit, often relaxed schema, in contrast to relational databases. Several papers focus on making the graph schema explicit (see, for example, [7,11,15]). Schema matching and mapping strategies are essential to compare arbitrary schemas or databases during schema transformation. A categorisation of matching techniques can be found in [28]. [12] converts schemas into graphs and performs graph matching. *Schema extraction resembles a prerequisite to schema transformation. Nevertheless, none of these focus on system-independent graph transformation.*

Schema Evolution and Transformation. Schema evolution and transformation rely on the same components. However, they differ in the unknown component. For schema evolution, the source schema and a set of evolution operations are used to derive the target schema. In contrast, schema transformation compares schemas to detect changes. There are two surveys available on schema evolution [8,10]. Furthermore, numerous publications on schema evolution and transformation of different types of databases are accessible, including [13,16,34] for relational, [33] for document, and [20] for graph databases. In [30], data warehouses are transformed into graph models. [27] focuses on schema transformation between RDF and property graphs, whereas [2] uses a meta level. A new declarative paradigm for describing detected changes is presented in [6]. *However, none of the existing solutions use a domain-independent language for graph transformations.*

Model-Driven Engineering and Co-evolution. Since we use a model-driven approach, we also analyse similar approaches to schema evolution, transformation and data migration. [35] aims to improve the quality of data extracted from schemas. Graph transformation is closely related to co-evolution. Several tools exist in the area of co-evolution of modeling languages. Representative approaches and tools are reviewed in, for example, [5,24]. The relevance of a model-driven approach for handling transformation tasks, especially at the meta level, is demonstrated in [25]. The approaches in both [25,35] are model-driven. *Nevertheless, existing approaches are not GQL-compatible.*

Summary and Novelty. In summary, no system-independent tool for model-driven property graph schema transformation exists. To address this gap, we present EVOLVEGDB, which builds on our previous work [19], where we introduced a GQL-based metamodel for extracting the schema of arbitrary property graph databases. Based on this conceptual model, schema transformation is performed by aligning source and target schemas with graph models. The tool generates migration scripts by mapping the identified operations to corresponding GEO (Graph Evolution Operation) statements [21]. However, a comprehensive tooling for our model-driven approach to schema transformation is still missing.

3   Model-Driven Schema Transformation in EVOLVEGDB

We present a model-driven approach to ensure transparency at a higher level of abstraction. Schema transformation is thus handled directly through technology-independent schema models, which are GQL-standardised metamodels, describing property graphs used in the transformation process described in [19]. EVOLVEGDB includes rules derived from this metamodel that describe possible or desired schema changes. These rules identify complex evolutions within the set of low-level atomic changes obtained by matching the source and target models during the comparison process. Increasing the level of abstraction enables schema transformation to be formulated in a reusable, technology-independent way.

This section describes the implemented workflow for a model-driven schema transformation, as shown in Fig. 1. EVOLVEGDB takes two versions of a graph database as input: a source and a target graph version. As an explicitly defined schema cannot be assumed to be present, implicit schema extraction is necessary (Step ①). As property graphs

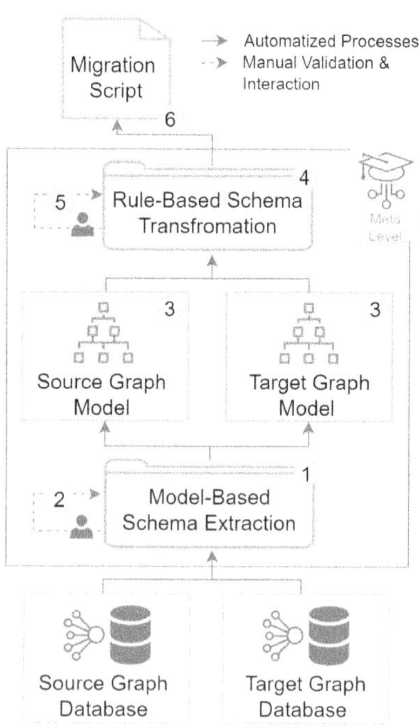

Fig. 1. Workflow description.

allow multi-labelling, i.e., nodes or edges with more than one label, ambiguities can occur. In Step [illegible], we use a human-in-the-loop to resolve such ambiguities by allowing a manual adjustment of properties to their associated label, thus adhering to the user's intention. Afterwards, both the source and target graph schemas are transformed into instances of our graph metamodel (Step [illegible]). During the mapping phase, the differences between the resulting graph models are automatically identified based on a set of rules derived from the metamodel (Step [illegible]). To validate the automatically detected changes, the results are forwarded to the user in Step [illegible], allowing adjustments. The mapping is then updated accordingly and translated into the graph evolution language Geo. All Geo statements are stored in a migration script (Step [illegible]), which is presented to the user. Although the GQL standard now exists, each database system uses a different query language: Cypher (Neo4j), Gremlin (Apache), and PGQL (Oracle), for example. Using Geo, a technology-independent evolution language, guarantees technology independence across all components of our workflow and reduces the extensive knowledge of these query languages that would otherwise be required.

4   Demonstration

The audience will experience the following tool demonstration:

Metamodel and Data Exploration. First, we present our metamodel to outline the generalised conceptualisation for property graphs. In this context, we highlight aspects of our GQL-based metamodel that are not supported by Neo4j, such as multi-labelled edges. Additionally, we provide statistical data on the schema and instance data of the dataset to illustrate the differences between them, together with the manually executed operations that serve as the gold standard.

Schema Extraction. Thereafter, schema extraction is presented using an example that also illustrates the need for manual user input. Figure 2 shows the extracted source and target versions of the example dataset. The screen dump depicts two versions of a graph dataset describing university courses, including elements such as **Person** and **Course**. A particular challenge in this context is multi-labelling, for instance **:Person:Professor**. Since properties of multi-labelled nodes cannot always be assigned unambiguously to one of the involved labels, manual refinements are required during schema extraction. In such cases, the user assigns the properties of multi-labelled nodes to their respective labels. The blue and green borders indicate the partitioning between the schema and data levels, thereby illustrating both schema evolution and data migration operations. Schema-level changes are shown within the blue-bordered parts, whereas data-level changes are shown within the green-bordered parts. In addition, the red boxes and arrows highlight the changes in the dataset between the two versions. For example, the property **dName** from **Professor** is moved to **Department**.

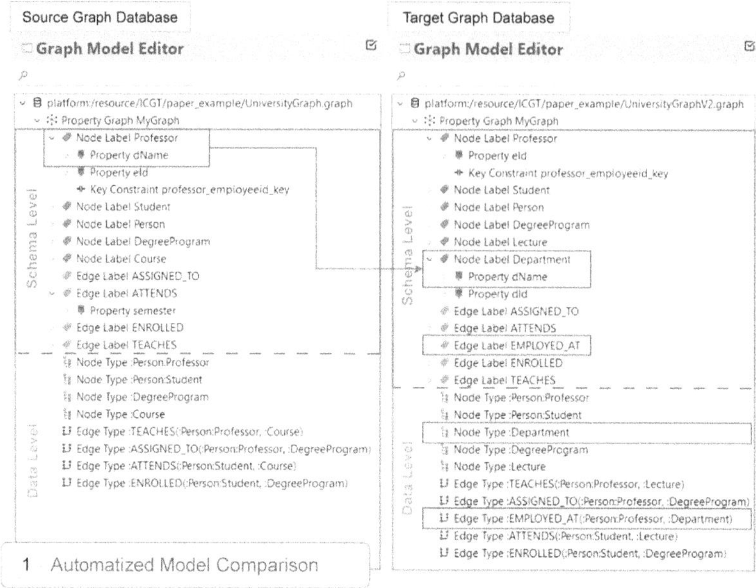

Fig. 2. The extracted source and target schema of the dataset.

Schema Mapping and Matching. The next step is to match both model versions and to identify the differences between the source and target versions. This involves displaying the automated schema mapping results for user validation (see Fig. 3). The blue elements indicate renames, while the green element indicates an unmatched element, meaning that it exists only in the target model and is therefore a new element. The user can then refine the mapping to ensure correctness and accuracy; here, the ✔ indicates that everything is correct and accurate. Afterwards, the mapping is aligned automatically. The resulting migration operations are represented in the migration editor shown in Fig. 4. A detailed view of each detected modification (see Fig. 5) ensures that the user can see which atomic editing steps are combined into semantic change sets representing complex operations. For instance, this may involve combining an `add` and a `delete` operation to define a `move`.

Migration Script. EVOLVEGDB generates a migration script that consists of all detected operations in our graph evolution language, GEO (see Fig. 6). This provides a clear understanding of the effect of an operation without the need for prior domain knowledge, thereby extending the accessibility of the tool to non-domain experts. Based on the migration script, we can show how conclusions can be derived from both schema-level changes and the data migration statements. For example, the property `dName` was moved to the newly created `Department` nodes at the schema level, in the cause of which the aligning data

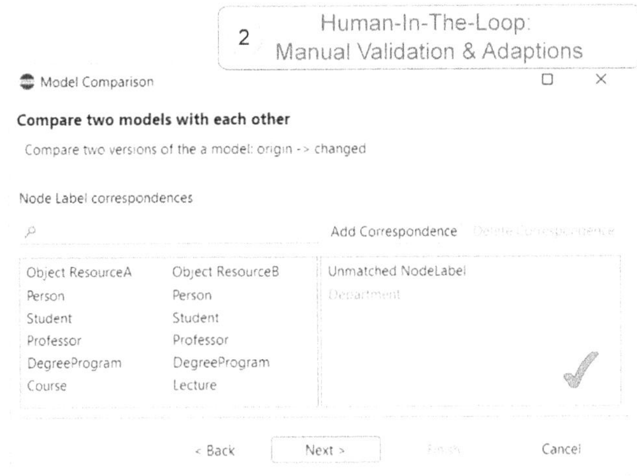

Fig. 3. Interface for manual user-sided adjustments with all renamed (blue) and added entities (green), showing 100% accuracy for the detected schema changes. (Color figure online)

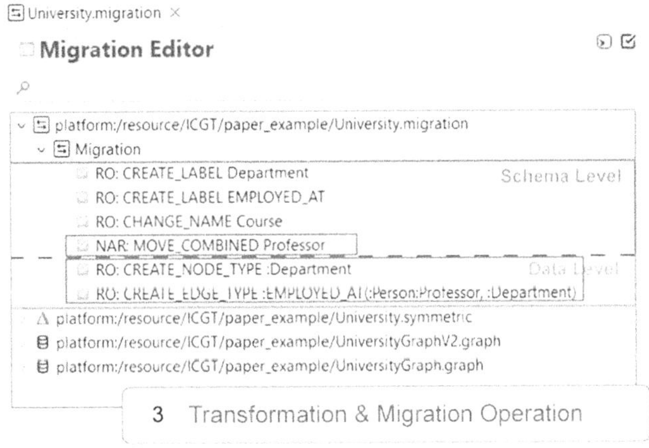

Fig. 4. Migration operations aligned with the manual refinements (Fig. 3), partitioned by schema and data level.

was migrated. To keep the connection between `Professor` and `Department`, the edge `EMPLOYED_AT` was added.

Novelty. Building on our previous work in [19], we have comprehensively aligned GEO with the metamodel, ensuring that both the metamodel and the evolution language are applicable to any property graph database. Specifically, GEO is now capable of defining schema changes as well as data migration operations. Decou-

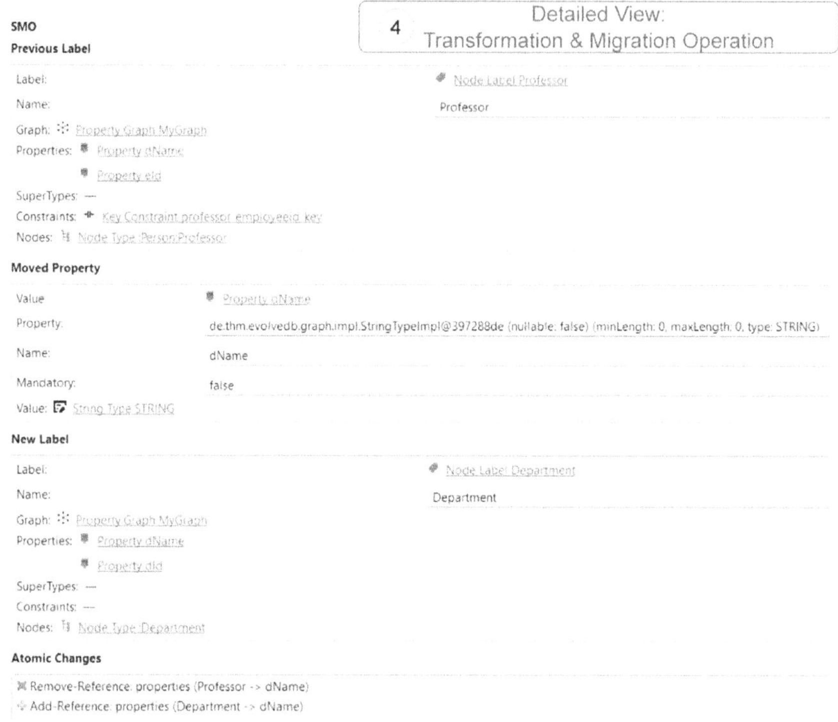

Fig. 5. Detailed view of the **move** operation, deconstructed into atomic changes.

pling these two levels enables users to instantly identify where an adjustment was made and the effects it caused at each level.

5   Implementation

This section describes the design and implementation of EvolveGDB, which is available as an Eclipse product. An Eclipse product is a packaged, installable application based on Eclipse that bundles the necessary plug-ins and configurations into a ready-to-run distribution. We chose the Eclipse platform because the Eclipse Modeling Tools and the Eclipse Modeling Framework [32] provide a powerful platform for creating, editing, and managing structured data models. For model comparison, we used the SiLift framework [23] based on Henshin. The SiLift framework supports model comparison, since it groups low-level changes into *semantic change sets*, each of which represents the impact of a user-level editing operation. Henshin supports in-place model transformations, i.e. direct changes of the existing model structure. In order to apply SiLift to our modeling language, a set of edit rules is required. These rules define the available editing operations and specify how the structure or content of a model may be modified or updated. They describe patterns of atomic changes, which are then grouped

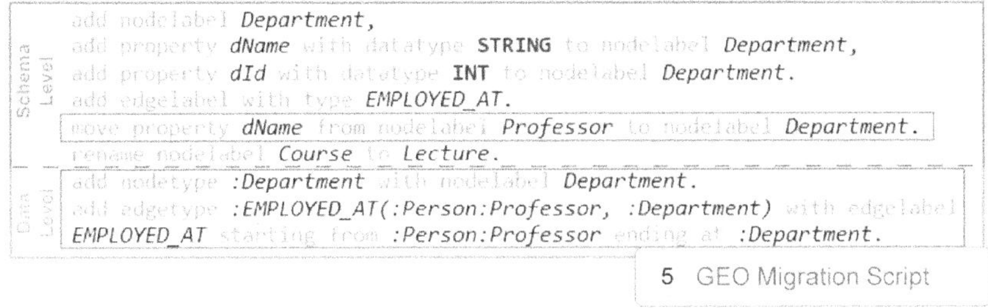

Fig. 6. Technology-independent evolution language, Gᴇᴏ, describing schema- and data-level changes in an intuitive manner.

into permitted or intended user-level editing operations. The rule set, which is specific to the metamodel used, was created once for our setup; it does not need to be redefined for each use.

The Gᴇᴏ generator is implemented in Xtend [1]. To support individual graph databases, it provides extension points, ensuring technology-independency. Currently, EᴠᴏʟᴠᴇGDB includes a plug-in that supports model extraction for Neo4j. We selected Neo4j because of its widespread use in industry and research. In addition, we used the APOC (Awesome Procedures on Cypher) library for our schema extraction algorithm. APOC provides access to useful procedures and functions that extend the use of the Cypher query language. The source code of our implementation is available on GitHub[1].

6   Initial Evaluation

In our previous work [19], we evaluated our approach using three Neo4j example databases[2], which differ in both schema size and number of nodes and edges. To simulate typical schema modifications, we applied schema evolution in a realistic way. Figure 7 shows the total number of operations executed, as well as the number of operations detected automatically and those requiring manual user input. During schema comparison, users were asked to review the matching results and, if necessary, add correspondences for previously unrecognised elements. To quantify the required manual effort, we use the interaction rate, which is the proportion of elements that are unmatched or incorrectly matched.

A small number of manual adjustments are caused by the current lack of full support for `split` and `copy`. However, including a human-in-the-loop enables the system to achieve 100% accuracy in detecting transformation operations. The following results occurred for the interaction rate during schema mapping: *Twitch*: 2.63%, *Pole*: 6.81%, and *Bloom*: 2.23%. These low rates demonstrate that the vast majority of operations can be identified automatically, leaving only minimal refinements for the user. Multi-labelling is the only concept that requires

---

[1] https://github.com/tekw24/EvolveGDB.
[2] Neo4j example databases: https://github.com/neo4j-graph-examples.

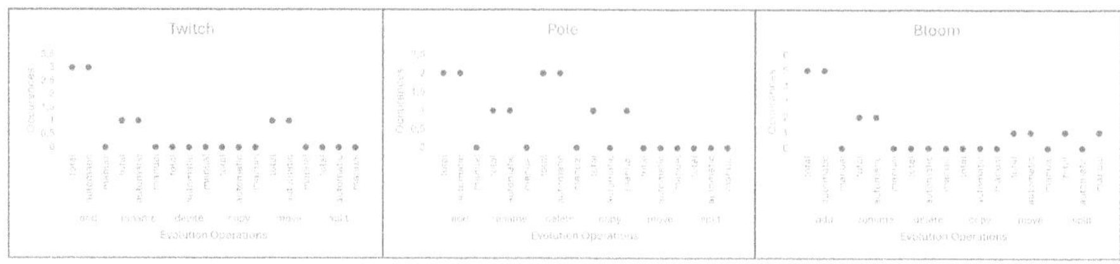

Fig. 7. The evaluation results are partitioned by dataset and depict the gold standard (i.e., the total number), the number of operations that were automatically detected by EVOLVEGDB, and the necessary manual input.

manual interaction. This occurs in 10 out of 250 occurrences during the schema extraction, corresponding to an overall rate of 3.84%. *Even though 96.16% of operations were detected automatically, reviewing the results is essential to ensure 100% accuracy.*

7 Conclusion

Modifications to a graph database can affect the implicitly defined schema and may result in data quality issues. Making the evolution between two schema versions explicit helps developers to understand and document these effects, control schema changes, and migrate existing graph data to match the target schema. In this paper, we introduce EVOLVEGDB, a tool that uses model-driven techniques to reconstruct the undocumented evolutionary process between two graph database versions. EVOLVEGDB extracts the implicit schemas as graph models and analyses the differences between the source and target models to derive a migration script in the graph evolution language GEO. Furthermore, the migration script offers traceability and reconstructability.

In addition to the use case discussed above, the tool may be applicable in other scenarios. One such scenario is migration in cases where only the target graph schema, rather than the data, is available. In this setting, the tool can detect all required evolution operations to transform the existing data according to the specified target schema. Another promising scenario is schema versioning, when comparing the current schema version with a previous one.

Our initial evaluation indicates that EVOLVEGDB provides significant support and shows high potential for practical use. In the future, these findings should be validated through a user study involving diverse real-world databases to evaluate the effectiveness, usability, and robustness of our approach more thoroughly. Furthermore, we plan to extend complex operations with conditions to align data migration with detected schema changes.

Acknowledgments. The work of Dominique Hausler has been funded by Deutsche Forschungsgemeinschaft (German Research Foundation) – 552691270.

Disclosure of Interest. The authors have no competing interests to declare that are relevant to the content of this article.

References

1. Xtend. https://www.eclipse.org/xtend/. https://www.eclipse.org/xtend/
2. Abdelhédi, F., Brahim, A.A., Atigui, F., Zurfluh, G.: UMLtoNoSQL: Automatic Transformation of Conceptual Schema to NoSQL Databases. In: AICCSA, pp. 272–279. IEEE Computer Society (2017)
3. Angles, R., et al.: PG-Schema: schemas for property graphs. Proc. ACM Manag. Data **1**(2), 198:1–198:25 (2023)
4. Angles, R., et al.: PG-Keys: keys for property graphs. In: SIGMOD Conference, pp. 2423–2436. ACM (2021)
5. Bettini, L., Di Salle, A., Iovino, L., Pierantonio, A.: Supporting reusable model migration with edelta. J. Syst. Softw. **212**, 112012 (2024)
6. Bonifati, A.: Versatile property graph transformations. Proc. VLDB Endow. **18**(12), 5516–5526 (2025)
7. Bonifati, A., Dumbrava, S., Martinez, E., Ghasemi, F., Jaffré, M., Luton, P., Pickles, T.: DiscoPG: property graph schema discovery and exploration. Proc. VLDB Endow. **15**(12), 3654–3657 (2022)
8. Brahmia, Z., Grandi, F., Oliboni, B.: A literature review on schema evolution in databases. Computing Open **02**, 2430001 (2024)
9. Ceri, S., Bernasconi, A., Gagliardi, A., Martinenghi, D., Bellomarini, L., Magnanimi, D.: PG-triggers: triggers for property graphs. In: SIGMOD Conference Companion. pp. 373–385. ACM (2024)
10. Cleve, A., Gobert, M., Meurice, L., Maes, J., Weber, J.H.: Understanding database schema evolution: a case study. Sci. Comput. Program. **97**, 113–121 (2015)
11. Comyn-Wattiau, I., Akoka, J.: Model driven reverse engineering of NoSQL property graph databases: the case of Neo4j. In: IEEE BigData, pp. 453–458. IEEE Computer Society (2017)
12. Ding, G., Sun, S., Wang, G.: Schema matching based on SQL statements. Distributed Parallel Databases **38**(1), 193–226 (2020)
13. Eckwert, T., Guckert, M., Taentzer, G.: EvolveDB: a tool for model driven schema evolution. In: MoDELS (Companion), pp. 61–65. ACM (2022)
14. Eckwert, T., Guckert, M., Taentzer, G.: Evolvedb: evolving relational database schemas in a model-driven way. Softw. Syst. Modeling, 1–26 (2025)
15. Frozza, A.A., Jacinto, S.R., dos Santos Mello, R.: An approach for schema extraction of NoSQL graph databases. In: IRI, pp. 271–278. IEEE (2020)
16. Giachos, F., Pantelidis, N., Batsilas, C., Zarras, A.V., Vassiliadis, P.: Parallel lives diagrams for co-evolving communities and their application to schema evolution. In: ER (Companion). CEUR Workshop Proceedings, vol. 3618. CEUR-WS.org (2023)
17. Grant, J., Parisi, F.: On measuring inconsistency in graph databases with regular path constraints. Artif. Intell. **335**, 104197 (2024)
18. Gutiérrez-Basulto, V., Gutowski, A., Ibáñez-García, Y.A., Murlak, F.: Containment of graph queries modulo schema. Proc. ACM Manag. Data **2**(2), 77 (2024)
19. Hausler, D., Eckwert, T., Klettke, M., Guckert, M., Taentzer, G.: Model-driven schema transformation for graph databases. In: ER. LNCS, vol. 16189, pp. 320–338. Springer (2025)

20. Hausler, D., Klettke, M.: Nautilus: implementation of an evolution approach for graph databases. In: MoDELS (Companion), pp. 11–15. ACM (2024)
21. Hausler, D., Klettke, M., Störl, U.: A language for graph database evolution and its implementation in Neo4j. In: ER (Companion). CEUR Workshop Proceedings, vol. 3618. CEUR-WS.org (2023)
22. Information technology— Database languages — GQL. Standard, International Organization for Standardization, Geneva, CH, April 2024
23. Kehrer, T., Kelter, U., Ohrndorf, M., Sollbach, T.: Understanding model evolution through semantically lifting model differences with SiLift. In: 2012 28th IEEE International Conference on Software Maintenance (ICSM), pp. 638–641. IEEE (2012)
24. Kelly, S., Tolvanen, J.P.: How metaedit+ supports co-evolution of modeling languages, tools and models. In: 2023 ACM/IEEE International Conference on Model Driven Engineering Languages and Systems Companion (MODELS-C), pp. 9–13. IEEE (2023)
25. Khelladi, D.E., Kretschmer, R., Egyed, A.: Change propagation-based and composition-based co-evolution of transformations with evolving metamodels. In: MoDELS, pp. 404–414. ACM (2018)
26. Pokorný, J., Valenta, M., Kovacic, J.: Integrity constraints in graph databases. In: ANT/SEIT. Procedia Computer Science, vol. 109, pp. 975–981. Elsevier (2017)
27. Rabbani, K., Lissandrini, M., Bonifati, A., Hose, K.: Transforming RDF graphs to property graphs using standardized schemas. Proc. ACM Manag. Data **2**(6), 242:1–242:25 (2024)
28. Rahm, E., Bernstein, P.A.: A survey of approaches to automatic schema matching. VLDB J. **10**(4), 334–350 (2001)
29. Reina, F., Huf, A., Presser, D., Siqueira, F.: Modeling and enforcing integrity constraints on graph databases. In: Hartmann, S., Küng, J., Kotsis, G., Tjoa, A.M., Khalil, I. (eds.) DEXA 2020. LNCS, vol. 12391, pp. 269–284. Springer, Cham (2020). https://doi.org/10.1007/978-3-030-59003-1_18
30. Sellami, A., Nabli, A., Gargouri, F.: Transformation of data warehouse schema to NoSQL graph data base. In: ISDA (2). Advances in Intelligent Systems and Computing, vol. 941, pp. 410–420. Springer (2018)
31. Sharma, C., Genevès, P., Gesbert, N., Layaïda, N.: Schema-based query optimisation for graph databases. Proc. ACM Manag. Data **3**(1), 72:1–72:29 (2025)
32. Steinberg, D., Budinsky, F., Merks, E., Paternostro, M.: EMF: eclipse modeling framework. Pearson Education (2008)
33. Störl, U., Klettke, M.: Darwin: a data platform for schema evolution management and data migration. In: EDBT/ICDT Workshops. CEUR Workshop Proceedings, vol. 3135. CEUR-WS.org (2022)
34. Vassiliadis, P., Karakasidis, A.: Time-related patterns of schema evolution. In: EDBT, pp. 310–323. OpenProceedings.org (2025)
35. Wischenbart, M., et al.: User profile integration made easy: model-driven extraction and transformation of social network schemas. In: WWW (Companion Volume), pp. 939–948. ACM (2012)

User-Defined Types and Operations in GROOVE

Arend Rensink[✉][iD]

University of Twente, Enschede, Netherlands
`arend.rensink@utwente.nl`

Abstract. The graph transformation tool GROOVE supports data manipulation through a signature with fixed sorts `int`, `real`, `bool` and `string` and a collection of pre-defined operators. Graphs can contain algebra values as special nodes; attributes correspond to edges to such value nodes.

This setup has limitations. For instance, it is awkward to model more advanced data calculations—for instance, advanced string or statistical operations. Moreover, the algebraic underpinning means that non-determinism (for instance, randomness) cannot be modelled. Finally, there is no support for structured data types, such as records.

In this paper, we describe an extension of GROOVE that allows *user-defined types and operations*, based on programmable Java classes and methods. Essentially, users can annotate their own classes and methods and make these available to GROOVE at runtime, after which they can be employed in rule systems. Moreover, methods can be declared as *indeterminate*, meaning that their outcome is not completely fixed by their arguments; this allows randomness and other forms of non-determinism.

1 Introduction

For graph transformation tools to be able to model practically relevant domains, they have to support a notion of data attributes. In the case of GROOVE, this support is rooted in algebra: there is a pre-defined signature with four primitive sorts (`int`, `real`, `bool` and `string`), with for each sort a set of constants and a collection of pre-defined operators. GROOVE offers a choice of four different algebras at various levels of abstraction (the `term` algebra, in which no computation takes place; the `big` algebra for unbounded-precision arithmetic; the `java` algebra, directly based on Java types; and the `point` algebra, where each carrier sort contains precisely one value). Data values are incorporated in graphs as special *value nodes*, typed by their sorts; attributes are edges from ordinary (non-value) nodes to value nodes. Rules can contain sort-typed variable nodes and expressions built from operators, constants and variable nodes.

This setup has clear limitations. For instance, it is awkward to model advanced data manipulation beyond the pre-defined types and operations; e.g., trigonometrical or statistical calculations. Moreover, the algebraic underpinning

© The Author(s), under exclusive license to Springer Nature Switzerland AG 2026
B. Archibald and O. Semeráth (Eds.): ICGT 2026, LNCS 16624, pp. 211–222, 2026.
https://doi.org/10.1007/978-3-032-29730-3_12

means that operations are *determinate*: their outcome is always completely determined by their arguments. This means that, for instance, randomness cannot be modelled. Finally, there is no support for structured data types, such as records; while this does not affect the modelling power *per se*, it does hamper the usability for practical purposes.

In this paper, we describe an extension of GROOVE to *user-defined types and operations*, based on programmable Java classes and methods, that eliminates these limitations. Essentially, rules can invoke methods of appropriately annotated Java classes, made available to GROOVE at runtime. User-defined types are limited to records with primitively typed fields; user-defined operations can have any signature based on the original primitive types plus user types. Moreover, methods can be annotated as *indeterminate*, meaning that their outcome is not completely determined by their arguments. This allows the inclusion of randomness and other forms of non-determinism.

Below, we discuss the choices we made and their rationale (Sect. 2) and we briefly recapitulate the theoretical underpinning of GROOVE attributes (Sect. 3) to show how user-defined types and operations fit into that. After that, we discuss the actual implementation and illustrate it on the basis of a toy example (Sect. 4). Conclusions and related work are presented in Sect. 5.

The functionality described in this paper has been incorporated in GROOVE release 7.5.2, and the Java code and GROOVE rule system of the example are available as part of this paper's repository.

2   Design Considerations and Decisions

The extension reported in this paper was motivated by the lack of convenience, reported by users, in modelling structured data using just graph nodes and primitively typed attributes. Some particular concerns are:

Representation. Using nodes and primitive attributes causes all data values to become part of the graph structure, making them less easy to recognise and represent textually. Essentially, a term such as `Date(6,6,1964)` is more immediately comprehensible than a `Date`-typed node with three outgoing `int`-typed edges.

Immutability. Manipulating structured data should not modify the existing values but create new ones. For instance, if one adds a year to a given `Date`, this results in a new `Date` and not in the replacement of the `year`-edge. To mimic that behaviour using standard graph transformation, one has to be careful in explicitly creating a new node whenever this occurs.

Equality. For data types, it is unintuitive to have multiple copies of the same value: if data values correspond to graph nodes, equality should correspond to node identity. This is hard to maintain when relying on standard graph nodes, in particular in light of the previous point: rather than blithely creating a new node whenever a new (structured) data value is required, one has to reuse the node with that new value if it exists, and create one otherwise.

Operations. A particular structured data type may come with a set of corresponding operations (in object-oriented programming typically provided as methods) for instance, in the case of a Date, one might want to obtain the next date value or to reason about the number of days since the beginning of the year. If the data type is modelled as part of a graph, there is no obvious way to encode and invoke such operations. Note that, since operations offer the possibility to "wrap" any complex calculation, they are convenient for primitive as well as structured data.

A final point at which the attribute support of GROOVE was found to be lacking is unrelated to structured data.

Randomness. All primitive GROOVE operations are deterministic. This makes it very awkward to model systems that may involve randomness or any other kind of indeterminacy in their behaviour. For instance, the only way to model the roll of a die is in modelling all possible outcomes explicitly, meaning that all resulting behaviours are part of the resulting state space.

In addressing these issues, the following questions had to be answered:

- *What kind of data types* should be offered, in addition to the currently available primitive types?
- *How should used-defined data types be integrated* into the existing attribute support architecture?
- *In what language* should users program their data types and operations?

Though these questions are not completely independent, we address them one by one.

Kinds of Data Types. An obvious source of inspiration are the data type structures developed for programming languages; see, e.g., [6]. Two kinds of data structure stand out as being potentially useful: *records* and *lists*. Other kinds of structured data types, such as *sum types* or *object types*, are reasonably compatible with node types and do not urgently require a different, data-specific solution, whereas the use of more powerful notions such as *function types* is less obvious in the context of graph-based modelling.

The current work focusses on record types; moreover, we have chosen to restrict fields to primitive data types. Both support for arrays and for nested records are left as future work.

Integration. The strength of GROOVE lies in the formal foundation of its models, based on typed attributed graphs, and its capability for state space generation, including automatic isomorphism checking. The extension to user-defined structured data means that the typing of attributes has had to be reconsidered. Ideally, the type system should be able to distinguish between different user types and so catch errors in the invocation of user-defined operators on the wrong user-defined type. However, the solution chosen for now is to group all user-defined types under a single algebraic sort user: erroneous invocations are caught at runtime by generating a special "user error value".

Language. To allow users full flexibility in their implementations, a natural choice has been to offer Java as source language, given that *(i)* it is also the language of GROOVE itself, *(ii)* the native `record` structure provides a lot of scaffolding, *(iii)* information about the types and operations can be imported through annotations, and *(iv)* invocation can be programmed through reflection.

Moreover, using Java this also enables the reuse of pre-existing code. On the other hand, from a formal reasoning point of view, a disadvantage is that it is impossible to restrict what may happen within user-defined operations: they may easily have side-effects that can lead to unpredictable results, also because there are no guarantees about the precise moment at which GROOVE invokes them. In other words, the correctness of the state space exploration partially depends on user discipline.

3 Theoretical Underpinning

Since this paper is especially meant to introduce a tool extension, we limit the theoretical exposition to the necessary minimum.

3.1 System Types and Operations

The attribute support in GROOVE is based on multi-sorted algebra. This starts with the concept of a *signature*, being a tuple $\langle S, C, O \rangle$ of disjoint sets S (*sorts*), C (*constants*) and O (*operators*); C and S are partitioned into $\{C^s\}_{s \in S}$ and $\{O^s\}_{s \in S}$, respectively. GROOVE offers only primitive sorts, in the form of $S = \{\texttt{bool}, \texttt{int}, \texttt{real}, \texttt{string}\}$; C consists of literals in Java notation; and O is a set of elementary arithmetic and string manipulation operators.

The *sort of* a constant or operator $p \in C \cup O$ is that $s_p \in S$ for which $p \in C^{s_p} \cup O^{s_p}$. Moreover, each $o \in O$ has an *input signature* $\sigma_o \in S^*$. In addition, there is a set of *variables* X, likewise partitioned into $\{X^s\}_{s \in S}$.

Given a signature $\langle S, C, O \rangle$ and a set of variables X, the set of *terms* T, once more partitioned into $\{T^s\}_{s \in S}$, is defined as the smallest set such that *(i)* $c \in T^{s_c}$ for all $c \in C$, *(ii)* $x \in T^{s_x}$ for all $x \in X$, and *(iii)* $o(t_1, \cdots t_{|\sigma_o|}) \in T^{s_o}$ for all $o \in O$, given $t_i \in T^{\sigma_o|i}$ for all $1 \leq i \leq |\sigma_o|$.

An *algebra* based on $\langle S, C, O \rangle$ consists of *carrier sets* D^s for all $s \in S$, *values* $v_c \in D^{s_c}$ for all $c \in C$, and *functions* $f_o \colon D_1 \times \cdots \times D_{|\sigma_o|} \to D^{s_o}$ for all $o \in O$, where $D_i = D^{\sigma_o|i}$ for all $1 \leq i \leq |\sigma|$. Given a *valuation* $\nu \colon X \to D$ (with $\nu(x) \in D^{s_x}$ for all $x \in X$), every term $t \in T^s$ gives rise to a value in D^s.

Out of the box, GROOVE offers four algebras: `term`, where $D^s = T^s$ for all $s \in S$; `big`, where the carrier sets are essentially the mathematical sets of booleans $\mathbb{B}$, integers $\mathbb{I}$, rationals $\mathbb{Q}$ and strings $\mathbb{S} = \mathbb{C}^*$ (for the set $\mathbb{C}$ of Unicode characters); `java`, where the carrier sets are the values of the Java types `boolean`, `int`, `double` and `String`; and finally `point`, for which all carrier sets are singletons. In addition, `big` and `java` contain special error values $\perp_s \in D^s$ for each sort $s \in S$ to ensure that all f_o are fully defined; for instance, a term t_1/t_2, denoting the division of t_1 by t_2, yields $\perp_{\texttt{int}}$ respectively $\perp_{\texttt{real}}$ if t_2 evaluates to zero.

It may be noted that the above formalisation does not include equations, and thus omits an ingredient that is essential in algebraic reasoning. Indeed, GROOVE does not offer equation-based analysis capabilities. If operators would have equational specifications, then term would not be a valid algebra.

We will not go into the formalisation of GROOVE graphs here, except to recall that nodes are taken from a universe that includes the combined carrier sets D (of the selected algebra) as so-called *value nodes*, and edges can have D-nodes as their target (but not their source). Rules can contain terms encoded as AST-like graph structures (see [4] for the encoding) that include variables as nodes. A *match* of a rule r into a host graph establishes a valuation ν_r for r's variable nodes, which is used to evaluate all terms contained in r. Part of the outcome of that evaluation serves as an application condition for r, another part determines the values in the target graph. Any combination of host graph G and match m of r into G that (when evaluated) satisfies r's application conditions gives rise, through the usual algebraic pushout construction (see [2,3]), to a target graph H, which is therefore uniquely determined up to isomorphism. The combined construction is denoted $G \xRightarrow{r,m} H$.

3.2   User Types and Operations

We introduce a single new sort user. User-defined operators come in three kinds:

- *Constructors* u, with $\sigma_u \in S^*$ and $s_u =$ user. As the name implies, from a sequence of primitive-sorted input values a constructor returns a unique user-sorted value, being essentially the *tuple* of input values—in other words, formally speaking, u is a product operator. Uniqueness here means that the corresponding function f_u is injective and the image sets img f_u are guaranteed to be disjoint for different constructors u.
- *Accessors* $a_{u,1}, \ldots a_{u,n}$ for every constructor u and $1 \leq i \leq n = |\sigma_u|$, with $\sigma_{a_i} =$ user and $s_{a_i} = \sigma_u|_i$. The accessor $a_{u,i}$ retrieves the i'th element of the tuple constructed by u; equationally this can be expressed as $a_i(u(x_1, \ldots, x_n)) = x_i$. Outside img f_u, the accessors $a_{u,i}$ are undefined—or rather, they yield $\perp_{\mathsf{user}}$.
- *Other operators*, of any signature and sort.

Let U be the collection of constructors; then the user-carrier set is defined by

$$D^{\mathsf{user}} = \bigcup\nolimits_{u \in U} \text{img } f_u \ .$$

This means that all user-defined values can be obtained through construction. In particular, though there may be "other operators" in $O^{\mathsf{user}} \setminus U$ that also return user-sorted values, those can always (alternatively) be produced by some $u \in U$, hence can be understood as tuples of which the elements can be retrieved using accessors.

An important additional feature is that the "other operators" may be designated as *indeterminate*, meaning that their result is actually not fixed by their inputs.

The prototypical example is a random generator, which has an empty input signature (it takes no arguments) but by its very nature produces an unpredictable result. Algebraically, an indeterminate operator $o \in O_\iota$ can be captured by a powerset function $F_o \colon D_1 \times \cdots \times D_{|s|} \to (\mathcal{P}(D^{s_o}) \setminus \{\emptyset\})$, rather than a simple function f_o as above; each time F_o is *invoked* on a set of values $v_1, \ldots, v_{|s|}$, it returns a *single* value from $F_o(v_1, \ldots, v_{|s|})$.

As a consequence, if a rule r contains an indeterminate operator, its actual application is no longer deterministic. Given a host graph G and a match m, the indeterminate operators of r are invoked based on the valuation ν_r, as part of the evaluation of the terms in r. The combined outcome may mean that r's application condition is not satisfied; and if it is satisfied, the graph H produced by the transformation $G \overset{r,m}{\Longrightarrow} H$ is likely to be partially determined by that indeterminate outcome. The overall effect is that explorations of the same rule system at different moments in time can have different results—which is precisely what one would expect from a system that includes a form of randomness.

4   Implementation

User types and operations are defined through annotated Java classes, made available to the JVM upon invoking GROOVE. Annotations come in two flavours:

@UserType. This is a class-level annotation, to be used on public **record** types with all field types taken from the java algebra (**boolean**, **int**, **double** or String).

```
@UserType
public record Nm(ty₁ fd₁, ..., tyₙ fdₙ)
```

defines an operator Nm $\in O^{\mathsf{user}}$ with $\sigma_{\mathsf{Nm}} = s_1 \cdots s_n$ (where the s_i are the sorts corresponding to the Java types ty_i) as well as operators $\mathsf{fd}_i \in O^{s_i}$ with $\sigma_{\mathsf{fd}_i} = \text{user}$ for all $1 \leq i \leq n$, together with corresponding functions $f_{\mathsf{Nm}}, f_{\mathsf{fd}_1}, \ldots, f_{\mathsf{fd}_n}$. In terms of Sect. 3.2, Nm is a constructor and the fd_i are accessors.

@UserOperation. This is a method-level annotation to define "other operators," to be used on public methods in arbitrary public classes. All parameter types as well as the return type are either taken from the java algebra, *or* may be @UserType-annotated records. If the containing class is not a @UserType, the annotated method must be **static**. Hence there are two cases.

- ```
  @UserOperation
  public ty op(ty₁ fd₁, ..., tyₙ fdₙ)
  ```

  in a @UserType-annotated class defines an operator op $\in O^{\mathsf{ty}}$ with $\sigma_{\mathsf{op}} = \text{user } s_1 \cdots s_n$, together with a corresponding function f_{op}.

- ```
  @UserOperation
  public static ty op(ty₁ fd₁, ..., tyₙ fdₙ)
  ```

  in *any* **public** class defines an operator op $\in O^{\mathsf{ty}}$ with $\sigma_{\mathsf{op}} = s_1 \cdots s_n$, together with a corresponding function f_{op}.

Table 1. Operators defined by the Date class of Fig. 1, with sorts and signatures. The *-marked operators are indeterminate

o	σ_o	s_o		o	σ_o	s_o	
Date	int int int	user		toString	user	string	
day	user	int		daysSince	user	int	*
month	user	int		next	user	user	
year	user	int		isLeapYear	int	bool	
				today	ϵ	user	*

Note that in the first of these cases, op has an extra argument of sort user: this corresponds to the **this**-value "on which," in object-oriented terminology, the method op is invoked. An example annotated class annotated is given in Fig. 1, defining the operators in Table 1. The intended meaning is self-explanatory.

To actually *use* annotation-defined operators, a rule system has to specify the qualified names of the annotated classes in its System Properties. From then on, they can be treated like built-in system operators.

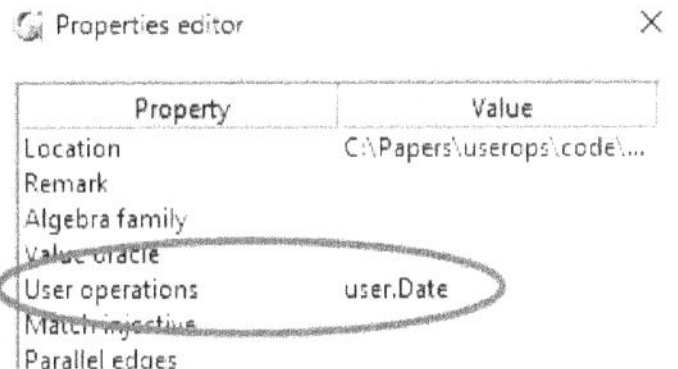

Figure 2 shows two example GROOVE rules using the operators of Fig. 1.

- create consumes a node d of (node) type **Date** and invokes the user-defined constructor Date, using d's node attributes as arguments. It then creates a node of type **Person** with that Date as their birthday. Moreover, the created **Person** is **pregnant** depending on a further condition, specified by the conditional quantifier young: this is satisfied if the number of days since the birthday is properly between 7000 and 15000.
- birth specifies that a **pregnant** person gives birth (and stops being **pregnant**). The newly born **Person** is a child of the first, and its birthday is based on the outcome of the today operator.

In both rules, the decoration **0** marks data nodes that serve as *rule parameters* (with number 0, meaning the first—here: only—parameter). Parameter values are part of the transition label when the rule gets applied. An example exploration is shown in Fig. 3: from the start graph on the left, using any of the rule application sequences of the transition system in the middle, eventually the final graph on the right is obtained. The indeterminacy of today causes the outcome of the exploration to depend on the day of execution.

```java
@UserType
public record Date(int day, int month, int year) {
  @UserOperation
  public String toString() { // Returns a String representation of this Date
    return "" + day() + " " + MONTHS[month() - 1] + " " + year();
  }

  @UserOperation(indeterminate = true)
  public int daysSince() { // Returns the number of days between this Date and now
    var cal = Calendar.getInstance(); cal.set(year(), month() - 1, day());
    long diff = Math.abs(new java.util.Date().getTime() - cal.getTime().getTime());
    return (int) TimeUnit.DAYS.convert(diff, TimeUnit.MILLISECONDS);
  }

  @UserOperation
  public Date next() { // Returns the next Date with respect to this one
    int day = day() + 1, month = month(), year = year();
    if (day > daysInMonth()) {
      day = 1; month += 1;
      if (month > 12) {
        month = 1; year += 1;
      }
    }
    return new Date(day, month, year);
  }

  private int daysInMonth() { // Returns the number of days in this Date's month
    return switch (month()) {
    case 1, 3, 5, 7, 8, 10, 12 -> 31;
    case 2 -> 28 + (isLeapYear(year()) ? 1 : 0);
    default -> 30;
    };
  }

  static private String[] MONTHS =
    {"Jan","Feb","Mar","Apr","May","Jun","Jul","Aug","Sep","Oct","Nov","Dec"};

  @UserOperation
  static public boolean isLeapYear(int year) { // Tests whether year is a leap year
    return year % 4 == 0 && (year % 100 != 0 || year % 400 == 0);
  }

  @UserOperation(indeterminate = true)
  static public Date today() { // Returns a Date object representing today
    var today = Calendar.getInstance();
    return new Date(today.get(Calendar.DAY_OF_MONTH),
        today.get(Calendar.MONTH) + 1, today.get(Calendar.YEAR));
  }
}
```

Fig. 1. Annotated Date class.

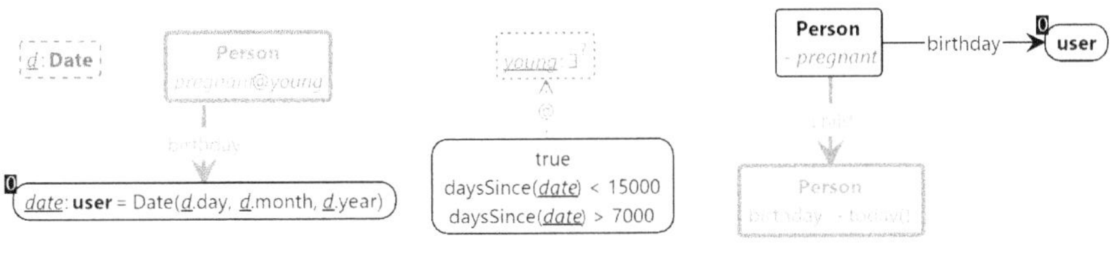

(a) create: a `Date`-typed node is transformed to a `Person`   (b) birth: a *pregnant* `Person` gives birth

Fig. 2. GROOVE rules using the operators defined in Fig. 1.

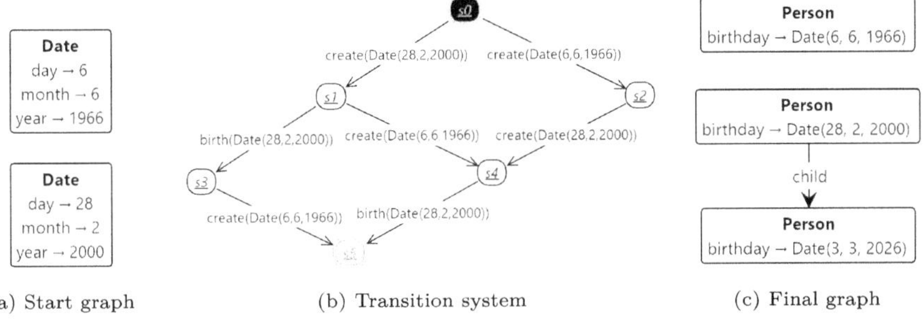

(a) Start graph   (b) Transition system   (c) Final graph

Fig. 3. Example exploration based on the rules in Fig. 2.

5   Conclusion

We have presented an extension of GROOVE that enhances the tool's practical usefulness in incorporating data, based on user-defined record types and arbitrary operations. The extension addresses all the concerns identified in Sect. 2 (representation, immutability, equality, operations and randomness).

This work was inspired by a feature request.[1]

5.1   Limitations

We list some practical limitations in the current GROOVE implementation.

- *User types and operations are only supported in the* java *algebra.* In other words, the choice of algebras (`term`, `big`, `java`, `point`) recalled in the introduction is currently not available for grammars with user-defined types. We expect that the extension to `term` and `point` will be straightforward; however, to also be compatible with `big`, the user types and operations would natively have to rely on `BigInteger` and `BigDecimal` rather than **int** and **double**.
- *User types are restricted to* **record**s. This is a choice motivated by the fact that Java **record** instances are inherently immutable and **record**s have well-defined constructors. We expect that this will not be a limitation in practice.

---

[1] Thanks to Reiko Heckel and Adam Machowczyk for their suggestions and feedback.

- *User type fields are restricted to primitive sorts.* Though there is no inherent problem in allowing user types to have user-typed fields, cyclic dependencies would necessitate the introduction of `null` values.
- *User type checking is weak.* The GROOVE type system cannot statically distinguish different (Java) user types: they are all values of the single `user` sort. Run-time type errors result in the special $\perp_{user}$ error value (see Sect. 3.1).
- *Operator names must be distinct.* The current implementation does not allow overloading. In particular, this means that also field names must be distinct across `@UserType` classes.
- *Indeterminate operations cannot appear in quantified rules.* For instance, it is not possible to simultaneously assign random values to a set of nodes by universally quantifying the nodes; or for the example in this paper, neither of the rules in Fig. 2 can be universally quantified so as to apply to all `Person` nodes simultaneously. Lifting this restriction will require a fairly major restructuring of GROOVE's rule matching engine.

5.2 Related Work

The seminal work of Ehrig et al. [3] embeds the theory of attributed graphs (in which actually not just nodes but also edges can have attributes) and their transformation into algebra. GROOVE's implementation is based on a variant of this embedding (see [4]); for practical purposes, the main difference is that only nodes can be attributed and that attribute types are restricted to the four primitive sorts recalled in Sect. 3.

Algebraic theory obviously allows much richer data types than just GROOVE's primitive attributes. However, once users are allowed to program their own types and operations, the equational reasoning that is foundational to algebra is very hard to uphold. This is also seen in the tool AGG[2] (see [8, 11]): they, too, essentially import Java types into graphs, at the price of disabling some of AGG's analysis capabilities, e.g., critical pair analysis.

Again based on the theory of algebraic node and edge attributes, Lambers and Orejas et al. [9] have developed a very powerful theory of symbolic reasoning, which in that paper is reported as having been implemented in a tool called AutoGraph. (Unfortunately, the tool itself seems to be unavailable.)

A different way of integrating attributes and graphs has been both theoretically worked out and implemented by Plump et al. in the context of the Graph Programming tool GP (see [5, 7]). Rather than aiming to be all-encompassing by allowing any algebraic type, they restrict data attributes to a compact, powerful but closed set of data types consisting of integers, strings and lists of those two, plus booleans.

---

[2] A more recent, open source snapshot of AGG can be found here.

On the other side of the spectrum, there are graph transformation tools that were conceived to be usable in practice, rather than to embrace theoretical concepts, and hence do not strive for a complete formalisation. Prime among these is Henshin (see, e.g., [1,10]), which actually shares many of GROOVE's capabilities regarding state space exploration and model checking. Citing [1], for data attributes they offer "flexible attribute computations based on Java or JavaScript."

Declaration of Interests. The author has no competing interests to declare that are relevant to the content of this article.

References

1. Arendt, T., Biermann, E., Jurack, S., Krause, C., Taentzer, G.: Henshin: advanced concepts and tools for in-place EMF model transformations. In: Petriu, D.C., Rouquette, N., Haugen, Ø. (eds.) Model Driven Engineering Languages and Systems (MODELS), Part I. Lecture Notes in Computer Science, vol. 6394, pp. 121–135. Springer, Cham (2010). https://doi.org/10.1007/978-3-642-16145-2_9
2. Ehrig, H., Ehrig, K., Prange, U., Taentzer, G.: Fundamentals of Algebraic Graph Transformation. Monographs in Theoretical Computer Science. An EATCS Series, Springer, Heidelberg (2006). https://doi.org/10.1007/3-540-31188-2
3. Ehrig, H., Prange, U., Taentzer, G.: Fundamental theory for typed attributed graph transformation. In: Ehrig, H., Engels, G., Parisi-Presicce, F., Rozenberg, G. (eds.) Second International Conference on Graph Transformations (ICGT). LNCS, vol. 3256, pp. 161–177. Springer, Heidelberg (2004). https://doi.org/10.1007/978-3-540-30203-2_13
4. Kastenberg, H., Rensink, A.: Graph attribution through sub-graphs. In: Heckel, R., Taentzer, G. (eds.) Graph Transformation, Specifications, and Nets — In Memory of Hartmut Ehrig. Lecture Notes in Computer Science, vol. 10800, pp. 245–265. Springer, Cham (2018). https://doi.org/10.1007/978-3-319-75396-6_14
5. Manning, G., Plump, D.: The GP programming system. Electron. Commun. Eur. Assoc. Softw. Sci. Technol. **10** (2008). https://doi.org/10.14279/TUJ.ECEASST.10.150
6. Pierce, B.C.: Types and Programming Languages. MIT press (2002)
7. Plump, D.: The design of GP 2. In: Escobar, S. (ed.) 10th International Workshop on Reduction Strategies in Rewriting and Programming (WRS). EPTCS, vol. 82, pp. 1–16 (2011). https://doi.org/10.4204/EPTCS.82.1
8. Runge, O., Ermel, C., Taentzer, G.: AGG 2.0 - new features for specifying and analyzing algebraic graph transformations. In: Schürr, A., Varró, D., Varró, G. (eds.) Applications of Graph Transformations with Industrial Relevance - 4th International Symposium (AGTIVE). LNCS, vol. 7233, pp. 81–88. Springer, Cham (2011). https://doi.org/10.1007/978-3-642-34176-2_8
9. Schneider, S., Lambers, L., Orejas, F.: Automated reasoning for attributed graph properties. Int. J. Softw. Tools Technol. Transf. **20**(6), 705–737 (2018). https://doi.org/10.1007/S10009-018-0496-3

10. Strüber, D., et al.: Henshin: a usability-focused framework for EMF model transformation development. In: de Lara, J., Plump, D. (eds.) ICGT 2017. LNCS, vol. 10373, pp. 196–208. Springer, Cham (2017). https://doi.org/10.1007/978-3-319-61470-0_12
11. Taentzer, G.: AGG: a graph transformation environment for modeling and validation of software. In: Pfaltz, J.L., Nagl, M., Böhlen, B. (eds.) AGTIVE 2003. LNCS, vol. 3062, pp. 446–453. Springer, Heidelberg (2004). https://doi.org/10.1007/978-3-540-25959-6_35

Benchmark First: Defining Tasks for Graph Transformation Learning

Adam Machowczyk[(✉)] and Reiko Heckel

University of Leicester, Leicester, UK
{amm106,rh122}@le.ac.uk

Abstract. Learning graph transformations from examples requires datasets for training and benchmarking. To establish which machine learning architectures are suitable for which kinds of problems, we need to experiment on a range of graph-computation tasks. In this paper, we propose a framework for defining such tasks and categorising them along four dimensions: complexity, input-output relation, graph type, and the structural changes they require. We apply the framework to 16 tasks for which we have implemented data generators or provided data sets in a unified interface. Our aim is to work towards a benchmark that supports the training and evaluation of graph transformation models in a framework that can be used by the wider community to support their own research, define more tasks, thereby extending and refining the framework.

1 Introduction

Research in machine learning models to perform graph transformations requires data sets for training and evaluation. Graph transformation tasks vary, so we need different model architectures to address different types of tasks. Benchmarks assessing such models should offer a range of tasks of varying complexity, working on different types of graphs, involving different graph manipulations and input-output relations. We are not aware that such benchmarks exist, and more fundamentally, that the different types of graph transformation tasks are well understood and agreed.

In graph machine learning, a *graph-to-graph transformation*, or a *Deep Graph Transformation* (DGT), is a mapping of graphs from the input domain to the output domain [20]. The three most common types of DGT tasks are *Node-level Transformation (NT)*, *Edge-level Transformation (ET)* and *Node-Edge Co-Transformation* (NECT). NTs generate node attributes or classifications, including the classification of nodes as deleted, created or preserved. Similarly, ETs update edges and their attributes, and NECTs combine both kinds of changes [20].

DGT models are typically purpose-trained for specific domains. For example, the Diffusion Convolutional Recurrent Neural Network—a node-level DGT model—was built for traffic forecasting and evaluated exclusively on the METR-LA and PEMS-BAY datasets [30,39]. Because these models are developed in

B. Archibald and O. Semeráth (Eds.): ICGT 2026, LNCS 16624, pp. 223–234, 2026.
https://doi.org/10.1007/978-3-032-29730-3_13

isolation to solve custom problems, the discipline lacks standardised engineering and evaluation frameworks. This situation mirrors well-documented reproducibility crises in other areas of machine learning, such as Deep Reinforcement Learning [23] and Generative Adversarial Networks [32], where inconsistent evaluation metrics and hidden hyperparameter optimisation frequently generated false impressions of architectural superiority. Within graph learning specifically, there is growing evidence that this lack of standards is a critical vulnerability. Recent findings highlight the fragility of experimental setups that rely on a single train, validation, and test split: When training procedures and hyperparameter selections are applied robustly over multiple data splits, simple models can surprisingly outperform supposedly sophisticated GNN architectures [40]. Consequently, researchers are forced into expensive, time-consuming replication efforts, sometimes deriving entirely different findings than the original studies [16]. Ultimately, lacking unified benchmarks, structured comparison between tasks and models remains difficult, imprecise, and prone to the same pitfalls that have historically plagued broader deep learning research.

To address these challenges, we propose the first version of a conceptual framework for defining and comparing graph-to-graph transformation tasks. While specialised benchmarks seek to establish competitive models in a given domain, our goal is to propose an extensible framework to support reliable and reproducible training and evaluation across a range of tasks. To demonstrate and populate the approach, we introduce 16 tasks from existing literature selected to cover a broad spectrum of complexities, input-output relations, graph types, and structural changes. By outlining these dimensions, we motivate the development of a unified benchmark interface to support clear task specification, implementation, and evaluation across diverse problems. This is intended as an evolving community resource as we invite others to contribute tasks and expand the taxonomy.

2   Task Categories

To provide a common framework for graph transformation tasks, we propose a categorisation based on four factors: *complexity, input-output relation, graph type* and *structural changes*.

Complexity is defined using standard classes such as linear, polynomial-time (P), NP-complete or NP-hard. Using established transformation tasks, their complexity is usually known from the literature. It is tempting, given our interest in rule-based graph transformations, to define transformation complexity in terms of the number of rule applications, but not all transformation tasks have established rule-based solutions.

The relation between input and output graphs can be *deterministic, nondeterministic,* or *probabilistic*. In a deterministic relation, the same input always produces the same output. In the nondeterministic case, a single input admits multiple valid outputs. Such tasks can be further divided: In unconstrained tasks, any valid output is acceptable (e.g., any spanning tree of a connected graph). In *optimisation* tasks, the goal is to find a valid output that minimises or maximises a given objective function, such as removing a minimal number of edges to eliminate all cycles. In *heuristic optimisation*, the task is to approximate such an optimum without guaranteeing it. In a *probabilistic* relation, each input graph induces a probability distribution over output graphs.

Graph machine learning architectures differ in which graph types are supported. Tasks can require *directed* or *undirected simple*, *multi-* or *hypergraphs*. Support for *homogeneous* graphs is more usual than for *bipartite* or *heterogeneous* (i.e., explicitly typed) graphs. However, *labelled* graphs are common, as are *attributed* graphs with numerical and textual features that models rely on to learn.

Structural changes are classified as *node- or edge-level transformation (NT or ET) or node-edge co-transformation (NECT)* [20]. Edge-level tasks include edge *addition* and *deletion*, and *edge attribute computation*. Node-level tasks involving *adding or deleting nodes* are challenging for neural networks since they change the shape of adjacency matrices [46], while *node attribute computation* is common in graph neural networks. Node- and edge-level attribute computation can be numerical (regression) or textual (classification). NECT tasks support node and edge-level transformation, and are especially useful for graph optimisation, error detection, and correction. An example is HOPPITY, a tool for detecting and correcting errors in JavaScript programs, which converts source code to graphs, learns a sequence of graph transformations to fix syntactically and semantically invalid code, and parses the results back to their original form [15].

3   Task Selection and Definitions

Existing graph machine learning models are evaluated against narrow, domain-specific datasets that do not comprehensively test topological generalisation. To address this gap, we conducted an exploratory search to curate a broad spectrum of problems. Guided by the four criteria above, we identified tasks that populate this multi-dimensional space, spanning the required structural changes, complexities, graph types, and input-output relations.

None of the selected tasks have as yet been solved using graph transformation learning. We specifically sought novel tasks because our objective is to evaluate the feasibility of different approaches. Several of the selected tasks represent problems for which efficient algorithms already exist. Applying machine learning to well-defined algorithmic problems is a choice in line with *neural algorithmic reasoning* (NAR) [43]. While NAR is motivated by practical considerations, such as improved efficiency and processing speed, we expect tasks with well-understood algorithmic solutions to provide insights into the nature of the challenges posed, such as their worst-case or mean complexity.

Due to the limitations of current models for NT tasks with dynamic sets of nodes, 13 out of 16 tasks are edge classifications, including edge creation and deletion, with the remainder covering edge regression, node regression, and node classification. This shared formulation across otherwise distinct problems underscores the feasibility of a unified benchmark interface.

Next, we define the 16 tasks, ordered by increasing complexity, except where subsequent problems build on their predecessors.

Symmetric Closure: Given datasets of directed simple graphs, the objective is to transform the network by adding an inverse edge for every existing connection, provided one does not already exist. Requiring a model to learn a logical OR operation purely from topology makes symmetric closure a strict test of structure-based learning [9]. This poses a specific difficulty for graph transformation models, as they will inherently fail if they rely on non-structural node or edge features rather than recognising the actual connectivity patterns.

Transitive Closure: The ability to uncover hidden, multi-hop relationships is a fundamental challenge in network analysis. Given datasets of directed simple graphs, the objective is to transform the network by adding a direct edge between any two nodes connected by a path of length greater than one [36]. This presents a twofold graph learning challenge: the model must learn to compute all missing closures simultaneously across the network, while also generalising to recognise and bridge paths of arbitrary lengths that exceed those observed during training.

Shortcut Elimination: The inverse of transitive closure, shortcut elimination forces a model to prioritise multi-hop routing over direct links. Given datasets of directed simple graphs, the objective is to transform the network by deleting any direct edge between two nodes if an alternative path of arbitrary length also connects them. As a learning problem, this is difficult because the model must accurately scan and verify the existence of longer, secondary routes within the broader topological neighbourhood before safely pruning a connection [21].

Shape Completion: Reconstructing localised geometric patterns tests a model's acute spatial awareness within a larger network. Given datasets of undirected simple graphs containing 3- to 6-cycles (triangles to hexagons) with specific cycle edges removed, the objective is to transform the network by predicting and restoring these missing links. The primary graph learning difficulty lies in context recognition—a model might misinterpret the surrounding structure, hallucinate a missing edge in a perceived square, and erroneously connect unrelated nodes to force a shape that geometrically does not belong [35].

Molecular Bond Inference: Determining the exact nature of chemical connections tests a model's ability to perform complex multi-class discrimination within structured data. Given datasets of undirected, attributed multigraphs representing molecules generated from predefined fragments, the objective is to predict and assign the correct bond type—single, double, triple, or aromatic—between pairs of atoms [12]. While compensating the model with access to domain-specific structural and numerical atom features, the core learning difficulty lies in effectively mapping these rich local node attributes to the correct categorical edge formations across diverse molecular topologies. A standard use of this inference is reconstructing a chemically valid molecular graph from 3D atomic coordinates, including bond orders, hybridisations, and formal charges [27].

Node Core Number Computation: Evaluating the hierarchical density of a network requires isolating heavily interconnected sub-structures from peripheral nodes. Given datasets of undirected simple graphs with node attributes, the objective is to compute and assign the core number for every node, defined as the largest k for which the node belongs to a k-core (a maximal subgraph where every internal node has a degree of at least k). This is challenging as a graph learning problem because the model must recursively evaluate degrees within dynamically shifting subgraphs rather than relying on static global connectivity, demanding a deep understanding of local neighbourhood density [5]. A common use case is finding influential spreaders in online social networks, since high-coreness nodes often sit in dense, diffusion-relevant parts of the graph [3].

Intra-Community Edge Prediction: Distinguishing whether structural links bridge distinct social groups or connect internal members is a key practical challenge in social network analysis. Given [28], the SNAP Facebook Combined dataset of undirected simple graphs with edge attributes, the objective is to evaluate each edge and predict whether it connects users from the same or different communities, as originally identified by the Louvain algorithm. Rather than allocating users to specific groups, the primary graph learning difficulty lies in recognising the topological signatures of intra- versus inter-community ties, compounded by the computational challenge of efficiently training the model to scale across a medium-sized, real-world dataset. A direct application of this task is predicting future links between users in the same community in a dynamic social network [38].

Edge Betweenness Centrality Computation: Identifying critical bottlenecks in network flow patterns requires a deep understanding of global routing dynamics. Given datasets of undirected simple graphs with edge attributes, the objective is to compute the Edge Betweenness Centrality for every edge, a continuous metric quantifying how frequently an edge lies on the shortest paths between all possible node pairs. As a graph learning problem, predicting this global property is particularly difficult because it rigorously tests a model's long-distance regression capabilities; the algorithm must accurately aggregate topological information from across the entire network rather than relying on immediate local neighbourhoods [8]. This computation is highly useful in community detection, where edges with high betweenness are treated as bridges between groups and removed to reveal isolated communities [19].

Feedback Edge Set Identification: Minimising edge deletions to break all network cycles is a notorious optimisation challenge where local decisions compound into immense global complexity. Given datasets of undirected simple graphs with edge attributes, the objective is to transform the network by deleting the fewest edges required to eliminate every cycle. As a graph learning problem, this is exceptionally difficult because individual edges frequently participate in multiple overlapping cycles; the model must therefore navigate an exponentially vast search space, dynamically optimising its deletions to achieve the exact global minimum without indiscriminately pruning essential connections [17]. A practical application of this problem is reducing scan-register overhead in circuit testing [17].

Spanning Tree Identification: Extracting a foundational skeletal structure from a dense network poses a unique challenge due to non-differentiable operations and non-unique solutions. Given datasets of connected, undirected simple graphs, the objective is to transform the network by identifying and extracting a valid spanning tree that connects all nodes without forming any cycles. This poses a significant graph learning challenge because thresholding a reconstructed adjacency matrix is non-differentiable, forcing the model to optimise a surrogate objective function that assesses the structural validity of the candidate tree rather than directly evaluating exact-match correctness. Furthermore, since dense graphs possess numerous valid spanning trees, carefully selecting consistent target structures for the training data is a critical requirement to prevent the model from being penalised for finding alternative correct solutions [41]. A practical application of this identification is configuring data aggregation and broadcasting pathways in distributed systems, where an arbitrary, loop-free topology ensures that messages reach all network nodes without creating redundant broadcast storms [33].

Graph Colouring: Finding the optimal chromatic assignment in a network is a classic, computationally demanding problem that tests an algorithm's ability to balance competing constraints. Using the DIMACS dataset (specifically the DSJC125.1 subset of undirected simple graphs with node attributes), the objective is to assign colours to nodes such that no two adjacent nodes share the same colour, while strictly minimising the total number of colours used to reach the graph's known chromatic number of 5 [24]. Training a model for this task is inherently difficult because it requires simultaneously optimising three distinct objectives: Potts and Entropy to statistically minimise conflicting adjacent assignments, alongside Usage to penalise excess colour allocation [22]. Even on this relatively simple dataset subset, achieving the absolute minimum number of colours under a standardised evaluation interface remains a formidable graph learning challenge. In real-world applications, graph colouring is used for frequency or channel assignment in cellular phone networks, where colours model frequencies and edges model interference constraints [7].

Minimum Chordal Graph Completion: Enforcing a triangulated structure across a network is a strictly constrained, NP-hard optimisation problem. Given datasets of undirected simple graphs, the objective is to transform the network into a chordal graph—where every cycle of four or more vertices contains a chord bridging non-consecutive nodes—by adding the absolute minimum number of new edges [18]. As a graph learning challenge, this is particularly formidable because the model must navigate an exponentially vast search space where a single network often possesses multiple valid minimal chordal completions, forcing the algorithm to learn an optimal global strategy for edge addition rather than relying on a single deterministic pattern. Practically, this completion finds use in triangulating Bayesian networks for exact junction-tree inference, where better triangulations significantly reduce inference costs [29].

Estimated Minimum Chordal Graph Completion: Approximating computationally intractable network triangulations provides a practical alternative to true minimum-fill problems. Given datasets of undirected simple graphs, the objective is to transform the network into a chordal structure by predicting the edge additions generated by a Maximum-Cardinality-Search-based triangulation (such as [6] implemented in the Python NetworkX library). This presents a unique graph learning dynamic: rather than hunting for the absolute, NP-hard minimum-cardinality completion, the model must learn to approximate a specific computational heuristic. The primary difficulty lies in accurately replicating an algorithmic process that produces a minimal set of non-redundant edges, rather than the absolute smallest possible fill, meaning the ground-truth objective itself is inherently heuristic rather than an exact mathematical optimum.

Algebraic Connectivity Maximisation: Addressing the chronic under-capacity of UK power grids poses a critical, highly complex global optimisation challenge. By modelling the grid as an edge-attributed directed multigraph, where edges represent electrical capacity. The core task is to apply specific graph transformations—adding new edges—to maximise the objective function of algebraic connectivity λ_2, the second smallest eigenvalue of the Laplacian. As a graph transformation learning problem, this is exceptionally difficult; maximising λ_2 is NP-hard, and models struggle to learn the global objective because training on too few edges fails to fully exploit optimisation capabilities, while training on too many leads to arbitrary selections due to the diminishing returns from later edge additions. This challenge is further compounded by extremely limited real-world data from the Power Graph Cascades dataset [42], which provides just four small UK power grid networks (three for training, one for evaluation), ranging from fewer than 100 to slightly over 400 nodes, culminating in the strict evaluation requirement to optimise the network's capacity by adding exactly 5 edges.

Graph Denoising: Filtering unwanted noise from structured datasets is essential for reliable data imputation, standardisation, and stability. Given the medium-sized ConceptNet dataset of directed simple graphs, the objective is to transform the network by identifying and removing erroneous edges, replicating the GOLD model's denoising process without relying on the original pre-mined rules [14]. As a graph learning problem, this tests both topological reasoning and system extensibility. The primary difficulty lies not just in predicting structural anomalies based on connectivity, but in successfully integrating external, pre-trained BERT embeddings within a standardised framework to evaluate the model's capacity for multimodal feature processing. An example application is predicting whether a user will retweet a post in a microblogging network based on social influence patterns within the user's ego network [47].

Retweet Prediction: Anticipating user interactions is a foundational mechanism for driving recommender systems in large-scale social networks. Given [11], the SNAP Higgs Twitter Retweet Network dataset—a massive directed simple graph with edge features—the objective is to predict the existence of a directed edge between two users, indicating whether one actively retweeted the other. The primary graph learning difficulty here stems directly from computational complexity: efficiently processing a continuous, real-world network with over 250,000 nodes demands rigorous memory management and highly scalable message passing, severely testing a model's ability to maintain predictive accuracy at scale.

4   Task Categorisation

Having defined all 16 tasks, we now categorise them in the following table according to the criteria outlined in Sect. 2.

Table 1. Summary of Task Complexities and Structural Requirements

Task	Complexity	I-O Relation	Graph Type	Structural Changes
Symmetric Closure Completion	Polynomial [37]	Deterministic	*Directed* simple graphs	*Edge* Structure Completion – Add Only
Transitive Closure Completion	Polynomial [10]	Deterministic	*Directed* simple graphs	*Edge* Structure Completion – Add Only
Shortcut Elimination	Polynomial [2]	Deterministic	*Directed* simple graphs	*Edge* Structure Completion – Delete Only
Shape Completion	Polynomial [4]	Deterministic	Undirected simple graphs	*Edge* Structure Completion – Add Only
Molecular Bond Inference	Polynomial [10]	Deterministic	*Undirected, attributed multigraphs*	*Edge* Attribute Computation – Classification
Node Core Number Computation	Polynomial [5]	Deterministic	Undirected simple graphs with *node attributes*	*Node* Attribute Computation – Regression
Intra-Community Edge Prediction	Polynomial [13]	Deterministic	Undirected simple graphs with *edge attributes*	*Edge* Attribute Computation – Classification
Edge Betweenness Centrality Computation	Polynomial [8]	Deterministic	Undirected simple graphs with *edge attributes*	*Edge* Attribute Computation – Regression
Feedback Edge Set Identification	Polynomial [1]	Optimisation	Undirected simple graphs with *edge attributes*	*Edge* Attribute Computation – Classification

(continued)

Table 1. (*continued*)

Task	Complexity	I-O Relation	Graph Type	Structural Changes
Spanning Tree Identification	Polynomial [26]	Nondeterministic	Undirected simple graphs	*Edge* Structure Completion – Delete Only
Graph Colouring	NP-hard [25]	Nondeterministic; can be deterministic	Undirected simple graphs with *node attributes*	*Node* Attribute Computation – Classification
Minimum Chordal Graph Completion	NP-hard [44]	Optimisation	Undirected simple graphs	*Edge* Structure Completion – Add Only
Estimated Minimum Chordal Graph Completion	Polynomial [6]	Heuristic optimisation	Undirected simple graphs	*Edge* Structure Completion – Add Only
Algebraic Connectivity Maximisation	NP-hard [34]	Optimisation	Undirected *multigraphs*	*Edge* Structure Completion – Add Only
Graph Denoising	NP-hard [45]	Deterministic	*Directed* simple graphs	*Edge* Structure Completion – Delete Only
Retweet Prediction	Polynomial [31]	Deterministic	*Directed* simple graphs with *edge features*	*Edge* Attribute Computation – Classification

5   Discussion and Further Research

Analysing the distribution of this initial task set reveals specific areas where the first version of the taxonomy requires future expansion. The categorisation results show that we have not defined any tasks with a probabilistic input-output relation, nor any that require hypergraphs. Only one task—Estimated Minimum Chordal Graph Completion—performs heuristic optimisation. There is only one task each for node classification, node regression, and edge regression; all other tasks fall under edge classification. With the partial exception of Molecular Bond Inference, which addresses edge typing via edge-attribute classification, all tasks operate on homogeneous graphs. Spanning Tree Identification is one of two nondeterministic tasks; however, optimisation tasks can also be viewed as constrained instances of a nondeterministic input-output relation.

By categorising 16 diverse, illustrative tasks, we aim to lay the groundwork for a standardised, extensible foundation that facilitates reliable and reproducible research. Our idea is to develop a unified ML interface that accepts task specifications defined by input graphs and corresponding output graphs. The pipeline is currently in the prototyping stage and supports both static graph access and dataset generation, covering all defined tasks. Pending work involves, but is not limited to, custom feature registration, automatic standardised feature computation, support for all complexity classes, required graph types, input-output relationships, and required structural changes outlined in Table 1.

This is where we are looking to involve the wider community. If you are currently working on or have in mind any tasks that align with our outlined categorisation criteria, please email us your suggestions and any limitations you encounter or are aware of. Edge classification and node attribute computation tasks are likely to be more interesting to us in the near future, whereas node-level transformation and NECT tasks will be of interest in the long term.

Disclosure of Interests. The authors have no competing interests to declare that are relevant to the content of this article.

References

1. Agrawal, A., Panolan, F., Saurabh, S., Zehavi, M.: Simultaneous feedback edge set: a parameterized perspective. Algorithmica **83**(2), 753–774 (2020). https://doi.org/10.1007/s00453-020-00773-9
2. Aho, A.V., Garey, M.R., Ullman, J.D.: The transitive reduction of a directed graph. SIAM J. Comput. **1**(2), 131–137 (1972). https://doi.org/10.1137/0201008
3. Al-garadi, M.A., Varathan, K.D., Ravana, S.D.: Identification of influential spreaders in online social networks using interaction weighted k-core decomposition method. XXPhys. A **468**, 278–288 (2017)
4. Alon, N., Yuster, R., Zwick, U.: Finding and counting given length cycles. Algorithmica (New York) **17**, 209–223 (1997). https://doi.org/10.1007/BF02523189
5. Batagelj, V., Zaversnik, M.: An o(m) algorithm for cores decomposition of networks (2003). https://arxiv.org/abs/cs/0310049
6. Berry, A., Blair, J., Heggernes, P., Peyton, B.: Maximum cardinality search for computing minimal triangulations of graphs. Algorithmica **39**, 287–298 (2004). https://doi.org/10.1007/s00453-004-1084-3
7. Borndörfer, R., Eisenblätter, A., Grötschel, M., Martin, A.: Frequency assignment in cellular phone networks. Ann. Oper. Res. **76**, 73–93 (1998). https://doi.org/10.1023/a:1018908907763
8. Brandes, U.: A faster algorithm for betweenness centrality. J. Math. Sociol. **25**(2), 163–177 (2001). https://doi.org/10.1080/0022250X.2001.9990249
9. Campbell, G.: Efficient graph rewriting (2021). https://arxiv.org/abs/1906.05170
10. Cormen, T.H., Leiserson, C.E., Rivest, R.L., Stein, C.: Introduction to Algorithms, Third Edition. The MIT Press, 3rd edn. (2009), [Molecular Bond Inference: Sect. 22.2, Transitive Closure: Sect. 25.2]
11. De Domenico, M., Lima, A., Mougel, P., Musolesi, M.: The anatomy of a scientific rumor. Sci. Rep. **3**(1), October 2013. https://doi.org/10.1038/srep02980
12. Dehof, A.K., Rurainski, A., Bui, Q.B.A., Böcker, S., Lenhof, H.P., Hildebrandt, A.: Automated bond order assignment as an optimization problem. Bioinformatics **27**(5), 619–625 (2011). https://doi.org/10.1093/bioinformatics/btq718
13. Delling, D., Görke, R., Nikoloski, Z., Gaertler, M., Brandes, U., Wagner, D., Hoefer, M.: On Modularity Clustering. IEEE Trans. Knowl. Data Eng. **20**(02), 172–188 (2008). https://doi.ieeecomputersociety.org/10.1109/TKDE.2007.190689

14. Deng, Z., Wang, W., Wang, Z., Liu, X., Song, Y.: Gold: a global and local-aware denoising framework for commonsense knowledge graph noise detection (2023). https://arxiv.org/abs/2310.12011
15. Dinella, E., Dai, H., Li, Z., Naik, M., Song, L., Wang, K.: Hoppity: Learning graph transformations to detect and fix bugs in programs. In: International Conference on Learning Representations (2020). https://openreview.net/pdf?id=SJeqs6EFvB
16. Errica, F., Podda, M., Bacciu, D., Micheli, A.: A fair comparison of graph neural networks for graph classification. CoRR abs/1912.09893 (2019). http://arxiv.org/abs/1912.09893
17. Even, G., Naor, J.S., Schieber, B., Sudan, M.: Approximating minimum feedback sets and multi-cuts in directed graphs. In: Balas, E., Clausen, J. (eds.) IPCO 1995. LNCS, vol. 920, pp. 14–28. Springer, Heidelberg (1995). https://doi.org/10.1007/3-540-59408-6_38
18. Fomin, F.V., Villanger, Y.: Subexponential parameterized algorithm for minimum fill-in (2011). https://arxiv.org/abs/1104.2230
19. Girvan, M., Newman, M.E.J.: Community structure in social and biological networks. Proc. Natl. Acad. Sci. **99**(12), 7821–7826 (2002). https://doi.org/10.1073/pnas.122653799
20. Guo, X., Wang, S., Zhao, L.: Graph neural networks: Graph transformation. In: Wu, L., Cui, P., Pei, J., Zhao, L. (eds.) Graph Neural Networks: Foundations, Frontiers, and Applications, pp. 251–275. Springer, Singapore (2022)
21. Heckel, R., Taentzer, G.: Graph Transformation for Software Engineers. Springer (2020)
22. Helaly, A., Sakr, N., Madkour, K., Torunoglu, I.: Unsupervised graph neural network framework for balanced multipatterning in advanced electronic design automation layouts (2025). https://arxiv.org/abs/2511.16374
23. Henderson, P., Islam, R., Bachman, P., Pineau, J., Precup, D., Meger, D.: Deep reinforcement learning that matters. CoRR abs/1709.06560 (2017). http://arxiv.org/abs/1709.06560
24. Johnson, D.S., Aragon, C.R., McGeoch, L.A., Schevon, C.: Optimization by simulated annealing: an experimental evaluation; part ii, graph coloring and number partitioning. Operat. Res. **39**(3), 378–406 (1991). http://www.jstor.org/stable/171393
25. Karp, R.M.: Reducibility among Combinatorial Problems, pp. 85–103. Springer US, Boston, MA (1972). https://doi.org/10.1007/978-1-4684-2001-2_9
26. Kruskal, J.B.: On the shortest spanning subtree of a graph and the traveling salesman problem (1956). https://api.semanticscholar.org/CorpusID:120068278
27. Labute, P.: On the perception of molecules from 3d atomic coordinates. J. Chem. Inf. Model. **45**(2), 215–221 (2005). https://doi.org/10.1021/ci049915d
28. Leskovec, J., Mcauley, J.: Learning to discover social circles in ego networks. In: Pereira, F., Burges, C., Bottou, L., Weinberger, K. (eds.) Advances in Neural Information Processing Systems. vol. 25. Curran Associates, Inc. (2012). https://proceedings.neurips.cc/paper_files/paper/2012/file/7a614fd06c325499f1680b9896beedeb-Paper.pdf
29. Li, C., Ueno, M.: An extended depth-first search algorithm for optimal triangulation of bayesian networks. Int. J. Approximate Reasoning **80**, 294–312 (2017)
30. Li, Y., Yu, R., Shahabi, C., Liu, Y.: Diffusion convolutional recurrent neural network: data-driven traffic forecasting (2018). https://arxiv.org/abs/1707.01926
31. Liben-Nowell, D., Kleinberg, J.: The link-prediction problem for social networks. J. Am. Soc. Inform. Sci. Technol. **58**(7), 1019–1031 (2007). https://doi.org/10.1002/asi.20591

32. Lucic, M., Kurach, K., Michalski, M., Gelly, S., Bousquet, O.: Are gans created equal? a large-scale study (2018). https://arxiv.org/abs/1711.10337
33. WDAG 1996. LNCS, vol. 1151. Springer, Heidelberg (1996). https://doi.org/10.1007/3-540-61769-8_9
34. Mosk-Aoyama, D.: Maximum algebraic connectivity augmentation is np-hard. Oper. Res. Lett. **36**(6), 677–679 (2008)
35. Pascual, R., Le Gall, P., Arnould, A., Belhaouari, H.: Topological consistency preservation with graph transformation schemes. Sci. Comput. Program. **214**, 102728 (2022)
36. Plump, D.: Reasoning about graph programs (2016)
37. Rosen, K.H.: Discrete mathematics and its applications. WCB/McGraw-Hill, 7th edn. (2012). [Symmetric Closure: Sect. 9.3, 9.4]
38. Rossetti, G., Guidotti, R., Miliou, I., Pedreschi, D., Giannotti, F.: A supervised approach for intra-/inter-community interaction prediction in dynamic social networks. Soc. Netw. Anal. Min. **6**(1), 1–20 (2016). https://doi.org/10.1007/s13278-016-0397-y
39. Shao, Z., Zhang, Z., Wang, F., Xu, Y.: Pre-training enhanced spatial-temporal graph neural network for multivariate time series forecasting. In: Proceedings of the 28th ACM SIGKDD Conference on Knowledge Discovery and Data Mining, pp. 1567–1577. KDD '22. ACM, August 2022. https://doi.org/10.1145/3534678.3539396
40. Shchur, O., Mumme, M., Bojchevski, A., Günnemann, S.: Pitfalls of graph neural network evaluation. CoRR abs/1811.05868 (2018). http://arxiv.org/abs/1811.05868
41. Tarjan, R.: Depth-first search and linear graph algorithms. SIAM J. Comput. **1**(2), 146–160 (1972)
42. Varbella, A., Amara, K., Gjorgiev, B., El-Assady, M., Sansavini, G.: Powergraph: a power grid benchmark dataset for graph neural networks (2024). https://arxiv.org/abs/2402.02827
43. Velickovic, P., Blundell, C.: Neural algorithmic reasoning. CoRR abs/2105.02761 (2021). https://arxiv.org/abs/2105.02761
44. Yannakakis, M.: Computing the minimum fill-in is np-complete. SIAM J. Algebraic Discrete Methods **2**(1), 77–79 (1981). https://doi.org/10.1137/0602010
45. Yannakakis, M.: Edge-deletion problems. SIAM J. Comput. **10**(2), 297–309 (1981)
46. You, J., Ying, R., Ren, X., Hamilton, W.L., Leskovec, J.: Graphrnn: generating realistic graphs with deep auto-regressive models (2018). https://arxiv.org/abs/1802.08773
47. Zhang, J., Tang, J., Li, J., Liu, Y., Xing, C.: Who influenced you? predicting retweet via social influence locality. ACM Trans. Knowl. Discov. Data **9**(3), April 2015. https://doi.org/10.1145/2700398

Author Index